Indigenism

A Yanomami girl holding the Brazilian flag. Photo courtesy of Claudia Andujar, Comissão Pró-Yanomami, São Paulo, Brazil.

Alcida Rita Ramos

Indigenism

Ethnic Politics in Brazil

The University of Wisconsin Press

The University of Wisconsin Press
2537 Daniels Street
Madison, Wisconsin 53718

3 Henrietta Street
London WC2E 8LU, England

Library of Congress Cataloging-in-Publication Data
Ramos, Alcida Rita.
    Indigenism: ethnic politics in Brazil / Alcida Rita Ramos.
    336 pp.   cm. — (New directions in anthropological writing)
    Includes bibliographical references and index.
    ISBN 0-299-16040-8 (cloth: alk. paper).
  ISBN 0-299-16044-0 (pbk.: alk. paper).
    1. Indians of South America—Brazil—Government relations.
  I. Title.
  F2519.3.G6R35   1998
  305.8′00981—dc21   98-15472

Contents

Illustrations

Acknowledgments

This book is the result of more than two decades of involvement with indigenist issues in Brazil. During this time many people, knowingly or not, contributed to the maturing of the ideas presented here. Although acknowledging each and every person who has influenced my thinking on the subject of Indigenism is impossible, I would like to thank my department colleagues at the University of Brasília, particularly Rita Laura Segato, Roque de Barros Laraia, Stephen Baines, and Wilson Trajano Filho, for their thoughtful reading of some chapters. I am also grateful to Aurélio Veiga Rios, Bruce Albert, Christine Alencar, Claudia Andujar, Dominique Buchillet, Jean Landgon, John Monteiro, Luis Eugenio Campos Muñoz, Maxim Repetto Carreño, Maria Helena Ortolan, George Zarur, Stephen Nugent, Peter Rivière, and Vincent Crapanzano for providing ideas, comments, bibliographic sources, and technical information. For their important strategic assistance I thank Wilson Hargreaves, Júlio Cezar Melatti, Jo Cardoso de Oliveira, Monica Pechincha, André Dusek, and the members of the Instituto Socioambiental, especially Fany Ricardo, Beto Ricardo, Márcio Santilli, and Adriana Ramos. I deeply appreciate Paul Little's time and effort in revising the English and making useful suggestions. I am equally pleased to thank Rosalie Robertson, senior editor of the University of Wisconsin Press, for her generous encouragement. My thanks also to Neil Whitehead, Jane Collins, and the anonymous reader, whose reassuring comments contributed to the acceptance of the manuscript for publication, for helping me find a more adequate focus for a non-Brazilian readership.

Excerpts from "A Hall of Mirrors: The Rhetoric of Indigenism in Brazil," published in *Critique of Anthropology* 11: 155–69, copyright © 1991 Sage Publications Ltd., and "The Hyperreal Indian," published in *Critique of Anthropology* 14: 153–71, copyright © 1994 Sage Publications Ltd., are reprinted with the kind permission of the publisher. Chapter 4, "Indian Voices" is reprinted from *Rethinking History and Myth: Indigenous South American Perspectives on the Past,* edited by Jonathan D. Hill, copyright ©

1988 Board of Trustees of the University of Illinois, with kind permission of the University of Illinois Press. Excerpts from "From Eden to Limbo: The Construction of Indigenism in Brazil," published by Routledge in *Social Construction of the Past: Representation as Power* are reprinted with permission of the editors of Routledge, copyright © 1994 George Clement Bond, Angela Gilliam, and contributors.

To the Indians of Brazil: my appreciation for their lessons on how to go on despite everything.

Indigenism

Introduction

Least but Not Last

The Fundamental Question

The question that prompted me to write this book is why Brazilian Indians, being so few, have such a prominent place in the national consciousness. Indeed, although they are a tiny minority—with the possible exception of Argentina's, the Brazilian Indians are the smallest indigenous population in the Americas—they have the power to burrow deeply into the country's imagination. The answer is not simple. I came close only after the long effort of writing this book, with all the thinking and analyzing it required. Like the hero's quest in a fairy tale, the pursuit of this answer has led me into unsuspected labyrinths of both individual and collective unfinished business regarding matters of identity. At the most visible level the discomfort that Indians provoke in the national population derives from their possession of well-defined cultures and territories of their own—too much land for so few Indians, it is often said—and their living apart from the national society and yet being part of the same country. But this pragmatic consideration is by no means the only or the strongest reason for the ambivalence that pervades interethnic relations in Brazil. Part of the Indians' conspicuous existence in the minds and lives of Brazilians is the result of the contradiction between a certain pride in the country's multiethnicity and the aspiration for national homogeneity. The late ethnologist, former indigenist, politician, and writer Darcy Ribeiro declared that the uniqueness of Brazil resides in its linguistic and cultural uniformity with no dialects or segments that claim autonomy (Ribeiro 1995, 20–23). Ribeiro thus sweeps under his poetic rug all Indian languages, all regional dialects, all the various immigrant influences, and some separatist movements.

Hard Facts

The estimates of the total indigenous population in Brazil vary from 236,000 to 300,000, constituting 206 different peoples speaking approximately 170 distinct languages (Montserrat 1992, 93). They represent no

3

more than 0.2 percent of the national population of more than 160 million people. Nearly half the indigenous societies living in Brazilian territory have 200 to 500 members; thirty-two have from 500 to 1,000; forty-four have 1,000 to 5,000; four—Potiguara, Sateré-Maué, Shavante, and Yanomami —have 5,000 to 10,000; three—Guajajara, Terena, and Makushi—have 10,000 to 20,000; and another three—Guarani, Kaingang, and Tikuna— have more than 20,000 people (B. Ricardo 1996a, xii). The total amount of Indian land is reckoned to be about 998,000 square kilometers, or 11.72 percent of Brazil's 8.5 million square kilometers (Fany Ricardo, personal communication) of which nearly 820,000 kilometers are officially designated as Indian land. Compare this with the United States's indigenous population of 1,959,234, representing 0.8 percent of a national population of nearly 250 million people, according to the 1990 census. The total amount of land held by indigenous peoples in the United States is about 45 million acres, or 160,000 square kilometers, a figure Native Americans have hoped to increase to 100 million acres (Kickingbird and Ducheneaux 1973, 1). In response to the argument that Brazilian Indian territories contain too much land for a small indigenous population, Áureo Faleiros, an administrator at the National Indian Foundation (FUNAI), replies by pointing out that the 307 largest landholdings in the country, owned by an infinitesimal portion of the national population, account for an area roughly equal to half the total amount of land occupied by indigenous peoples (Gondim 1996, 15).

Brazil seems to be unique in the Americas in that its Indians receive a great deal of national attention. In contrast, consider that

> To the great majority of the inhabitants of the Republic of Argentina, the Indians represent a mere remembrance from their school books that narrated the episodes of Conquest and national expansion. Many among this [national] population (over fifty percent of which is urban) are surprised when they hear that more than 150,000 Indians survive in Argentina, or when they read any brief news item about legal claims by some obscure Guarani "cacique," or territorial demands by a forgotten Araucanian leader. Not even sensationalist magazines are interested in the Indians, for their high degree of acculturation makes them much less "exotic" than Amazonian groups. (Bartolomé 1972, 341)

Nothing could be more different in Brazil where the Indians stand as a powerful symbol of nationality. It might not be altogether preposterous to say that, except for Argentina's, the smaller the indigenous population, the greater claim it has on the national consciousness.

1. A one thousand cruzeiro bill from the 1980s, no longer in circulation. On one side it shows a Karajá Indian couple, and on the other side, Marshall Rondon, the creator of the Indian Protection Service.

Defining Indigenism

The political field of relations between Brazilians and Indians—call it contact zone, middle ground, or colonial situation—acquires in Brazil a magnitude that is not explained by a single cause, such as competition for material and symbolic resources. Rather, this field that I call Indigenism is the result of many overlapping factors that history has compounded in an extraordinary case of collective overdetermination. Hence, the need for a broader definition of the concept of indigenism.

Before I continue I must clarify to non-Brazilian readers my use of the term *Indian*. Unlike other American countries (such as, for instance,

Ecuador and the United States) where Indian has become so offensive as to be carefully avoided (and replaced by terms such as *nativo* or *Native American*), in Brazil Indian has gone through phases of denigration and of regeneration. The indigenous movement of the 1970s and 1980s reappropriated the term and infused it with a substantial dose of political agency. Hence, to say Indian in Brazil is, among other things, to acknowledge the existence of social actors who are ethnically and culturally differentiated from the national population.

In my use of the term *Indigenism* I depart from authors who limit it to dominant official policies toward indigenous peoples (Gnerre and Bottasso 1986; Arze Quintanilla 1990; Favre 1996). My notion of it comes closer to that of Souza Lima, for whom Indigenism is "a set of ideas (and ideals) concerning the incorporation of Indian peoples into nation-states" (1991, 239). But I differ from him in that I expand the concept well beyond state incorporation of indigenous peoples to include the vast realm of both popular and learned imagery among the national population onto which are carved the many faces of the Indian. The force field generated in the interethnic realm creates a conceptual and practical reality that is perhaps uncommon outside Brazil. Indigenism is a political phenomenon in the broadest sense of the term. It is not limited to policy making by a state or private concern or to putting indigenist policies into practice. (Readers should be aware of the difference between *indigenous*—referring to the internal affairs of the Indians—and *indigenist*—pertaining to the realm of interethnicity.) What the media write and broadcast, novelists create, missionaries reveal, human rights activists defend, anthropologists analyze, and Indians deny or corroborate about *the* Indian contributes to an ideological edifice that takes the "Indian issue" as its building block. Lurking behind the images of *the* Indian composed of this kaleidoscopic assortment of viewpoints is always the likeness—or, more appropriately, unlikeness—of *the* Brazilian. Indian as mirror, most often inverted, is, as we shall see in the pages that follow, a recurrent metaphor in the interethnic field. In other words, Indigenism is to Brazil what Orientalism is to the West. The parallels between Indigenism and Orientalism are easy to draw: just as "the Orient is *Orientalized*," so is the Indian *Indianized*. "To the Westerner . . . the Oriental was always *like* some aspect of the West" (Said 1979, 67), just as to the Brazilian the Indian has always been like some aspect of Brazil. One also hears echoes of Indigenism in Orientalism in such passages as "It is Europe that articulates the Orient; this articulation is the prerogative, not of a puppet master, but of a genuine creator, whose life-giving power represents, animates, constitutes the otherwise silent and dangerous space beyond familiar boundaries" (Said 1979, 57).

Indigenism diverges from Orientalism in at least one important way, namely, the participation of the Indians in the construction of Indigenism. In the case of Brazil, Indians and Brazilians are part of one nation in the sense that they live in temporal and spatial contiguity, the laws, attitudes, and actions that set them apart notwithstanding. For this reason, if for no other, the Indians are equally agents in the country's indigenist project, no matter how constrained their agency may be. Moreover, when Indians seize the notion of "culture," an artifact of Western thinking about the Other, to further their cause for ethnic recognition and self-determination, they contribute significantly to the design of Indigenism. This being so, we cannot say, as Said does for Orientalism, that Brazil (read: the West) is the actor and the Indian (read: the Orient) a passive reactor (Said 1979, 109). In short, in my conception Indigenism amounts to an elaborate ideological construct about otherness and sameness in the context of ethnicity and nationality. Within this vast symbolic and practical field one finds many ways in which Indigenism is manifested. It can take the shape of regional prejudice, urban commiseration, state control, anthropological curiosity, religious commitment, sensationalism in the media, or indigenous verbal, written, or gestural discourses. Every one of these manifestations is like a brick laid in the process of building an edifice of ideas and actions that lodges some of the most revealing aspects of Brazilian nationality. What follows is dedicated to opening a few doors to this edifice; I hope it will let itself be fully disclosed by the time we get to the conclusion.

Reading This Book

I have structured the book so that the chapters can stand alone, which gives readers access to them in any sequence. I translated and expanded some chapters from published versions in Portuguese (for Chapter 3 see Ramos 1990; for Chapter 6 see Ramos 1994); in fact, unless otherwise noted, I did all the translations of referenced works originally published in other languages. Chapter 2 is a blend of two articles published in England, whereas Chapter 10, also published in England, is reproduced here with few alterations. Chapters 4 and 5 appeared in the United States, the former in a collection of essays on history and myth (Hill 1988), the latter as part of collected working papers on otherness (Domínguez and Lewis 1995). I expanded on both for this book. The remaining chapters and the conclusion are new.

The two chapters in Part I—"Setting the Stage"—provide a conceptual and political background for the problems of Indians in general and Brazilian Indians in particular. The unequal number of chapters in Parts II and III—"Speaking to the Whiteman" and "Speaking through the Indians," respectively—reflects somewhat the realities of interethnic contact:

Brazilians usually do the speaking and usually not *to* the Indians but *through* them, whereas the Indians have fewer occasions to speak to and be heard by the rest of the population. In the conclusion the reader will find a commentary on the ambivalence that permeates relations between Brazilians and Indians, and my answer to the question posed at the beginning of this introduction.

I am aware of the problems the terms *Whiteman* and *whites* bring to the minds of a North American audience. But considering the ethnographic reality of the interethnic relations in Brazil, I cannot avoid it altogether without the risk of distorting this reality. I find myself in a position similar to that of Robert Berkhofer Jr., who titled his 1978 book *The White Man's Indian* and, more specifically, to Keith Basso's in his book *Portraits of "The Whiteman"* (1979), where he justifies the use of the term by the Apache:

> Conforming to no Whiteman in particular, "the Whiteman" is an abstraction, a complex of ideas and values, a little system of what Alfred Schutz called "taken-for-granted typifications and relevances" that Indian people use to confer order and intelligibility upon their experience with Anglo-Americans. (p. 4)

Basso defines the Whiteman as a social category and a cultural symbol, a multipurpose instrument for rendering Anglo-Americans meaningful. "More specifically, 'the Whiteman' may be viewed as an unformalized model: a model *of* Whitemen (in the sense of defining who Whitemen are, how they contrast with other forms of humanity, and what, given these contrasts, they stand for and represent) and a model *for dealing with* Whitemen" (p. 4).

In this sense Whiteman resembles the Portuguese term *branco*. But there are some differences. Whereas in the United States the indigenous use of Whitemen refers to Anglo-Americans, in Brazil brancos encompasses all non-Indians—Brazilians and foreigners, regardless of racial features. Moreover, branco is used by both Indians and non-Indians and thus constitutes a "native" category of Brazilian society in general. As a polar category to *Índio*, branco is as necessary an element in the Brazilian model of interethnic relations as Whiteman is to the Apache. Any ethnographic analysis devoted to the interpretation of this model must conform to it.

Writing This Book

The entire book is the result of my personal commitment in the realm of Indigenism. It is based on lived experience, and its flavor is definitely anthropological, even if the writing style departs from the familiar canon expected from a social scientist. I have drawn heavily on textual materials, but the thrust of all the chapters springs directly from nearly thirty years of being exposed to the problems of Indian-white relations. Even my first prolonged field experience with the Yanomami in 1968–1970, geared toward basic ethnographic research, was pervaded by political concerns involving protection of land rights and critical appraisals of missionary action. During the 1980s I was intensely involved with the Indian cause, spending a great deal of time and effort on steering committees, in interminable meetings, drafting documents, and raising money. In early 1985 my living room became a makeshift office for Indians and their supporters who were preparing an indigenous policy proposal for the transition government from military to civilian regime. As host to a number of Indian leaders, I heard stories told in private about the personal suffering that goes on backstage in interethnic politics and witnessed some hair-raising incidents, such as the attempt of a demoralized Tikuna man to commit suicide by jumping from my sixth-floor window. My activism receded during the late 1980s when I and all other Yanomami ethnographers were denied access to the field by the National Indian Foundation while a massive gold rush was devastating both the environment and the lives of the Brazilian Yanomami. In the early 1990s I returned to the field on a medical team that tried desperately to brake raging malaria epidemics that were killing hundreds of Yanomami. During the two years that I worked as interpreter for doctors and nurses in the most harrowing situations I had ever experienced (Ramos 1995a, 1995b), I felt the need to withdraw from the forefront of indigenist activism. Although I had been writing about interethnic contact for about twenty years, I longed for the emotional and intellectual distance necessary for a more ambitious analysis. Thus I devoted the next two years to creating a mental retreat that might allow me to digest a rich and often overpowering experience in the field of Indigenism.

Now a few final words about writing anthropology and writing in a foreign language. I was well into the last chapters when I began to read Michael Herzfeld's 1997 book on cultural intimacy. I began to hear echoes of his reflections on the "poetics" of doing anthropology in my perception of it. A good example of this resonance appears in this passage from Herzfeld:

> For me the pleasures of writing have throughout sustained an absorbing tension between the essentialism entailed in giving shape to ideas and impressions, and the taunting vertigo of skeptical doubt without end. This has been the "militant middle ground" on which I have engaged with the conventions and assumptions of my profession. (1997, 36)

Would I be able to express my own thinking on the subject in a different or better way? I think not.

The strain of writing an entire book in a foreign language has been an exhausting eight-month enterprise that seemed to plunge me into an interminable expanse of mental moving sand. But it is a strain not devoid of its own pleasures. To track down the precise word, to force to the surface some dimly remembered idiom, to conquer unwieldy tantalizing figures of speech, to search for culturally apt metaphors, or to fight one's way through "unreasonable" spellings are toils that can provide gratification when finally mastered. Here too I hear a familiar echo (of Joseph Conrad in *Lord Jim*) through the sometimes ponderous landscapes of the English language: "I had to work like a coal miner in his pit quarrying all my English sentences out of a black night."

Now, on to Indigenism.

Part I
Setting the Stage

1
Keywords for Prejudice

Writers often cast certain words about in both professional and lay contexts without much thought for their connotations. One of the most interesting ways of elucidating underlying meanings is found in *Keywords* by Raymond Williams. He perceives the problem as one of vocabulary "in two senses: the available and developing meanings of known words . . . and the explicit but as often implicit connections which people were making, in what seemed . . . [to be] particular formations of meaning" (1985, 15). For more than two decades he collected words with these characteristics in order to analyze "some of the issues and problems that were there inside the vocabulary." These key words are "significant, indicative words in certain forms of thought" (p. 15). He then examined the historical trajectory of 131 words related to the field of culture and society.

Following Williams's lead, I shall focus on a set of words that, together or separately, have contributed to a specific "formation of meaning" in the field of Indigenism. But, unlike Williams, I do not intend to trace the etymological history of these words; rather, I seek to uncover hidden meanings behind notions that are often used uncritically. The set I have selected is small and can easily be expanded. Some words or word clusters are used more widely than others; some display a thicker veneer of neutrality than others, but none is devoid of value judgments.

One purpose of this exercise is to show how anthropology not only is not immune to semantic contamination but actually contributes to the canonization of particular notions about indigenous peoples through its indiscriminate use of received ideas disguised as scientific concepts. Allowing the common usages of words to enter the ranks of disciplinary concepts amounts to what Bourdieu describes as the smuggling of received ideas into sociological discourse in the clear view of unsuspecting social scientists. Much scientific subject matter, he says, is no more than "social problems that were smuggled into sociology" and that "vary according to the fluctuations of the moment's social consciousness. Here is one of the mediations by

13

means of which the social world constructs its own representation, making use of sociology and the sociologist." How, Bourdieu asks, can one escape from this "clandestine persuasion"? To this end he suggests one should pursue "the social history of the problems, the objects, and the instruments of thinking which construct social reality" (1989, 36). As an example he decodes *profession,* "a word from common language which entered scientific language as contraband" (p. 40). In the domain of Indigenism an equivalent word would be *nomadism,* a recurring attribute of the indigenous way of life decried by a wide range of outsiders, such as missionaries, administrators, businesspeople, and settlers. Transposed to anthropological discourse, nomadism was hoisted from plain stereotype to scientific truth. A critical look at idées reçues should be part and parcel of any analytical enterprise. In the field of music, for instance, Stravinsky (1996) exercises his fine critical power to demystify modernity, among other things. If this exercise is crucial to the arts, what do we say of social sciences whose task it is to take "reality" as an object of study and not as a model in itself? To analyze is to pull apart, to scrutinize what is behind the obvious, to catch dogmas in their contradictions, or to unveil covert meanings in statements and actions that are the opposite of their stated intentions. Without critically evaluating the concepts one uses in a field such as anthropology, one risks simply repeating reality. Actually, the risk is greater than that. The risk is that the repetition of a concept without critical evaluation of it lends the concept an aura of scientific legitimacy. Just as tropes surface insidiously in language, as Hayden White (1973) demonstrated for history, so received ideas tend to adhere to one's discourse on the Other with so much ease that it takes a great deal of effort to break their hypnotic pull. But once we manage to break free, we find a Pandora's box scattering fragments of unanticipated meanings around our field of critical vision. Although the risk is that the social scientist will be immobilized, rummaging through words and their explicit and implicit messages is worthwhile.

What follows is an exploration of the surreptitious meanings of notions attributed to Indians by non-Indians. The idea is to break the picture of *the Indian* of the interethnic imagination into as many of its components as possible. We will see the Indian as child, the Indian as heathen, the Indian as nomad, the Indian as primitive, and the Indian as savage. No doubt the reader will immediately think of myriad other terms also applied to Indians, such as *native, exotic, noble, natural,* and *pure,* not to mention the term *Indian* itself, which has indeed been amply reviewed as a dictionary entry (Reissner 1983). One must, however, be selective, lest the project grow into a full-sized dictionary, outweighing the present undertaking. The words chosen have great power to set the background for the realities of Indigenism in Brazil. They are all part of the explicit vocabulary used by the actors of the Brazilian interethnic universe. Excluded are metaphoric terms that come to the surface by means of analysis, such as the Indian as woman in Chapter 5. I refer to a number of adjectives in my analysis, although I do not make them separate entries: *dirty, lazy, unreliable,* and other stereotypes such as *cannibals, warriors,* and *tribal.* Because these words are often associated with more inclusive images—heathen, child, nomad, primitive, and savage—I take them to be distinctive features of these images. As I said, my concern is not to search for the origin and development of the words as such but to track down the ideological underpinnings of their current usage. The alphabetical order is a mere convenience of presentation.

Child

The term *child* is commonly used in relation to Indians in spoken language but more rarely so in writing. Instead of explicitly using the word child, speakers refer to such traits as absence of malice, incompleteness, credulity, innocence, and candor in regard to Indians, which brings them close to the usual idea one has of Western children. These attributes fit the definition of *childlike*. According to *Webster's Encyclopedic Unabridged Dictionary of the English Language,* the adjective childlike is to be 'like a child, as in innocence, frankness, etc.; befitting a child; *childlike candor.* . . . **Syn.** young, ingenuous, simple, guileless, trusting, innocent. . . . **Ant.** sophisticated, adult'.

European thinking seems to have been inspired by Aristotle, who applied the notion of children to adults of other cultures. But Aristotle's children were not simply the epitome of a joyful phase of innocence in one's life cycle:

> Children . . . were regarded by Aristotle as little more than animals so long as their reason remained in a state of becoming. . . . "While the heir is a child," said Vitoria quoting Saint Paul, "he does not differ from a slave." So, too, with the Indian. Like the children of other races he will one day grow into a free and independent citizen of a true *polis*. Until that time arrives, however, he must, for his own benefit, remain in just tutelage under the king of Spain, his status now slave-like, but not slavish. (Pagden 1982, 104)

Aristotle, then, provided the intellectual justification for Europeans to regard "the American Indian as a 'natural man' incapable of rational and hence moral choice"; hence, it was Europeans' "Christian duty to care for peoples who were still in a condition of childlike imbecility" (p. 3).

Not surprisingly, the image of the Indian as child was duly carried to Brazil in 1500. Pero Vaz de Caminha, the scribe of Pedro Álvares Cabral, "discoverer" of Brazil, was enthralled by what he called the Indians' innocence of both body and soul. The candid and handsome nakedness of sixteenth-century Tupinambá was visual evidence of the native peoples' ingenuous and virginal minds. Caminha saw a glorious panorama of future Christians just waiting for proper training. Like children, they needed to be initiated in the arts of true humanity. "They seem to me of such innocence that, if we understood their speech and they ours, they would soon be Christians . . . because these people are certainly good and of beautiful simplicity" (Caminha 1963, 60).[1] They were beautiful, simple, innocent children of a paradisiacal land capable of yielding anything one would care to sow. Just as the land was "so gracious that, if we want to use it, it will yield everything" (p. 67), so were the Indians gracious and pliable. But if Caminha gazed at the new land and its inhabitants with admiration, he also regarded both as so rudimentary as to incite the mastering impulse of the Europeans. The supposed simplicity of native customs was quickly translated as intellectual inferiority. The Portuguese were struck by the absence in Tupinambá language of the f, l, and r sounds. This linguistic feature helped the conquerors explain to themselves why the Indians had no faith ($f\acute{e}$), no law (lei), and no king (rei). Lack of religion, laws, and government attested to the primitiveness of the Indians and thus became a major trope of conquest (Giucci 1993).

With the arrival of the Jesuits in the midsixteenth century, the Portuguese drew up special legislation for the Indians because of their "mental undevelopment" that made them unequal to the rest of the population. According to this legislation, the Indians were the immature children of the colonial powers. The authorities "must take the position of parents, charged with correcting and protecting their social offspring. After all, [Indians] were in the 'infancy of humanity,' in a 'new world,' and had proved . . . that they were not of the same age (= maturity) as the Christians" (Baêta Neves 1978, 121).

Thus, as decades and then centuries advanced, Caminha's seemingly lyrical vision gave way to concerns that were expressed more pragmatically. The job of taking possession of the new colony sent the Portuguese in pursuit of indigenous slave labor, first in the extractive industry of brazilwood, later on sugarcane plantations, in gold mining, and the like (Monteiro 1994). The Indians' indifference to commodities such as gold made them look puerile in the eyes of the conquerors. As McGrane explains,

> The Other is inferior to the European because he is not, as the European is, capable of having a responsible relationship with this gold that

1. Caminha's letter, written on the first of May 1500 and addressed to D. Manuel I, king of Portugal, has had a number of published versions. I am freely translating from the text edited by Leonardo Arroyo published in Brazil in 1963.

surrounds him, and hence the European appropriation of it is justified. This formulation we may term the Other-as-Child. . . . In reference to gold and spices the non-European Other is a child, but an adult child, a man-child, i.e., he is not equal to his own desires. (1989, 25–26)

In the mideighteenth century the colonial Portuguese Law of Liberties converted Indian slaves into indentured servants. In the province of Grão-Pará, then a separate colony from the rest of Brazil, the government required Indians to remain for six years with their former masters or wherever they happened to be working. The idea was that, because indigenous ex-slaves had no experience other than total freedom and slavery, they needed time to become accustomed to the new order, according to which they were paid for their labor. Moreover, to prevent the now-free Indians from simply abandoning the work, the colonial government placed them under the Regulation of Orphans. This rule was to be applied to the " 'rustics,' the 'ignorant,' and the 'vagrants who do not want to do any sort of work' " (Farage and Carneiro da Cunha 1987, 108). It excluded Indians who earned their living as artisans and those who still lived in their traditional villages. Although the measure was pragmatically designed to ensure the continuity of the labor force after slavery was banned, not to declare Indians as debilitated children (p. 111), it is revealing, to say the least, that the rule associated the official termination of the master-slave relationship with orphanage, the rupture by death of the parent-child link. The orphanage metaphor was a potent forerunner of legislation that would declare all Indians, laborers or not, isolated or not, known and yet to be known, as relatively incapable and hence wards of the state.

Lest one form the idea that state orphanage is an exclusively Brazilian phenomenon, it is worth making a quick mention of another colonial country. Early twentieth-century Australia declared the offspring of European men and Aboriginal women (the possibility that Aboriginal men and European women would cohabitate simply was not entertained) to be orphans. Because of the "British blood" they carried in their veins, these "half-breeds" or "half-castes" were pulled away from their maternal home and influence as a way of rescuing them "from the degradation of the blacks' camp."

> Assuming the legal authority of the parent, without transmitting 'blood', the state turned its wards into orphans, cut off from their Aboriginal kin without acquiring European kin. Uncertain about what it was creating, and fearful of atavism, it often repeated the separation of parents and children in subsequent generations, while limiting the scope of relationships that were allowed to exist. Such practices seemed to envisage a population of perpetual orphans. (Beckett 1988b, 198)

Apparently keener to absorb "the 'mixed blood' population into the white majority" (p. 199) than Brazil was, Australia put a much greater emphasis on the notion of blood—European blood, that is—as a powerful solvent that could "whiten" Aborigines and thus make more palatable their sharing of the nation European Australia was eagerly trying to build. As we will see in Chapter 2, for Brazilians blood—Indian blood this time—translates as a potent marker for an emerging Brazilianness that was distinct from the culture of the European colonizers.

As indigenous labor lost its importance for the national economy as a whole, the image of the Indian as childlike became sharper. Early in the twentieth century,

> indigenous societies appeared as infantile forms . . . which should be guided by means of guardianship toward the civilization of our society. Guardianship, which above all was to have been a state instrument to defend indigenous lands, was then discussed in terms . . . that took for granted the infantile character of Indians and their societies. . . . [The] protection conferred on the Indians [was] based on their alleged infantility at the expense of public guardianship of their goods and, particularly, their lands. (Farage and Carneiro da Cunha 1987, 114)

Always treated in Brazilian legislation as a residual category, Indians were inserted in the 1916 Civil Code as objects of guardianship to last until they became adapted to national society. They remained as orphans until 1928 when the Indian Protection Service, created in 1910, took over their guardianship from the judge of orphans. In the 1960s married women, who had been included in the category of the relatively incapable, were liberated from this humiliating condition, but the Indians continued as before. Article 6 of the Civil Code, still current, establishes who is relatively incapable to exercise certain acts:

> I—Minors between sixteen and twenty-one years of age.
> II—Prodigals.
> III—Indians (*silvícolas*).
>   The Indians (silvícolas) are subjected to the guardianship regime, as established by special laws and regulations, which will cease as they become adapted to the civilization of the country. (Farage and Carneiro da Cunha 1987, 117)

The legal insistence on the Indians' status as relatively incapable derives from the notion that Indians need protection because they are ill equipped to live in modern society. Thus, although they are unqualified to exercise full citizenship, they have the right to the exclusive use of their lands. Thus protection of indigenous territories is a result of the Indians' infantile condition rather than a historical right for having occupied them before any

Brazilians (Carneiro da Cunha 1987, 28–32). If an Indian person or group chooses to become "emancipated" from the condition of relative incapability, the person or group can gain full citizenship, but this will be accompanied by the loss of the right to exclusive land use, for only as civil minors are Indians entitled to the possession of their territories. Once people are declared non-Indians, their lands lose their feature of inalienability. Perceiving this as a Catch-22, no Indian person or group has ever seriously requested emancipation. Indians would rather continue to bear the humiliation of being labeled as incompetent children than lose the right to their communal lands. All things considered, and given the resistance of the Brazilian judiciary to acknowledge communal property rights, guardianship seems to be the lesser of two evils.

Brazil's 1988 Constitution introduced a discordant note into the tradition of regarding Indianness as a preadult, temporary condition. According to the new constitution, the Indian is no longer a child to be promoted into ethnic adulthood. Article 231 specifies that Indians have the right to their own social organization, customs, languages, beliefs, and traditions, as well as usufruct of the lands they traditionally occupy; the union is obliged to demarcate and protect these lands and ensure that the indigenous ways of life are respected. This constitutional change was in large part the result of a strong pro-Indian lobby active during the Constitutional Assembly held in Brasília. Large numbers of Indians, nongovernmental organizations, and professional associations, such as the Brazilian Anthropological Association and the Association of Geologists, successfully influenced members of Congress to legally recognize indigenous ethnic differences and an attendant set of rights to natural resources, subsoil excluded.

But although the Constitution grants Indians the right to remain Indians, the Civil Code, in specifying their special status, declares that such status will eventually be suspended. The expectation is that the Indians will "adapt" to Brazilian civilization and hence stop being Indians. The assumption is that one cannot be "adapted" and continue to be an Indian. Adaptation would mean a change in ethnic identity. While Indians are not adapted, they will remain under the wardship of the state. The Constitution is mute about guardianship, so in practice the 1916 Civil Code and the 1973 Indian Statute, both of which are under revision, continue to regulate the legal status of indigenous peoples. For all the advances of the new constitution regarding indigenous rights, one has the nagging feeling that plus ça change, plus c'est la même chose. From orphans of slavery to wards of the state, Indians in Brazil continue to endure the stigma of being eternally immature in the name of a protection that often exacerbates that stigma.

In some quarters of the Brazilian state, most explicitly—but not exclusively—among the military, the Indian-as-child is in fact taken to be a liability to the nation. Regarded as both ignorant and gullible, with no commitment to patriotism, the Indians who live in frontier areas, especially in the Amazon, are considered a potential hazard to national sovereignty because they can easily fall prey to the greed of foreign groups or individuals interested in Amazonian natural resources. Researchers and missionaries are the most common targets for accusations of manipulating indigenous innocence in order to take over the region. In a 1990 document the Superior School of War (Escola Superior de Guerra, ESG) proposed that "anthropological cysts" that grow among indigenous groups be crushed by warfare, for they operate as beachheads for the takeover of Amazonia. Army general Antenor Cruz Abreu later repeated this notion in an interview, which bore the headline "Amazonia May Become a Vietnam, Says a General. ESG's 1990 Document Admitted the Hypothesis of Warfare in Case of the Internationalization of the Region" (*Folha de São Paulo* 1991). The specter of the internationalization of the Amazon has become a major topos in the discourse of national security, persisting well beyond the military regime that lasted from 1964 to 1985.

Each renewal of this national anxiety invariably evokes two figures: the military and the Indians. The Indians, viewed as unconscious facilitators of alien encroachment, come under the surveillance of the military. Because Indians are not responsible for what they do, the military needs to watch them, lest the Indians cause harm to the nation's interests. To the military the Indians, who do not have full citizenship, are as suspect as foreigners. Convinced that only nationals can protect the country's borders, the military has attempted to remove all Indians from the frontier zone and to open to colonization indigenous areas located within a 150-kilometer-wide strip along the northern border. Imputing childish irresponsibility to the Indians who therefore endanger the nation's autonomy is but a strategy to expropriate their lands for occupation by Brazilians. "The world has changed, but for the military the 'enemies' of Amazonia continue to be the same as in the sixties, seventies, and eighties" (Nogueira and Figueiredo 1996). The syndrome—fear of loss of state sovereignty by internationalization—may be relatively recent, but the ultimate goal—appropriation of Indian lands—is as old as Brazil. We will see in Chapter 8 some military strategies to control the Indian issue in the Amazon.

But the supposed immaturity of the Indians arouses more than a basic telluric greed. It can also reflect the condition of the country as a whole. Hélio Jaguaribe, a well-known political scientist and former minister of science and technology, stated in 1994 that Brazil will have no more Indians by the twenty-first century. By sending all Indians to school, Brazil will turn the native peoples into Brazilian citizens. Infantile Indians would thus come of age by means of formal Western-style education. Schooling would thus be the magic stroke that would reduce undesirable differences to a uniform sea of citizenship. Bringing Indians to "cultural maturity" would therefore end the "Indian problem," and Brazil could then claim to be a civilized country. Just as a belief in sympathetic magic assumes that equal attracts equal, the fear behind Jaguaribe's statement seems to be that childlike Indians might infantilize Brazil (more about Jaguaribe later and in Chapter 6).

The equation of adults and children can summon different responses. It can evoke arrogance or humility. So far we have explored the arrogant aspect of the Indian as child. Turning now to the use anthropology makes of the image of childlikeness, we can see how apparent humility may, although not necessarily, conceal arrogance. At the risk of digressing it is worth looking into the way anthropologists have dealt with the image of adult as child.

The respect generated by the intimate knowledge of native societies is an antidote to crude biases such as those just considered. Nevertheless, the image of the child is often present in ethnographic writings but in an inverted way. For now the children are the ethnographers themselves. Just to give a few examples, we find this in Evans-Pritchard: "That means you are their pupil, an infant to be taught and guided" (1976, 253). We find it in Seeger: "[The Suyá] treated me like a child—which I was, for I did not know how to speak or to see as they saw. . . . They treated me like a 12 year-old boy . . . for I knew how to paddle, to fish and hunt nearby as a 12 year-old does. . . . There is much to laugh about a couple of clumsy adults who act as children and the Suyá love to laugh" (1980, 34, 35). We find it in Ramos: "I burst with pride when they complimented me for my progress in language learning, comparing me to a five-year-old child" (1995a, 5). What is behind the seemingly natural simile of an awkward foreign adult and a native child in the context of interethnic differences? Does the ethnographer experience the same constraints that Indians do when they are called children? Or is it just a rhetorical artifice to put across the feeling of inadequacy when one plunges into someone else's culture? The metaphor of the child's coming of age by means of ethnographic knowledge is by now a cliché. Ethnographers have explored imagery drawn from ethnographic accounts of rites of passage to fashion the discipline's own fictions. Beyond the aptness of the simile, apparently so obvious as to not require commentary, one might find some interesting innuendoes that can help us understand that other fiction of the Indian as child. For embedded in the simile is the silent distance between promoting and demoting individuals or collectivities to childhood.

One question raised by this simile is the cross-cultural meaning of *child*. Do the Suyá laugh at their twelve-year-olds as they do at their ethnographers? Is a twelve-year-old Suyá, or a five-year-old Sanumá equivalent to a North American or Brazilian child of the same age? If I may refer to my experience as a member of a "Western" society, I would say that in the

West children are encouraged to be puerile for as long as possible. A vast and complex industry of infantility pours millions of gadgets, television programs, and magazines into the market designed to maximize the child-ishness of children, often infantilizing adults as well. The ultimate affront is to use the Indian as a plastic toy (*The Indian in the Cupboard*) to entertain Western children. The old North American tradition of "playing Indian" has now reached cyberspace (the *Pocahontas* debate; see Strong 1996). It is the Indian as child in more ways than one.

Although the West creates a whole world to be peopled by children, children are not allowed to enter large areas of adult society. The gulf be-tween Western children and adults has, among other things, opened a huge field on the psychopathology of growing up and the malaise caused by the generation gap. At certain times and in certain places the matter is so seri-ous that it becomes the object of public policy.

A Munduruku Indian has written a book for Brazilian children. In telling amusing anecdotes about his encounter with national ignorance re-garding Indians, the author exposes much discrimination and prejudice among urban populations. His style is light and humorous, infused with the candor and sweetness with which one addresses the young. Charming as it may be, Daniel Munduruku's 1996 book does little to offset the strong tendency to infantilize the Indian. Its simplified language has the mimetic effect of simplifying the subject matter. One may well ask why the Indian is so rarely the theme of serious adult writing in contemporary Brazil.

Western children have a long and rather painful history. At least since classical Greece, their status has been rather dubious, 'little more than animals'. Do these children of the West resemble the children of indige-nous peoples? The ethnographic record says no, and so does Lévi-Strauss: "Every fieldworker who has had concrete experience of primitive children will undoubtedly agree that . . . in many regards the primitive child ap-pears far more mature and positive than a child in our own society, and is to be compared more with a civilized adult" (1969, 92). Significant dif-ferences in socialization result in significant differences in social product. Again drawing from my experience among the Sanumá, a Yanomami sub-group, a child is given the respect of a future adult. The basic difference between Sanumá children and grownups is that the children have not yet had time to accumulate as much knowledge. Sanumá children have ac-cess to every domain of sociability, all the way from shamanic sessions to sexual encounters. No cultural areas are prohibited to children. No indus-try prolongs their immaturity. Most of their toys are miniatures of objects they will use in their adult life. Infants are not addressed in baby talk but in normal speech, including vocabulary and intonation. In short, children are not infantilized beyond their natural capacities to speak and act.

The learning process, also known as childrearing, most commonly refers to the socialization of children, of reproducing the sociocultural apparatus in the new generations. Children are totally dependent on adults to pass on knowledge. This dependence means that children are literally at the mercy of grownups to acquire skills, including those necessary for survival; without them, children would not have a chance. This aspect of helpless dependence is what the dominant society appropriates in characterizing indigenous peoples. The latter's knowledge is irrelevant to Brazilians. Because Indians are thought to be unable to speak the national language, drive cars, or put money in the bank, they are inferior incomplete beings, just as children are in the national society. And when Indians show themselves capable of doing all these things, a certain widespread common understanding says they are no longer Indians. From this point of view Indians *as* Indians are by definition in a permanent state of ignorance, in need of learning from civilized teachers, forever caught in the Caliban-Prospero trap (Shakespeare [1611] 1987; Baêta Neves 1978; Retamar 1989; Mannoni 1990).

But when ethnographers go into the field to learn the local cultural code, their dependence is of a different sort. Their residence is a voluntary act, frequently for a short time, which results in manifest benefit to the ethnographers. Their survival is rarely dependent on the knowledge they are there to acquire. Moreover, the trade goods that most of us carry are efficient guarantees of fair treatment. In the same piece in which Evans-Pritchard declares himself a pupil of the Azande, an infant to be instructed and guided, he also says that his main Zande informants were his two "personal servants" (1976, 247). Our dependence is thus more symbolic than real, for if fieldwork aborts, we can simply pack up and leave, an option no longer open to indigenous peoples anywhere in the Americas. Perhaps in the effort to counterbalance the negative image of Indian as child, ethnographers put themselves in the same position—as if to show that anyone who has something to learn is bound to fall into the slot of childhood. However, the lighthearted childlikeness of the ethnographer is reduced to a witticism when compared to the predicament of Indians in the profoundly unequal world of interethnic relations. In posing as children to their hosts ethnographers are far from stepping into the Indians' interethnic shoes. In fact, I dare say that the ethnographer as child is the epitome of a perverse rhetoric that, whether consciously or not, has the effect of diluting the gravity of the stereotype of native as child. This clumsy relativism—"you say they are like children when among us, but look, we are too when among them"— misses the political point of interethnic inequality. The image of the infantile ethnographer is at most cute, whereas the image of the infantile Indian is a stigma at the service of the native person's subjugation. It is, in other words, a matter of differential power.

The native as childlike is therefore far from being an innocent image that emanates mere condescension. "Aside from the evolutionist figure of the savage there has been no conception more obviously implicated in political and cultural oppression than that of the childlike native" (Fabian 1983, 63).

Heathen

Again we can begin with what the dictionary says about *heathen:*

> *n.* 1. an irreligious or unenlightened person. 2. an unconverted individual of a people that do not acknowledge the God of the Bible; one who is neither a Jew, Christian, nor Muslim; pagan. 3. (formerly) any person neither Christian nor Jewish, esp. a member of the Islamic faith or of a polytheistic religion: *Many a knight joined the crusades to fight the heathens. -adj.* 4. irreligious or unenlightened. 5. pagan; of or pertaining to the heathen . . .—-**Syn.** 5. heathenish, barbarous. HEATHEN, PAGAN are both applied to peoples who are not Christian, Jewish, or Muslim. HEATHEN is often distinctively applied to unenlightened or barbaric idolaters, esp. to primitive or ancient tribes: **heathen rites, idols.** PAGAN, though applied to any of the peoples not worshipping according to the three religions mentioned above, is most frequently used in speaking of the ancient Greeks and Romans: *a pagan poem; a pagan civilization.*

This is the province par excellence of organized religion in most of its Christian persuasions. The distinction between heathen and pagan, and the subsequent assimilation of both, opens an interesting field of discussion about the change of mood in the colonizers regarding the status of the indigenous soul, whether a blank page where Christianity could be easily written, or a tortured spirit peopled with demons. In his "discovery letter" Caminha insists on the tabula rasa aspect of the Tupinambá people, clearly a religious empty slate, "for they neither have nor understand any belief, judging from appearances" (1963, 60).

Soon, the first Jesuits on the Brazilian coast realized that the Indians were not devoid of beliefs and idols. From then on, the future of the demonized native was to be a long one.[2]

For the Jesuits one of the most unnerving features of Tupinambá reli-

2. Of the vast literature on the Jesuits in sixteenth-century Brazil I shall make special reference to Baêta Neves 1978; Mello e Souza 1993; Vainfas 1995; and Viveiros de Castro 1992. See also Bettencourt 1992; Gambini 1988; Hemming 1978; S. Leite 1993; Meliá and Nagel 1995; Monteiro 1992; Nascimento, in press; Raminelli 1996; Ribeiro 1993; Shapiro 1987; and Thomas 1982.

gious behavior was the lack of fidelity. One moment the Tupinambá had the missionaries believing they gladly accepted the word of God, the next moment they would fall back to their barbarous drinking and cannibalistic feasts. The "inconstancy of the savage soul" drove the Jesuits to propose the use of force against the Indians:

> Thus he [converted leader Tibiriçá] manifested the deceit of his faith, which he had pretended to have, and he and all the other neophytes fell back without rein to their old customs. One cannot therefore expect or succeed to convert the heathens in all this land without the arrival of many Christians who . . . subject the Indians to the yoke of slavery and force them to accept the flag of Christ. (Anchieta, quoted in Viveiros de Castro 1992, 50)

A master move in the direction of total control was the Jesuits' change of strategy from visiting Indian villages to the "reduction" of indigenous populations into large concentrated settlements totally run by the missionaries. The "missions" or "reductions" had many advantages over the previous itinerant pattern of individual priests or small groups of priests that would go from village to village, dispensing various kinds of sacraments, the most important of which was baptism. No longer did the missionaries have to go to the Indians. The Indians came to the missionaries, albeit not spontaneously. Massive recruitment into missionary settlements was far from being an indigenous decision, and it was achieved with the help of the colonial powers (Marchant 1942, 115), particularly by means of the infamous *tropas de resgate* (*resgate* in Portuguese means both 'rescue' and 'ransom') and *descimentos* (forced removals) so recurrent in Brazilian colonial history; "even our heroic Nóbrega, uncompromising defender of indigenous freedom, came to propose just wars as a solution to the evangelization of rebellious Indians" (Montero 1996, 62).

A mission was a total institution (Goffman 1961) with a hierarchical distribution of power that closely resembled the state itself. The Jesuits were sovereign and grew so powerful that the colonial government became alarmed. As Baêta Neves points out, the missions were a first step the Jesuits took to distance themselves from colonial society. "The Villages [i.e., missions] seek to have maximum autonomy with regard to their internal affairs, and take on an autarchic character which makes them less vulnerable to the political game of the colony at large" (1978, 162).

For uprooted Indians the advent of the missions was also a turning point from autonomous village life to a regime of utter dependence on colonial society. Thousands of Indians were removed from their villages to live under complete Jesuit control in the most capillary Foucauldian fashion. Using a rigid and full daily schedule the missionaries administered the Indians' lives all the way from hygienic habits to schoolwork, regimented work, and leisure. Latin leveled the language differences in school, Portuguese in social situations, and "Tupi" in "external use." The mission was thus "a vast total pedagogical project" by means of which indigenous life was literally reduced to the commandments of the reduction (Baêta Neves 1978, 162).

The mission system offered many advantages. Not the least important was that missionary autonomy amounted to a quasi-state within the colonial state, not only in terms of control over large indigenous populations but also in terms of land tenure and other material resources. Physical comfort replaced the long, hard, and often lonely walks through swamp and forest. The priests' newly fixed abode provided an easy lesson for the *brasis,* as the Indians were then called, on the merits of a sedentary life. The total control of indigenous activities resulted in a thorough resocialization of the young and with it the longed-for "conversions." The mission succeeded in breaking the back of Tupinambá culture: no more intertribal vengeance, warfare, shamanism, polygyny, or cannibalism or the tattooing associated with it. The Jesuits had finally harnessed the slippery souls of the Indians.

Although they had many "benefits," the reductions had two major drawbacks: the frequent epidemics that ravaged the indigenous population and the constant slave raids by colonists in search of free labor. Both profited immensely from the high population density of the missions. The astonishing mortality rate—in the late sixteenth century the 40,000 Indians in fourteen Bahia "churches" were reduced to 3,500 "souls" in three churches (Anchieta, quoted in Ribeiro and Moreira Neto 1993, 28)—demanded continuous replacements, and thus the missionaries conscripted more Indians, who were equally subjected to deculturation, contagious diseases, and/or slavery in an infernal spiral of pestilence and death. In about two centuries of mission life on the coast of Brazil the Jesuit "utopia" succeeded in first eliminating cannibalism—the quintessence of missionary abhorrence—then intertribal warfare—the quintessence of Tupinambá culture—and finally the Tupinambá themselves. By 1759, when the marquis of Pombal, Portugal's prime minister, expelled the Jesuits from Brazil, the Tupinambá were virtually extinct. So much for the first heathens of the land, a tragically real instance of throwing the baby out with the bathwater.

The Tupinambá vanished, the Jesuits came and went, and Franciscans, Capuchins, Carmelites, Salesians, and Benedictines—just to mention some Catholic orders—populated what were considered still vacant spiritual spaces throughout Brazil, but the vision of the heathen or pagan Indian was to remain as a symbolic commodity in the country's interethnic landscape.

Until quite recently, the Roman Catholic Church did not show itself to be very comprehending of cultural differences, apart from the dividing line between "tame" Indians and "wild" Indians—the former regarded as legitimate ingredients of the nascent Brazilian nationality, the latter a threat to this same nationality. As late as the nineteenth century, Catholic missionaries applied physical punishment to force the Indians to comply with their regulations. They defended the procedure quite explicitly as the only way to subdue the natives, for, in a priest's words, "rigor is more useful than kindness; because they (the Indians) are more prone to fear than to respect, to the stick than to Rhetoric, to castigation than to disguise" (Galvão 1979, 141). Stereotypes that were current among colonists, administrators, and the like were also freely dispensed by missionaries. An example is the description of Uaupés Indians by Father Alcionílio Brüzzi Alves da Silva as late as 1962. In his "observations of the psychology of the Indian" he says:

> Since the Indian is physically sluggish in his movements, he is also slow to give us the most obvious answer. Lethargic to understand an order we give him, he finds it difficult to accompany our thinking. . . . Thus, one should not expect from the Indian great tenacity of will. One cannot count on him for regular, identical work. [Because the Indian] feels inferior to the white, [when he faces] the *civilizado* whose superiority he recognizes and feels, he always shows docility. . . . [The] Indian is neither a hero of fatigue, nor the prototype of laziness, although by temperament he is slow of movements. He will, however, produce reasonable work under two conditions: a fearful respect for the whites, and constant surveillance. (quoted in Ramos 1980b, 2)

Here the widespread theme of the lazy native (Alatas 1977) is given ontological status. Brüzzi shows himself totally oblivious to the historical irony of attributing indolence to the Indians simply because they—like anyone else—loathed forced labor. Brüzzi's Indians have filled their minds with illusions that distort their thinking and render them prone to silly superstitions. But, he adds, "one can easily understand that this is so for he [the Indian] lacks control of a more developed and educated intelligence; to the contrary, his mind is informed by childish tales and beliefs, incoherent and even absurd." But Brüzzi's Indians have their good qualities too. They are stoic, keen observers, pragmatic, and artistically sensitive; most noticeable is the Indians' "charming naïveté. They are a jolly race" (quoted in Ramos 1980b, 2).

For more than fifty years the Salesians constructed a solid dominion in the Upper Rio Negro region of Brazil's northwest Amazon. Somewhat similar to the sixteenth-century Jesuits, the Salesians based their control of the indigenous population on the educational system of boarding schools. Children were recruited into the mission and visited their families only during vacation. The traditional village layout and ornate constructions were completely obliterated and redesigned in regional style. Also like the early Jesuits, the Salesians selected a local language, Tukano, as their lingua franca, at the expense of the fourteen or so other indigenous groups in the area under missionary influence (Oliveira 1983).

Only in the early 1970s did the more progressive wing of the Catholic Church begin to change its outlook regarding cultural diversity and the role of evangelization. A new concept was introduced into the missionary project, namely, "enculturation." This project was inspired by the anthropological concept of acculturation, but the church has nevertheless transformed it to its own purposes. "Enculturation inverts . . . the direction of contact: whereas 'acculturation' describes the movement from the native to civilization, enculturation attempts to move toward native culture, defined as a 'process according to which the Church inserts itself in a given culture' " (Montero 1996, 120). In actual practice this tactic is like a return to the peripatetic premission times, now with a strongly relativistic flavor. The branch of the Catholic Church that is active in indigenous rights, the Conselho Indigenista Missionário (CIMI), has exalted what has been referred to as "incarnation," the mimetic effort of missionaries to blend themselves with indigenous peoples in order to carry out an agenda of "presence and annunciation." Presence means the direct participation of the missionary in indigenous daily life. Again one finds echoes of anthropological inspiration, as this idea of presence brings to mind the ethnographic motto of participant observation. By sharing the Indians' problems as they are experienced, particularly regarding land issues, the missionaries are better equipped to propose solutions. But their presence must never be dissociated from "the *annunciation*—the properly religious and spiritual dimension of pastoral action where preaching the Gospel is central—of the Christian message" (Rufino 1996, 162—63; see also CIMI 1979).

Although the policy of enculturation has led to an atmosphere that is a far cry from that of the early Jesuit missions, it is not devoid of contradiction. Despite its urge to redeem the past of physical and spiritual violence, its ultimate goal is to transform the Indians into Christians, albeit "indigenous Christians." Enculturation is the " 'effort to have the Gospel penetrate a given cultural milieu by calling upon it to grow according to its own values, so long as they are compatible with the Gospel.' Embedded in this definition is the whole dilemma of 'enculturated evangelization.' It wants to preserve the universal and the particular at the same time" (Montero 1996, 120). No matter how politically correct, evangelization is always an endeavor to turn native cultures into Christian cultures.

Protestant missionaries, lacking the compunction of the progressive Catholics and much newer to the indigenist scene, have maintained a general policy of noninterference in the political issues of interethnic contact while carrying out their persistent work of Christianizing the heathens.[3] The ubiquitous trade goods are their constant allies in convincing the Indians to abandon shamanism, polygyny, infanticide, drug taking, and all those features rated as offensive to Christendom. In the late 1970s a member of the Unevangelized Fields' Mission candidly reported to me that the missionaries withdrew a full load of trade goods, payment for indigenous labor for the mission, from Yanomami workers because they refused to comply with the missionaries' directive to stop shamanizing and having more than one wife. But let us hear a Yekuana (Maiongong) man from the Brazil-Venezuela border area tell his tale of Protestants:

> It was in Venezuela. He [the missionary] arrived speaking a different language that nobody understood. He didn't speak Spanish, anything. We figured he belonged to other people. Then [the missionaries] learned a little Maiongong. The Maiongong had many feasts and they [the missionaries] got very angry. They would go and break the record player. They spoke little Maiongong and didn't even speak Spanish. They would drink *cashiri* [manioc beer], get dizzy and said that was a thing of Satan, that Maiongong had Satan in them, and we would say that it was a Satan thing for them, not for us, that they could go away if they wanted. They would come saying that everybody was a brother, but we would tell them they were different, spoke different, not even Spanish did they speak. There was a Maiongong man who was ill and the Americans said: "be a believer and you'll recover." Then the man became a believer and recovered and everybody else wanted to be a believer too. But Americans are always angry with the Maiongong. At night they would put a book on a Maiongong's mouth and would say: "Look, it's your food, the history of God!" and they quarreled. . . . In Venezuela there are many Americans. The Maiongong fought a lot with missionaries because they said that Maiongong history was wrong. After five years they spoke Maiongong well. The Maiongong in Venezuela are all believers. (Ramos 1980b, 79)

Disease has been the great ally of the missionary enterprise. The sixteenth-century Tupinambá came to consider baptism, the quintessence of sacra-

---

3. A characteristic feature of Protestant missionaries in Indian areas is to avoid any involvement with political actions in defense of indigenous peoples. Their tacit policy is not to rock the boat, not to antagonize national authorities so as not to jeopardize their residence among the heathens. On several occasions North American fundamentalist missionaries have been linked to expansionist projects of the United States, sometimes with the collaboration of the receiving country's authorities (Stoll 1982; González 1989; Colby and Bennett 1995). Some scholars question this judgment (Fernandes 1980; Gallois and Grupioni, in press), but it remains to be explained, for instance, why the fundamentalists were the only people working with the Yanomami who were not expelled from the Indian area in 1987 at the beginning of the gold rush. All others—Catholic missionaries, medical teams, and anthropologists—were banned from Yanomami territory for three years (Ramos 1995a).

mental practices, as the source of lethal epidemics, perhaps with good reason. "The Jesuits themselves frequently pointed out this particular horror the Indians felt for the Catholic sacrament, especially for the baptisms *in extremis,* common in the Missions during smallpox epidemics. The shamans then proclaimed that 'baptism killed' as they verified that the Indians died as soon as they received the 'sanctified oils' " (Vainfas 1995, 121). Epidemics, the "Secret Judgments of God" (Cook and Lovell 1991), have had as strong, if not stronger, an effect on the control of indigenous peoples as have warfare, persuasion, or any other tactics of conquest (Ramos 1995b).

The same Unevangelized Fields' Mission (known in Brazil as MEVA), operating among the Yanomami in the northern Brazilian state of Roraima, also covers Wai Wai territory in the border region between Brazil and Guyana (former British Guiana). Beginning in the late 1940s the Hawkins brothers worked hard to convert the shaman Ewká, the leader of the Wai Wai in Guyana, for if Ewká converted, the others would follow suit. It was a time of epidemics (flu, pneumonia, tuberculosis, measles), and the shamans were unable to cure the sick. "When they saw their power fail . . . the shamans committed suicide" (Queiroz, in press). Those who abandoned shamanism to try the new religion also died, so it became a general belief that conversion would mean death.

> The missionaries promised to "save" the Wai Wai with western medicines and with a new religion. The preachers said that "the world would end in a huge fire and that they could show the way to salvation and a better life." They proposed that leader Ewká abandon his beliefs and guaranteed that he would not die of it as his people's tradition sustained. If he died the missionaries would leave the village. Otherwise, Jesus' superiority over Wai Wai spirits would have been proven, and the Wai Wai should accept the new faith. (Queiroz, in press)

Ewká did not die and in fact became one of the first Wai Wai to embrace the career of indigenous itinerant preacher. "Ewká was sent on various expeditions with the purpose of bringing the Indians on the Brazilian side to the village created in Guyana, for the Mission considered the number of evangelized Indians still small" (p. 226). Since then the Wai Wai have turned into the most active indigenous evangelizers in the Amazon. They are often recruited by the National Indian Foundation (FUNAI) on pacification expeditions, which was the case with the Waimiri-Atroari in the 1970s. Paraphrasing Whitehead's concept of "ethnic soldiering" (1990), I would say that the Wai Wai are a clear case of "ethnic *bibling.*" They serve as beachheads on the evangelical front, pushing their way, Bible in hand, through the uncivilized undergrowth of their heathen brethren to save souls. The big village of Mapuera in the state of Pará has a large temple with twelve indigenous preachers. The village is inhabited by more than one thousand Indians of various ethnic origins attracted by the Wai Wai and all speaking Wai Wai as lingua franca (Queiroz, in press).

Competition between different Christian religions or sects for native souls can be profoundly damaging to the Indians. The tug-of-war between Catholics and Protestants among the Terena Indians of Mato Grosso do Sul in the 1950s is a case in point. There the missionaries' efforts, combined with the work of the Indian Protection Service (SPI), the state agency for Indian affairs, succeeded in dividing the community into Catholic Terena and Protestant Terena and thus created favorable conditions to rule them more effectively.

> The Protestant missionaries came to organize groups of Indians relatively convinced of the doctrine and practice of the Gospel through whom they proceeded to convert a considerable number of individuals in certain villages, to the point of generating some hostility between the Protestant converts and the non-Protestant or Catholic. . . . In those villages . . . a division into two groups occurred: the "Catholics" and the "Protestants." (Cardoso de Oliveira 1960, 104–105)

The split in the communities was aggravated by conflicts between SPI agents and Protestant missionaries. The SPI agents favored the Catholic mission, which had a much longer history in the area. But here we find another example of the "inconstancy of the savage soul," as the Terena played at being either Catholic or Protestant according to their interests of the moment. Quarrels between individuals or families could result in a split along the lines of missionary influence or dissatisfaction with SPI administrators might lead someone to join the Protestants. These were ephemeral allegiances, "for at the first opportunity they would change category again, crossing over from one group to the other with relative ease, depending on the moment's political conjuncture" (p. 106). Strict moral rules were also cause to leave the Protestant group, at least temporarily: "The express prohibition of the Protestants to drink alcohol created situations in which a Protestant convert . . . gave up [the faith] when he had the urge to drink; we thus have the curious fact of individuals who remained in one religious group (in this case Protestant) for a year, then a few months in the other while his craving for alcohol lasted!" (p. 106). Indigenous communities divided because of Catholic-Protestant competition are common in Brazilian ethnographic literature and often are much more serious than the Terena case (Wright 1996, in press; Pereira, in press; Andrello, in press).

One of the most tragic situations at least partly created by the interference of conflicting religious missions is that of the Kaiowá of Mato Grosso do Sul. Both the Brazilian and international press have frequently reported the suicides of young people from this Guarani-speaking group. Since 1986, 191 suicides have been reported (Gomes and Atunes 1995). CIMI counted 85 suicides between 1991 and 1993, 40 percent by people younger than twenty (1994, 37). In 1995 alone FUNAI reported 55 cases of suicide. The reasons for this calamity seem to be several. Almeida cites "missionaries, fundamentalist sects, landowners, the proximity of towns, compulsory labor sometimes coming close to situations of slavery, forced removals from their traditional lands, impoverishment of their ecosystems, and other variables" (1996, 725). Indeed, nearly nine thousand Indians try to make a living in a cramped area of less than four thousand hectares (Neri 1996). But would a nine-year-old girl kill herself for that reason?

A few years ago I happened to see on television a session of exorcism in one of the cult houses on the Kaiowá reserve. A teenager was in contortions amid the nervous screaming of all present, including the missionary who shouted angrily at her and slapped her repeatedly to shake away the demons possessing her. Her eyes were closed, and the girl's face and her whole body were the living picture of fear and helplessness. The scene made me shudder, and those images remained in my mind for a long time, causing me perceptible mental discomfort. How does it feel to live with that on a permanent basis?

A Presbyterian mission has been among the Kaiowá since 1928. More recently, the Kaiowá have been invaded by other opposing sects, most of them rather obscure: "The Word of God to Brazil," "God Is Love," "Bethel," and "an infinitude of fundamentalist evangelical sects that intensely practice their proselytization" (Yafusso 1995; Almeida 1996, 726). The interference in indigenous lives is substantial:

> In the late 1970s, the missionary at the Ramada village committed the offense of snatching a *mbaraka,* a Guarani sacred instrument from the hands of a *pa'i* (Kaiowá priest), and, "in the name of God," tossed it in the fire in a gesture of repudiation of the Indians' religiosity. This caused outrage and the moving of the Guarani priest's family to another area, running away from the incendiary missionary and his fanaticism. (Almeida 1996, 726)

Guarani suicides are not a new phenomenon. They are known to have occurred during colonial times because of slavery and mission life (p. 727). Cultural loss, psychological confusion, and cosmological void are some of the disturbances one finds in the wake of the "sacred fury" (Ribeiro 1970, 32) that has propelled most missionary action since Caminha urged the king of Portugal to hurry up and Christianize the brasis.

Nomad

Let us again begin with a couple of entries from the dictionary:

> **nomad,** *n.* 1. a member of a race or tribe which has no fixed abode, but moves about from place to place according to the state of the pasturage or food supply. 2. any wanderer.
>
> **wandering,** *adj.* 1. moving from place to place without a fixed plan; roaming; rambling; *wandering tourists.* 2. having no permanent residence; nomadic: *a wandering tribe of Indians.* 3. meandering; winding: *a wandering river, a wandering path. n.* 4. an aimless roving about; leisurely traveling from place to place: *a period of delightful wandering through Italy.* 5. Usually, *wanderings.* a. aimless travels; meanderings: *His wanderings took him all over the world.* b. disordered thoughts or utterances; incoherencies: *mental wanderings; the wanderings of delirium.*

The association of *nomad* with *wanderer* is interesting if we consider that a dictionary is a collection of notions assembled to inform the public at large. The popular character of a dictionary's content is what makes it so revealing about received ideas.

What do the two words have in common? First, a negativity, an absence. Nomads and wanderers have *no* fixed abode, moving from place to place *without* a fixed plan. The most outstanding trait is the absence of fixity, of permanent residence. Second, both words embrace the idea of an open-ended, "destination unknown," type of movement; neither implies the return to the point of departure. Third, both entries refer explicitly to indigenous peoples: a nomad is the member of a *"race or tribe"*; a wanderer refers paradigmatically to *"a wandering tribe of Indians."* Curiously enough, the plural noun wanderings evokes something verging on madness as *"disordered thoughts"* or *"incoherencies,"* as in the model phrases *"mental wanderings"* and *"wanderings of delirium."* And last, but by no means least, the thread of thought that links both entries is a movement away from order into unpredictability. Contrasted with a sedentary life, a fixed abode, an established residence, a nomadic/wandering existence evokes an undisciplined loose way of life over which control is not easily exerted.

What is the general public going to make of the close association of aimless movements of body and mind with indigenous peoples? What other natural conclusion would one draw from these canonical descriptions but that indigenous tribes are always nomadic? That the uninformed public so deduces is neither surprising nor shocking, given the catalogue of information contained in dictionaries. Surprise and shock come when specialists in "indigenous" peoples use terms such as nomads and nomadism without a critical appraisal of the words and the pejorative load they have in common

language. Statements such as the following are bound to enter the reper-
toire of prejudiced language and imagery regarding indigenous peoples:

> Under this simple form of social and political organization, the Tasmani-
> ans lived the life of nomadic hunters. They were ignorant of agriculture
> and possessed no domesticated animals—save the vermin which throve
> on their bodies and were from time to time picked off and eaten! Even
> the dog, the almost universal companion of savage man, was unknown
> until introduced by the whites. The quest for food, in brief, was confined
> to collecting, fishing, and hunting. (Murdock 1934, 4)

Not the least of the overwrought features in this pathetic passage from *Our
Primitive Contemporaries* is the exclamation mark capping the description
of a vermin-based diet. One can almost envision the expression of disgust
on the author's face as he comes to the end of that sentence and frees his
reaction in a punctuation mark. Thus described as a negative example of
humanity, the Tasmanians, before being wiped out by Europeans, showed
themselves to be even lower than the average "savage man" because they
lacked not only a fixed abode but "the dog." The same book calls attention
to other examples of the primitive nomad/wanderer: the Semang of the
Malay Peninsula "pursue a life of nomadic hunters and collectors. Rarely
remaining in one place for more than three days, they wander restlessly
about in search of game and the wild roots and jungle fruits which constitute the mainstay of their existence" (p. 88). The Polar Eskimos also have
"a nomadic mode of life. A family rarely remains in one settlement for
more than a single year" (p. 196). The Crow of the Western Plains "subsist
mainly on the products of the chase and lead the life of nomadic hunters"
(p. 267). And, of course, pastoralists such as the Kazak of central Asia,
are pictured as a generic individual who "is primarily a nomadic herder.
His whole existence centers about his domesticated animals" (p. 138). One
wonders how many undergraduates in North America and perhaps elsewhere were fed this book in its heyday, how many dictionary makers used
it as an expert reference to compose their entries.

According to *Webster's Encyclopedic Unabridged Dictionary,* nomad comes from the Greek *nomás,* meaning 'pasturing flocks'. But no
pastoralists known to anthropology are so random in their spatial movement as to render them nomads in the sense of moving about from place
to place as if with no defined destination. By all accounts, routes, sites, and
purposes of herders are well demarcated and structured according to a refined knowledge of both herds and environment. Barth (1964) provides a
superb example of the elaborate design in pastoralist mobility, exploiting
different seasons and ecosystems for different animal flocks in southwest
Asia. From his and innumerable other ethnographic reports, pastoralists

do not fit the notion of aimless wanderers haphazardly following the grazing urges of their animals. Barth, however, insists on the term *long-range nomadism,* as distinct from *transhumance,* because of the long distances involved, often more than a thousand miles. But sheer distance seems to me to be neither a sufficient nor a necessary condition for rendering such well-defined activities as nomadism. Pastoralism has been so fused with the idea of nomadism that reluctance to disengage the two sometimes results in ambiguous statements such as Forde's:

> Nomadism is justifiably associated with a pastoral life, but its extent and character are very variable. Eternal wandering in which no spot is deliberately sought a second time is never found. Everywhere a unit community, whether it be a kin group, a larger clan or a whole tribe, has a fairly well-defined territory which it oversteps at its own risk just as invaders transgress it at theirs. . . .
>
> Moreover, the range of the seasonal movement is extremely variable. While some of the central Asiatic pastoralists . . . cover several hundreds of miles regularly every year, they are not wedded to this wanderlust. (1949, 406)

If the matter requires so much qualification, it surely is a sign of mismatch between the two terms, in which case one might as well drop the idea of nomadism for characterizing the spatial mobility of pastoralists.

Old World "nomads" enjoy a certain reputation as aloof, proud, and independent peoples. Arabs, with their horses, camels, and sheep, and northern reindeer herders epitomize the image of freedom and autonomy romanticized in books and films. In contrast, when the term nomad is applied to Native Americans, it is laden with notions of savagery, primitivism, and cultural indigence. In crossing the Atlantic the word seems to have suffered a slippage of meaning from a technical concept related to a mode of livelihood—the pasturing of flocks—to a moral judgment—a wandering tribe of Indians. This semantic metamorphosis would not be particularly problematic if it had not been appropriated by the dominant society to despoil dominated Indians. Let us examine some cases in which the notion of nomadism was used against indigenous peoples.

The United States, 1854

Article 6 of the Omaha Treaty, designed to allot individual plots of land to Indians, rules that the Indians should be settled in permanent homes on tracts of land specified by the government:

> And if any such person or family shall at any time neglect or refuse to occupy and till a portion of the land assigned, and on which they have located, or shall rove from place to place, the President may, if the patent

shall have been issued, revoke the same, or if not issued, cancel the assignment, and may also withhold from such person or family, their proportion of the annuities . . . or other moneys due them, until they shall have returned to such permanent home, and resumed the pursuits of industry; and in default of their return, the tract may be declared abandoned, and thereafter assigned to some other person or family of such confederated tribes, or disposed of as is provided for the disposal of the excess of said land. (quoted in Kickingbird and Ducheneaux 1973, 16–17)

As Kickingbird and Ducheneaux point out, the "true purpose of the section on allotment is of course revealed in the words 'rove from place to place,'" that is, those "wandering tribes of Indians" were, first, occupying too much land that could be profitably colonized, and, second, as they roved from place to place, controlling them was more difficult. Requiring that the Indians adopt a sedentary life on established portions of land and fixed residence killed two birds with one stone: it liberated land for whites and brought the "tribes" more easily under the authority of the federal government. The individual allotments left a "surplus" of land that was "then sold to the immigrant settlers brought west by the railroads or opened to homestead settlement" (p. 17).

Brazil, 1784

After three years of intense attacks by the Portuguese, the Mura Indians of the Madeira River, a southern tributary of the Amazon, surrendered and allowed themselves to be settled in permanent villages. In Marta Amoroso's fine 1992 description the Mura appear in Brazilian history, together with the Guaikuru horsemen of the Chaco, as the archetype of ferocious nomads. Their reputation as barbarians was built on the strength of their raids on riverboats, colonial settlements, and other Indians who had been forced into a sedentary way of life by the Jesuits. Considered the scourge of the region, the Mura were also hosts to runaway Christianized Indians— ladinos—who fled the poor conditions of life and work at the colonial settlements. In sheltering these refugees the Mura aggravated the hostility of the Portuguese, who officially declared them to be their enemies. With this justification the colonial authorities organized war parties against the Mura and, whenever possible, took them as slaves. The Mura were so bothersome to the government that it made an exception to the Law of Liberties, authorizing their persecution and enslavement (also launched against the equally recalcitrant Munduruku and Karajá).

But what really disturbed the whites was the Mura's supposed nomadism. "The 'uncertainty as to their place of residence,' added to their predatory action, convinces the whites, who do not know where the Mura live, that they are everywhere" (Amoroso 1992, 305). Being everywhere amounts to being nowhere from the point of view of control. They represented an unruly force more akin to baffling nature itself.

> To the eyes of the colonizers, the Mura were attacking all those who moved away from the narrow circle of "police and civility" which represented the urban space drawn by the colonial administration. Agriculture did not prosper because the fertile soil, lying out of hamlet bounds, remained unproductive for being the territory of those Indians. The "pirate heathen" (*gentio de corso*), the barbarian who was not in villages or in hamlets, of whom no one knew the whereabouts, was part of untamed nature. (p. 303)

Fear of uncontrollable Indians, an eighteenth-century truism, spilled over to the next century, recast as contemptuous discourse about the defeated:

> The eighteenth-century images projected onto the nineteenth century comprise a radical ideology in the negative representation of the Mura: demilitarized as enemies, they survive as derogatory images of an incomplete, inept humanity. Thus, the Mura use of the *paricá* hallucinogen, their dances, and their "nomadism" are the features selected by these travelers as evidence of the depraved customs of a population with corrupted habits. (p. 300)

The Mura reached the late twentieth century still complaining of persecution by shopkeepers, landowners, and the police (ISA 1996a, 377).

Using the notion of nomadism against native peoples is by no means a weapon of centuries past. In 1992 a retired general of the Brazilian army, concerned with the prospect of the government's granting a large contiguous area to the Yanomami, told an interviewer for *Veja* magazine exactly what he thought:

> VEJA: Don't you think the Indians deserve a reservation?
> [THE RETIRED GENERAL]: Of course we have to protect the Indians. What is wrong is the way the beer-loving anthropologists (*antropólogos de chopinho*) want to do it. In the case of the Yanomami, there are studies by serious anthropologists who question whether they [the Yanomami] are really nomads. If this is true, why then would they [the Yanomami] need a 9.4 million–hectare area, and, to top it all, along the border with Venezuela? (Júnior 1992, 8)

Leaving aside his interesting system for classifying anthropologists, the general chooses to cloud the issue by associating the need for a large area with nomadism. No nomadism, no large area. The appeal to nomadism—or to lack of it—is part of a broader concern by a large segment of Brazilians who insist that there is too much land for so few Indians, a monotonous refrain intoned whenever the demarcation of Indian lands is at stake. "It is said that it is a waste to 'give' so much land to so few Indians who, moreover, don't occupy all of it, don't know how to exploit its natural resources, are even responsible, albeit indirectly, for the misery of legions of deprived landless Brazilians, and end up opening a flank to foreign cravings" (Ramos 1996a, 18).

I do not know in what category I would fit (I am certainly not a beer lover), but I object to the epithet of nomad perhaps as much as the general does, although no doubt for different reasons. I object equally to application of the concept to the Yanomami or to any other indigenous group in South America. Nomadic (see, for instance, Holmberg 1960; Maybury-Lewis 1974) and seminomadic (see, for instance, T. Turner 1992) are inadequate terms for referring to the spatial mobility of indigenous peoples. *Trekking*, a concept explored in detail by Maybury-Lewis to describe Shavante seasonal movements, like *herding*, says a lot more about the activities in question than the prejudice-laden nomadism. The Shavante's extensive treks along hunting and gathering grounds were never random and open ended. The ethnographer uses the word nomads but recognizes its inappropriateness:

> They were nomads, but not in the sense that their home was wherever they happened to be at a given moment. They had their villages, which they thought of as semi-permanent settlements. Such settlements might be abandoned without too much difficulty and similar half-circles of huts erected on a new site; but they did not generally abandon them without good reason. . . .
>
> A trek starts from the base village and may last as little as six weeks or as much as three or four months. It is deliberately planned by the elders in the men's circle so that the community may move over certain country with a view to exploiting specific resources. (Maybury-Lewis 1974, 53)

Let us return to the Yanomami so that I may clarify in what way my rejection of the term nomadism does not coincide with that of the general. The Yanomami's spatial mobility is a response to the by-now generally acknowledged characteristics of that other part of Amazonia in which they live: extremely poor soils and widely scattered game. One can identify various types of mobility among the Yanomami: seasonal movement from village to summer camp, not very different from the Shavante trekking; the search for new grounds for gardening and hunting in a radius of about 2 kilometers every two or three years, during which previously worked areas lie fallow; and a move farther away, encompassing 10 to 30 kilometers approximately every generation, as the result of the accumulated drain on natural resources in a given area. Moreover, intervillage conflicts and, after contact with European diseases, the outburst of epidemics, are additional reasons for a community or cluster of communities to move away. Considering that nearly ten thousand Yanomami in Brazil are grouped in more than two hundred communities, these movements, some of which are actual migrations, amount to the effective occupation of a considerably large area. The 9.4 million hectares demarcated as Yanomami area in Brazil contemplate precisely this: the exploitation of natural resources, such as soil, game, forest products for food, construction materials, and the like *and* their rejuvenation. One does not need to be "nomad" in order to require an appropriate amount of land to carry on life as usual. Yanomami moves cannot be confused with nomadism, a notion that is too often evoked by dominant society in regard to the exotic primitive. It is against common sense to take any kind of indigenous mobility as a sign of nomadism; I cannot overemphasize that the Yanomami are *mobile,* not nomadic (Ramos 1996a, 18).

Neither the Shavante nor the Yanomami, to limit the examples to two indigenous societies, "rove from place to place" with "no fixed abode" and "without a fixed plan." To insist on the term nomadism to describe what these Indians do when they move in space is to smuggle a word from common parlance and launder it as scientific concept. To use nomadism is to give mobility a bad name, for the term has become associated with a stigma against peoples who simply do not comply with the Western ideal of sedentary life. Nomadism is anathema to the exercise of control. As Fisher properly remarks, "Indian mobility in the nineteenth century was derided because it made for an elusive labor force" (1995, 177). In addition,

> Accusations of nomadism were often tantamount to accusations of "paganism," since nomadism effectively curtailed organized Christian worship. There is no small irony that even indigenous peoples who cooperated with rural officials should be derided for their nomadic lifestyles in nineteenth-century accounts, since colonial administration increased the need for many indigenous peoples to be more mobile. (Fisher 1995, 177)

One presumes that Fisher chose his words carefully. His expression "accusations of nomadism" says volumes and highlights the point I have been trying to make. For one is not accused of something that is approved and legitimate; one is accused of an offense or of a crime. Being nomadic amounts to being vagrant, and police records are brimming with arrests of vagrants with no defined domicile. To accuse Indians of nomadism is tantamount to calling nomadism an offense or a crime and the Indians offenders or criminals. Offenses and crimes must be corrected, and that is what officialdom has been doing in Brazil since 1500.

There are, then, two major problems with the notion of nomadism. First, as a value judgment it opens the way for criminalization of indigenous peoples who somehow evade control, be they Mura, Kayapó, or any other group. Second, as a concept nomadism is far from covering what it is meant to cover, as the passages from Forde and Maybury-Lewis make clear.

If, as defined in dictionaries and in common usage, nomadism does

not exist among indigenous peoples, does it exist at all? What human populations would fit the description of wanderers with no point of reference,
moving about from place to place at random in search of a means of subsis-
tence? The Gypsies? No, as they also have a well-defined circuit of mobility,
returning regularly to the same places (Yoors 1967; Sutherland 1975). Seasonal agriculture workers of the *bóia-fria* type in Brazil or strawberry pick-
ers in the United States? Apparently not those groups either, for they too return to the same workplaces at harvest. Perhaps those who come closest to
qualifying as true nomads with no defined trajectory and destination are the
masses of unemployed from the European job markets who go from country to country in search, not of "pasturage or food supply" as such but of
paid labor. It is ironic that an idea developed in Europe to separate Western
civilization—the hub of civitas, the ultimate form of sedentary life—from
barbarism—iconically cast in the image of nomadic barbarians or medieval
outcasts roaming the countryside (Le Goff 1977)—turns onto itself and
comes to characterize a phenomenon that is a direct result of an excessively
sedentary life. The polis is no longer a guarantee against nomadism.

Primitive

The concept of *primitive* has supplied anthropology with one of its major
narrative threads (Kuklick 1991). Although contemporary authors have insisted that primitive is "essentially a temporal concept, . . . a category,
not an object, of western thought" (as critiqued by Fabian 1983, 18), that
" 'primitives' are made, not found," that " 'primitive peoples' are not a
fact, but an interpretation" (McGrane 1989, 99), the anthropological history of primitive reveals a long experiment in essentializing. Cultures that
were labeled primitive did exist on the periphery of the civilized world,
exhibiting primitive institutions, primitive ways of life, primitive modes
of thought. The result of this experiment has entered common usage in a
variety of interrelated meanings. *Webster's Encyclopedic Unabridged Dictionary* has a rather long entry for primitive:

> *adj.* 1. being the first or earliest of the kind or in existence, esp. in an
> early age of the world: *primitive forms of life.* 2. early in the history of the
> world or of mankind. 3. characteristic of early ages or of an early state
> of human development: *primitive art.* 4. *Anthropol.* of or pertaining to a
> race, group, etc., having cultural or physical similarities with their early
> ancestors. 5. unaffected or little affected by civilizing influences; uncivi-
> lized; savage: *primitive passions.* 6. being in its or the earliest period; early:
> *the primitive phase of the history of a town.* 7. old-fashioned: *primitive
> ideas and habits.* 8. simple; unsophisticated: *a primitive farm implement.*
> 9. crude; unpolished: *primitive living conditions.* 10. original or radical,

as distinguished from derivative. 11. primary, as distinguished from secondary. 12. *Biol.* a. rudimentary; primordial. b. noting species, varieties, etc., only slightly evolved from early antecedent types. c. of early formation and temporary, as a part that subsequently disappears. *n.* 13. someone or something primitive . . . [< L *primitiv (us)* first of its kind . . .].

From the original Latin meaning of "first of its kind," in the sense of initiator, the term was transformed to mean, among other things, savage, crude, uncivilized. Of special interest is the explicit citation of anthropology as a field that correlates "a race, group, etc., having cultural or physical similarities with their early ancestors." In short, *Webster's* identifies the launching pad for the anthropological enterprise, namely, the tenancy of the "savage slot" in the European division of intellectual labor (Trouillot 1991). The search for a civilized identity led the Western mind to look for a mirror. Diamond traces it to Plato's *Republic,* the utopia that was everything that nonurban society was not: "In opposing the primitive, Plato helps us define both it and the state" (1981, 177). From then on, other "races or groups" were all negativity, they were noneverything: no state, no cities, no writing, no history, no money, no market economy, no differential distribution of power, no enlightenment, no . . . Like a sort of inverted prophecy, civilized thinkers looked at "our primitive contemporaries" as if they were looking back into the remote past and saying, "We've come a long way, we are you in the morrow." Or, as Fabian puts it, "What could be clearer evidence of temporal distancing than placing the Now of the primitive in the Then of the Western adult?" (1983, 63). And so anthropology began in earnest its search for the primitive. From the nineteenth-century inclination to slip into the connotations of primitive that *Webster's* provides for biologists' use of the word—"rudimentary; primordial," "of early formation and temporary, as a part that subsequently disappears"—anthropological research has consistently elaborated upon the primitive. A cursory glance at major works in the discipline finds *Primitive Culture* (Tylor), *Primitive Mentality* (Lévy-Bruhl), *Primitive Marriage* (McLennan), *Primitive Classification* (Durkheim and Mauss), *Primitive Art* (Boas), *Primitive Religion* (Lowie, Radin), *Primitive Society* (Lowie), *Primitive Man as Philosopher* (Radin), *Our Primitive Contemporaries* (Murdock), *Primitive Social Organization* (Service), *Primitive World and Its Transformations* (Redfield), *The Father in Primitive Psychology* (Malinowski). The term continues to permeate the field: "In all current standard narratives of contact along the Brazil shore, the Amerindians are presented as 'primitive', 'stone age', or 'naked nomads' " (Whitehead 1993, 198). Among the profusion of meanings anthropologists have appended to the word, the "most troublesome meaning of the term 'primitive' is that connected with various shades of inferiority" (Hsu 1964, 174).

With more or less editorial appeal, more or less embarrassment, more or less critical posture, more or less theoretical sophistication, the primitive has been at the center of the anthropological "master narrative" for more than a century. Kuper traces the crystallization of the idea of primitive in anthropology to the 1860s and 1870s (1988,1), again as a Western specular necessity: "The anthropologists took this primitive society as their special subject, but in practice primitive society proved to be their own society (as they understood it) seen in a distorting mirror" (p. 5).

We reach the second half of the twentieth century still fumbling with the pros and cons of using the notion of primitive. Some consider it to be quite acceptable, together with *barbarian, pagan,* and *savage,* because nothing pejorative is found in their etymological origins:

> *Primitive, pagan* and *savage* are, then, three perfectly respectable words. But *primitive* is the most widely disseminated, in the most recognizable forms, in major languages and has, even today, the least pejorative associations, signifying merely a prior state of affairs, a relative sense of origins. Therefore, I see no reason for abandoning the word, as is periodically suggested, hedging it with quotes, prefacing it with the inexplicit irony of "so-called" or replacing it with limited and misleading expressions such as "pre-literate." The task is rather to define it further and so help to reach agreement on what *primitive* means. (Diamond 1981, 125)

Apart from the contradiction between the statement that primitive, pagan, and savage are perfectly respectable words and the admission that primitive has, even today in major languages, the least pejorative associations (how little pejorative can pejorative be?), the passage displays a rather disquieting feature of these "major languages," namely, the incapacity to denote otherness without connoting inferiority. How are we to refer to that part of humanity, sometimes dubbed the Rest of the West, without applying words laden with value judgments or becoming entangled in complicated circumlocutions that try in vain to skirt prejudice? The silence of these major languages regarding "perfectly respectable" expressions for legitimate otherness is more revealing than the effort to circumvent idées reçues. Diamond continues:

> What I mean to say is that the anthropological term *primitive* applies, or should apply, to the condition of man prior to the emergence of civilization and following those earliest periods of cultural growth culminating in the Upper Paleolithic. . . . *Primitive,* then, refers to widely distributed, well-organized institutions that had already existed just prior to the rise of ancient civilization. . . . [However] contemporary primitives can be roughly conceived as our contemporary, pre-civilized ancestors. (pp. 126,127,131)

He concludes with the rather cryptic remark that "we cannot abandon the primitive; we can only outgrow it by letting it grow within us" (p. 173).

Service, another twentieth-century defender of the primitive, seems to have fewer qualms about its implications. He disagrees with other anthropologists who object to the notion that contemporary primitives shed light on "our" past by retaining cultural traits long lost by civilization. He criticizes Herskovits for wishing that anthropologists had abandoned the habit of "calling such cultures 'primitive,' 'simple,' or 'preliterate' " and justifies his position with an ominous argument:

> What else can explain such a culture, then, but that there have been survivals into the present of ancient cultural forms which because of relative isolation have maintained a relatively stable adaptation. Many primitive societies have changed greatly in modern times and ultimately all will be changed, assimilated, or obliterated, but that only makes the point more clear. Where an Arunta-like way of life is not yet significantly altered by modern influences it is a culture that is primitive, ancient, and preliterate. And it has a very long history, too, for the Arunta culture is paleolithic in type, although the paleolithic *era* ended when and where higher stages arose—a long time ago. . . . In this sense anthropology possesses a time machine. (1962, 8–9)

"Modern influence" translates as the all-powerful Western demiurge capable of transforming the primitive into the civilized when, of course, the demiurge does not mismanage and cause the obliteration of his earthlings, "our contemporary ancestors" (Service 1962, 8). Anthropologists would then be engaged in a race against their own times to collect as much evidence of the cultural big bang as they could before the doom of the primitive. Surely, whoever possesses a time machine is, to all intents and purposes, a demiurge, as science fiction often demonstrates. Curiously, because of his "neo"-evolutionary emphasis, Service transposes to twentieth-century anthropology a feature that McGrane associates with the nineteenth century: "Nineteenth-century anthropology is in many respects precisely a time machine" in its search for the Western past in contemporary non-Western cultures (McGrane 1989, 103).

Service's effort to characterize "primitive society" is an exercise in essentialism. Primitive societies not only exist but can be tangibly described in their constitutive parts. A similar essentialist concern is easily perceived in Diamond's book *In Search of the Primitive*. What he says on page 212— "The idea of the primitive is, then, a construct"—does not revoke previous statements about the substantive ontology of the primitive: private property in primitive society consists of "breechclouts, back scratchers and similar 'extensions of the personality,' "; "primitive economies are natural economies"; "primitive societies abound in 'chiefs' "; in primitive societies "laws as we know them do not exist"; "society to the primitive is apprehended as a part of the natural order" (malgré Durkheim); primitive society "changes its essential form only under the impact of external circumstances or in response to drastic changes in the natural environment," and so on and so forth (Diamond 1981, ch. 4).

Kuper's 1988 book, *The Invention of Primitive Society,* is an attempt to deessentialize the primitive:

> There is not even a sensible way in which one can specify what a "primitive society" is. . . . The history of the theory of primitive society is the history of an illusion. . . . The theory of primitive society is about something which does not and never has existed. One of my reasons for writing this book is to remove the constitution of primitive society from the agenda of anthropology and political theory once and for all. (pp. 7, 8, 18)

But, because old habits die hard, Kuper begins his book with an oddly paradoxical proposition: "The persistence of this prototype for well over a hundred years is the more remarkable since empirical investigation of tropical 'primitive' societies only began in a systematic way and on any scale in the last decade of the nineteenth century" (p. 1). This reminds me of the old Spanish joke about whether witches exist: "I don't believe in witches, but I'm sure they're around." No matter how many quotations marks are put around the word, the message remains that primitive societies do exist after all and they are in the tropics, to boot. Having guessed the existence of primitive society before it materialized in ethnographic writings, the founding fathers of anthropology only bestowed on the concept an aura of inexorability.

Kuper affirms that the anthropological vision of the primitive is either a thing of the past or of the discipline's academic fringes: "The orthodox modern view is that there never was such a thing as 'primitive society' " (1988, 7). Because Kuper does not tell us what anthropological orthodoxy consists of, or when "modern" began, we are at a loss to place Service and Diamond—would they be premodern or fringe academics?

All this is to make the point that anthropology is one inspiration that feeds the Western imagination about Indians. It is an obvious point but by no means trivial. Anthropological discourse is not sufficiently sheltered to be incomprehensible by average readers. It is serious enough that some statements, such as those quoted in this chapter, are issued by professionals for professionals or students. It is worse when anthropologists deliver radio lectures, give television interviews, write newspaper articles, and pop up in other popular media known to spread the anthropological word among the public. The distance between the cultural complexities that churn in the back of the anthropologist's mind and the receiver's simplification process of cultural understanding is sufficiently large to produce a public reality that is often unrecognizable by the discipline's professional. The result is usually unfavorable to the people being discussed. For example, *Newsweek,* in a 1981 article titled "The Vanishing Tribals," quoted anthropologist Francis Huxley as saying that tribal peoples "will have to join the human race eventually" (p. 30). How else would the public interpret this but as implying that tribal peoples do not belong to the human race? Let us take the more complex and perhaps more damaging example of the Yanomami Indians of northern Brazil and southern Venezuela.

In 1976 *Time* had a piece titled "Beastly or Manly" that told readers:

> Implied in Chagnon's findings so far is a notion startling to traditional anthropology: the rather horrifying Yãnomamö culture makes some sense in terms of animal behavior. Chagnon argues that Yãnomamö structures closely parallel those of many primates in breeding patterns, competition for females and recognition of relatives. Like baboon troops, Yãnomamö villages tend to split into two after they reach a certain size. (p. 37)

In 1990 *O Estado de São Paulo,* a major Brazilian daily, published a re-markable article under the headline "Feminists Attack Yanomami" (Sotero 1990). It comments on the reaction of a teacher and students in a com-munications classroom at Menlo College in Menlo Park, California, to Yanomami male violence toward women. The teacher, Marilyn Faulken-burg, responded as follows to a newspaper report about the effect of the gold rush on Yanomami lives:

> According to distinguished anthropologist Marvin Harris, the Yano-mami were nicknamed as fierce people because they practice wife bat-tering and female infanticide. Our question is: does that society deserve to be protected against the twentieth century? Or, put it another way, would the [invading] gold miners be the real bandits in this story as sug-gested in the article? (Sotero 1990)

Sotero quoted the teacher as having said that preserving "so brutal and primitive" a culture would benefit only anthropologists. Her comments were originally published in the letters section of the *Wall Street Journal.* The crudeness of such a view reflects the most virulent form of misappro-priation that can be made of anthropological materials. No anthropologist is immune to this kind of confiscation of ideas. The trade of translating cultural differences into the idiom of the Western world is fraught with peril. It displays the logic of "exotic" realities in a way that generates anything from deep respect to insulted abhorrence. By and large, efforts such as Kuper's to put certain value-laden concepts under analytical scrutiny should be routine in anthropological practice.

Although anthropology may be a major source of ideas about the primitive, it should by no means be held responsible for the political use and abuse of the notion of Indians as primitive, as something of the past that should be eradicated. Laypeople often pontificate about the stage of development of indigenous cultures, but the matter becomes more serious when these laypeople hold positions of authority and therefore feel confident in displaying their value judgments. On April 19, 1989, the National Day of the Indian, the Brazilian army minister Leônidas Pires Gonçalves declared to the House of Representatives' Committee for Foreign Relations in Brasília that the Indians should not be protected because, after all, "Indian cultures are very lowly and therefore are not respectable" (quoted in M. Barbosa 1989, 1026). The barrage of criticism that followed in the media forced some countermessages from other military officers, but the army minister's crudeness rang throughout the country as an example of the obtuseness and arrogance of the powerful. "The Army minister's statements can only disturb us for the prejudice and arbitrariness they contain. We feel distressed for the sad figure of the minister himself, for the Country, for what this means in exposing us to discredit vis-à-vis the enlightened international community, for the Indians themselves" (M. Barbosa 1989, 1026).

Arrogance and obtuseness are by no means limited to the military. Civilian intellectuals such as the writer Osman Lins and political scientist Hélio Jaguaribe have tried their hands at spontaneous ethnography by also declaring that indigenous culture, in the singular, is "so little evolved" (Lins 1979, 27) and that through education the Indians should disappear by the onset of the third millenium. A former minister of science and technology, Jaguaribe shocked the public when he declared: "There will be no more Indians in the twenty-first century. The idea of congealing man in the primeval state of his evolution is, in fact, cruel and hypocritical" (Mõssri 1994; see also Jaguaribe 1994). The occasion was his conference during a seminar, "Education Policy for the Army: The Year 2000," that took place at army headquarters in Brasília. A high-ranking army officer enthusiastically agreed with the speaker: "It is a sociological fatality." Jaguaribe's vulgar evolutionism is one of the explicit expressions of equating cultural diversity with underdevelopment. Like a contagious disease, the Indians' ignorance must be eradicated if Brazil is to grow into a fully developed nation.

Unfailingly, such statements are met with a volley of protests by nongovernmental organizations (NGOs) and other concerned groups and individuals, driving state authorities into the uncomfortable position of having to downplay or even refute their colleagues' damaging forays into futurology.

More often than not, the notion of primitiveness appears in Indigenism as an inverted mirror for the nation at large. For a country like Brazil with a short history, mentions of primeval-ness necessarily evoke a temporal proximity of Indians and Brazilians that verges on having the latter polluted by the former. Hence, primeval lifestyles are no cause for pride but, to the contrary, are reminders of the long road to civilized development. Having primitives within the national territory is like having embarrassing wilderness in one's backyard. If Brazil is to fulfill its self-ascribed prophecy of greatness, it first has to rid itself of all signs of primitiveness.

Savage

A ubiquitous stereotype, the Indian as savage has a history that is far longer than the notion of Indian itself. Well before Europeans ever saw an inhabitant of the Americas, the European mind had centuries of elaborating on the theme of the savage and savagery; "during the fifth century B.C. wild men already formed a well structured though complex stereotype that embraced centaurs, cyclops, satyrs, and giants" (Bartra 1994, 13). Associated with the term savage is the idea of wilderness, raw nature, absence of civilization. Let us see the various ways in which savage is conceived in the dictionary (*Webster's Encyclopedic Unabridged*):

> Savage. *adj.* 1. fierce, ferocious, or cruel; untamed: *savage beasts.* 2. untamed; barbarous: *savage tribes.* 3. enraged or furiously angry, as a person. 4. unpolished; rude: *savage manners.* 5. wild or rugged, as country or scenery: *savage wilderness.* 6. *Archaic.* uncultivated; growing wild. *n.* 7. an uncivilized human being. 8. a fierce, brutal, or cruel person. 9. a rude, boorish person [ME *savage, sauvage* < MF *sauvage, salvage* < ML *salvati(us),* r. L. *silvaticus,* equiv. to *silv(a)* woods + *-aticus* adj. suffix] ...
>   —Syn. 1. wild, feral, fell; bloodthirsty. See **cruel.** 2. wild. 3. infuriated. 5. rough, uncultivated. 9. churl, oaf.
>   —Ant. 1. mild. 2,4. cultured. 5. cultivated.

Although savage has come to be associated with barbarian, the two terms have had different applications. Returning to *Webster's,* we can see both similarities and differences:

> Barbarian *n.* 1. a man in a savage, primitive state; uncivilized person. 2. a person without culture, refinement, or education; philistine. 3. (loosely) a foreigner. 4. (in ancient and medieval periods) a. a non-Greek. b. a person living outside, esp. north of, the Roman Empire. c. a person not

living in a Christian country or within a Christian civilization. 5. (among Italians during the Renaissance) a person of non-Italian origin. *adj.* 6. uncivilized; crude; savage. 7. foreign; alien. [< L *barbari(a)* barbarous country + -AN].... **Syn.** 3. alien. 6. rude, primitive, wild, rough, coarse, ignorant, uncultivated. BARBARIAN, BARBARIC, BARBAROUS pertain to uncivilized people. BARBARIAN is the general word for anything uncivilized: *a barbarian tribe.* BARBARIC has both unfavorable and mildly favorable connotations, implying crudeness of taste or practice, or conveying an idea of rude magnificence and splendor: *barbaric noise.* BARBAROUS emphasizes the inhumanity and cruelty of barbarian life: *barbarous customs.* Ant. 6. cultivated, civilized.

On one level the terms are treated as synonyms; both connote lack of civilization (that is, Western culture), inhumanity, wildness, roughness, cruelty. But while savage is linked to nature's wilderness, barbarian is associated with foreigners, non-Christian lifestyles, but nevertheless humanly created. We might say that savage is to heathen as barbarian is to pagan, the main difference being that the former is devoid of customs, a tabula rasa, whereas the latter pertains to uncivilized but still human traditions.

The two figures—the barbarian and the wild man—were clearly separated in European thinking until the New World was discovered. Barbarians were originally the peoples from far-off lands who did not speak Greek. "For Aristotle, for instance, the barbarian did not have access to *logos,* or reason, because man can only acquire moral capacities in the city.... From a term originally denoting a foreign language, it came to mean non-Greek peoples, and, following the wars with the Medes, it acquired the meaning of cruel" (Bartra 1994, 9–10).

Europeans made war on barbarians but not on wild men, for wild men were not in the same category as full human beings. In contrast to barbarians, wild men existed in nature but in proximity to the civilized. They were in fact an invention of the civilized for the civilized. In his delightful biography of the European wild man Roger Bartra asserts: "History has shown that the explanation of monsters and myths is intrinsically linked to the definition and wisdom of oneself: the I and the Other are inseparable.... Renaissance Europe began to perceive the great utility of a game of mirrors based on the image of the wild man" (1994, 169, 174). Eventually, wild men became associated with peasants (the Greek *agrios*). "From the twelfth century, the term *wild man* (*homo sylvaticus, homo agrestis*) itself became a concrete image referring to an easily identifiable character in medieval iconography and mythology" (p. 63). The image of the wild man was ultimately attached to the socially and politically marginal segments of medieval society. The peasant, the poor, the *rusticus* of the European world represented danger to the integrity of the inhabitants of the polis. "Vicious, dangerous, illiterate, [the peasant] will remain closer to beast than to man. [Medieval] literature mostly excludes him or puts him in its teratological bestiary. Turned realist, literature will then furnish him with the figure which the very High Middle Ages would abstractly define as a medieval Caliban" (Le Goff 1980, 133). The wild man was, however, a necessary evil to the construction of a self-image of the civilized, as it provided an inverted mirror that favorably reflected Christian values. Thus fused with the rustic, the notion of the savage as untamed remote past persisted for centuries.

> In its initial explorations and investigations of the non-European, or rather, non-Enlightened world, the Enlightenment at first encountered mostly "the savage" the "barbarian," and the "idolatrous semicivil" of the East. Then in a complex, obscure and confusing modification, the *savage* as he was mixed with the *ancients* (pagans and Jews) became the *primitive*. (McGrane 1989, 68)

Eyewitness reports from the New World became primary data for a multitude of Old World analyses linking the dwellers of the Americas to the inhabitants of Europe's antiquity in an attempt to assimilate "exotic peoples into their own universe of discourse" (Ryan 1981, 521). As "the discovery of new worlds coincided with the Humanists' recovery of the ancient world," soon the ancients were being explained in terms of the newly discovered "Indians," and vice-versa, "because observers believed that a real, not simply a metaphorical, relationship inhered between the exotic and the antique" (pp. 526, 527).

On a more down-to-earth, pragmatic key, the wild man was good not only for reflecting the superiority of Europeans but also for serving them as, among other things, a beast of burden.

> Guibert of Nogent, the historian who left us with vivid descriptions of a sinister and violent world of wars, relates how the armies of the first Crusade were accompanied by a cannibal troop of professional beggars who went barefoot and weaponless. This troop of wild vagabonds . . . were led by a Norman noble who lost his horse and organized them as a parallel army, providing secondary but invaluable services as carriers of provisions and fodder in exchange for alms and tributes, or managing the heavy apparatus used for siege warfare. (Bartra 1994, 127)

Transposed to America, the wild-man-turned-Indian was also a convenient means of transportation as Taussig (1987) has so dramatically exposed. In what was to become the Brazilian state of São Paulo and the neighboring Spanish-speaking countries, people took produce for sale "on the backs of male and female Indians who carry it as if they were mules, even when they are raising children. . . . The beasts rest in the fields and the Christian

Indians, faithful to Your Majesty, carry the loads" (Buarque de Holanda 1986, 33, quoting the Spanish priest Antonio Ruiz de Montoya).

Historian Buarque de Holanda attributes to this human means of transportation "the main reason for the high prices in São Paulo, given the scarce capacity of the carriers" (1986, 33; also see Monteiro 1994, 122–26).

The mixture of idealization of the exotic with the pragmatic exploitation of the inferior, what Bartra describes as European "horror and fascination for wildness" (1994, 206), was and still is responsible for some of the most gruesome episodes in human history.

> Many centuries later, in the clamor of modern colonialism could be heard the ancient echoes of that Western distaste for peoples submerged in nature, and that fear of a political vacuum accompanied by an absence of statutes and regulations. The nineteenth-century hunt for what Armand de Quatrefages was also to call wild men . . . acquired a brutal and sanguinary character: the so-called Black War—the extermination of Tasmanians by English colonists, who considered the aborigines as little more than animals to be hunted. George Arthur, the governor of the island, attempted to "civilize" the hunt for wild men as a measure to prevent their extinction and offered a reward of five pounds sterling for each adult captured live and unhurt (two pounds for each child). . . . In 1876 Lalla Rookh the last Tasmanian wild woman died, and with her disappeared a people who for many ethnologists were considered to be the most primitive ethnic group known to modern Western man. [Here Bartra refers readers to Chapter 1 of Murdock's *Our Primitive Contemporaries*.] The fact is that the Tasmanians were treated in much the same way medieval man had treated *homo sylvaticus*. The myth materialized into history. (Bartra 1994, 111–12)

Elsewhere in Australia the Aborigines could expect a similar fate. "Behind [the pastoral frontier] they were once again *sauvages*, children of nature, doomed to disappear as the wilderness was brought to order, and meanwhile useful devices in poetic and graphic compositions" (Beckett 1988b, 196).

Back in the fifteenth century the discovery of the New World precipitated the blend of savage and barbarian. Contrary to European expectations, the antipodes were not the monsters that peopled the minds of the old continent. In fact, Amerindians were often praised for their physical attractiveness. They thus came to combine two features that had been kept separate in the European imagination: human appearance (like the barbarians) with natural wildness (like the savage wild men). Hence Caminha's perplexity as he faced the beautiful Tupinambá whose bodily tidiness could only be attributed to their "natural" state:

I deduce they are bestial people and of little knowledge, that is why they are so shy. But despite everything they go about very becoming and clean. And for this I am even more convinced that they are like birds, or mountain beasts, to which the air makes better feathers and better hair than the tame, because their bodies are so clean and so full and so lovely as there can be no better! And this leads me to presume that they have no houses nor dwellings to which they retreat; and the air where they grow makes them so. (Caminha 1963, 50)

From then on the "naturalization" of the Brazilian Indian has been a constant topos in interethnic discourse (see, for instance, the astute analysis by Viveiros de Castro and Andrade 1988).

The Portuguese language makes the passage from wildness to Indian more direct than in English. *Selvagem* (savage) is the inhabitant of the *selva* (woods, jungle, forest) who is then called *selvícola* or *silvícola*. *Silvícola* is actually the official term for Indians in Brazil as it appears in the 1916 Civil Code, the 1967 Constitution, and in the 1973 Statute of the Indian: "Article 1. This Law regulates the judicial situation of the Indians or *silvícolas* and of the indigenous communities, with the purpose of preserving their culture and integrating them, progressively and harmoniously, into the national communion." The text of this law lets it be understood that Indian and *silvícola* are synonyms, but there is no discussion to make this explicit (Agostinho 1982, 61). In any case, the term *silvícola* is enticingly similar to the notion of "the *homo sylvaticus,* who lived in the woods and mountains of Europe" and whose outstanding features were dictated by nature rather than by culture—"nakedness, consumption of raw food, loss of memory, and life in the open" (Bartra 1994, 89, 133). Transposed to literature, these features resolved themselves into characters such as Shakespeare's Caliban, himself a composite of the European wild man and the American "cannibal."

Carried over to anthropology, cannibalistic savages and barbarians stood for the lowest stages of human development. One of the most influential nineteenth-century anthropologists, Lewis Henry Morgan, stated: "The diminution of cannibalism, that brutalizing scourge of savagery, was very marked in the Older Period of barbarism" ([1877] 1963, 541).

Whether stated explicitly or merely suggested, the notion of Indian as savage has been rather frequent in anthropological writings in general and in South American ethnography in particular. "All the South American tribes," said Morgan, "with the exception of the Andean, were when discovered either in the Lower Status of barbarism, or in the Status of savagery" (1963, 188). In the ingenuous prepolitically correct days ethnographers were more candid about their views of the natives, judging by their descriptions of indigenous peoples, including fieldwork hosts. Let us see some examples from the ethnographic record on Amazonian Indians:

> It may well seem that Urubu life is basically ignoble, and the Indians are aptly described as savages. Indeed, though this is something of a rude word, it is no use denying that the Urubus are savage. They were well known for their cruelty and vindictiveness in war, in the days before they were pacified; their rites, among which was the killing and eating of an enemy prisoner, were savage with a vengeance; and their manners are often both crude and barbarous. . . . An Indian may well be savage, but this does not mean that he is unprincipled.
> Savages in fact have morals, and their world, irrational though it may be, is neither disorderly nor pointless. (Huxley 1956, 13)

> Except for a very poor development of the lower legs, the Siriono are well-constructed physical specimens. Ontogenetically, they seem to fall within the normal human race . . . most men and women possess well developed prehensile toes. (Holmberg 1960, 8)

> An old Caliban of a man, dressed in the remains of a sack, was issuing dishes of salt and cakes of brown sugar to the women and girls who crowded up to him. The [Sherente] men were perched like vultures along a pole which ran the length of the room and served as a sort of bench. They kept a sharp eye on those of their numbers who were sorting out the knives and the cloth, the fishing tackle and the bottles of cheap perfume. . . .
> [The author, his wife, and small child] had lived with some of the wildest Indians in Mato Grosso [the Shavante] and even come to like them after a fashion. (Maybury-Lewis 1965, 40, 265)

Nevertheless, anthropological sobriety stands out in comparison with the treatment the press has reserved for the savage, particularly when it aims at vilifying and even criminalizing the Indian. One of the most forceful examples of the Indian as savage ever drawn by the mass media involved a well-known Kayapó man, Paulinho Payakan. In early June 1992 the Brazilian version of *Time* magazine, the weekly *Veja*, had a cover story on him. The cover photograph showed him in full Kayapó regalia and was captioned "*O Selvagem,*" calling attention to the main story, which was headlined, "The Explosion of Savage Instinct" (Gomes and Silber 1992, 68). The long report focused on the scandal that involved Payakan as the alleged rapist of a young white woman from the town near his home village. Neither *Veja* nor the rest of the press seemed concerned about presenting the accusation for what it was: an accusation; they were condemning him in advance of a fair trial. Payakan and his Kayapó wife, Irekran, were accused of having "savagely" raped an eighteen-year-old virgin after a party at his ranch on the outskirts of the town of Redenção. Stories on the case ran relentlessly for two months, with much emphasis on the brutality of the assault. "Payakan and Irekran join their hands and introduce them into the student's vagina. They drink the blood and spread it on their bodies," *Folha de São Paulo* told its readers (1992b). Sadistic sex (Webster's "primitive passions") and cannibalism were fused in a single emblematic act involving offending male and female Indians and a white female victim. At first Payakan admitted having had intercourse (not rape) with the young woman as a result of the festive mood of his barbecue-beer party but then denied it and blamed his wife for the physical aggression.

Whether the accusations were justified or not, the extraordinary repercussions of the case elevated it to a cause célèbre in the history of interethnic relations in Brazil. *Payakan* became a household word as his story transfixed the nation for many weeks. He was the source of erotic jokes. Rhetorically, he was associated with the political scandal of the day, which culminated in President Fernando Collor de Mello's impeachment.

By coincidence the case broke during the Rio Earth Summit, which lent it an extra dramatic quality. The executive secretary of the Brazilian NGOs Forum remarked: "It is curious that amidst the Conference one chooses a case that has not been proved, but is already judged by the press to serve as reportage" (*Folha de São Paulo* 1992a). Payakan was expected in Rio for the 1992 Global Forum when the news of the rape broke.

Paulinho Payakan's political visibility was catching up with him. In 1988 he had received a great deal of publicity for having been tried (with another Kayapó leader and North American anthropologist Darrell Posey) on charges of having denigrated the image of Brazil abroad after a series of meetings with World Bank officials. At one of those meetings he had pleaded against the Brazilian plans to build a series of dams in his Xingu homeland. He and the other Kayapó were ludicrously framed under the Law of Foreigners, the absurdity of which led to the shelving of the case. Two years later Payakan was awarded the United Nations' Global 500 prize and, together with Jimmy Carter, the prize from the Society for a Better World for his defense of the environment.

However, Payakan had also caught the attention of the media for the wealth he had accumulated by selling mahogany and from the levies collected from gold miners within the Kayapó indigenous area. This combination of Indian and wealth offended many a Brazilian. In the 1992 episode news reports constantly mentioned his cars, bank account, and an airplane donated by the *Body Shop,* the British cosmetic chain. For instance, the *Veja* article had a section on "Rich Indians" that expounded on how the Kayapó became the richest Indians in the country, "owners of a fortune in hardwood and gold which sprouts generously from the 3.2 million hectares of their reserve" (McCallum 1994, 3). Payakan's wealth was not lost on the young woman's family. Her attorney declared that if Payakan was considered guilty by the judge, the family would sue for $1 billion in damages. "The leader possesses wealth and can pay the compensation" (*Folha de São Paulo* 1992d).

The publicity also exploited the ambiguity of Payakan's status as "relatively incapable," pointing out the contradiction between his capacity to manage wealth and his legal condition as nonresponsible Indian. One FUNAI lawyer insisted that only "an anthropological report showing that Payakan was an Indian integrated into civilization [could] make him accountable to a penal process" (Gondim 1992a). As for Payakan's wife, who, according to the police, was obviously "primitive," no one doubted that she was unimpugnable. The deputy in charge of the case declared her to be "a real Indian" who could not be punished (*Folha de São Paulo* 1992e). More than two years later, "during the trial, Irekran was not heard because she was considered an Indian with no understanding of the customs of non-Indians" (Gondim 1994). It is possible, although it was never made explicit, that Payakan and/or his lawyers took the course of placing the blame exclusively on Irekran, counting on the unanimous opinion that she was legally unaccountable and thus saving both from conviction.

The attacks on Payakan generated much concern about the risk of jeopardizing the Indian cause while Congress was processing important legislation. "One cannot transform his trial into the trial of the indigenous societies" (Carneiro da Cunha 1992). Feminists tried to disconnect the criminal issue of rape by an Indian from the political issue of indigenous rights. Humanist writers stressed the evil influence of civilization that spoils the innocence of the Indians. Editorials pointed out the change of national mood from tolerance for the Indian condition of silvícola to the discomfort engendered by Indians capable of amassing U.S.$60 million, living in cities, and participating in the world of finance (*Folha de São Paulo* 1992c). Much rhetoric both for and against Indians swept across pages and pages of newspapers, some focusing on the unfair treatment the Indians suffer from national society, others on the privileges they enjoy from the government, which gives them land and impunity. Again from *Veja*:

> The stereotype of savage purity will resound in many places in the world when news of the crime of Paulinho Payakan spreads. Payakan incarnated like nobody else the modern Hollywood Indian, that idealized savage, full of ancestral wisdom, virtuous in his primitive and perfect ecological universe. He is a new generation Indian, created in films like "Dances with Wolves." (quoted in McCallum 1994, 2)

Beneath the outrage against a wild man who dared assault a virgin white woman—as opposed to the much cherished figure of the Indian grandmother who was once lassoed by one's white grandfather to produce splendid offspring (Munduruku 1996, 35)—interethnic tension was on the verge of exploding into armed conflict. At Redenção the baffled non-Indian population staged a demonstration against the Kayapó, their rich indigenous neighbors, and carried placards that said *"Lugar de índio é na aldeia e de estuprador é na cadeia"* (Indian belongs in village, rapist belongs in jail; Gondim 1992b). Rumors had it that the Kayapó were preparing for a counterattack. When the judge in charge of the case—according to whom "Payakan is very dangerous and puts the public order at risk" (Gondim 1992a)—ordered Payakan's arrest, the military police of the state of Pará sent two hundred men to Redenção, "prepared for a war operation within the reserve" (Gondim 1992c).

As it turned out, Payakan was under house arrest in his home village for two years. In 1993 the white woman married a local man who ended up in jail for murder. In November 1994 Payakan was acquitted on the ground of insufficient evidence. He was then "congratulated" by the judge with the exhortation: "Go back to your people" (Gutkoski 1994). That judge interpreted the scratches found in the woman's vagina as having been made by Irekran's fingernails. But because Irekran was "primitive" and therefore could not be held accountable for what she did, the case was closed. Some said the verdict was a tactic to avert a major confrontation between the Kayapó and the non-Indians of the region that was likely had Payakan been found guilty. Predictably, the decision was openly criticized. One female attorney declared: "In Payakan's case, Justice was intimidated by Kayapó pressure" (Nunes 1994).

One of the most striking features of the Payakan affair is the total blend of his act with his ethnic identity. He was not simply a man accused of raping a woman. He was a savage Indian, an attribute that increased exponentially the virulence of the sexual crime with which he was charged. With rare exceptions—such as journalist Gilberto Dimenstein, who commented on how "the image of the rapist is muddled with that of Indian, the eternal victim of savagery" (1992)—there was no attempt to separate male violence from Indian identity. Payakan was the sexually unbridled wild man incarnate, *"o cacique tarado que estuprou uma garota"* (the sexually perverted Indian leader who raped a young girl), as a journalist described him six months before the trial (Machado 1994). The image is disquietingly evocative of the wild man of the Middle Ages, "a monstrous force that nature had unleashed to assail civilized men with a bestial humanity, and who enwrapped whoever he so desired within his colossal embrace" (Bartra 1994, 100).

Then there was the public's reaction to Irekran. *Veja* and *Folha de São Paulo* matter-of-factly informed their readers that in 1991 a surgeon from

Redenção had tied off Irekran's fallopian tubes during a delivery without her or Payakan's consent. This same doctor, who later made the medical report on the rape, was being sued by Payakan for the unethical operation. The press, unable to make sense of a woman who contributed to the unfaithfulness of her husband, attributed Irekran's aggression first to sheer jealousy and then to a quaint Kayapó custom: "The deputy . . . who handles the case, declares having heard from FUNAI employees that there is a legend in Kayapó culture according to which the woman goes back to being fertile only if her man has sex with a virgin. 'I'll look into this story,' says [the deputy]" (Gondim 1992d).

One may well ask why, amid the generalized sexual violence in Brazil and elsewhere, this Kayapó man was selected as the prototype of the rapist. Cecilia McCallum suggests an arresting answer:

> The *Veja* Payakan is a usurper, an Indian rancher, financier and businessman, a pilot and car driver, an international traveler. He is a pervert conqueror, an enemy of Brazil who has taken the place—and the land—that should belong to true Brazilians. Yet this is not his worst crime. This is that he has colonized not only the space and rank of the conqueror, but also the processes of conquest itself. If a surgeon in Redempção [sic] sought to emasculate him by sterilizing his wife, he struck back through the monstrous rape of a "white woman." . . . By so invading the trajectory of the processes of legitimate conquest, he turns the nation against its own history. The *Veja* Payakan and his "tribe" loom in the imagination, threatening to divert the course prescribed by modernism, and to relegate the nation forever to the murky depths of savagery. (McCallum 1994, 7–8)

Far from being relegated to the Middle Ages, the idea of the savage is alive and well in the minds and guts of civilized Brazilians.

I would like to make three final comments by way of summary. The first relates to the construction of the images represented here as entries in a dictionary of prejudice. What do the images of the Indian as child, heathen, nomad, primitive, and savage have in common? Bestard and Contreras attempt an answer: "The assimilation of the Other to a hierarchy in which, for one reason or another depending on the case, the other is always assigned a position of inferiority" (1987, 11). Administrators, missionaries, anthropologists, and journalists are the main producers and/or consumers of these images. State administrators attempt to control "Indianness" through the construction of the Indian as a dependent child; missionaries transform Indians into heathens to justify their mission; anthropologists construct a universe of differences based on concepts such as nomad and primitive in order to theorize about human diversity; and journalists capture Indians at their most exotic as a stunt. All these agents, with their own agendas, have in common an underlying feature: they help build Indigenism up as a multilayered, multifaceted mosaic. Each of these images reflects the differential power that has marked Indian-white relations since the invasion of the Americas. Whether consciously or not, by accident or by design, with good or bad intentions, the net result of the projection of the Indian as child, heathen, and the like has been to foster the conquest of indigenous peoples.

My second comment has to do with the spirit of the age of discovery and its consequences for the future of interethnic contact in the New World. Brazilian Indians, like all other original inhabitants of the Americas, were made to fit molds of otherness cast in medieval Europe and earlier that were simply carried over to the New World in the acts of "discovery." As Bartra says, "In order to understand and value the strange inhabitants of the New World, sixteenth-century Europeans had to rummage in their own cultural memory to find archetypes that could catalogue them" (1995, 219). The Portuguese, like the Spaniards and the English, personified the trend that prevailed in Europe in the sixteenth century, that is, the conviction that the "exotic" Amerindians were simply echoes of the "antique" (Ryan 1981, 527). The European experience with Old World "barbarians" served as a template for interpreting all cultural differences. It was "as if *real* discovery were not the exoticism of the other but his ultimate similarity with peoples already assimilated into European consciousness" (p. 529). Thus "the Spaniards treated the Aztecs and the Incas according to their experience with Muslims in the Iberian Peninsula. The treatment given by the English to the Indians of the Massachusetts Bay colony seems to have been based on what they had previously done to the Irish" (Bestard and Contreras 1987, 21–22). Every idea and every image about Indians had already been concocted back in Europe. Rather than being overturned by the radical novelty found in the new environment, this imagery was simply adjusted to it. Transatlantic travel fused the European wild man with the inhabitant of the Americas, pagans with heathens, sabbat witches with cannibal Tupinambá women, destitute medieval peasants with "nomadic tribes." Even the name *Brazil* seems to derive from an amalgam of two separate notions—Irish and Portuguese—about the existence of a certain enchanted Isle of Brazil, which first appeared on maps in the fourteenth century (Weckmann 1993, 29–40). What European eyes saw as unexpected otherness (human beings with their own customs), European brains processed as expected exoticism (monsters, if not in the physical sense, certainly in terms of customs). Too much was at stake in terms of their own self-identity for Europeans to acknowledge the existence of a whole universe of differences that had not been conceived in Europe. With a certain dose of what was to be identified as Latin American magical realism, Europeans then proceeded to update their vision of otherness as they faced "the very real presence . . . of human communities which seemed unlike anything known in Europe" (Pagden 1982, 4). But the changes were mere finishing touches that did not alter the basic mold of the old structure.

Transposed to the domain of anthropological discourse, this resilience in maintaining old habits in the face of radical differences manifests itself in the permissiveness with which anthropology has allowed terms such as nomad, primitive, and savage to enter its disciplinary vocabulary. This uncritical incorporation of received ideas, smuggled into the profession from the ideologically laden realm of common usage, is a constant reminder of the spirit of an era that anthropology was expected to counteract.

My third comment refers to the specular value of otherness. Several authors cited in this chapter point out the mirror effect of New World peoples on Western self-perception. Diamond affirms that the "idea of the primitive is, then, as old as civilization, because civilization creates it in the search for human [read: Western] identity" (1981, 211). On the primitive as the antithesis of the civilized, Kuper suggests that primitive society "therefore must have been nomadic, ordered by blood ties, sexually promiscuous and communist" (1988, 5). McGrane's analysis of nineteenth-century anthropology concludes that "regarding these savage and barbarous tribes, we're not trying to explain them; we're trying to explain ourselves" (1989, 95). Bartra remarks that "Caliban's lewd and sarcastic aggression profiles a monster who, as a creation of nature's delirium or God's tolerance, exists only to foil Prospero's humanizing and civilizing values" (1994, 194). Considering that "European" was and still is a diffuse identity indeed—a collection of whites of various shades and Christians of many persuasions— the quest for a mirror with the power to reflect a positive and unified image of the Westerner is not at all surprising. Although Christianity provided the thread that tied all western Europeans into an apparently uniform pattern, the split between Catholics and Protestants was wide enough to produce deep antagonisms and cultural differences. "The demographic history of most of Europe," says Hobsbawm, "was such that we *know* how multiform the origin of ethnic groups can be" (1991, 79). Virtually each European kingdom had its own identity and political agenda, which in turn were reflected in their respective styles of colonization in the New World (Seed 1995).

Nevertheless, European countries had at least one thing in common: the quest for world power. Their tactics and immediate aims might have differed, but they agreed on one fundamental thing, namely, that they should conquer the Americas and their native peoples. But Christianity being what it is, conquest needed to be duly justified, and the only justification possible was to elevate Christian values to universal commandments. The exotic native of the New World had to be proved humanly inferior lest the European conquistador incur the sin of doing unto others what he would not do unto himself. Hence the symbolic magnitude of mirrors. On the flat surface of the European-made looking-glass, the more degraded the image of the Other, the more elevated its creators would see themselves to be. Is it sheer coincidence that the appearance of Snow White's likeness in the magic mirror sets off the demise of the all-powerful stepmother? Like a Freudian slip, this fairy tale tells worlds about its authors, particularly the discomfort of the powerful vis-à-vis the powerless, or the anxiety of confronting the Other for fear of turning out less than becoming. Appropriately "European," Snow White, Little Red Riding Hood, Cinderella, and other children's stories have been important telltale clues to the workings of Western imagination regarding alterity. Consider, for instance, the hyperbolic pun depicted in the title and original dust jacket of a modern anthropological classic, *La Pensée Sauvage*. Could it be otherwise?

2
The Paradise That Never Was

If we were to pick a single word to characterize the attitude of the Portuguese toward the newfound land of Brazil and its inhabitants, that word would surely be *ambivalence*. We might begin with the name of the land — Brazil. Originally thought to be an island, the subcontinent received a Christian name from the first Portuguese "authority" to set foot on it, Admiral Pedro Álvares Cabral. Terra de Vera Cruz (Land of the True Cross) soon became Terra de Santa Cruz (Land of the Holy Cross), but neither caught on, and they soon were replaced by the profane designation of Brazil.

Brasil has been associated with brazilwood, the valuable dye that is as red as a hot ember (*brasa* in Portuguese). The new colony's exports of brazilwood helped maintain the crown's economy, so it was something of a consolation prize for the absence of the gold and silver that the Portuguese expected and in which the Spaniards delighted. But the name has a much more complex origin. As early as the fourteenth century the Isle Brasil was part of at least two distinct European traditions. One was the notion of "a moving island that existed somewhere west or south of Ireland; it was one of the many islands that medieval imagination had set on the periphery of the known world" (Weckmann 1993, 29). Thus the word brasil may be derived from the Celt "*Bres,* meaning 'noble' or 'fortunate' [not to be confused with the Fortunate Islands, later renamed Canary], and also 'happy' or 'charming'" (Weckmann 1993, 31).

In the fourteenth century other islands with the name Brasil appeared on European maps. One of these was near the Azores, which after 1500 became associated with the land discovered by Pedro Álvares Cabral. The red wood itself had been known in Europe since the thirteenth century as a product imported from the East primarily by the Italians who called it *verzino*. Brazilwood then "derives its name (*brasil, braxilis, bresdilsi,* etc.) from the Isle Brasil of medieval cartography, according to the belief that this dye wood was its main product" (Weckmann 1993, 36). A blend of fable and fact regarding the word brasil circulated in Europe for nearly two centuries:

> Accumulating legends, moving them in space, re-fusing them, the European imaginary also encompassed the archipelago of the Isles Brasil, a possible transformation of the Isle of San Brendan. From 1351 to 1508, it was to know a multitude of variations: Brazi, Bracir, Brasil, Brasill, Brazil, Brazile, Brazille, Brazill, Bracil, Braçil, Braçill, Bersill, Braxil, Braxili, Braxill, Braxyilli, Bresilge. In 1367, Pizigano's letter mentioned three isles Bracir which, from then on, would be recorded in most maritime charts; their position would be unaltered: "the southernmost of the isles can be found marked in the Azores group, approximately on the latitude of Cape São Vicente; the second remains to the NW of Cape Finisterra, on Britain's latitude; the third to the W and not too far from the coast of Ireland." (Mello e Souza 1987, 27–28)

From the coast of Brazil, Pero Vaz de Caminha, Pedro Álvares Cabral's scribe, wrote the first report of the land: "The soil is very bountiful in yielding to them what they require" (1963, 67). Shortly afterward Amerigo Vespucci declared: "I fancied myself near the terrestrial paradise" (Vespucio 1951, 290). Reports such as these contributed to the creation of the legend of Brazil as an earthly Eden (Buarque de Holanda 1992). But Fray Vicente do Salvador, Brazil's first historian, had a different opinion. The new land was no paradise, and its diabolical character was epitomized by the choice of the name Brazil. He lamented that the original reference to a saintly wood—the "Holy Cross"—was superseded by a designation for the profane commerce of brazilwood (Laraia 1993, 41–42). He also attributed its immaturity to its being possessed by the devil; "He poured over the nascent colony the whole load of the European imaginary where the devil had an outstanding role since at least the eleventh century. . . . Brazil, a Portuguese colony, was thus born under the sign of the Devil and the projections of western man's imagination" (Mello e Souza 1987, 28).

Regarding the inhabitants of the Americas, the first sign of European ambivalence is, of course, the misnomer *Indian*. In his search for India Columbus found "Indians," an appellation that took on a colossally negative load for centuries to come. The Indian as Indian could easily fill many pages of a dictionary entry, as it in fact does. "From the beginning, the dictionary has contributed to the construction and later diffusion of a stereotyped image of the Indian" (Reissner 1983, 137).

When I mention European ambivalence toward Brazil's original inhabitants, I am referring to attitudes that oscillate between an Edenic admiration and an urge to civilize them. We see this ambivalence both today and in the earliest reports by the European discoverers. Consider the

first descriptions of indigenous peoples on coastal Brazil, such as the letter by Pero Vaz de Caminha and the letters written by Amerigo Vespucci,
all about the Tupinambá. Although he praises their innocence, their cooperation in work and desire to trade, Caminha envisions them as fertile
ground for Christianization. Just as the land "is so gracious that, if one
wants to use it, it will yield anything because of the waters it contains,"
so the natives, so blameless and unfettered, present themselves as the ideal
virgin soil for conversion: "One can easily imprint on them any mark we
choose, for Our Lord has given them good bodies and good faces as befits good men" (1963, 67, 60). The Indians were good but not yet good
enough: "Therefore, if anyone is to come here, let a clergyman come along
to baptize them" (p. 65). In fact, as the days of that memorable week of
April 1500 went by, Caminha's letter showed "a progressive degradation
of the image of the Other" (Barreto 1983, 181).

Amerigo Vespucci was similarly impressed by the land. But unlike
Caminha, who had a very confined and brief stay in Brazil and perceived no
internal differences among the natives, Vespucci, who traveled widely along
the coast, was exposed to various faces of the numerous Tupinambá, albeit
reducing them to two types: the gentle and the brutes. With the gentle he
traded, with the brutes he made war and took them home as slaves.

This double image of the good Indian and the bad Indian—"the 'noble
savage' and the 'dirty dog'" (Marchant 1942, 22)—living in equally ambivalent surroundings—from blissful wilderness to Amazonian green hell—
was to remain a constant theme in the history of Indian–non-Indian contact.
But while in the early days of European conquest both images were blended
into the same discourse, especially so in Caminha's case, in later years and
centuries they separated, with different groups espousing either the Edenic
discourse or the civilizing discourse. The former emphasizes the purity of
Indians in communion with nature; the latter takes the Indians to be as
much objects of domestication as the land itself. But, as Retamar points
out, "both ways of considering the American, far from being in opposition,
were perfectly reconcilable" (1989, 8). Indeed, they are opposed only in appearance, for while the Edenic discourse exalted the Indians as children of
Paradise, its proponents did nothing to prevent real Indians from being an-
nihilated by European diseases and unrelenting slave raids or beleaguered
by Christianizers intent in eradicating their indigenous identities. For the
Edenists flesh-and-blood Indians were an abstraction. The real thing was
the idea of the noble savage, the avatar of Europe's lost innocence.

In an alluring essay on the influence of Brazilian Indians on the formulation of ideas that led to the French Revolution, Melo Franco traces
the editorial trajectory of some travel writings, including Vespucci's 1503

Mundus Novus letter to Lorenzo di Medici, and the letters' enormous repercussions in propagating the image of the good savage. Melo Franco does a
rather selective reading of Vespucci, omitting passages about cannibalism,
for instance, where the navigator says: "We endeavored to the extent of our
power to dissuade them and persuade them to desist from these depraved
customs" (Vespucio 1951, 303). Nevertheless, Vespucci's and many other
writings by eyewitnesses described alien customs and compared and contrasted them to the European status quo; thus the Indians' customs were
interpreted as proof that humans, living in a natural state, are essentially
good. As a result, European institutions were questioned, and the days of
teratological fears that haunted the European imagination until the Middle
Ages came to an end. "The notion of the cruel and monstrous savage
was completely superseded by the idea of the good savage" (Melo Franco
1976, 30). Reports of the ways of life of the Tupinambá and other indigenous groups on the Brazilian coast would have been responsible for the
formation of a new European attitude regarding good and evil in human
nature. The outcome of all this was "an evolving movement of European
public opinion toward the formation of a theory of natural goodness"
(p. 30). The political consequences of such movement were truly momentous. "In the field of political ideas, the theory of the good savage was to
set a definite course, or rather, give a more conscious theoretical meaning to the confused feelings of revolutionary individualism which presides
over and guides the whole conception of Renaissance" (p. 17). The praise
of the noble savage in sixteenth-century reports made a particular impression on such writers as Montaigne, "and also, nearly two centuries later,
on the fiery work of Jean-Jacques Rousseau" (p. 27). Events such as the
"Brazilian feast at Rouen," held in 1551 with a simulation of the quo-
tidien life of a Tupinambá village in which real Tupinambá and French
actors performed comme il faut, contributed to cement the notion of the
noble savage (pp. 46–49). The remarkable illustration reproduced from a
book by Ferdinand Denis is a sort of microcosmic rendering of the European vision of the inhabitants of the New World. Against a paradisiacal
background of woods and sea a multitude of natives engages in various activities: couples lie romantically in hammocks, stroll leisurely among the
trees holding hands, or otherwise court in the nude; men haul tree trunks
to the shore; others paddle canoes, climb trees, or shoot birds with bow
and arrow, enter huts surrounded with low suburban-style fences, dance in
a circle, and fight each other while bodies lie on the ground. Interestingly
enough, the illustration contains no sign of cannibalism, which often appears in sixteenth-century drawings. The minds of Renaissance Europeans
were not troubled by their simultaneous fascination with the good natural

life of the Indians and abhorrence of cannibalism, but Denis's rendering of the Brazilian feast at Rouen duly expunged anthropophagy, perhaps in deference to the royalty for whom the event was organized.

Meanwhile, the legion of civilizing agents in direct contact with the Indians proposed that they be turned into civilized persons, even as these Indians were being killed or shoved into the fringes of society. For the civilizing agents Indian was a passing condition with no future in the world of Europeans, and because Indians showed themselves to be inept at becoming civilized, they might as well die out. Although it may seem paradoxical, the civilizing rhetoric concludes that the Indian has no place in civilization.

Let me give a few examples to illustrate how the Edenic and the civilizing discourses have become part of Brazilian interethnic relations. These are brief sketches of the Indian of romantic literature, the Indian of regional society, the Indian of the missionaries, and the Indian of the state. Each image deserves a detailed and extensive discussion, but for introducing how the Indian has populated the national imagination, even before the Brazilian nation existed as such, I believe they give a basic idea of how various types of Brazilians have used the Indian and in so doing added another layer of meaning to the ideological edifice of Indigenism.

The Noble Savage in Three Acts

The nativist moment of the eighteenth century and the romantic moment of the nineteenth century are best depicted in paintings, music, and especially in literature. The difference between them is subtle and may even be somewhat artificial, but it is useful in attempting to identify the similarities and differences in the political and ethical approaches of those centuries to the Indian issue.

In a sense the nativist era reflects the shock waves of the Enlightenment as they reached Brazil: the fascination with the unspoiled native, the aesthetic value of nobility of character, the spiritual potential of the pristine purity of the New World. One of the most outstanding examples of this phase is the poem *Caramuru*, first published in Lisbon in 1781 by an Augustinian friar, José de Santa Rita Durão. The poem is an epic about a Portuguese man, Diogo Alvares Correia, who, so the story goes, survived a shipwreck in 1510 off the coast of Bahia, went native, and married Paraguassu, the daughter of an Indian leader. In the poem Diogo Alvares, one of the most famous squawmen in Brazilian history, is portrayed as a nobleman and Paraguassu as an Indian princess. Durão's writing enhances Alvares's nobility through his metamorphosis into the native Caramuru. He becomes the hero in Paradise (Barros 1968). In glorifying his hero the friar suppressed some embarrassing traits of Alvares's character, such as accepting the sexual favors of young Tupinambá girls and passing on to the Portuguese crown large plots of land he acquired through his marriage to Paraguassu (Candido 1967, 201–202).

The Diogo Alvares of historians seems to have been anything but a nobleman. Mendes de Almeida, for instance, points out his obscure origins, adding that "it is not certain whether he was the survivor of a shipwreck, a convict, or a deserter from Crown or private ships" (1876, 21). He attributes "this legend or pious fraud" to the efforts of Alvares's apparently numerous illegitimate offspring to erase the "irregularity of their origin" (p. 18). Caramuru, he says, "had no greater importance than that which resulted from his knowledge of the Indians' language; but like him there were others on the shores of Brazil" (p. 21). Other historians are equally critical of the "Caramuru myth" (Varnhagen 1848; Marchant 1942). Paraguassu in turn was described as the Brazilian equivalent of La Malinche, "an instrument to best dominate Bahia" (Rocha Pitta 1950, 53).

By a stroke of Durão's pen Paraguassu, when taken to the Court of Paris, brings along the innocence and purity of the Indian and adds to these virtues the indispensable qualities of wifely dedication and fidelity, all enhanced by a Christianized persona. "Like the most authentic heroine of European tradition," she is depicted as having white and rosy skin, rejecting the nudity of her companions, and displaying a pious concern for the spiritual fate of her relatives and neighbors. In changing her name to Catarina, a homonym for the queens of both France and Portugal, she completes her civilizing process "in an opposite and symmetrical movement" to that of her husband. They are together in "the same ideal situation of ambiguity" (Candido 1967, 208). Paraguassu represents the much cherished image of the Indian princess who marries into European society. One is only too aware of the remarkable similarities between Paraguassu's literary trajectory and that of the North American Pocahontas (Hulme 1986, 137–73; Stedman 1982).

Caramuru, then, is the story of a European man who went native and of an Indian woman who went European. The characters are allowed to cross the cultural boundaries only because the Indian is portrayed as holding those qualities treasured by Europeans—dignity, courage, monogamy, impeccable honesty, unspoiled by greed or any other sin. The couple represent the best of two worlds. But the fusion of these worlds is possible only because the Europeans—represented here by Friar Durão—projected their ideal virtues onto the Indians. The proclaimed nobility of Europeans was thus heightened by their social and sexual intercourse with the noble savage, so long as that savage was domesticated by Christianity. Only thus was it possible to create *Caramuru,* the European with the strength of character and psychological malleability required to colonize the new land. This image of the easily adaptable Portuguese who populated the colonies of Africa and America, thanks to their lack of prejudice toward black and Indian women, was to remain one of the strongest ideological artifices of Portuguese colonization vastly praised by such authors as Brazilian sociologist Gilberto Freyre (1953, 1992; see Araújo 1994). To this day we find statements praising the fecundity of the Portuguese and their ability to merge with the natives. Ribeiro writes:

> The Portuguese was the Jesuit lime and the genetic oil which cemented the Indian sand and the black gravel in the edification of Brazil. He was the nerve of those fleshes and bones; from a small bunch of people, they multiplied in a prodigious way, lusitanizing the world, in a feat as unbelievable as grandiose, impossible to imagine if it had not been accomplished. (1993, 43)

Caramuru is the quintessence of the Edenic discourse at the service of exalting the feats of the colonizers to the benefit and appreciation of the colonized Indians. Europeans and Indians are thus inextricably intertwined in the same glorious destiny, that of an emerging nation. It is no mere coincidence that "the Portuguese dominion in Brazil was showing the first signs of declining, and the colonial system itself was beginning to run into contradictions with local realities" (Candido 1967, 202). In such a context the literary elite of the colony was encouraged to promote a "Brazilian historical tradition, in order to justify the political individuality of the country" (p. 203).

In the next century we find the "Indianist" moment also glorifying the Indian, again an abstract Indian whose real life was never directly observed by these artists. Two major writers, José de Alencar and Gonçalves Dias, are perhaps the main representatives of "Indianism," a literary movement that used indigenous imagery and whose thrust was to create a style of literature with a distinctly Brazilian flavor, free from European influence. They sought inspiration in what they regarded as authentically Brazilian—the Indian. These authors were engaged in a more or less conscious enterprise of making a culturally independent Brazil, following its political and administrative independence in 1822. Their endeavor was no longer to show the nobility of the Portuguese but the vitality of the Brazilian. Such vigor was not imported from Portugal but inherited from the natives of the land. From the Indians, or what they imagined the Indians to be, they extracted the ingredients necessary to compose a recipe for Brazilian nationalism: "Brazilian Indianism glorifies the Indian as the original inhabitant of Brazil and proclaims him the main source and origin of the new, superior race and civilization that has originated in Brazil, thanks to the miscegenation of two races and cultures: the Indian and the white, European" (Lemaire 1989, 59).

In making ample use of the exotic these writers aroused the reader's imagination not with ethnographic accuracy but with the equipment they knew how to handle best, which ironically was the European imagery of the Indian, heavily shaded with erotic innuendo, astonishing surroundings, or unbelievable displays of bravery. Gonçalves Dias excels at this formula, mixing female beauty, titillating women's attire, grandiose landscapes, and intrepid male courage. It is, in Candido's expression, a "cocktail of medievalism, idealism, and fantasied ethnography." Gonçalves Dias's poem, *I-Juca Pirama* (1851), about the lament of a brave Tupi prisoner facing death at the hands of his enemies, is, continues Candido, "one of these undisputed things which have been incorporated into the national pride, it is the very representation of the country together with the magnitude of the Amazon, the Ipiranga cry [of Independence by Emperor Pedro I], or the green and yellow national colors" (1993, p. 75). Candido praises Gonçalves Dias as a great poet, "in part for his capacity to find in poetry the natural medium for the feeling of fascination for the New World of which Chateaubriand's prose had been the main interpreter up until then" (pp. 73–74).

José de Alencar's *O Guarani* (1857) is about a Guarani Indian, Peri, whose dedication to his white masters rescues them from the rage of his enemies, the Aimoré, a society of warriors and, of course, cannibals. Peri falls in love with the young woman Ceci, but no sanctioned union is possible between them. Here we find again the asymmetry of miscegenation: white man + Indian woman = yes; white woman + Indian man = never. In Brazil as in the United States (Stedman 1982) or elsewhere interethnic romance is always a one-way affair, for "miscegenation, especially between white females and nonwhite males, must never occur" (Torgovnick 1990, 53). It seems to have been out of the question to conceive of white women who "lowered" themselves to the appeal of colored men, let alone who were responsible for generations of mestizos. At the end of the novel Peri heroically saves Ceci from death in a portentous storm that killed her family and destroyed their property, to end up platonically beside Ceci on the frond of an uprooted palm tree, placidly drifting down the torrent. Peri is almost as strong as the natural elements and the epitome of abnegation, altruism, and strength of character. A true noble savage who knew his place, that is, a social outcast, he was never allowed to enter white society as an equal.

The ambivalence of the nascent Brazilian society toward the Indians becomes very clear in these literary works. If, on the one hand, Indian blood is a necessary ingredient in the formation of nationality, on the other, the mixture of indigenous and Portuguese blood must not be effected at random. Brazilian ideology of miscegenation may at first seem to be a straightforward case of racial inequality. But it is best understood as a basically political and moral issue. Otherwise, why permit — if not actually encourage—Indian females to cohabit with European males while strongly barring unions between Indian males and European females? Brazil is an example of gender speaking louder than race. Important as it may be, the racial factor is not sufficient to explain the way in which the Brazilian nation has handled the question of miscegenation.

Alencar dedicated two more books—*Iracema* (1865) and *Ubirajara* (1874)—to the theme of Indianism as his search for a truly Brazilian persona and distinct intellectual identity. Candido vividly points out the relevance of the fictional Indian to the self-perception of Brazilians:

> Just as Walter Scott fascinated Europe's imagination with his castles and knights, so did Alencar establish one of the most cherished models of Brazilian sensitivity, namely, that of the ideal Indian as developed by Gonçalves Dias, but projected by him onto daily life. The Iracemas, Jacis, Ubiratãs, Ubirajaras, Aracis, Peris—who every year for about a century have disseminated the "genteel bunch of lies" of Indianism through baptismal fonts and registry offices—translate the deep will of the Brazilian to perpetuate the convention that gives to a country of mestizos the alibi of a heroic race, and to a nation with a short history the depth of legendary times. (1993, 202)

In a form of domination the romantic figure of the noble savage, as promoted in literature, painting, and music, has been benign only in appearance. In order to sustain itself literature needs to keep the Indian in the bush and in purity of sentiment. A demoralized drunken Indian lying in some town gutter would be unthinkable to writers such as José de Alencar or to musicians such as Carlos Gomes, the author of the opera *O Guarani*. Equally unthinkable to these artists would be the image of a politically active, vociferous Indian accusing national authorities of murder, theft, and immorality, as the twentieth century was to witness.

The self-sacrificing Peri of Alencar's novel and Gomes's opera, along with other Indian heroes, is a useful ingredient for brewing the powerful fiction of the melting pot to which Ribeiro refers. Somehow, this fiction succeeds in the remarkable juggling act of keeping the noble savage both noble and isolated while mingling him with the rest of the population to beget this miracle that is the Brazilian nation. Again, Ribeiro: "Brazil is more than a mere ethnic unit, it is a national ethnic unit, a nation-people, settled in its own territory and framed within the same State. . . . Brazilians are integrated into one single national ethnic unit, thus constituting one single people incorporated into a unified nation, in a uni-ethnic State" (1995, 22). In an afterthought that tries to accommodate his blunder, Ribeiro concludes: "The only exception are the multiple tribal microethnic groups, so imponderable that their existence does not affect the national destiny" (p. 22).

Part of the mindset that reduced the Indian to a component of the great national makeup is a series of verbal and gestural statements, both popular and official. For instance, folkloric to a fault is the much repeated story (by all sorts of people, including São Paulo taxi drivers) of the Indian grandmother who was caught with a lasso. It is a little half-joke usually told in the most candid of moods and as if it were highly original to people who are perceived as having anything to do with Indians or even to Indians themselves (Munduruku 1996, 35). It goes without saying that the joke never involves an Indian grandfather or father (too humiliating for a man) or an Indian mother (too close for comfort) who was lassoed. To have a wild Indian grandmother is reason for pride; it is a valid passport to authentic Brazilianness.

A more recent rendering of the Indian as an ingredient of nationality is a television advertisement for army recruiting. A fully clad young soldier has his face slowly and subtly transformed from white to black to Indian, the three shapes and colors of which the Brazilian citizen is made. The Indian fades into a soldier's uniform as the old myth of national origin enters the electronic era.

Both the nativist and the Indianist modes use Indian imagery to construct non-Indian identities, be they of the indomitable colonizer or of the proud nationalist. We find a rather sardonic version of these trends during the modernist movement of the 1920s. The figure of the Indian Macunaíma, created by writer Mário de Andrade, who sought inspiration in a myth cycle of the Makushi Indians in the northern state of Roraima, represents the amoral hero (*herói sem caráter*) who uses his magic powers to play tricks of all kinds on both friends and foes. As a sort of comical trickster Macunaíma has become a symbol of the self-derision in which Brazilian nationalists often engage as a way to set themselves apart from European hegemony. In the movie version of the story of Macunaíma, the Indian hero metamorphoses into a wicked black man. The soldier of the army ad might as well be a latter-day Macunaíma without the original sense of humor.

Why does nationalism draw so much of its imagery from the Indians? Benedict Anderson argues that "this need to indigenize American nationalism seems only to have appeared as a conscious project well after political independence was achieved." Moreover, because "the ascendancy of creoles and mestizos" was based on the extermination, domination, and/or marginalization of indigenous populations, " 'indigenization' almost everywhere was necessarily constructed in bad faith and as a kind of political theater" (1988, 404). A robust, autonomous, indigenous population would perhaps keep the conqueror too busy with weaponry to give him imaginative leisure to invent ethnic metaphors.

Advocates of the romantic vision of the Indian are a resilient lot, not at all confined to the past. They still exist, increasingly shocked by the spectacle of fast change—the pure Indian is steadily disappearing behind pants and shirts, transistor radios, pocket calculators, sun glasses, video cameras, and cynicism. For them a good Indian is still a naked Indian, unspoiled by the evils of civilization. Those Indians seen on television delivering fiery speeches in Congress (Chief Juruna in the early 1980s), threatening to throw the president of the National Indian Foundation (FUNAI) out of a window or occupying FUNAI's presidential office (Shavante men in the early 1980s and late 1990s), denouncing missionary excesses at the Fourth Russell Tribunal (Álvaro Tukano in 1980), or waving a machete in the face of top-level executives (Tuíra, the Kayapó woman, during the 1989 Altamira meeting; see C. Ricardo 1995, 47) are not really Indians and are no longer a redeeming race but subversives, a threat to civilization. Only in the condition of natural purity can Indians be raised to the honor of ancestors of today's Brazilians.

A modern version of the romantic mode of Indigenism is the attitude of some "friends of the Indians," among university people, journalists, lawyers, artists, anthropologists, and the like, who seem to demand from the Indians an unshakable integrity. Indians must defend to the death, if need be, the firmness of their convictions, be these fighting for land, resisting official or private development plans, refusing bribes, or rejecting dubious deals. These friendly professionals have shown themselves willing to lend their solidarity only to Indians who demonstrate ideological purity. In 1982 I witnessed an instance of intransigence to indigenous political autonomy. During the first national meeting of indigenous leaders held in Brasília, most of the dozen or so anthropologists in attendance rebelled against the Indians' decision to invite the president of the National Indian Foundation to deliver a speech. Because national opposition to the military, in power since 1964, was gathering momentum, the move by the Indians to pay tribute to a man such as Colonel Paulo Moreira Leal, head of FUNAI and a member of the National Security Council, the biggest symbol of military repression, was taken as an affront to the friends of the Indians at the meeting. For decades sympathetic Brazilians had directly or indirectly confronted the Indian policy carried out by the military. Moreover, these militants thought that because they had helped the Indians organize and run the event they had the right to tell the Indians who were the good guys and who were the bad guys. Some felt personally betrayed by the indigenous leaders who showed no consideration for the political commitment of Brazilian citizens struggling to put an end to the military dictatorship. The Indian cause at that time was a vehicle for dissatisfied Brazilians to vent their political grievances. The problem was that the Indians seemed to have a mind of their own—they were attuned to issues that did not quite coincide with those of their friends.

Virtuous principles, purity of ideology, and disposition to die heroically are, of course, Western fantasies, but it does not occur to these militant indigenists that in demanding such moral high standards from the Indians they are in fact looking for the ideal of the idealist who does not crumble under pressure. The contrast between the martyred Indian and the sold-out Indian becomes the contrast between honorable and corrupted Westerners. The one-way ideological mirror is typical. To expect the Indians to resist pressures and die in the name of unattainable principles is as intolerant an attitude as that which denies Indianness to Indians who wear Western clothes and speak Portuguese.

A more recent trend cuts across national boundaries and focuses on environmental preservation. The ecological movement shares two main features with the nativist and the romantic discourses—emphasis on the Indian-as-part-of-nature and affirmation of Indians' purity. Because Indians are closer to nature, the assumption is that they are purer, less affected by the evils of this world, and therefore should always demonstrate the integrity of the unspoiled. To fall from the purity of nature is to be lost to humanity and, as such, to be undeserving of protection. A latter-day Edenic discourse in search of a threatened Eden, the ecological movement in its most naive incarnation (although relatively recent, the movement already shows considerable internal differences) takes Indians as a monolithic figure, the companion-cum-keeper of beast and plant; as an integral part of nature they are also threatened and, like fauna and flora on the verge of extinction, need to be protected by the enlightened few of Western civilization. Thus the protector comes full circle in five hundred years: from invader to savior. Widely publicized international campaigns involving prominent political figures, show business stars, religious leaders, and news media experts cry out for the saving of Amazonia and, by extension, the Amerindians.

Comparing the romantic attitudes of the nineteenth and twentieth centuries, we can detect an interesting difference underlying their common denominator, which is the image of the noble savage. Whereas nineteenth-century romantics used indigenous imagery to highlight the virtues of Western civilization—Alencar, among others, was searching for the foundations of a genuine Brazilian nationality—twentieth-century environmentalists, intent on the preservation of wilderness areas such as Amazonia, embrace the cause of the forest and the Indians as an instrument to criticize that same Western civilization. One century later the promises of industrial society have turned into polluted nightmares for critics of progress and technological expansion. For them the Indian has maintained a pristine innocence and wisdom and is therefore a fitting symbol for the Paradise on earth that is about to be lost.

The reasoning seems to follow a straightforward exercise in Cartesian logic: unspoiled nature is pure; the Indian is part of nature; therefore the Indian is pure. Such purity then becomes associated with the wisdom that Westerners once had but have lost in the deluge of technological progress and its by-product, the destruction of the environment. Now the West badly needs to recover its lost wisdom in order to rebuild, no longer a single nation but the entire planet. The Indian enters this gloomy picture as the wholesome reservoir of wisdom, ready to be reappropriated by the dominant society. In this trajectory of the Edenic discourse, from Paradise Found to Paradise Lost, the figure of the immanent Indian has been a crucial instrument for the transcendental Westerner. For it is Westerners that "find" Paradise, transform it to the point of ruining it, and then, again through their volition, rescue the Earth from their rapacity by tapping indigenous resources that seem to exist for no other reason than to serve the needs of Westerners. As sovereign agents of the world, they have reduced the Indians to mere hostages of economic terrorism.

For all its apparently sympathetic and benign inclinations that the environmentalist rhetoric (and the less sophisticated side of ecological activism) displays toward the Indians, it conceals an element of paternalism and intolerance that can easily come to the surface whenever the Indians fail to meet its expectations. If a good Indian is a pure Indian—and here, as usual, the definition of purity is given by the dominant society—an Indian who falls prey to Western seduction by, for instance, selling lumber to foreign companies (such as the Kayapó leader Payakan), making pacts with the military (such as Álvaro Tukano), or striking deals with corporations (such as various factions of the Gaviões, Kayapó, and Tukano) is denigrated and doomed to fall lower than the wheeler-dealer. An Indian who has sold out is, in short, much less deserving of understanding or forgiveness than a Brazilian in the same situation. Assigned the absurd role of guardian of humanity's reserves of both natural resources and moral purity, Indians become charged with the "white man's burden" in reverse, whether they want it or not. In Chapter 1 we saw in Payakan's case an exemplar of the condemning disposition of the dominant society regarding alleged offenses by Indians. We shall see other examples in the chapters to come. It might be an instructive exercise to imagine the reverse situation—of Indians judging the purity or corruption of Brazilians. The Shavante Mário Juruna made a few incursions in that direction and, as will be apparent in Chapter 3, paid a high price for it.

The Civilizing Project and Its Contradictions

Running parallel to the eulogizing eloquence of the Edenic rhetoric is the civilizing discourse, which contains a series of images of the Indian with as long a history but which exploits features that are diametrically opposed to those of the children of Paradise. The idiom of conquest and control has as its basic premise the inferiority of the Indians. They are the creatures of barbarism, either renegades or ignorant brutes, much in the vein of Vespucci's image of the "bad" Tupinambá or of the Jesuit Manoel da Nóbrega's "filthy dogs" (Mello e Souza 1987, 64).

The civilizing discourse began with the first encounter between the Portuguese and Brazil's coastal Indians in 1500, when Caminha urged the king of Portugal to quickly send Catholic priests to convert the innocent people of the land. But it took a few more years before Europe was confident that the Indians were human and had souls to be conquered by the faith. The papal bull of 1537 signed by Paul III declared the natives of the Americas to be humans and therefore open to Christianity (Bestard and Contreras 1987, 11; Bosi 1989).

The job of taming the wilderness began just a few decades after the discovery of Brazil. Once the Portuguese got over their initial surprise at meeting mere people and not the monsters conceived by European imagination, the ordinary physicality of the Indians was countered by the monstrosity of their customs, namely, incest, cannibalism, and nudity (Baêta Neves 1978, 56). Hardly thirty years had gone by since Cabral's memorable landing on the coast of Bahia, and early traders and settlers were already waging wars against the Indians, enslaving them, looting their resources, and dislodging them from their lands. The new colony had an Aristotelian attitude, regarding the Indians as natural slaves; they might be human, but they certainly were the Europeans' inferiors and more suitable for hard work, if properly managed. Indigenous slavery began and was to last for more than two centuries (Schwartz 1995; Zavala 1964).

By means of "just wars" colonists and colonial authorities circumvented the crown's prohibition against enslaving indigenous peoples. Prohibition notwithstanding, "a just war was easy to provoke" (Ellis 1965, 50). A war was qualified as just when it was a matter of combating cannibalism and whenever the Indians resisted capture or attacked invaders. "Even after the Portuguese Crown prohibited indigenous slavery, in 1570, cannibalism continued to provide a 'just cause' to put them in slavery" (Schwartz 1995, 41). The practice of *resgate* (ransom, rescue), inspired by Roman custom, justified enslavement. It was the principle according to which the victor had the right "to spare the life of the vanquished, enslaving him as compensation" (Melo Franco 1976, 34).

Fray Vicente do Salvador, the seventeenth-century historian, describes the outcome of one such just war, waged against a group of Indian villages that occupied fertile lands in northeastern Pernambuco. Governor General Duarte Coelho "ordered them evacuated by war." Twenty thousand "tame" Indians were recruited for the raid.

> With all these people Duarte de Albuquerque Coelho left, marching to the first enemy fences where they had the first clashes, and there were some casualties among both parties, and as [the enemies] saw that it would be impossible to resist so many, they broke into a quick flight so as to have our people follow them with equal speed, thus missing the chance of destroying their houses and fences. . . . But Duarte Coelho, having guessed their thoughts, ordered some houses burnt down and left troops with the order to take all of their supplies, with which he forced them to make peace, which was conceded under the best conditions and he allotted the lands to people who immediately began to cultivate it and who, finding so much food planted, did no more than eat it and plant from the same shoots in the same holes.
>
> And thus they made their sugar plantations and sugar mills with which they became very rich, for the land was extremely fertile. (Salvador 1954, 186–87)

A second successful raid consolidated the power of the sugar planters:

> With the fame of these two victories, all heathens of this coast all the way to the São Francisco River were so frightened that they let themselves be tied to the whites as if they were sheep and ewes. And thus they went on boats along these rivers, loaded with Indians, selling them for two *cruzados,* or a thousand *réis* each, which is the price of a sheep. (p. 188)

Worse than slavery were the recurring epidemics that could kill as many as thirty thousand Indians in two or three months (Ribeiro 1993, 28). In the past as today indigenous communities assaulted by lethal epidemics suffer the extra penalty of lack of able hands to feed the sick (Ribeiro 1970, 272–307). Famine usually follows epidemics. Frequent reports describe how in total despair survivors of smallpox, measles, and other plagues offered themselves into slavery as a means of survival (Marchant 1942, 117–18; Ribeiro 1993, 28; Schwartz 1995, 52).

While Indians tried to escape starvation by giving themselves into slavery, Jesuits engaged in a most unseemly debate regarding the theological justification for such an extreme attitude. Far from condemning slavery as an institution, the priests were troubled by whether individuals had the right to sell themselves or their family into slavery. The theological quandary revolved around the following questions:

I, whether a father may sell his child; and II, whether one may sell oneself. In case I, [Father Quiricio] Caxa decided in the affirmative, assuming extreme necessity, because of the aid from the child to which the father is entitled. In case II, the answer was also affirmative, provided the person was over twenty, because each is the master of his own liberty.

Nobrega's response began with a strict interpretation of the law *de Patribus* in question, and pointed out that the law spoke only of great poverty and the need to eat, not of extreme necessity. . . . Thus, the powerful natural law of self-preservation . . . permitted the sale of the children and the loss of one's own liberty in order to maintain oneself alive.

A series of corollaries followed from this point, not all of which were strictly pertinent. . . .

Then, in a fifth corollary he appealed to historical instances familiar to the Portuguese of Bahia. The instance chosen was that of the Potiguares, who, during a famine in 1550, sold their children to get food. These children, [Nobrega] decided, were legitimate slaves, for they were sold to relieve the distress of the parents.

On the other hand, in a sixth corollary, he found that the instances of the selling of children around Bahia between 1560 and 1567 were not comparable. Famine, he said, had not been sufficiently severe. The children were sold for reasons other than the approved one of relieving extreme need and therefore were not to be considered slaves. This part of the discussion he concluded with an injunction that all royal officials should most carefully examine cases of enslavement in the light of this reasoning in order to determine the legitimacy of the enslavement. . . .

[H]e took up the enslaving of parish Indians during and following the Caaeté war. These parish natives could not be slaves because they had already begun to be civilized. . . . [T]hese Indians were now both converted and somewhat civilized, they were no longer in the lowest state of human existence, and, consequently, were not fit subjects for enslavement. (Marchant 1942, 141–3)

By contemporary standards this debate would verge on the immoral, but the mores of the day were not concerned with the morality of slavery itself. What strikes one as the epitome of injustice or callousness on the part of these Jesuits is the impassive tone of the debate, the casuistic argumentation to safeguard *their* Indians' "freedom," and the inane ruling that the more extreme the victim's necessity, the more legitimate his enslavement was. Thus adding insult to injury, the theological intelligentsia of colonial Brazil made a decisive contribution to the demise of many an indigenous people and to the flavor of indigenous policies yet to come.

In the next five hundred years one finds variations on the same theme: taming the Indians in the name of Western values, be these religious, political, economic, or social. The civilizing discourse took on new local colors, both in terms of time and space, but the message has been strikingly uniform: Indianness is a temporary undesirable condition and must be eradicated from a country such as Brazil that is trying to make it into the community of civilized nations. The treatment of indigenous peoples as pests lingered well into the twentieth century and well beyond the limits of the Brazilian nation or of the South American continent. It has been routine for many regional settlers and represents the crudest manifestation of the dominant society's arrogance and impunity. We find a particularly striking example in 1967 in Colombia, where "settlers treacherously massacred fifteen Indians and were acquitted in a jury trial because it was considered customary to kill Indians. In his own defense one of the admitted killers stated, 'I didn't believe it was wrong since they were Indians'" (Bodley 1975, 28).

Of all the rhetorical styles uttered in the interethnic arena, perhaps the most blunt, frank, and sincere has been that of the regional population. For them the Indians are undesirable and should either be killed off or pushed back into the wilderness of the jungle where they belong, away from civilization. It is the most candid way of naturalizing the Indian. One can hear regional people comment on the incredible skills the Indians have in hunting, tree climbing, negotiating thick vegetation, in being part of the physical environment. These same regional people are unambiguously clear when they describe how awkward the Indians are when they come to town and try to be "civilized"; they do not know how to work, cannot handle the most trivial affairs, are hopeless, useless, and a constant irritation. Moreover, even if they wanted to become civilized they could not, for it is in their nature to be Indian, and Indians belong in the bush.

On the outskirts of Indian areas in Amazonia, for instance, one hears regional people advocating the extermination of the Indians in the name of past attacks on non-Indian settlers. Stories are told of atrocities committed by Indians on someone's grandparents, uncles, and aunts, but nowhere in these stories is there a hint of acknowledgment that the Indians were reacting to land invasions. They killed people simply because they are savages, animal-like. This is the backward Indian, the Indian of the regional population. Called by different names according to the regions—*caboclo* in Amazonia, *bugre* in the south—the backward Indian, whether living in the jungle or in towns, is inherently incapable of becoming an upstanding member of mainstream society. These Indians are also, by and large, the government's or, more specifically, FUNAI's Indians. Semiliterate FUNAI employees commonly boast of having taught the Indians how to work the land—how to plant manioc, of all things! It is a manifestation of the pecking-order syndrome, the convenience of always having someone below you to lift you a little above the rock bottom of society. But while FUNAI aims to bring Indians out of their backwardness by integrating them into the national society, their regional neighbors keep them at arm's length. While official policy says "Integrate!" regional people say "Keep away!" This head-on collision between integration and segregation makes indigenous peoples a permanent target for prejudice, discrimination, and sheer persecution and is responsible for many conflicts that occur in areas where the indigenous population is large or especially visible. This situation is most acute in the case of uprooted Indians identified as caboclos. Although the term caboclo extends far beyond displaced indigenous peoples (Nugent 1993, 1997), I am referring specifically to them. Having lost their ethnic base along with their territory, these village-less Indians bear the brunt of their futile attempt to integrate into regional society. FUNAI's officials hardly respect them for trying to pass as *brancos* (non-Indians), and regional people despise them for the same reason. The Brazilians are civilized—the Indians should be wild. Anything in between is sheer pretense. These caboclos are Indians who play at being brancos but convince nobody. Perhaps even more than the wild Indians, the ex-Indian caboclos, because of their proximity and inevitable competition for jobs and services, are subjected to heavy doses of prejudice and discrimination (Figoli 1982). They are the "bad" Indians in another sense than Vespucci's. They epitomize the unhappy conscience of people who see themselves through the eyes of their detractors: no skills, no pride, no capacity to rise from their miserable condition of neither Indian nor branco. Having lost the marks of their ethnicity (language, dress, eating habits, etc.), they are looked upon as losers in both Indian and national society. The caboclo is the embodiment of the paradox contained in the civilizing project: the effort to wipe out Indianness while closing the doors to their full citizenship. What is left in the wake of such ambivalence seems to be no one's concern. Masses of displaced caboclos, illiterate, in poor health, and hardly capable of earning a living on the fringes of the precarious job market of poor towns is not exactly the conventional idea of a civilized population. And yet neither official policy nor the practice of daily life indicates any awareness of the failure of the civilizing project. No doubt it is an example of how old habits die hard, for the urge to transform Indians into Brazilians is as old as Brazil itself.

Papal bulls were powerful instruments in the West's civilizing project for Indians and for other "pagans" before them. In 1454 Nicolas V passed the Bula Romanus Pontifex, allowing the king of Portugal, D. Afonso Henriques, full power to invade, conquer, and subjugate any enemies of Christ, reducing them to slavery. In 1493 Pope Alexander VI signed the Bula Inter Cetera, including the kings of Spain in the deal that had been granted the king of Portugal. By this bull the Iberian powers were free to subjugate and "reduce to the Catholic Faith" the inhabitants of all the islands and firm lands already found and to be found, their European "owners" having "full, free, and total power, authority, and jurisdiction" over them (Ribeiro 1993, 16–17). Since then church and state have shared the task of civilizing and integrating the Indians; their discourses may differ in tone, from religious to secular, but both have been decisive in the conquest and control of indigenous affairs.

An arm of civilization, the church is muscular and far reaching. Missionaries of all Christian creeds rejoice in the Indians' paganism as the epitome of virgin soil in which the seeds of Christianity can be sown. Missionaries by and large take for granted that the Indians are basically undeveloped. Some may actually become so familiar with Indians as to admire their culture, but that does not deflect the missionaries from the goal of winning Indian souls, transforming them into well-behaved, obedient serfs of the Lord and, by extension, of officialdom, including the missionaries themselves.

Much damage and abuse has been committed in the name of Christianity. From boarding schools run by Salesians that deprive indigenous children of a proper socialization to the cold wars between Catholics and Protestants that, as we saw in Chapter 1, divide entire indigenous societies, missionaries of various persuasions exercise one of the most efficient modes of control over indigenous lives. As assured as any Westerner, or even more so, of being unquestionably right and superior, missionaries have in Indian populations a fertile ground on which to practice their righteousness and superiority. The arrogance of the conversion enterprise is justified precisely by the conviction that the Indians are crude clay in search of a skilled sculptor of souls, a cultured and enlightened manipulator capable of molding raw nature into a divine creation (Baêta Neves 1978; Rafael 1988). In many parts of Brazil missionaries, either Catholic or Protestant, have been the first members of the dominant society to come into contact with indigenous peoples, and they have paved the way for the arrival of more pragmatically oriented intruders (Hvalkof and Aaby 1981; Stoll 1982; Colby with Dennett 1995).

Missionary action has sustained the notion that the Indians are helpless without assistance—their customs are so primitive that they endanger their spiritual salvation. Of these customs, cannibalism became the banner for the church's pious intervention. The civilizing discourse benefited immensely from deploring the man-eating habits of the Tupinambá. Cannibalism provided perhaps the most potent weapon for European control. It had the power to erect with a single stroke two of the handiest images for the colonizing of the New World: European martyrs and Indian heathens. While martyrdom justified the political domination of the "cannibals," paganism justified the right to subject the Indians to Christian indoctrination.

The arrival of the Jesuits in midsixteenth century (later than Caminha had wished in 1500), with the mission of Christianizing the natives, had a rather ambiguous result. By gathering large numbers of Indians in densely populated settlements, both to protect them and as a convenient strategy for conversion, the Jesuits provided settlers with a ready reserve of cheap or slave labor. Interested in building up the Indians' Christian spirituality (despite the "savage's inconstant soul"; see Viveiros de Castro 1992) rather than preserving their physical integrity, within a couple of decades the Jesuits had adopted the policy of force instead of the time-consuming techniques of persuasion. José de Anchieta and Manoel da Nóbrega made their mark on the history of Brazil with a reputation for extraordinary fervor and determination to spread the true religion among the natives. Both resorted to the expedient procedure of "placing the Indians under the yoke." To make Christians out of them, Nóbrega writes: "I also wish . . . to see the heathen subjugated and placed under the yoke of obedience to the Christians, so that we could imprint on them all that we desire. . . . Nothing can be done with them if they are left at liberty, for they are brutish people." Also Anchieta: "We now think that the gates are open for the conversion of the heathen in this capacity, if Our Lord God would arrange that they be placed under the yoke. For these people there is no better preaching than by the sword and iron rod. Here more than anywhere, it is necessary to adopt the policy of compelling them to come in" (both are quoted in Hemming 1978, 106). Catholic priests closely accompanied the westward expansion of Portuguese-Brazilian dominions. They followed the often devastating assaults on Indian lands and the capture of slaves by the *bandeirantes*, seventeenth-century adventurers, most of them *mamelucos* (the offspring of Portuguese men and Indian women) in search of wealth, and turned the Indian villages along the way into permanent sites of settler occupation. The Indians who did not flee were captured by the bandeirantes or concentrated in large settlements (*reduções*) run by the missionaries.

With regard to the Catholic Church, the last few decades have witnessed new trends in the style of interaction with the Indians. Under the influence of liberation theology some missionaries have become defenders of indigenous rights to land and to ethnic identity and have openly confronted economic groups and the government. This attitude, humane as it may be, is not, however, the result of humbleness in light of Indian wisdom. It is, rather, one more manifestation of the missionaries' certainty of being right, of knowing what is best for the Indians. Frequent complaints by some indigenous leaders about the control of Catholic missionaries over native actions provide plenty of examples of this brand of Christian paternalism. Like children, the Indians need to be guided, even to remain Indians.

As an active representative of the state, the military has had a long and intensive participation in indigenous affairs. Beginning in the early seventeenth century the military founded forts in Amazonia that became the birthplaces of important towns such as Manaus.

In 1910 the first national agency for the protection of the Indians was created by an army officer, Cândido Mariano da Silva Rondon, a true believer in positivism as a humanist philosophy. Faithful to the Comtean version of evolution, he was convinced of the need to preserve the lives of indigenous peoples so that they could ultimately decide to abandon their primitive ways and embrace Western civilization. As a civilizing strategy, Rondon applied some army devices, such as furnishing titles and olive uniforms to Indian men who often had no local legitimacy. It was the modern period of the village "captains." Official indigenism was thus created, and the destiny of the Indians was sealed: slowly but surely, they were to relinquish their lifeways and integrate into national society. They received a special status: they were now considered "relatively incapable" by law — the 1916 Civil Code — along with married women and children, a triad disturbingly reminiscent of Aristotle's inferior categories: slaves, women, and children. Although legislation in the 1960s freed married women from this stigma, the Indians continue to be wards of the state. Their first "tutor" (guardian), the Indian Protection Service (SPI), replaced by FUNAI in 1967–1968, was assigned to the Ministry of Agriculture (Gagliardi 1989). Since then, protection of the Indians has made the rounds of several other ministries, such as labor, industry and commerce, back to agriculture, then to war (as the Army Ministry was then called), interior, and, more recently, justice. In none of these bureaucratic bodies did this duty feel right or comfortable; in none did it command enough respect and interest to be given sufficient attention and funding. Since the 1960s protection of the Indians has been steadily downgraded. Not even the humanism and humanitarian intentions of the early Rondonian days have survived the decline of this official institution for the guardianship of Indians.

In 1978 Rangel Reis, the minister of the interior under whom FUNAI was uneasily accommodated, declared that Indians should have the right to become important people, even to aspire to the country's presidency. But for that to happen they would have to be "emancipated." Emancipation, in this special and deceptive reading, meant the termination of the Indians' special status, created in the Rondon era as a legal device to protect their lands as a collective possession in a country that had no legal provisions for communal landownership (Comissão Pró-Índio 1979a). It became clear that to emancipate the Indians meant, and still means, to emancipate their inalienable lands and open them for sale. It happened in the United States after the 1887 Dawes General Allotment (Severalty) Act with well-known catastrophic consequences for Native Americans (see Chapter 9) and was hinted at in Australia with more than a touch of cynicism by its minister of the interior in 1939: "The raising of their [the Aborigines] status so as to entitle them by right and by qualification to the ordinary rights of citizenship, and to enable them to help them to share with us the opportunities that are available in their native land" (quoted in Beckett 1988b, 200). Although "this became the national policy" in Australia after World War II, in Brazil the "emancipation decree" was shelved because of strong public response and resurrected a few years later in the form of "criteria of Indianness" devised by the military officials who ruled FUNAI at the time. According to these criteria, FUNAI was to decide who was eligible to be classified as Indian. The criteria included a long lists of items, among which were manners of clothing, food, language, and, ludicrous as it may seem, presence or absence of the Mongolian spot, a birthmark (see Chapter 9). Again, public protest against the absurdity of these criteria exposed FUNAI at one of its particularly acute moments of bureaucratic delirium (CEDI 1982a).

In the 1980s FUNAI fell to its lowest levels of competence and legitimacy. It became the headquarters of coercion and the favorite target of irate Indian leaders and indignant supporters who joined the Indian cause. FUNAI has long been drowning in red tape and suffering corrupt presidents who plunder indigenous resources with impunity, from the transfer of large plots of land to private hands to the sale of lumber, and medical doctors who sit around in town offices while entire Indian villages suffer from diseases transmitted by outsiders, such as tuberculosis, malaria, and measles. In short, either through outright criminal action or through omission the Indian foundation has been part of the problem more often than part of the solution.

In 1985 the military handed the federal government over to civilians during what was known as the "New Republic," a civic interlude when the Brazilian people's high hopes for better times were proportional only to their subsequent disappointment. The Indian issue was a sort of microcosm of the national climate: great expectations that one by one were dissolved into thin air by the surreptitious maneuvers of politicians and interest groups in the mining and lumbering business, for instance, for whom indigenous rights were a serious inconvenience (Comissão Pró-Índio 1981, 1985; CEDI/CONAGE 1988). Amazonia came to the fore once again as the last frontier; its abundant resources were now envisioned as the remedy to the cancerous growth of foreign debt. Backstage, the military planned grandiose projects, such as the Calha Norte (North Watershed), designed to bring development to the northern region while controlling international borders and enclosing the indigenous populations within small pockets of their original lands. From behind the scenes the military continued to run indigenous policy, which for the military is inextricably tied to the development of Amazonia (Albert 1992; Ramos 1995a, 271–312; also see Chapter 8). From the recesses of their offices in the National Security Council army officials in particular directed the most important moves taken by the Indian foundation: bureaucratic decentralization, the appointment of top-level personnel, and even the prohibition of anthropological research in the northern Indian areas. Before 1985 FUNAI *was* military. Under the New Republic the Indian foundation became a mere puppet of the military. These same military officers had their army minister play the role of éminence grise in the José Sarney government. That powerful man in olive green, Leônidas Pires Gonçalves, was the author of the notorious statement that said that protecting indigenous peoples amounts to a waste of time, for their cultures, being so base, are undeserving of respect.

The first nationwide indigenous organization, the Union of Indian Nations (UNI), was created in 1980. At that time FUNAI, like many other government bodies, was run by the military. Neither the military nor a good many others in the country's central administration accepted the designation of "Indian Nations." Brazil, they repeated, could not afford to have nations within the nation (see Chapter 6). Besides, they insisted, the Indians are Brazilians and must define themselves as such. They are entitled to participate in the benefits of a developing country, so long as they don't attempt to create enclaves; they should cooperate in developing the Brazilian nation by having their natural resources properly exploited, preferably by non-Indians.

In the early eighties the Indian issue was at a peak of visibility. One Indian, the Shavante Mário Juruna, was elected in 1982 to the House of Representatives; another, Marcos Terena, was made chief of staff to the president of FUNAI; and another, the Kayapó Megaron, became the director of the Xingu National Park. At the time such concessions were impressive and were historical firsts. In the long run, however, they appear to have made no difference in the trajectory of the Indian movement, or perhaps they have, in the sense of smoothing sharp edges that might have cut a clearer figure of the Indian as an empowered political actor. Still, the official policy has not been changed from integration to self-determination, despite what the 1988 Constitution says about the right of the Indians to maintain their ethnic identity. The state policy for the Indians is still as covertly ethnocidal as ever, although it has been insidiously dressed up in a robe of liberalism.

The civilizing discourse does not appropriate the Indian as an image but rather as an essence. Indians belong to the Brazilian nation, and therefore those in power can do to Indians as they see fit, regardless of what Indians may want for themselves. Here the Indians are not only nature's creatures but also the nation's children. Their "special" status as relatively incapable individuals and collectivities under the wardship of the state reveals in unequivocal terms the disparity of power manifested in the civilizing rhetoric. In metonymic fashion it wraps the relationship between the national state and its indigenous peoples in a cloak of established truths about the nature of the Indian as well as of the civilized. The Indians' alleged unpreparedness and the protective zeal of the state have become the most recurrent message of the way things are and should be. With a single stroke this message delivers two of the cardinal commandments of the dominant interethnic truth: Brazilians—that is, adults—know what is best for the infantile Indians, and for Indians to reach adulthood they must relinquish their Indianness. What sort of adulthood awaits emancipated Indians remains to be spelled out in more honest terms than the insidious hyperbole of government ministers. With such forceful semantic weapons in their hands the rulers of the country have controlled the Indians, giving them little recourse to other sorts of more literal weaponry, as happened in past centuries and other countries.

Neither the Edenic nor the civilizing discourse has any concern for what the Indians might be on their own or might say about projected images of themselves. The representation of Indians as nobles or villains requires that they remain mute about themselves and about Brazilians, passive figures to be molded by Euro-Brazilian ideologies, conflicting as these may be.

The voice of the Indian, if heard at all, is devoid of timbre or echo, is rendered a flat, vague, and incomprehensible murmur attached to no specific language, no recognizable tradition. The anonymity of indigenous utterances serves as background noise for the dominating voice of the national society. Even when speaking the national tongue, usually with a strong accent and incorrect grammar, the Indian's voice is not willingly heard. Cultural misunderstandings apart, much of the Brazilian interpretation of indigenous discourses is distorted by the undisputed certainty regarding the superiority of Western ways of thinking. Indian languages are not usually acknowledged as "real" languages with their own logic and lexical richness. In Brazilian Amazonia, for instance, regionals refer to Indian languages as *gíria*, slang, and seem utterly incredulous when told that those languages are as sophisticated as Portuguese. To learn an Indian language is to lose prestige among one's peers. Rather than risk a change of mind about indigenous inferiority were one to penetrate their worldview, people find it safer to perpetuate the comfortable assurance passed on from generation to generation that the Indian is culturally retarded.

As would be expected, this syndrome of elite status is derived from a spontaneous or cultivated ignorance of indigenous languages and customs and is not limited to Amazonia. "The problem [with bilingual interpreters] was that to know enough Algonquian to ensure accurate and reliable interpretation they [Virginia colonists] had to be so steeped in Algonquian culture that their very identity as Englishmen, and therefore their political reliability, became suspect (Hulme 1986, 142).

As unintelligible, literally or ideologically, the Indian's voice is more easily disposed of for being a spurious human expression. It is thus possible to speak for Indians, to dictate what is best for them, and the best for them is to do as brancos say. Because the dominant society is not a monolith, the colonization of the Indian's worldview takes the shape of the specific colonizer, giving rise to the church Indian, the army Indian, the Indian service Indian, and, more recently, the nongovernmental organization Indian (see Chapter 10). Thus gagged, Indians are then judged to be naive or pure, ignorant or innocent, treacherous or defenseless, depending on one's inclination toward Edenism or civilizationism.

There are also those who, after contributing to the impoverishment of indigenous traditional cultures, proceed to lament the loss of authenticity, a phenomenon Rosaldo (1989) has aptly called "imperialist nostalgia." By authenticity they mean the naked Indian with bow and arrow in hand, living off what Mother Nature alone provides. Such a quest for the authentic Indian—here closely associated with the Indian as exotic—is never pitched against the civilizing quest. Why Indians are now covered with clothes, often rags, why they no longer hunt with bow and arrow, or with anything else for that matter, on their badly shrunk and depleted patch of land, are questions that the nostalgic invaders hardly ask, and when they do, they never link the condition of the Indians to the effects of missionizing, land usurpation, and consequent economic dependence. Rather, these questions are dismissed as the result of the Indian's inability to learn how to be civilized. Missionaries, military personnel, and regional shopowners usually provide abundant examples of this type of double standard, but residents of the country's largest city can supply magnificent stereotypes as depicted in the humorous passage that follows. For our purposes it does not matter whether the episode happened the way it is told or whether it was embroidered for effect.

> One time I took the subway to Praça da Sé. It was during my first days in São Paulo and I liked to go by subway and bus. I felt a special delight in displaying myself to feel people's reactions when they saw me go by. I wanted to be sure that people identified me as an Indian so that I could form my own self-image.
> On that occasion I heard the following dialogue between two ladies who stared at me up and down when I entered the subway:
> — See that young man? He looks Indian, said lady A.
> — Yes, he does. But I'm not so sure. Haven't you noticed he is wearing jeans? He can't be an Indian and wear Whiteman's clothes. I don't think he's a real Indian, contested lady B.

— Yah, maybe. But can't you see his hair? Straight, straight hair. Only Indians have hair like that. Yes, I think he's an Indian, lady A said, defending me.

— Gee, I don't know. Have you noticed he wears a watch? Indians see time by the weather. The Indian's watch is the sun, the moon, the stars. . . . He can't be an Indian, argued lady B.

— But he has slit eyes, said lady A.

— And he also wears shoes and shirt, said lady B ironically.

— But his cheeks jut out. Only Indians have a face like that. No, he can't deny it. He can only be an Indian and a pure one, it seems.

— I don't believe it. There are no pure Indians any more, affirmed lady B full of wisdom. —After all, how could an Indian be riding the subway? True Indians live in the forest, carry bow and arrow, hunt and fish and plant manioc. I don't think he is an Indian at all. . . .

— Have you seen the necklace he's wearing? Looks like it's made of teeth. Could they be people's teeth?

— I wouldn't be surprised. I've heard that there are still Indians who eat people, said lady B.

— Haven't you just said you didn't think he was an Indian? And now it looks like you're scared?

— Just in case . . .

— How about talking to him?

— What if he doesn't like it?

— Tough luck. . . . At least we'll have more precise information, don't you think?

— Yes, I do, but I must admit I don't have much courage to start a dialogue with him. Will you ask?, said lady B who by now showed herself somewhat uncomfortable.

— I'll ask.

I had my back to them as I listened to their conversation and couldn't help laughing from time to time. Suddenly I felt a light touch of fingers on my shoulder. I turned around. Unfortunately they took too long to call me. My stop was coming up. I looked at them, smiled and said
— Yes! (Munduruku 1996, 34)

Brazilian Indians live in a social limbo between a paradise of purity and a hell of savagery. Whereas the Edenic discourse denies ethnic legitimacy to Indians who defy the image of purity, the civilizing discourse denies that there is purity or any other redeeming value in being Indian. Because they are Indians, they are incapable of performing properly and hence need to be perpetually tutored. The civilizing project is therefore analogous to *Mission Impossible*: it will never destroy itself because its goal will never be met. So long as the Indians are not allowed to reach full citizenship *as Indians*, the notion that they are relatively incapable, and thus must be subjected to state guardianship, will remain a self-fulfilling prophesy.

Part II
Speaking to the Whiteman

3

The Indian against the State

This chapter deals with three notions—ethnicity, citizenship, and universalism—and the role they play in the field of interethnic relations in Brazil. I do not seek to undertake an exegesis or deconstruction of these notions as academic concepts pertaining to disciplines such as political science, philosophy, and history. I simply intend to observe them "ethnographically," that is, how they behave in the context of interethnic affairs and how they add to the complexity of Indigenism. In turn, Indigenism, regarded as an ideological province of interethnicity, provides the "middle ground" where this triad of concepts meets. The meanings generated by ethnicity, citizenship, and universalism will depend on the specific context in which Indians, nationals, and foreigners pursue their interests. The concept of middle ground has been used to designate the social and political space of the broader phenomenon of Indigenism as I envisage it (Conklin and Graham 1995). It is a softer version of the dense concept of "colonial situation" as developed by Georges Balandier (1955) to account for the complexities of African colonialism. If we replace "colonial situation" with "internal colonialism" (Stavenhagen 1972, chap. 1; Cardoso de Oliveira 1978), Balandier's concept is by and large applicable to Indigenism, at least in its Brazilian manifestation.

To ease presentation I discuss these concepts in contrasting pairs. Arbitrary as this arrangement may be, it is, for better or worse, the unavoidable price of analysis. I focus on the interaction between universalism and citizenship and between citizenship and ethnicity and then all three in the context of the humanistic claims professed by the indigenist movement in Brazil. To demonstrate how the confluence of these various notions can empower Indian activists I shall bring up the case of the Fourth Russell Tribunal in which the Indians provoked a confrontation between the logic of universal human rights and that of the nation-state. But first I would like to make a few comments on the problematic of relativism regarding the issue of human rights.

Universalism and Relativism

This theme has had the attention of various social scientists, including Habermas (1989), Dumont (1985), and Geertz (1984). Renteln (1988) provides a long list of references on the subject. I approach it here specifically to highlight the way in which indigenous peoples have used the notions of relativism and universalism in their attempts to protect their rights to cultural diversity.

According to the Universal Declaration of Human Rights, "all men are born free and equal in dignity and rights." This declaration institutes the great aporia faced by anthropologists and other defenders of cultural relativism. For if, on the one hand, it denies the principle according to which a vast number of indigenous peoples declare themselves the chosen people to the detriment of all other human beings, on the other hand this declaration, among others of the same statute, is the basis for the defense of Indian rights vis-à-vis the national societies to which indigenous peoples are subjected.

Europe, exercising the reason of the Enlightenment, endowed the world with perhaps the most finished product of humanism. This centuries-old stimulus for the Declaration of Human Rights had several versions. The first, the Declaration of Rights of Man and Citizen, appeared in 1789. Although its inspiration was the North American colonies' Declaration of Independence, the colonies were still an America of the Pilgrims and thus directly associated with Old World ideals (Dumont 1985, 109–14). The current Declaration of Human Rights was proclaimed in December 1948 after World War II opened to the world the macabre spectacle of racism by fascist governments, another European product. The universal rights of humankind emerged then "as the common ideal to be achieved by all peoples and all nations." The human, faceless and devoid of cultural specificity, exercises these rights as an individual rather than as a member of a group, society, or nation, that is, "without any kind of distinction, be it of race, color, sex, language, religion, political opinion or of any other nature, national or social origin, wealth, birth, or any other condition" (Article II, Paragraph 1). This means that, beyond cultural diversity, a single set of norms should apply to all societies and cultures.

Meanwhile, another European precept, with equal humanist impetus, sprang up in contradistinction to normative universalism. It was the notion of cultural relativism, according to which no absolute values exist in the absence of a specific cultural matrix, and therefore each culture is sovereign in dictating its norms, immune to value judgment by other cultures, and unbending to outside ethical or moral standards. To impose values that are purportedly universal is an act of ethnocentrism or, more specifically, Eurocentrism. To condemn infanticide as it occurs among some indigenous peoples because it disrespects the third article of the Declaration of Human Rights ("All men have the right to life, freedom and personal security") would amount to judging others by Western standards.

What does the confrontation between these virtually contradictory positions tell us? First, that the West—and not only the West—is capable of generating such disparate propositions that, taken to their logical conclusion, would cancel each other out. The outcome would not be so serious if the West, in dominating other peoples, did not make them pawns of its contradictions. Second, that either position, taken to its ultimate consequences, would entail the danger that it aspires to abolish. On the one hand, by condemning all cultural practices that might affront its individualistic principles, extreme humanism would obliterate flesh-and-blood people. On the other hand, extreme relativism would defend the indefensible by supporting such policies as genocide. Obviously, absolute universalism would be as disastrous as absolute relativism. Third, to be politically feasible and ethically prudent both positions would need to be nuanced and perhaps transformed in what Todorov calls *"universalisme de parcours"* to which, by extension, one might add *"relativisme de parcours."* This would amount to changing the positions from constraining postulates into strategies, that is, into courses of action rather than established models to be rigidly observed. In short, they would refer "not to the fixed content of a theory of mankind, but to the need to postulate a common horizon to the interlocutors of a debate if this debate is worth anything" (Todorov 1989, 427–28). Universalism, continues Todorov, "is an analytical tool, a regulating principle which permits the fertile encounter of differences; its content cannot be fixed, it is always open to revision" (p. 428). Taking his lead, I would then say that relativism is an analytical tool, a regulating principle that permits a fertile comparison of similarities, save the differences, and its content cannot be diluted in order to pulverize social and political responsibility. It is always open to ethical scrutiny. Relativism would then be the politics of possible differences.

Thus regarded, universalism and relativism lose much of the contradictory character they take when perceived as absolute propositions. They acquire vigor as concepts and agility in practice. From radical ideological principles steering in opposite directions, they become pragmatic means for the resolution of concrete problems generated by the uncomfortable coexistence of postulates that are potentially if not actually antagonistic, such as citizenship or, rather, nationality, and ethnic specificity.

As a matter of fact, what seems to be a universal, because of its vast cross-cultural dissemination, is not the sameness of humans everywhere but ethnocentrism, of which patriotism is a specific manifestation. For Dumont, "in traditional holism humanity is co-terminous with the society of the *we*, foreigners are devalued as, in the best of hypotheses, imperfect men—and, by the way, all patriotism, even modern, is more or less impregnated with this sentiment" (1985, 127). The sentiment is that our society is better than any other, if for no other reason than that of providing the mechanisms necessary for self-preservation that are inherent to any human group that is socially constituted. Anthropology is brimming with examples of peoples the world over who take their ethnonym as coterminous with human being; all other peoples, not being thus denominated, are left out of the category of humans. Nevertheless, this does not mean that the self-identification of such peoples presupposes the elimination of Others because of their differences—quite the opposite. What the ethnographic experience has shown is that the legitimacy of many peoples is assured and reinforced precisely because they are culturally and ethnically differentiated. We might call this phenomenon a sort of ethnicity-cum-relativism. In stark contrast with national societies such as those of the New World that insist on erasing ethnic plurality, indigenous peoples have exhibited an extraordinary will to pluralism and acceptance of cultural diversity, beyond whatever stereotypes, antagonisms, and conflicts they may nourish about Others. The Others may not be quite as human, but they certainly have the right to be what they are. They may be criticized, looked down upon, attacked, defeated, or even ingested, but no indigenous society, in Brazil or elsewhere, has been known to have a policy of eradicating the differences that alterity produces (Ramos 1980b).

Relativism, in the sense of a pragmatics of possible differences, would lean more comfortably toward ethnicity—the practical outcome of the option for human diversity—than toward the universality of rights. When universalism, citizenship, and ethnicity come together, relativism plays the role of moderator, attenuating generalizations, contextualizing specifics, and advocating the transit between different ethoses and ethics.

Let us now turn to the crossroads at which universalism, citizenship, and ethnicity act out their potency in the tangled field of interethnic relations.

Universalism and Citizenship

In the spirit of the illuminist principles that created them, universalism and citizenship should be components of a single voice. Nevertheless, in practice they often come apart and in some cases are put in opposite camps. As Todorov remarks, they may actually engender two distinct voices, that of the universal rights of mankind and that of the rights of the citizen as a legitimate member of a given nation-state. That both are Eurocentric does not make them univocal. Depending on the historical juncture, they may come together in a harmonious duet, or they may diverge in a strident cacophony. Charles Taylor makes this point: "Where the politics of universal dignity fought for forms of nondiscrimination that were quite 'blind' to the ways in which citizens differ, the politics of difference often redefines nondiscrimination as requiring that we make these distinctions the basis of differential treatment" (1994, 83). Taylor continues: "These two modes of politics, then, both based on the notion of equal respect, come into conflict" (p. 84).

Every state needs to distinguish itself from all others, for it "cannot afford failing to make a difference between its citizens and foreigners from the moment it assigns certain duties and grants certain rights to some but not to others" (Todorov 1989, 277). Todorov continues,

> Our philosophers ignore . . . the conflict between man and citizen and imagine that states will conduct a policy which will be of interest to the world—which is excluded by definition, as it were. . . . To belong to humanity is not the same thing as to belong to a nation. . . . Indeed, there is a covert conflict between the two which may become overt the day we are forced to choose between the values of one or the other. Man, in this sense of the word, is judged on the basis of ethical principles, whereas the behavior of the citizen is judged from a political perspective. (pp. 286, 422)

Furthermore, in totalitarian states where the means of force overtake the rights of citizenship, the discrepancy between citizenship and universalism becomes all the more acute.

If universalism leads to individualism, to the supremacy of humanity, and to the hegemony of the generic human—which, according to Dumont (1977), is a feature of Western individualism that grew out of the hegemony of the economic domain—citizenship, the sociological effect of the constitution of the nation-state, may produce the reverse. As Anderson affirms, "No nation imagines itself coterminous with mankind" (1991, 7). The elements that give substance to citizenship are always linked to shared experiences, be these language, history, territory, government, religion, material and nonmaterial symbols, or even a sport such as soccer or baseball. But if the nation-state brings with it citizenship (or is it the other way around?), the nation-state will not necessarily forge a cultural uniformity that will guarantee a homogeneous and tranquil course through history. In fact, this is rarely the case. For instance, Smith (1981) follows the track of ethnic persistence through the history of the formation of European nation-states to demonstrate that the match between ethnicity and state, strategic as it may be politically, is so imperfect as to be incapable of overcoming internal ethnic diversity within each nation. By dictating norms for citizenship, the state excludes whoever fails to share those common experiences.

If such obvious dissonances exist between citizenship and universalism, both products of the same tradition, what to say of the contradictions generated from the encounter of ethnic groups bearing cultures of their own with the nation-state that has encompassed them? As ethnic groups are conquered by expanding national societies, the level of stridency can be so high that it arouses a third voice. Ethnicity, the third voice, is then compelled to join in the orchestration led by citizenship and universalism.

In the case of Brazil a fourth voice emerges from the encounter of these three voices—universal human rights, Brazilian citizenship, and the ethnicity of indigenous peoples. The fourth voice is Indigenism. At once an ideology and a praxis, Indigenism congregates both Indians and non-Indians in the battle over the recognition of human diversity. Indigenism's actors play their roles on a stage that has been erected on the ruins left by the internal conquest of the Indians. This stage is animated by the most discordant points of view and by divergent ethical, social, and political interests. At times in chorus, at other times in counterpoint, or even in utter disharmony, these four voices have been composing a historical score with a multitude of variations. In typical Rashomon fashion each rendition can be so different that it is unrecognizable by the others, and yet in addressing the same event they are interlocked in a plot they continue to weave. Such complexity simply reflects the intricate play of agents, postures, and interests bouncing off each other as the country's conjunctures change. The multivocality that resounds through the ideological province of Indigenism is the quintessence of interethnic contact writ large. It is where universalism, citizenship, and ethnicity appear as the master tropes that underscore the fate of indigenous peoples in twentieth-century Brazil.

Citizenship and Ethnicity

The novelty of double citizenship aside, Brazil offers three legal possibilities: to be Brazilian, foreigner, or Indian. The foreigner may become a citizen by a legal-bureaucratic act revealingly named *naturalization*. Indians cannot become naturalized, for they are already "naturals of the land." What they can do is be "emancipated," that is, relieved of their special status. The nation's defense against exotic bodies—the foreigners—is relatively simple; all it takes is an appeal to nationalist feelings or to the exclusive rights of its citizenship. But this special status of the Indians engenders a defense mechanism that is different from that aroused by foreigners (which is often identifiable as xenophobia); the conquest of indigenous peoples has created a more complex problem, for if the Indians are exotic it is not in the sense of being foreigners. Are they citizens? And, if deemed citizens, what kind of citizens would they be, given that they do not share the national language, history, symbols, and the like, except in the specific context of interethnic relations? The special status given to the Indians as a result of their political conquest and cultural colonization contains a great deal of ambiguity manifested, for instance, in the lack of consensus about whether the Indians are Brazilian. For that matter, a still more drastic question is often asked: Is being Brazilian necessarily to be a citizen of Brazil? One answer is no, if we consider commentaries such as the following:

> This situation . . . of quasi-illegitimacy of the conflicts lived by indigenous peoples throughout this century is also shared by various other groups of dominated people in Brazilian society, although, obviously, in a different way, due to their different life situations. Despite all their differences, blacks, women, minors, the elderly, rural and urban workers with no defined occupation, peddlers . . . have in common the non-recognition of their legitimate existence as common and active collective identities, or, what amounts to the same thing, the non-recognition of their struggles as politically relevant amongst other national problems. (Paoli 1983, 25)

In this regard, leaving the ethnicity question aside, not all Brazilians are de facto citizens (Dallari 1983). If vast segments of non-Indians are excluded from full citizenship by the perverse effects of social inequality, the Indian case is even more complex. "The Indian as a Brazilian citizen . . . is a fiction," asserts attorney Carlos Frederico Marés, because Indians would have to surrender their Indian identity in order to become Brazilian citizens. Marés continues: "So long as the Indian keeps his cultural identity, he will belong to a nation that is different from the Brazilian nation. He will be Guarani, Nambiquara, Yanomami, Patasho, etc., because each one of these nations has its fundamental operation of norms that have been established for longer than the rules adopted by the Brazilian constitution" (Marés 1983, 50). Note that Marés insists in using the term *nation* to refer to ethnic groups, in clear defiance of the ban by Brazilian politicians and the military to applying this concept to Indian peoples.

One might suppose that being born in Brazilian territory automatically confers Brazilian citizenship, but the matter is not so simple when it involves Indians, for it goes well beyond the mere accident of birth. Living according to their own norms, which not only differ from those of the Brazilian state but can actually collide with them, indigenous peoples find themselves in the odd position of being internal outsiders. Denied the status of nations by the Brazilian government, their position is kept in a liminal ambiguity that is fertile ground for legal experiments and interpretations. The condition of the Indians as "relatively incapable" and the attribution of their wardship to the state are two such examples. In declaring the Indians as relatively incapable (or relatively capable, in a seemingly more positive reading) to practice certain civil acts (basically, involving property rights), the state took upon itself the role of "guardian" of the Indians until they come civically of age and are "emancipated." What it means to be emancipated from an ethnic condition is something Brazilian legislation has never attempted to clarify.

Before the 1988 Constitution, being an Indian was a passing condition, like a child whose inexorable destiny, if it survives, is to grow into adulthood. The premise, unshaken for centuries, was that sooner or later the Indians would become Brazilians like the idealized rest of the national population. Generations of "indigenists" were guided by this premise, from the sixteenth-century pioneer Jesuit José de Anchieta to Marshall Cândido Mariano da Silva Rondon and the official Indian agencies in this century. As we shall see in Chapter 9, the new constitution has changed the definition of Indianness in this respect—to be an Indian now is to be an Indian forever—but written law and actual practice hardly ever meet. In the hearts and minds of many an employee of the National Indian Foundation (FUNAI) their job is still to train Indians to become Brazilians. Until then their wards remain in a civic limbo. For these managers of ethnicity it is just a matter of time and effort. The push toward integration

> should not be understood as an altruistic gesture on the part of the state in its quest for the integration of the "Brazilian people." It is rather a way of not recognizing the Indian nations and their territories and, as a consequence, of precluding their self-determination and their capacity to establish their own pace and means of development within their territories. It is, in fact, a way of not recognizing the Indian as a citizen, while considering his land as Brazilian territory and . . . denying the existence of Indian nations capable of attributing citizenship to their own nationals. (Marés 1983, 44, 46–47)[1]

One characteristic of citizenship is that it is temporalized and territorialized. "The concept of citizenship, as any juridical concept, has to be understood within a given society at a given time" (Marés 1983, 44). But this territorialization, demarcated according to the geographical boundaries of the nation-state, leaves in its interior a vast zone of indifferentiation and legal, as well as cultural, uncertainty. For indigenous peoples this conception of citizenship is potentially dangerous. In the first place, it affects their relationship to land. The Brazilian state denies the Indians the full property of their territory. Instead, they are allowed to *possess* the land, that is, they have the exclusive usufruct of all resources that exist on their land but—and this is crucial—not the subsoil. The Union is the proprietor, the Indians are the possessors (note that Brazilians apply the Portuguese term *posseiros* to non-Indian squatters). By law this should suffice to guarantee the Indians control of their territories, but in actual fact their lands

---

1. On the problematic of pluriethnicity, also see Maybury-Lewis 1984.

are taken to be public goods, and, as is notorious in the country, a public good is good for private appropriation. This being so, Indian lands are constantly invaded, reduced in size, and depleted of their resources.

Another danger, already put to the test on several occasions, is the social marginalization of the Indians because they are denied their cultural and ethnic specificity. Attempts by the government to "emancipate" them in the 1970s and 1980s were aborted only because of intense protests by both Indians and non-Indians, inside the country and abroad, but the nagging possibility always exists that in more propitious circumstances it will be done against the Indians' will.

If Brazil needed a looking-glass to contemplate the consequences of such emancipation, it would do well to borrow one from the United States, prodigal in legislation, old and new, designed to deprive indigenous rights of ethnic specificity and, most important, of land. "In 1854 a decision was made to begin a general policy of breaking down tribal societies through the deliberate use of individual allotments of tribal land. . . . The Government planners felt that if the tribes were restricted to certain land areas of limited scope in an orderly fashion, they could eventually merge the Indian communities into the developing rural society of the Middle West" (Kickingbird and Ducheneaux 1973, 16). The Dawes General Allotment (Severalty) Act of 1887 was passed in the same spirit. Massachusetts senator Henry Laurens "Dawes was convinced that within a very short period of time the magical qualities of individual property would transform the stolid warriors into happy churchgoing farmers" (p. 19). Traps such as these are also constantly placed in the path of Brazilian Indians. The question of citizenship is never separated from the question of rights to land, in Brazil and elsewhere.

If special status has its drawbacks, the Indians also need the legal protection of the state in order to maintain communal land rights and benefit from specific health and education programs. The proper social and political space for these rights to be claimed and observed is the field of interethnic relations. When Indians confront national society, they appreciate the advantages of being a citizen. Within their own societies, having an identification card, a voter's card, or any other sign of legal Brazilianness is perfectly irrelevant and dispensable. But it is not when they face the civic requirements of the nation.

What is missing in the Brazilian version of citizenship is the notion of rightful difference. Not only would it be thoroughly intelligible to the Indians, but it would also give them ethnic security by putting them on an equal footing with the majority population. Such equality, however, would not be based on similarity, for one cannot force an Indian to become a non-Indian, but on equivalence, that is, to have the right to full participation without abdicating one's specific identity. In short, what is missing in state territorialization is a legitimate ethnic space that would only be suitable for a de facto multiethnic country. It would mean opening up a space so that the Indians could be Brazilian citizens in the interethnic context while remaining full members of their respective societies. Would this represent having the best of two worlds? No more or less than for foreign-born individuals who opt for double citizenship. What is permitted to foreigners is denied the Indians. The Brazilian minister of justice, Nelson Jobim, publicly acknowledged the granting of double citizenship to people who are born in Brazil to foreign parents (*jus soli*) or who are born abroad to Brazilian parents (*jus sanguinis*). "The passport is a right which results from citizenship—whether by 'jus soli' or by 'jus sanguinis' " (Jobim 1996). As we will see in the last part of this chapter, the symbolic power of a passport goes far beyond a mere bureaucratic expedient. Although double citizenship is granted to non-Indians, nothing in present-day Brazil points to a similar solution for indigenous peoples. It is true that, for the first time in Brazilian history, the 1988 Constitution ensures that indigenous identities are a legitimate permanent state and no longer a temporary condition. But it does not mean that it confers on them full citizenship, much less a double one. The Indians are still under the wardship of the state and are still legally relatively incapable, even when they show themselves to be utterly familiar with the country's civic codes and fully capable of steering through the meanderings of national life. For all the advances of the new constitution over previous ones, it still falls short of exorcising the specter of marginalization that is sometimes camouflaged under the euphemism of emancipation.

Indigenism: The Fourth Voice

The context of interethnic relations lays bare some fine points that deserve attention. One is the interesting inversion of citizenship by nationals and by Indians. Whereas for the nationals, according to national ideology, citizenship is a natural result of having been born and raised in the country, for Indians citizenship is a tactic of survival amid the national population. While Brazilians naturalize citizenship, the Indians instrumentalize it. What is natural to the Indians is their ethnic specificity: once a Shavante always a Shavante. This is the feature that until recently the Brazilian state insisted on formally treating as a temporary condition, and the attitude still persists unofficially.

Picking their way through the twists and turns of the nation's logic has trained some indigenous peoples in the art of exploiting symbolic and political resources that are not accessible to most Brazilians, represented by such institutions as legal agencies, mass media, the National Congress, nongovernmental organizations, and power groups of various sorts (church, military, industry). The Indian groups most successful in the politics of interethnic contact have been those who have best played the natural-versus-instrumental game by pragmatically manipulating these categories as strategic devices. Let us examine some recent scenarios in which the polyphony of ethnicity-citizenship-universalism has been orchestrated and in which Indigenism operates as the music master that brings together those three voices.

First, the media. The fascination the media have had for Indians has brought a great deal of visibility to the indigenous issue in Brazil, which is rather amazing, considering the minute number of Indians in the country—indeed, the smallest in the Americas, excluding Argentina. No other American country in which Indians are demographic minorities pays so much public attention to them. Perceiving the attraction they exert on the press, the Indians have learned to use it to their advantage as a sort of amplifier of their own voice, a voice the government is reluctant to hear and for which the channels are far from clear. The media have become a key factor in contemporary Indigenism, even when they are less than sympathetic to the Indian cause. The media rarely miss an opportunity to bring out some feature of exoticism in indigenous questions. But in exploiting the native as exotic, the press has perhaps inadvertently provided the Indians with yet another means of ethnic expression. In a phenomenon similar to what happened to the term *Indian*—which the Indians appropriated, purged it of much of its derogatory undertones, and turned it into a political tool—they have instrumentalized exoticism and turned it into a decoy to first attract national attention and then put across their own message. One often sees in the capital city of Brasília groups of Indians from the northeast, long despoiled of ethnic emblems, appearing before Congress in feathered outfits in a generic rendition of what the "original Indian" might have been. In the field of Indigenism even the exotic is politicized.

Politics and power can take on unexpected overtones. I am referring to a particularly spirited line of exoticism struck by the media and transformed into one of the most cherished symbols of what one might call "pulp Indigenism." It is the supernatural aura surrounding the use of certain indigenous objects by Brazilian public figures. Particularly in electoral campaigns (it was especially evident during the Constitutional Assembly), Indians—most commonly men but also women—often place a splendid feather headdress on the head of some politician. For reasons that remain implicit, this act of crowning personalities with indigenous attire has become associated with bad luck. In 1989 a Brasília newspaper (*Correio Braziliense*, September 26) printed headshots of famous people, such as union leader and presidential candidate José Inácio Lula da Silva; the honored

2. The late House Representative Ulysses Guimarães "crowned" with a Kayapó feather headdress. Photo by André Dusek, 1987.

great man in Congress, Ulysses Guimarães; and another presidential candidate, Fernando Collor, all sporting magnificent headdresses from various origins, especially Shavante and Kayapó. The headline read: "Collor and Lula Defy the Cursed Headdress." Lula lost the 1989 election, Collor won but was later impeached, and in 1992 Ulysses Guimarães disappeared at sea in a helicopter crash. By now a relatively long list of politicians and other public people (including the first lady) has passed through the feather headdress ritual. The press created the belief in the bad-luck headdress, and the Indians subtly encourage it by not disavowing it and by continuing to perform the rite; it gains them mileage in their quest for political visibility, even if it means resorting to folkloric cheap thrills or to a cliché catering to the power of the weak.

Indigenous discourses in the interethnic context, whether spoken with a strong accent or in impeccable Portuguese, display an exceptional sense of political syncretism. With remarkable shrewdness, as we shall see in the next chapter, the Indians assert their alterity while appropriating symbols and images that are dear to the majority population's feelings of nationality and humanism. Learned in a fairly short time—in many cases less than two decades—the rhetoric of indigenous contact blends in a single ideological crucible the ingredients of ethnicity, citizenship, and universalism. One can still remember the inflamed speeches by Shavante leader Mário Juruna when, as a member of Congress in the early 1980s, he lumped together Indians and Brazilians who had in common the misfortune of enduring the same climate of oppression and poverty. Because of some of those speeches during the military regime, when he explicitly accused Brazilian politicians of being corrupt, Juruna nearly lost his office.

To Catch a White Thief
Alcida Rita Ramos

This was originally published in the weekly column of the Brazilian Anthropological Association in the *Jornal de Brasília,* November 8, 1983, p. 15, about the repercussions of Mário Juruna's speech. At the time he was a deputy in the House and accused members of the military government of stealing Indian lands, among other things. He made the speech at a time of great tension between the military-controlled executive and the civilian-controlled legislative branches.

To the nation's relief, the "Juruna case" was closed last Tuesday. Censure by the House of Representatives and Deputy Mário Juruna's "letter of retraction" halted a crisis that threatened to pit the executive branch against the legislative. Everybody seemed to be pleased, even those who had insisted on the immediate removal of Juruna from office. This general contentment leaves up in the air the question of why this particular speech created so much fuss—after all, it did not differ much from others Deputy Juruna had delivered and that had gone unnoticed. Because it has multiple meanings, this question lends itself to a variety of interpretations, and it is not my intention to go into them now. I would like to emphasize only two aspects of the "letter of retraction."

The first is the very need for such a retraction. In early October news coverage repeatedly mentioned that some of those implicated—the minister of transportation, for instance—would be satisfied if Deputy Juruna made a public apology to those who felt attacked by his speech. We can only take this as an attempt to "bend" this indigenous congressman who has stood out in the House for his integrity and commitment to defending the interests of the dispossessed—to "break" him, for Deputy Juruna puts his responsibility toward indigenous and Brazilian people above the interests of the current government.

With rhetoric that has swung from condescending paternalism (he is Indian, therefore he is not responsible for what he says) to overt authoritarianism (because he offended the government, he must be summarily punished, regardless of the House's internal rules), government representatives inflated the importance of Juruna's speech to, it seems clear, teach the legislature a lesson: if it could break Juruna, the government could break other members of Congress. This was the strategy of a desperate government that sees the legislature voting against its decrees and the press revealing scandals involving the government's representatives (as pointed out, for example, by Senator Fernando Henrique Cardoso in his statement to *Jornal de Brasília* on October 1, page 2: "With these actions the government is trying to cover up and dodge the numerous accusations of dishonest deals and irregularities widely denounced by the press based on a vast amount of evidence").

The second aspect of Deputy Juruna's "letter of retraction" has to do with its content. Two points stand out: first, that he had not intended to personally offend any member of the government. Because Juruna had already expressed these sentiments, which were widely publicized, one presumes that the main reason for the retraction was something else. The other point, in my opinion, is crucial. The letter says that the speech Juruna delivered on September 26 "addresses the situation of the Brazilian Indian who sees his lands being invaded and unduly occupied."

What does this mean? Who has noticed the underlying implications that such a "retraction" is satisfactory not only to members of the government but to everybody else? Why is it that, the moment the emphasis on Juruna's speech turned from the mass of dispossessed Brazilians to the exploited indigenous populations, it stopped being so offensive and everything settled down? What this means is that whoever steals from Indians is not considered a thief, for this is the normal (and accepted) thing to do. What sort of "civilized" conscience feels redressed of an accusation of robbery so long as the victim is Indian?

Let us put ourselves in Deputy Juruna's place as he signed the letter. Can it really be a retraction? Any Indian who finds himself evicted from his land, as in the case of the Patashó in the state of Bahia, sees in this episode the full confirmation of what Deputy Juruna said in his September 26 address. Only non-Indians do not see it, because they for a long time took on the role of "thieves of indigenous lands." Robbing public coffers and robbing indigenous possessions are regarded by the so-called *civilizados* as totally distinct, incomparable things. The former is a crime. The latter is standard practice. Hence, the general relief conveyed by the "letter of retraction," for if robbing Indians is not a crime, Deputy Juruna's accusation against the government is rendered meaningless. Is it really?

In the late 1970s we entered the age of nongovernmental organizations. Most of the so-called NGOs play the role of switchboards between universalism and citizenship. When dedicated to the Indian cause, they imprint Indigenism with a distinctive style. When Indian voices were hardly heard on the national scene, particularly during the military regime, the Indian support groups spoke out in defense of indigenous rights. As they pleaded for the Indians, the NGOs forced open important spaces within the state machine where indigenous complaints could be aired. Increasing red tape transformed NGOs into professional agencies of private Indigenism as they amassed considerable amounts of funds, most of them earmarked to promote the opening of political channels. The NGOs created centers of Indian law, circulated documents through indigenous communities, organized meetings of Indian leaders, and launched campaigns within and outside the country to inform the public of the problems afflicting indigenous peoples. As one of the political goods available to them, the Indians relate to NGOs basically as they do to other support groups, such as the church, and to professional organizations, such as the Order of Brazilian Lawyers, the Brazilian Anthropological Association, and the Association of Geologists. There actually seems to be a certain social (or would it be ethnic?) division of labor in the Indians' instrumentalization of their allies. Some indigenous peoples are more inclined toward some support groups than others. This reflects in part the specialization of certain NGOs. For example, the Center for Indigenist Work (CTI), based in São Paulo, has concentrated on development projects for the Krahó Indians in the state of Goiás, for the Sateré-Maué of Amazonas, and for the Waiãpi of Amapá, among others. The Pro-Yanomami Commission (CCPY) is dedicated to defending the Yanomami exclusively. In turn, the Socio-Environmental Institute (ISA, formerly CEDI) has opted for a wide range of problems regarding both indigenous and environmental issues. Its work includes the publication of documents, books, journals, maps, and a rich collection of photographs and videos. It covers virtually the entire country but puts some emphasis on specific areas, such as the Upper Rio Negro region. Beyond this specialization, however, one notices a tendency toward different loyalties, particularly with regard to the Catholic Indigenist Missionary Council (CIMI). There was a moment, for instance, when "CIMI Indians" did not mix with Indians associated with certain NGOs and the Union of Indian Nations, a pan-Indian organization.

As translators of the language of universalism to the idiom of citizenship and ethnicity, the NGOs inject into Indigenism not simply material resources but also a libertarian rhetoric easily digestible by Indians who are involved in the country's pan-Indian movement. The humanist stimulus of NGOs awakened many a political vocation among Indians. The NGOs have introduced the distinct tonality of universalism to the chorus of Indigenism, even if they sometimes show little talent for modulations and, as we shall see in Chapter 10, a tangible bent toward moral purism.

Let us now examine a case in which ethnicity put the nation-state in the docket before a universalist court. It shows how the power of a state can be converted into an empowering strategy for the powerless. It involves all the actors discussed earlier, plus all three branches of the state machine and international human rights activists. I turn now to the political drama precipitated by the episode of the Fourth Russell Tribunal held in the Netherlands in 1980.

The Russell Tribunal: The Indian against the State

In November 1980 the Bertrand Russell Peace Foundation Ltd. organized the Fourth Russell Tribunal in Rotterdam to consider crimes of genocide and/or ethnocide against indigenous peoples in the Americas. The foundation selected three cases from Brazil involving the breach of human rights of the Nambiquara, the Yanomami, and the Indians of the Upper Rio Negro region. In the first two cases the accusations were aimed at the Brazilian government, which was responsible for major economic projects involving road building. Both the Nambiquara and the Yanomami were being seriously affected by epidemics resulting from contact with road workers as well as invading lumberjacks and cattle ranchers (Nambiquara) and gold miners (Yanomami). The third was a case against Salesian missionaries who were accused of ethnocidal practices. The organizers invited both Indians and Brazilians to be part of the jury. Among the Indians was the Shavante leader Mário Juruna.

His invitation triggered one of the most remarkable episodes in the recent history of Brazil's interethnic relations. The Indian issue stuck out like a sore thumb in the country's self-consciousness regarding its image abroad. The incident involved a minister of state, twenty-four judges or ministers of justice, various members of Congress, and the many journalists eagerly flooding the mass media with a continuous stream of reports, opinions, jests, and ironic and sometimes distasteful remarks. In examining newspaper clippings of the event I am now much more aware of its extraordinary force than I was when it happened. Hindsight has the effect of intensifying the affair as a cause célèbre by placing the consequences of certain acts or speeches in the flow of history. Whatever is lost of the fervent flavor of day-to-day involvement is more than compensated by the composed exercise of intellectual understanding. Having the whole picture in front of me, as it were, I can now more easily tell the incidental from the recurrent than I could in the heat of the moment.

In 1980 the military held virtually all positions of power, including the control of the National Indian Foundation. Juruna was fast gaining renown for his frequent incursions in the corridors of power, always armed

3. As House Representative, Mário Juruna "crowns" House President Flávio Marcílio at the plenary room, 1987. Photo courtesy of the Archive Coordination, House of Representatives, National Congress, Brasília.

with a tape recorder to catch officials and politicians in the act of making false promises to his demands for better treatment of the Indians. He then played these recorded conversations with the powerful back to journalists. As an Indian he was somewhat protected by his special status as "relatively incapable," which ironically conferred on him greater freedom of speech than that then enjoyed by the full Brazilian citizen. Juruna's tape recorder— which literally became the title of a book about him (Juruna, Hohlfeldt, and Hoffmann 1982)—became a badge of his daring and an object of envy for many Brazilians muzzled by the repressive military regime.

The press had first announced the organization of the Fourth Russell Tribunal in July 1980, during the annual meeting of the Brazilian Society for the Advancement of Science. About three months later Juruna received an invitation from the foundation's secretary to be part of the jury scheduled to convene from November 24 to 30. It struck Brazilian authorities as an outright affront. When Juruna, a ward of the state, asked FUNAI to assist him in getting a passport, he, perhaps unwittingly, precipitated a crisis that was to assume unexpected proportions. Carrying his tape recorder, Juruna went to see Colonel João Carlos Nobre da Veiga, then the president of FUNAI, who agreed to help Juruna with his passport. During the long conversation Nobre da Veiga repeatedly warned Juruna not to denigrate Brazil abroad. Here is a portion of the transcript, which appears in Juruna, Hohlfeldt, and Hoffmann (the speaker is Nobre da Veiga):

> I only hope you'll remember that you're Brazilian, you're a Brazilian Indian, you can't sell out Brazil abroad. . . . You must work for Brazil and not against Brazil. . . . You must defend Brazil, don't attack Brazil. . . . If you're not Brazilian, go to Bolivia, if you don't want to defend Brazil, go to Bolivia. If you don't like Brazilian people, go away. . . . If you bad-mouth the Brazilian people, when you come back no one here will like you, Mário, don't do such nonsense. . . . You're a man who doesn't know white things very well. . . . You're against a Government that is defending you, because if it weren't for FUNAI you know what would happen. You have no right as a Brazilian to go out there and attack the Brazilian Government, or the Brazilian people, especially the Brazilian people. You can't do this out there, or else you'll see what'll happen to you when you come back. . . . I'm warning you as your guardian, don't make any attack against the Brazilian people. (1982, 150–51)

Juruna's request for a passport went to FUNAI's Indigenist Council, which had among its members the famous Indian tamer Orlando Villas Bôas. At its meeting on October 21 the council denied permission for Juruna to participate in the tribunal, either as part of the jury or as a mere observer.

The minutes of that meeting reveal some noteworthy details. The council's president, Nobre da Veiga, argued that "to agree with the participation of a representative would obviously mean to acknowledge the accusations and recommendations of those individuals of the jury in question, which is not to the interest of the Brazilian government." Father Angelo Venturelli, a Salesian missionary among the Shavante, was emphatic in declaring that "Brazil doesn't need any international meddling to solve its problems and those of its indigenous communities." Moreover, "Mário Juruna . . . is not a natural chief of his village let alone of his tribe or of the whole of the Brazilian Indian nations," and "he is an individual dishonestly integrated, for he possesses material goods and a bank account of dubious origin, according to information from the missionaries." Linguist Charlotte Emmerich argued against Juruna's participation because he was a Shavante speaker, and the cases in question involved indigenous peoples from other language groups; he would be merely a decorative figure whose participation might be diluted in the overall context of the tribunal. Therefore she suggested that members of the Russell Tribunal be invited to come to Brazil to see the national reality and its problems in loco.

Villas Bôas said, "An individual who has no knowledge of Brazilian problems could never participate in a jury." Counsellor Jayme de Albuquerque showed great concern for Juruna's special status: Juruna "may not be adequate to consciously represent [Brazil] as member of the jury, unless he requests his emancipation so that he can freely express himself without any legal impediment. . . . Juruna is still a ward of the state; therefore, his participation in that Tribunal could only be as a mere observer, giving his personal opinions, never positions in the name of the Brazilian government or of his guardian, so long as he goes with the assistance of a guardian's representative." A little later Albuquerque put the whole issue in a curious way: "Brazil has nothing to fear, unless it does."

About two weeks later the newspapers published a statement by Mário Andreazza, the minister of the interior to whom FUNAI reported, in which Andreazza barred Juruna from traveling to Holland on the ground that "the Brazilian government recognized neither the existence nor the competence of the Russell Tribunal to pass judgment on Brazil's indigenous policy" (*O Dia* 1980). Therefore, the minister insisted, there was no reason to send a representative. Besides, "chief Juruna, as a ward of the state, couldn't be such representative, anyway" (*O Globo* 1980). A lawyer affiliated with an indigenist NGO immediately filed a suit against the minister on Juruna's behalf in the Federal Court of Appeals. The court deliberated for nine hours over two days a week apart before deciding in Juruna's favor. It handed down its ruling on November 27, three days before the close of the tribunal.

While the judges debated the case, news from Rotterdam appeared daily in the press. The Salesians were under heavy attack, as were the Brazilian government and the World Bank because of the negative effect of road building on the Nambiquara Indians. On the second day of the tribunal, with Juruna still held in Brazil without a passport, its organizers exacerbated the situation by electing Juruna president of the jury. As Juruna said later, the pressure from the organizers was decisive in the court's positive ruling and the subsequent order to issue him a passport. "They Are Afraid of Me, Says Juruna" was one headline in *Correio Braziliense* (November 30, 1980).

It is worth examining the proceedings of the Federal Court of Appeals in Juruna's case, published in the *Revista do Tribunal Federal de Recursos* (83 TFR 248–301 [1982]), because it contains some of the most emblematic features of Brazilian Indigenism. Fifteen judges voted to grant Juruna a writ of habeas corpus, and nine voted against it. (During the debate two judges had changed their minds and ended up supporting Juruna.) Of the nine judges voting against Juruna, one had no declared justification, three justified their vote on strictly procedural grounds—they said habeas corpus was inappropriate for the case—and five declared Juruna ineligible for a passport because he was relatively incapable, a ward of the state; whether to grant him a passport was for FUNAI to decide.

Behind the highly stylized etiquette of legal professionals the session was a battle of opinions or, hermeneutically speaking, a conflict of interpretations (Ricoeur 1978). Both sides eloquently invoked John Stuart Mill, Shakespeare, the seventeenth-century Jesuit Antonio Vieira, Sultan Harum Al Rachid, and even poet Pereira da Silva (in a long passage about the doom of the vanquished). The Universal Declaration of Human Rights was brought up several times and of course the Brazilian Civil Code, according to which the Indians are considered minors, as well as the 1967 Constitution and the 1973 Indian Statute, which define the terms of Indian wardship. The controversy about the limits of the wardship was discussed at length, as it had been on many previous occasions (Dallari 1978; Agostinho 1982; Marés 1983). What purpose the wardship serves, what it means to be relatively incapable, how much power the guardian can exercise, and what protection the ward has against a bad guardian were central questions occupying the judges.

In the context of this chapter some statements made in the appellate court merit attention. Regarding the intersection of ethnicity, nationality, and universalism, one reads between the lines a reluctance to acknowledge full rights to ethnics when nationality is at stake. One sympathetic judge, Washington Bolívar de Brito, declared:

> No Nation has the right to prevent its children from freely leaving or returning, and this has already been said here, when the passage from the Declaration of the Rights of Mankind was evoked. Would there be any doubt that the Indian is a man? Evidently not. Since there is no such doubt, and since the Brazilian Nation co-signed the San Francisco Letter which spells out these rights, one cannot prevent a Brazilian man from leaving the country, be he an Indian or not. (83 TFR at 258)

Here internal affairs—where multiethnicity is acknowledged de facto but not de jure—are superseded by the concern that the nation is required to honor supranational commitments. The argument hinges on that impeccable Cartesian logic: Indians are men, Juruna is an Indian, therefore Juruna is a man. The quality of being human is what entitled Juruna to the benefit of universal human rights. His ethnicity is thus rendered irrelevant because it is eclipsed by nationality.

Judge Aldir G. Passarinho was confident of the power of nationality:

> I am absolutely certain that the Shavante chief's feeling of Brazilianness will speak louder abroad than any restrictions that might be made to indigenous policy. If he is apt to go abroad to discuss the Indians' problems it is because he equally understands the need to safeguard Brazil's name abroad, which is the first duty of any Brazilian. . . . I am sure he

will perceive the importance of, in the Concert of Nations, respecting the dignified name of Brazil. This is also his duty, for he is perhaps more Brazilian than all of us, because he has no mixture of races in his blood. Being this confident, I grant him habeas corpus, for I am sure that when he returns we will have to admit that, really, there was no reason for any fears of whatever nature about his going abroad. (83 TFR at 261)

In his view, Juruna's Indianness is still visible but attenuated by the compelling notion of Brazilianness. This being so, how could Juruna possibly betray a country that aspires to a place in the sun among the "Concert of Nations"? This judge's reasoning, rather than appealing to supranational arguments, leans on the power of nationalist feelings that in turn are the natural result of racial purity. Because Juruna has no mixture in his blood, he is more Brazilian than anyone else. He is, in other words, entitled to the highest degree of Brazilianness. This being so, there would be no grounds to fear that Juruna might denigrate his mother country (*Pátria*). It is of no concern whether Indians have their own agendas that do not coincide with the national one. What matters is that Brazil cannot be slandered by its own children, pure or not so pure. Whereas in the speech by Bolívar de Brito to be an Indian is to be a human, here to be an Indian is to be Brazilian. To *be* an Indian simply as *Indian* seems to be an unthinkable proposition.

A third, not-so-sympathetic judge, Geraldo Andrade Fontelles, asked this question: "Admitting that, for some reason, this Indian who is relatively incapable, while abroad inflicts some harm on somebody, who would repair this harm?" (83 TFR at 261). The Indian as clumsy child, unaware of civic behavior, cannot be let loose in the world. The bad boy would be a source of embarrassment to the nation. Here the Indian is not cloaked as either a national or a generic human. He is regarded as a deficient being with his relative incapacity, his naïveté, his quaintness, and his disconcerting unpredictability. For this reason the nation cannot afford to expose its flaws—the Indians—to the judging eye of an international assembly.

Judge Jarbas Nobre presented an interesting twist:

Mister President: Regarding the merit [of the case], it is my opinion that Chief Juruna, my Indian brother, has the right to what he requests, that is, to go to Rotterdam to meet with his equals of the Americas and say what he thinks and even denounce what may seem to him to be wrong in what has been done against the primitive and exclusive owners of the various countries they represent. Without being orthodox I say that to tutor is to protect, to uphold, to defend.[2] In this sense the institute of

2. The Portuguese verb is *tutelar*, translated in the Michaelis dictionary as "to tutor, protect, defend, patronize."

wardship should not be used to discriminate, to separate, to differentiate. It seems that this is exactly what is being done, the attempt to separate the Indian from the white in detriment of the former. (83 TFR at 286)

This argument raises an interesting point that deserves a little more attention precisely because it was made by a sympathizer of the Indians. One can convey prejudice even when affirming otherwise. In the same breath his honor declares himself a brother of Juruna and then retreats from such close kinship by evoking Juruna's equality to other Indians of the continent. The patronizing tone of his speech comes to the fore when he adds that "to tutor is to protect, to uphold, to defend." He regrets the treatment Indians have had at the hands of the majority population but proposes that internal differences should be leveled out. The invocation of his brotherhood with Juruna is a rhetorical device to attest to the univocality of Brazilianness. The betraying bit of discourse regarding the brotherhood between Brazilian Indians and non-Indians is Judge Nobre's statement that Juruna should attend the Russell Tribunal "to meet with *his* [not my] equals of the Americas." If we presume, as is usually done, that *brother* means *equal,* once again Western logic will reveal the vacuity behind Nobre's posture of an apparent ethnic liberality. If Juruna is my brother, Juruna's equals should also be my equals. But because Juruna has equals who are *his,* not my, equals, brothers and equals do not necessarily coincide.

Indeed, native as brother has become a cliché in the rhetoric of equality in Brazil and elsewhere. The phrase is most often used for sheer emotional effect. In his weekly column in *Folha de São Paulo* on October 28, 1996, anthropologist-senator Darcy Ribeiro applauded a particular move by a Shavante group by saying: "One of the greatest joys I've had lately was to see on TV my Shavante brothers, painted in red and black, invade Funai." It is often heard in patronizing speeches of politicians who have some vested interest in indigenous resources. Roraima congressmen, for instance, profess to have Indian blood in their veins as an alibi to defend development schemes on Indian lands; their argument runs as follows: since I have Indian blood, I know what is good for the Indians. This sophism of brotherhood, with its benign veneer, is not limited to Brazil. Richard Price describes how a Suriname government official, under the heavy volley of questions from the Inter-American Commission on Human Rights about the massacre of Saramaka (Maroon) people, declared that "the president and his political party consider the Maroons as their brothers" (1995, 456).

In reading the proceedings of the Federal Court of Appeals in Juruna's case one can apply verbatim Aijaz Ahmad's words when he analyses Nehru's and other statesmen's speeches during the 1955 Bandung conference of the so-called nonaligned nations: "Language itself came to have a peculiarly overdetermined, archaic character, perfectly transparent to the initiated, always in need of decoding by the others, with words constantly exceeding their meanings, at once slippery and hermeticized" (1992, 297). Indeed, to cut through the highly ornate style of judicial parlance is to unwrap successive layers of meaning, which make sense only if one is aware of the subtleties of Indigenism in Brazil. Overt phrasing often disguises its antithetical covert meaning. It is curious that it was the judges sympathetic to Juruna who most often used convoluted oratory and imagery to defend his right to participate in the international forum. Perhaps this was their embroidered way of covering up the dilemma of supporting his plea in the name of freedom and democracy without having to acknowledge the reality of ethnic diversity within the Brazilian nation.

While all this was taking place, another Indian quietly got his passport and flew unnoticed to Holland to attend the Russell Tribunal. It was Álvaro Sampaio, later known as Álvaro Tukano, invited to participate in the event as a witness. Brazilian journalists and authorities were so startled—first by his unexpected presence at the tribunal and then by his denunciations of the Salesian missionaries—that some reactions were simply baffling. FUNAI refused to believe he was a real Indian because the Indian agency had no record of him. He "must be a mere Brazilian citizen who went to the Federal Police to request a passport" after presenting the usual documents: birth certificate, social security card, voter's card, and a draft card. Furthermore, his Portuguese surname was evidence of his non-Indianness, as "any Indian, according to FUNAI's technicians, has an indigenous surname, is registered at birth by FUNAI. For this reason he does not receive a conventional birth certificate" (*O Estado de São Paulo* 1980). Besides the blatant falsity of the information about FUNAI's ubiquitous issuing of indigenous birth certificates, the notion that to be an Indian is to have an Indian surname was only fitting for the agency's plans—as later transpired—to apply the infamous "criteria of Indianness" (see Chapter 9).

But it was *Veja* magazine that carried the most malignant tone in condemning Tukano's purported boldness. Under a headline of "Perfect Crime: Tukano Deceives Funai and Travels to Rotterdam," the magazine produced a report dripping with sarcasm:

> The prohibition of Shavante leader Mário Juruna from traveling to Holland will not, after all, prevent jungle[3] emissaries from doing damage to the image of Brazilian indigenist policy in the ears of foreign audiences. Last Wednesday, evading Funai's vigilance, an Indian of the Tukano tribe in the Upper Rio Negro, Amazonas, traveled to Rotterdam to star in

3. The Portuguese word used was *taba*, a demeaning way of referring to Indian houses.

the Amazonian chapter of the spectacle produced by the "Russell Tribunal" with its debut scheduled for this week. To get his passport, the Tukano exhibited his white name — Álvaro Fernandes Sampaio — plus ID card, voter's card, draft card, and the declared profession of nursing technician. On Friday, Funai, startled with a trip it had not authorized, informed that it had decided to "officially ignore that Mr. Álvaro Fernandes Sampaio was an Indian." But he is, lives in a village and, like Juruna, cannot perform any act without the approval of his trustee, in this case, Funai itself. As a state ward, Sampaio's acts are juridically void, but he may be punished when he returns from Holland. It was, therefore, a perfect crime committed with the help of members of the Indigenist Missionary Council (CIMI), a section of the Catholic Church which actively militates against the government. . . . Fearing he could not fly to Rotterdam, the Tukano concealed his trip with elaborate caution. Invited by the "tribunal," Sampaio did not reveal his intention to travel even to the Salesians who assist the Tukano. Neither did he tell his friend Juruna, busy talking to the press and besieging courts. . . .

In the end the "Russell Tribunal" will have no difficulty in hearing exactly what it wants to hear. (1980)

Veja, notorious for its anti-Indian stories (McCallum 1995), took this opportunity to first misinform the public about the actual status of the Indians, making them seem absolutely incapable, and then to attack the Catholic organization that in the early 1970s, inspired by liberation theology, planted the seed of the pan-Indian movement in Brazil (see Chapter 6).

Álvaro Sampaio, who was to become a major pan-Indian leader, was vehemently critical of the Salesians' policy and actions in his homeland, particularly regarding the culturally disastrous consequences of boarding schools and the sending of Tukano girls to serve as maids-turned-prostitutes in Manaus, a major Amazon town.

Prostitution and hunger continue, as do diseases. Many Indians cannot be interned in hospitals because they do not have the documents required by the hospital in São Gabriel and FUNAI does not take care of them. I ask: how is it that we can transform the Indians into Brazilians if there is so much moral criminality against the Indians?

For 66 years, we have suffered the pressures of certain priests and nuns to abandon our culture, but we have resisted. (Tukano, quoted in Ismaelillo and Wright 1982, 69)

Upon his return from Europe Sampaio refused to go back home and for some time lived in fear of retaliation both from the missionaries and from other Tukanoans who took the Salesians' side. As it happened, the Salesians refused to take the children of his family group into their boarding school and so harassed his people that his entire community had to move elsewhere in the Rio Negro region.

If Sampaio got his passport without any problem, why the fuss about Juruna's? This question raises some interesting points regarding the exercise of state power over the growing potential of certain indigenous figures. The issuing of passports to Indians has been used as an instrument to control their political influence. In 1979 FUNAI prohibited Daniel Matenho Cabixi, a prominent Pareci Indian, from attending a meeting in Puebla, Mexico, organized by the Catholic Church. The case was made public but its effect was minimized either because the degree of political repression was higher then or because Cabixi was less willing to pursue it to its final consequences. Most likely, it was a combination of both. A few months later, just before the Juruna affair, FUNAI took two "tame," cooperating Indians to a meeting in Mexico City, duly providing them with passports.

Sampaio's and Juruna's cases raise two issues. One is the false assumption that FUNAI can legitimately exercise exclusive power over such matters as providing the Indians with documents. The other issue is, given that, why was it necessary to take Juruna's case to an appellate court? Among the many answers possible is one I deem irrefutable, namely, the quest for political visibility on the part of the Indians, a crucial feature of Brazilian Indigenism. Juruna, already a well-known character on the Brazilian public scene, seized the opportunity prompted by his confrontation with FUNAI's president to publicize a case of repression in times of military dictatorship and to implicate top-level members of the Brazilian state, such as the minister of the interior and the twenty-four ministers of the Federal Court of Appeals. It was a move that was bound to attract the public's attention to the Indian cause, with the added touch of putting the military government on the spot. Although Sampaio exposed FUNAI's false pretenses as the absolute master of the Indians, Juruna showed that, in Darcy Ribeiro's words, "the only way to defend the Indians in Latin America is to appeal to national and international public opinion" (Juruna, Hohlfeldt, and Hoffmann 1982, 146). Indeed, the visibility of the Indian issue in Brazil and abroad has been one of the most effective tools in the defense of Indians' ethnic rights against the abuses of the nation-state.

The Russell Tribunal reverberated in the Brazilian press for months afterward. In December a politician from the state of Amazonas repudiated the tribunal's accusations and defended the Salesians who, he said, contribute to "protect the Indian from human evil" (*A Crítica* 1980), the Catholic Church spoke out in support of the Salesians, arguing that it was "a true violation of human rights to have a Tribunal accuse without giving the possibility of defense" (*O Globo* 1981a). (Months earlier the press reported that the bishop of the Upper Rio Negro had been invited to participate in the Russell Tribunal and declined.) Juruna in turn complained that FUNAI was trying to defeat him by promoting a change of headmanship in his village. He declared that after his return from the Russell Tribunal his leadership among the Indians had been weakened (*Correio Braziliense* 1981).

In April 1981 FUNAI's president visited the Salesian mission in the Upper Rio Negro and was quoted as saying that the Salesians did "serious work such as I have never seen before. They educate, there is a spirit of Brazilianness in teaching, health, order, and discipline" (*O Estado de São Paulo* 1981). *O Globo* explicitly linked this visit to the denunciations made at the Russell Tribunal (1981b). Nobre da Veiga not only reacted to the charges against the Salesians in the Upper Rio Negro region but also took some ludicrously timid steps to respond to the accusations that the Brazilian government was violating the human rights of the Nambiquara in the state of Rondônia. He signed an agreement with the Anthropology Museum at the University of Goiás to provide "assistance in health and research to the indigenous communities who live near the BR-364 highway that links Cuiabá to Porto Velho" (*O Globo* 1981b).

Behind the government's anxiety about the international accusations was the fear that multilateral agencies such as the World Bank and the Inter-American Development Bank, themselves pressured by human rights activists, might stop financing Brazilian projects, such as the paving of the BR-364 highway. Haunted by the aftermath of the tribunal, fidgety Brazilian authorities made token attempts to mend their rather tattered image as bad custodians of the Indians, a charge that might jeopardize the flow of international funds. The country was feeling the effects of the potency that ethnicity can acquire under certain, albeit rare, auspicious circumstances. In the ranks of universalism the Brazilian nation did not pass muster.

Indian as Political Banner

The commotion generated by Juruna's case provided an opportunity to air grievances against the military by members of the opposition. Noteworthy is the statement made at the federal House of Representatives by Gilson de Barros of the Partido do Movimento Democrático Brasileiro opposition party:

> Overstepping its prerogative as trustee, the Government of the Brazilian military dictatorship, through FUNAI and, in the last few days, more specifically through the mouth of the Minister of the Interior himself, the also Colonel Mário Andreazza, publicly denies—and all Brazilian press recorded—authorization for Mário Juruna to travel to Holland. The arguments are the most base and mediocre. . . . I don't know if this

makes me laugh or cry, in this Republic where there are no more tears for those who want to shed them. . . . Now FUNAI, an Executive agency at the service of the Brazilian military dictatorship which has much to hide—and doesn't want Juruna to go to Holland and tell of the misery his people are enduring, the persecutions he suffers together with his white brothers, the squatters, in my state of Mato Grosso—says Mário Juruna is not even a leader. . . . Neither the Shavante people nor the Mato Grosso people nor the Brazilian people have any tears left, having already shed so many for the wretchedness of this dictatorship which crushes the most legitimate demands of the Brazilian people, including the most legitimate of Brazilians which are the Indian people in the Country, in spite of being marginalized, betrayed and vilified by the agency supposed to be their guardian. (*Diário do Congresso Nacional* 1980a, 13905)

A few days later the same representative continued:

The Nazi-fascist groups infiltrated in the Government or who count on its omission or consent begin to arm their sinister and nearly invisible tentacles in the explicit attempt to eliminate the courageous Shavante whose only crime, as far as we know, is to possess a perfect and multiform vision of his people's problems. . . . Indeed, it seems, Mr. President, that there is a plan astutely designed to discredit and dismantle the indigenous movement in Brazil. . . . Now there are statements by FUNAI employees saying that Juruna may be murdered by his own people. . . . In denouncing these facts to the Nation I intend to follow up with a series of accusations made weekly in this House to show the way in which the Brazilian Government, utterly illegitimate, intends to perpetuate itself in Power, while it eliminates leaders who most eloquently defend the interests of the suffering Brazilian people. (*Diário do Congresso Nacional* 1980b)

Representative Barros was a citizen against the state, or rather, against the improper use the military were making of the state. In launching his violent attack on the military government he raised the issue of legitimate ethnicity. In the hands of the dictatorship Brazilian citizens were as defenseless as indigenous peoples. But here the Indians, for all the specific rights to which they are entitled, are still put in the same slot as their Brazilian "brothers," squatters or otherwise.

The contours of indigenous peoples as political agents in their own right become sharper in the speech of Representative Modesto da Silveira, also from the opposition:

If in fact FUNAI, through its president, and the Brazilian Government are worried and so zealous that a people or a nation should not intrude in the affairs of another people or nation, as FUNAI's attorney declared to me . . . why then doesn't the Brazilian Nation worry about respecting the rights of the Indian nations? And, if the concern is really about intervention, why do they intrude in the interests of the Indian nations or of any Indian? If the Brazilian Government is worried about this self-determination and non-intervention, it might be the case, for instance, . . . of the nations themselves and indigenous peoples issuing their own passports, since they constitute nations that are absolutely established and recognized. (*Diário do Congresso Nacional* 1980c)

At that political moment the military was in its final years in government since the 1964 coup. In 1985 official power returned to civilians, although the Indian question was to remain, directly or indirectly, in the hands of the military. In 1980 protests such as those heard in the National Congress were increasing. As had happened before during the worst years of dictatorship, the Indian cause continued to be used opportunistically as a platform from which to launch attacks concerning the breach of rights of the Brazilian citizenry at large. Although the military tried to conceal the embarrassment that Indians represented to the nation, the opposition took them as an emblem of suffering and as such Indians played a significant role in the definition of an antimilitary ideology.

One way or the other, indigenous peoples, minute as their numbers may be in Brazil, seem to represent an endless reservoir of images that serve the most disparate convictions. No other segment of the country's population possesses the double feature of both proximity and distance that makes the Indians so specially evocative in the construction of ideological imagery. Episodes such as the Russell Tribunal are bound to precipitate a confrontation between the state and its discontents, and that is why they take on the aspect of political dramas brimming with analytical promise.

Brazilian Indians have appealed to other international forums, such as the United Nations and the Organization of American States, charged with the protection of human rights when nation-states fail to observe these rights. As a strategy recourse to the Universal Declaration of Human Rights ignores the contradiction between the logic of cultural diversity—the right of the Indians to practice "crimes" or "offenses," such as infanticide, the execution of witches, or polygamy (Price 1995)—and the logic of the Eurocentric universal rights. Depending on the grievance and the context, cultural differences are either emphasized or underplayed by Indians who have learned enough about the contradictions of Brazilian laws and legislation to pit Brazilian against Brazilian to the Indians' advantage. Paraphrasing Todorov once more, we have here a case of *indigénisme de parcours.*

As for the Brazilian state, it defends itself abroad against accusations of the breach of human rights by evoking its legislation, which—enlightened as it may be—is routinely reduced to dead letter. In its domestic confines the state counterattacks with pressure and retaliation. The Catholic Church, NGOs, researchers, and Indian leaders have often paid a high price for provoking a confrontation between Brazilian nationalism and international universalism. Curiously, state backlash violates citizenship rights, such as the freedom to move about (Indians are prohibited from traveling abroad) or to exercise one's profession (periodic bans on anthropologists from Indian areas). In the eyes of the state, especially in its military guise, the question becomes one of treason, to the benefit of foreign interests. The state is then caught in a spiral of transgressions suggestively akin to the schismogenesis effect as described by Bateson—"a process of differentiation in the norms of individual behaviour resulting from cumulative interaction between individuals" (1958, 175).

Lest we are left with the impression that state-as-bad-guardian is an exclusively Brazilian phenomenon, let me quote from two native North American authors: "It would be fair to say that if a private trustee were discovered acting in the same manner as the Interior Department does toward the Indians, he would immediately be indicted for gross violation of his trust" (Kickingbird and Ducheneaux 1973, xxvi). In this particular respect the difference between Brazil and the United States is that no amount of national or international protest against breaches of indigenous rights seems to make the U.S. government feel the scratches in its image, whereas Brazil's reputation abroad, regularly tainted by scandals at home involving massacres of homeless children, landless peasants, and Indians, is a constant government concern. The United States was also condemned by the Russell Tribunal but, to the best of my knowledge, domestic repercussions, if any, were not comparable to those in Brazil.

Defensive as the Brazilian state has been about what it takes to threaten national security—the military continues to handle the Indian question—it is nevertheless highly sensitive to international opinion and rather ambivalent toward foreign presence in the country. When challenged abroad, the nation's rulers brandish their indigenist legislation—of which they are proud—like an elegant storefront display, although their legislation is hollow in its application. Internally, these rulers, be they military or not, maintain an explicitly patriotic posture with recurring outbursts of repudiation of foreign coveting of national resources while inviting foreign investments and participation in the country's wealth.

It is at the crossroads of these contradictions that Indians find fertile ground to act out their strategic indigénisme de parcours. When Indians seize NGOs' humanistic guidelines and set in motion their own ethnic resources as political instruments, they are mixing levels and dimensions in a way that few Brazilians would imagine or dare do. By proceeding in this manner, the Indians steer anthropologists toward an exercise of distancing by means of which we learn to regard what seems fixed as moving, or, to put it another way, to avoid congealing what is actually fluid. Interethnic

Indians lead us to relativize concepts that, because they are ideologically laden, have come to be crystallized as unimpeachable precepts. This returns us to the initial discussion of the absolutism of universalism and relativism. Oblivious to the weight of such crystallization, the Indians are free to improvise, invent, or experiment with notions that for them are no more than tools to be used according to specific circumstances. If in their demands it is useful to evoke the distinctively ethnic, the nationally local, and the generically universal all at once, why not? They have no special allegiance to any ideological standpoint propounded by non-Indians.

One learns that in the political field of interethnic contact the Indians will have their right of access to state goods guaranteed only because of the universality of human rights. As a strategy, universalism is called upon as a mediator between the logic of ethnicity—the social product of cultural diversity—and the logic of citizenship—the social product of the nation-state. If we take citizenship as a social and political strategy rather than as a natural and monolithic ascription, we can maintain that it is on the strength of being *human beings* that the *Indians* must be acknowledged as having the right to also be *citizens*.

4
Indian Voices

In the 1950s Brazilian anthropologist Darcy Ribeiro prophesied that the Indians would become so deculturated by contact with Brazilians that they would lose their ethnic identity and be transformed into "generic Indians," stigmatized by the national society and left with none of their specific cultures or traditions (1970, 222). Ribeiro's pessimism was understandable, given the constant depopulation, loss of territory, exploitation of resources and labor, and armed persecution. For nearly five centuries people after people faced the same problems, which led many to extinction and others to precarious survival. But the image of the alienated generic Indian is a fiction. Ribeiro's prophecy has not come true.

What has happened since the 1950s is the birth and growth of a political pan-Indian movement in Brazil. The first regional Indian meetings took place in the early 1970s and initially were sponsored by the Catholic Indigenist Missionary Council (CIMI). At these meetings Indian leaders organized around the need to claim rights granted by the Constitution and by law but constantly threatened by both private and official actions. The União das Nações Indígenas (Union of Indian Nations, UNI), the first pan-Indian organization in Brazil, was created in 1980.

As a result of this pan-Indian movement, gatherings and speeches by Indians clearly demonstrated the persistence of Indian identities embedded in specific traditions. These peoples are not just Indians. They are Shavante, Terena, Kaingang, Makushi, Guarani of such and such a place, and so on. They often evoke the past, when their cultures were different from what they are now, before the effects of contact, but nowhere in their discourses is there a trace of the cultural void imagined by Ribeiro. The common cause forged in the political arena has unified the Indians and reinforced their ethnic distinctions.

They have transformed *Indian* from a derogatory term to a key concept in their politics of contact. The "generic Indian" is no longer the last stage of a defeatist, down-and-out, no-future-in-sight existence; rather, it has become a mark of otherness vis-à-vis the nationals. The appropriation of Indian by the Indians has exorcised the heaviest spells of discrimination associated with the term. Of course, this does not mean that discrimination no longer occurs. What it means is that discrimination is now expressed in other ways, for example, *bugre* in the south, *caboclo* in the north. (Neither term has an equivalent in English.) But Indian is no longer a dirty word. In fact, it has gained legitimacy by the use to which it is put and the context in which it is used. The Indian is now a well-known political figure on the national scene.

For the purpose of discussing some ways in which the national society has affected indigenous traditions of symbolic expression, I shall present three speeches delivered by Brazilian Indians to Brazilian audiences at meetings organized by Brazilians in major cities of Brazil. These meetings took place during the military government when both Indians and nationals felt the weight of repression and censorship. For better or worse the indigenous question was one of the few political issues that could be discussed in relative safety without automatically incurring the risk of imprisonment. Many nationals took advantage of this to air their frustrations, whereas the Indians used the unexpected opportunity to vent centuries-old grievances. Sympathetic Brazilians crowded into formal convention halls or improvised auditoriums to hear and applaud Indian speeches, often delivered in garbled Portuguese but always potent, vivid, and aimed at the common enemy—those in power.

When carefully scrutinized, these speeches acquire an extra density as texts. If we focus on the rhetorical matter that makes up the individual styles, we can find a number of clues about the speakers' viewpoints, expectations, life trajectories, and political options in the realm of interethnic relations. We can better understand these speeches if we examine them in the context of the symbolism of contact. All this leads me to reflect on what anthropology has offered by way of theoretical guidelines on this subject and to question some deep-rooted assumptions, particularly about history and "peoples without history" (Wolf 1982).

What follows is a sequence of three indigenous speeches, transcribed and published by various organizations, and then my analysis, first, of what is implied in turning spoken word into written text and, second, of the political significance of both speeches and speakers for the politics of contact. Running through the three speeches are recurring themes, comparable moods, and similar images of the Whiteman (see the Introduction for discussion of this term). Of the hundreds of Indian speeches available in written form, those selected here are as telling as any. I do not intend to explore these speeches fully, for a symbolic interpretation as such is beyond the scope of this chapter. I collected no life histories, but my familiarity with the last two speakers has allowed me to go beyond the personal traces they left in their speeches.

Listen, White!

The first speech was delivered by Augusto Paulino, a Krenak Indian from the state of Minas Gerais, to an audience of forty-four Indian leaders, six anthropologists, three lawyers, and one Catholic bishop, under the sponsorship of thirty-seven support groups, professional associations, and university branches. The meeting, organized by the Pro-Indian Committee of São Paulo, was held from April 26 to 29, 1981, in the city of São Paulo.

Dear brothers, I'm here to present this weak figure who has been suffering for many years. He has been suffering for twenty-two years. I'm going to tell you the little story of the Krenak, what has been happening for twenty-two years. Over there in our territory, since the time of the SPI [Indian Protection Service], the Post Chief began. . . . We had many head of cattle, we had 900 head of cattle, 600 sheep, 300 animals, it was well organized, we had everything. Then they began to sell away till there was nothing left; they took us away from there to Maxacalis. We didn't like it, went back, on foot, ninety-two days to go back. We arrived, camped on an island. There arrived Captain Pinheiro and said he was going to liberate our headquarters. Our liberation began again, he took us there and we began to work, making gardens and gathering cattle, we were starting again. He built a jail, opened up everything. We began to organize the land again. But then the *fazendeiros* [landowners] got suspicious that we would occupy the whole territory. They began to wander around, took us away again, now to Fazenda Guarani. Well, they took us to Fazenda Guarani way over at Crenaque. At that time they built a jail, everything, then they brought Indians from Amazonas, Indians from all over the place, were arrested, beaten up. That was in 1968, they took us away to Fazenda Guarani. The Indians didn't want to go, but they tied them up, put them in jail, left them there two, three days starving. They took us to Fazenda Guarani. We stayed there seven years. In seven years we began to discover the law, went back again. We were camping in our own territory again, we got there and they had destroyed everything. We went on camping and they wanted to remove us again. But then we began to know the law, going this place and that. They left us alone. We are camped there in thirteen *alqueires* [630,200 square meters]. We want to organize the territory, to get ahead. Then they came up, gathered together, came up and asked us how much land we wanted to organize as our territory, saying that our land up there is 1,950 alqueires. We are only eighty people, used to be 600, to get organized, to get the work done. People died out . . . the older ones were missing the place, wanted to come back but couldn't. Talked about it, they arrested, beat us up, and

people died. And there we are, eighty people in thirteen alqueires. Some
people tried to get us 250 alqueires, which would be fine for us, but they
didn't agree. Then, we went to the police chief in Valadares [the town of
Governador Valadares] and he said, "But what do Indians want so much
land for? Indians are lazy, don't work, this Krenak Indian who doesn't
work, what does he want land for, he can eat fish and game." Well, in
the old days the Indians had game to eat, had a lot of fish. Nowadays,
how can the Indians live, eighty people within thirteen alqueires of land?
What is there to eat? Then, I ask all of you, brothers here, to participate
and we will be very grateful. And I ask you all not to weaken, face the
battle, for the toad that stops is eaten by the snake. The toad always hops
a little bit forward. We can never stop, for I've been suffering for twenty-
two years, but now, with God's will, I'm getting ahead, even if I hop one
meter today, two meters tomorrow and, with God's will, I'll get there.
Even if it is to leave to my children, my nieces and nephews, my cousins,
to my community, I want to leave something. Thank you very much, all
of you. (Comissão Pró-Índio 1982, 26–27)

The second speech was delivered by Álvaro Sampaio, the Tukano
Indian from the Uaupés region who a year earlier had attended the Fourth
Russell Tribunal in Rotterdam (see Chapter 3). He spoke to an audience
of Indians, lawyers, anthropologists, and other professionals who work on
Indian issues. The panel was organized by the Brazilian Bar Association,
Rio de Janeiro chapter, and took place in the city of Rio de Janeiro on
November 18, 1981.

I'll stand up because I can't talk while I sit here. Usually at the Indian
assemblies I have attended, the chief stands up when he speaks to give
a better audience. I was born in mid-village in the state of Amazonas
where there was no auditorium, no doctors and I had never imagined
that I would speak to intellectual people like these present here. And why
is this? My presence here has a meaning, precisely to give a message. It
is a message that will serve many people well, but for others it will be
an alert. The discrimination the Brazilian Indian has been suffering from
the times when this country was discovered to these days means that our
country knows in fact—and conceals—that which is called racism. In
this sense the great mass of whites and the small number of Indians and
the way of subordinating our fellow men is not in accord with the dic-
tates of law and justice. FUNAI [the National Indian Foundation], lately
using the Indian Statute just like in the first times the white civilization
used, in front of them, its word, has disarmed us so that we lose our
lands. And FUNAI continues to do this. It places the Indian under the
Indian Statute in order to do a better control. No one likes to be subordinated to others, listen to words, or be alienated, since man's principle
is freedom. To be unable to participate, or to speak to one's superiors as,
for example, the Indian to FUNAI, right in the middle of a country like

4. Álvaro Tukano delivers a speech. Photo by Beto Ricardo/ISA, 1987.

Brazil, right in the times of democracy, this is not called democracy. To us it means imperialism and anti-democracy. The way of regarding the Indian, when the Indian begins to discover that his way and his destiny are not right, that's what makes us come to the big cities and give the public opinion a different knowledge from that it would never have. For, when we arrive here you're forced to listen and take this message to your families. Because the problem of the Brazilian Indian is not his alone, but of the Brazilian people. I'm speaking in this way because very often my word has been useful to many people. Emancipation and, lately, these criteria that FUNAI is throwing over the Indians, what does that all mean? Are we in full harmony? Myself and Marcos Terena, who is the president of the União das Nações Indígenas, are working, in the meantime, in the indigenous communities because many, as I have told you, are still asleep. And we are a proof of it. That the indigenous communities are exploited, omitted in every way and that they are innocent compared to people like us. For instance, I know what tricks FUNAI is playing over us; and nobody defends the other in this case. We are forced to speak like this, not because we want to, but because somebody forces us. It is the Indian Statute: the justice which is not done, and the law which these men ignore. And, unfortunately, gentlemen, lawyers, we have within FUNAI lawyers who study all day long to change the Indian Statute, and this

Statute can't be changed because what it contains has never been put into practice. Even a few days ago, on the 12th of this month, Marcos Terena, my cousin Carlos Fernandes Machado, and myself were having an interview with this new president. In accordance with our non-governmental organization, we wanted to have been received as members of the board of directors of the União das Nações Indígenas. Unfortunately, our organization is a pejorative being to the nation. And we don't understand why. We don't understand why. To be an Indian inside this nation means to be shameful for other nations. It means a regression to the progress of Brazil. But to steal the Indian's land, to commit injustice against him, that's what the people don't consider in fact. By people I mean men who are competent, who say they are competent, but to the Indian's eye they are not. Our conversation with the new president was like this. He found the word "Nations" can't be used. In fact, we also know this. He said to us: "you must have the spirit of Brazilianness [*brasilidade*], Brazil is great and must be still greater." I answered: "That's why we came here to talk. Because very often we, Indians, the leaders, have most responsibility, more than any president of FUNAI or perhaps even of the Republic. If Brazil is great, it must be equal for all, not just for some people." I wanted to say this to him because so far the Indian had not spoken up and been heard in his international and national demands. That's why the Indian has his problems with land. That's why we go on insisting until he listens to what we want to do. He also said, the president, that we are picking a fight within the nation. No one is picking no fight, when he's making a claim. A son, when he goes to his father to claim his rights, the father gives. Many of them were misunderstood. On the other hand, the Indian becomes that who existed in the old days. But, in reality, the Indian continues to suffer under our eyes; it is the Indian himself who is looking for a way to self-determination. Self-determination doesn't mean separating from Brazil and be in the government. It means a desire of the Indian to participate in what the Whiteman is participating, in the national communion, for we have the same ambitions as any Whiteman and the same rights, but we can't say that we'll turn into whites from one day to the next. Because that's not up to us. This is outside our principle. I can't change, transform the president of the Republic into a Tukano overnight, because that's impossible. There is no law for it. Many of those military men who are in high positions, at the top of FUNAI, want to use the Indian as military and we feel ashamed. What will other military men say about these people? They have a pejorative idea of the indigenous communities. We can't stand being exploited any longer. No one likes to be exploited. For these words I've just said I take responsibility. Anyway, I think the Brazilian Bar Association will also join the Indian struggle to put Order and Justice in our Brazilian society. (Ordem dos Advogados do Brasil 1981, 81–84)

The third speech was delivered by Marcos Terena from the state of Mato Grosso do Sul, on the same occasion as Sampaio's speech.

I'm very pleased to be here amid scientists from law, anthropology, and social fields. Having heard these remarks about the Indian issue in the country I feel a bit shy because we have just heard that, according to the criteria of Indianness, the Indian has to have the primitive mentality. Well, in front of a podium of wise people in the relevant subject matters, I have to declare myself an Indian and I proudly say this to you and say another thing; something that in my heart, in front of all this pile of papers which I know what it is, but many Indians don't even know exists. Well, what I have to say is that I feel highly honored with the opportunity you give me tonight; in this opportunity I can speak and I hope I will also be heard so that everything that has been debated here will be useful for our work, but that it can also be reverted as a concrete benefit for all Brazilian Indians who, who knows, would like to be here, but can't. The privilege given to me provides me with the chance to, in my name and in the name of my family, the Indian family, also thank all of you who are in this house, a house I consider to be of men dedicated to the law and to what is right.

For several centuries those men who were named Indians were able to live in peace, with their own customs, their own traditions, what is called culture. But one day into their homes, Indian homes, came men who at first showed themselves to be friendly, but later, deceitfully, betrayed the trust put in that relationship. Until very recently, only a few years ago, I think in the 70s, we heard—perhaps many of you have also heard—that right now, in the twentieth century, there were people proud of saying that they were Indian hunters, a fact I consider shameful for a nation that sees itself as potent as many others and which I consider the greatest in South America.

Although, since 1910, there has been a federal agency for the protection of these people who were the first inhabitants of this country called Brazil; although powerful instruments have been created which the Whiteman respects (and if he does not respect, at least he fears) which are called laws; although this kind of support exists, the Indian continues to be abused in his rights, respect for which very often depends less on the law, I think, than on solidarity and human respect. Today, looking around me as an Indian, as a Brazilian, knowing two societies, two civilizations, I have worried a lot about law, about justice, because many times I've heard that people who have killed a fellow human being have not been imprisoned. On the other hand, I have also heard of people who were in jail for a long time without having committed any fault or murder. In analyzing things of this kind I only think, not as an expert like you, gentlemen, but with the sensitivity of a human being who has always respected the most basic things, from a small twig falling off a tree, to the whole universe, I know that there is in the country a law called Constitution; I also know that there is a law called Human Rights; also another called Geneva Convention, and, particularly to deal with Indian affairs, there is a law number 6001 called the Indian Statute, not to speak of the various international agreements and recommendations to which

Brazil subscribed and took a position vis-à-vis other countries. In all this tangle of laws, decrees, recommendations, of endless legal paperwork, is the person of the Indian, an Indian who, even though massacred, cheated and forgotten, reappears as a myth, as a thing that doesn't exist. Very often, in the minds of Brazilians, what I call the majority society, there is that Indian who comes armed with arrows and clubs, painted in various colors, good to be photographed, to be made stories over, who makes pretty crafts and who is a source of funds both to FUNAI and to those who exploit that sort of thing. For some he is naive, savage, stubborn; for others he is an obstacle obstructing progress. Everybody talks, everybody debates the Indian issue, but no one has ever shown concern or, if he has, has not been heard, with what was really in the heart of the Indian, besides distrust or perhaps fear. FUNAI is here a guardian of the Indian. The laws are here to protect the Indian, and I ask you: where is the Indian? Today you're here, listening to my speech. My hope is that, by talking to you, I am contributing to alert you about things Indian. The Indian is also a Brazilian, although he has his own language, his own customs, his own world, a totally different world. I act and speak like an Indian because the Indian wants to speak and be heard; to respect but be respected too; and to participate, gradually and harmoniously, somehow, as a Brazilian; and more, as a native Brazilian. His culture, his customs, his traditions must be respected as sacred and valuable for each and every people. Why does the Whiteman use malice to cheat the Indian? Why doesn't the Whiteman respect the value the Indians put on land, according to their conception of it? Land is a fundamental element for the survival of Indian peoples. I believe the mere fact of your being gathered here, under the roof of the Brazilian Bar Association in Rio de Janeiro, is in itself an attempt to comply by exercising real Justice in the application of the laws in defense of these peoples called forest dwellers [silvícolas]. The demarcation of Indian land is essential for the definition of what Indian territory is, but I think it will have been useless to demarcate if there is no Indian to inhabit it. And a population will have a chance to grow and be strong if it has medical assistance and education. I also think that FUNAI's role is clear in the law. There is a specific law about it. It wasn't the Indian who invented it. It wasn't the Indian who asked for it. But it's there. I think the law exists and FUNAI exists. They're there. What is lacking then? I think that what is lacking is to find effective ways for FUNAI to defend its wards, to defend the Indians. When I see the Brazilian development programs I feel that Brazil is moving, at a fast pace, toward development, toward its interior, toward what is called progress. Will the law and goodwill alone be enough to give security and self-defense to peoples who only know how to make a living off the land? I hope that, within your possibilities, something concrete can be done, something that is really geared toward the Indian populations, which are few. As someone here said, demarcation should be easy, but it isn't. I would like you to think of those Indians who, right at this moment, who knows, are sleeping with empty bellies. Perhaps it doesn't depend completely on FUNAI, but on all those who feel themselves to be Brazilian and who can say so with pride. What I can say to you is that I am proud of being able to speak as an Indian and transmit this message because, in the same way as you're listening to me, there are many people who call themselves Brazilians and don't like to raise the subject. I hope that you of the Bar Association, anthropologists, sociologists, all of you who can hear me tonight will make of the Indian movement or of the Indian cause not just an excuse to say "I'm defending the Indian," but think of means for you to help the Indian, the Indian who is in his village. I consider myself privileged because I've learned your language while you haven't learned mine. I consider myself privileged for going to the University, while many of you struggle for years to do the same and don't succeed. Thus, my message is that you must regard the Indian from the point of view of the law, based on the organizational structure such as FUNAI, the government agency, to find a way for you to collaborate toward the growth of the Indian side by side with you, and not as an isolated society, as someone has said. A different society, by all means, but with the same feelings as any Brazilian, who knows how to love, to feel, and who wants to find in you also the thought that it is possible to join efforts to make our country less small, less mean about the Indian issue. (Ordem dos Advogados do Brasil 1981, 76–80)

Frozen on the page, these speeches lose a whole gamut of communicative links with the audience — fleeting facial expressions, voice inflections, pitch, pause, speed, gestures, stutters, looks, innuendos of all sorts — to gain the permanence of the recorded message, untrimmed, unqualified, unaltered. In the written version there is no mediating gesture, no sympathetic glance, no emphatic silence. We who read them have to content ourselves with this impoverished rendering of the speakers' presentation of self and dialogic effort. But, although the gesture is unseen, the silence unheard, and the glance no longer caught, the speech turned into text acquires a force of its own. We who were not there to see and hear the speakers, although away from them in space and time, are able to appreciate their message, understand their plight, and interpret their posture.

The ephemeral moment of the spoken word is transformed into fixed discourse to which we can turn again and again to discover new, even surprising, meanings. The congealed text, a contribution from the Western world (Goody 1968), can then become an effective tool in the struggle of the Indians against the Westerners. An equivalent device, the tape recorder, was used effectively by Shavante leader Mário Juruna in his meetings with government authorities. For most Indians in Brazil and elsewhere speech is the privileged medium of communication. But they increasingly recognize that the written word is more powerful and appropriate in contexts such as legal claims, political manifestos, or whenever the only way to be heard is through literacy.

The three speeches translated here can be displayed and commented upon, reaching a different, if not wider, audience simply because they were written down. In contrast to the speed of events surrounding the politics of contact, these speeches, in their textual tangibility, have gained a permanence in some ways equivalent to the memory of peoples without writing. The fixity of the written text fulfills a Western need that the Indians comply with in their attempt to hold Brazilians as their interlocutor. Writing is thus transformed into one more political tool.

For the English-speaking reader I have translated the speeches from Portuguese. This raises another set of considerations. Particularly in Álvaro Sampaio's speech, I had to face the problem of its incongruities, some grammatical, some lexical, some semantic, but on the whole much subtler than those in the first speech. These discrepancies give his speech a special flavor, but how does one convey special idiomatic flavors in a foreign language, such as English is to me? Given that translation is always an act of treason (captured in the shrewd Italian saying *traduttore, traditore*), I faced two alternatives: find equivalent incongruities in the English language, which I am ill equipped to do, or ignore them, translate the text in straight English, and point out that there are incongruities in the original. In the end I opted for a third alternative: a translation as literal as possible. The oddities thus produced are probably greater than the Portuguese text deserves, but my intention is simply to call the reader's attention to the disjointed yet catchy character of some of the utterances. Sampaio's speeches, which in a grammatical sense are usually slightly out of sync, have always seized his audiences in a more powerful way than, for instance, Terena's addresses in nearly flawless Portuguese.

Let us now examine each speech and try to capture some of the components of individual style in this political genre. Each reveals something about the speaker, his political trajectory and his position vis-à-vis Brazilians, the multifaceted contact situation, and the Indian movement.

The first speaker, a Krenak Indian from the state of Minas Gerais, presents a mode of expression quite common among Indians who are making their first appearances in the field of interethnic politics. The well-being of his people, kinship ties, parochial referents, repetitions, and the humble demeanor toward his audience betray his inexperience in handling the rhetoric of contact. Nothing in Paulino's discourse reflects a commitment to the indigenous movement at large; rather, he uses his audience as sympathetic shoulder on which he laments his people's sufferings. His speech has the same inflection as so many others uttered in similar circumstances: a long list of grievances against the non-Indians, responsible as they are for the depletion of resources, the invasion of traditional territories, anxiety about the future, lack of communication, and disrespect for indigenous ways of life. This Krenak man is representative of those Indian leaders whose point of reference is their immediate community and who have not as yet grasped the sociopolitical meanderings of the national society.

The passage from the traditional politics of persuasion to the imposed politics of coercion, exercised by the Brazilian state, is vehemently portrayed by Paulino in terms of stark raw violence. Arrests, beatings, forceful removals, expropriation—these are some of its ugliest faces. The epitome of such violence was the establishment, referred to in his speech, of the Crenaque jail for Indians, which was in operation for several years. In just a few words Paulino summarizes the long history of that treatment, common to so many other indigenous groups and intensely lived by his people in a matter of two decades. The condensed language, the use of metaphor and parable—the toad and the snake—give his individual style a candor that is so often the strength of indigenous discourses when delivered in Portuguese. Rather than a simplified stereotyped opponent, Paulino's Brazilian is a complex multifaceted Other: the captain who helped relocate his people, the police chief who disdained the Indians' capacity for work, those anonymous friends who tried to get more land for his people. For more than twenty years this man has continually had to expand his horizon to accommodate all these figures and situations previously unknown to him. He reaches forward in search of a solution to his people's problems, hoping to achieve a satisfactory modus vivendi, good enough to be passed on to the coming generations, for the "good old days" are forever gone. Punctuating this tragic story of unrelenting disruption is the poignant theme of the longing that kills, the well-known tale of old people who miss home and, unable to adjust to a new environment, simply give up and die.

The other two speakers exhibit a much greater fluency in political discourse and a much greater familiarity with the ways of the national society. The second speaker, Álvaro Sampaio, a Tukano from the Uaupés region in the northwestern Amazon, was educated by Salesian missionaries. As a youth he went to Manaus, was in the army for a while, then tried to enter the university before becoming involved in the Indian movement. He made his debut in the national and international politics of contact in 1980 at the Fourth Russell Tribunal where he denounced Salesian activities as ethnocidal. This cost him much anxiety because of the campaign the missionaries launched against him and his family, leading to their exile to a distant location. Expelled from home, Sampaio spent several years moving around Brazilian and other South American cities where he closely interacted with other emerging Brazilian Indian leaders and learned about the experiences of the Peruvian and Ecuadorian Indian movements. Heavy drinking was but a symptom of a deep sense of social malaise that resulted in Sampaio's cutting sarcasm and frequent aggressive moods. As a vehement spokesman for the defense of Indian rights against FUNAI, missionaries, and nationals at large, he had an important role in Brazil, having been elected as a director of UNI. Then, in the late 1980s, after years of struggling in vain for the demarcation of the Uaupés Indian area and removal of invading gold prospectors, he shocked both Indians and friends of the Indians with his pact with a powerful mining company and with the military officials who were launching the Calha Norte Project in the vast region of the Amazon watershed. He traded his "ethical integrity" for a less than satisfactory solution to both problems — demarcation and invasion — as well as promises of an adequate health program for his people (Buchillet 1990). As it turned out, none of these promises was fulfilled, and Sampaio lost his prestige as an Indian leader and the confidence of practically all his former political companions (C. Ricardo 1991, 101–103). I shall return to his case in Chapter 10.

But back in the early 1980s Sampaio's public appearances were always received with great enthusiasm and usually had plenty of media coverage. The assertive tone of his discourse, as transcribed here, reveals much of his life history. His sometimes vociferous speeches betray his personal drama as a young Indian: the conflict between his ideal of returning to his people and the urge to go on with his political involvement at the national and international levels.

Sampaio's discourse also shows his effort to involve the audience by using expressions and references that come from the political context of Brazilians themselves. The imagery is forthrightly political and full of "civilized" overtones. The military, self-determination, imperialism and democracy, the quest for equal opportunities — all were powerful symbols in political discourses by Brazilians who opposed the military government. The appeal to these symbols is particularly effective for an audience made especially sympathetic by the common experience of being ruled by a regime of force. Despite frequent semantic ramblings, Sampaio delivered a powerful message, and his anger was not lost on his listeners/readers. In this formal sense his discourse suggests a difference between sense and meaning. While at times the sense is fuzzy, the meaning of his point is quite clear.

Most important in his speech is the reference to "nations within a nation." Banning the designation União das Nações Indígenas, the military authorities — and, I must add, the civilian government that followed — have argued that such a proposition conflicts with national security in representing a potential danger to the country's sovereignty. They argue that to propose the establishment of nations within the Brazilian nation is to encourage internal cleavages, which is therefore unpatriotic, particularly in the case of the Indians as bearers of different traditions, speakers of different languages, and supposedly highly susceptible to foreign interests. Furthermore, to create Indian nations would go against the state's aspiration of integrating indigenous peoples definitively into the national society. The reference to brasilidade by the president of FUNAI is a condensed way of expressing this policy: from first occupants of the land the Indians have been turned into a threat to national security. The confrontational tone of Sampaio's speech is a reaction to such distortion. His discourse also reveals a most cherished notion that Indians should be equal to Brazilians while maintaining their cultural differences, a proposition that is entirely at odds with the interpretation of what integration should be, namely, the complete dilution of the Indian population into the undifferentiated mass of Brazilians.

As deeply involved in the Indian movement as the Tukano, the third speaker shows a completely different style. As a youth he too left his Terena village in Mato Grosso do Sul to study in the city—first Campo Grande, then Brasília. Marcos Terena joined the movement just before the creation of UNI, which he served as one of its first presidents. As a pilot he tried for a long time to work for FUNAI but was turned down repeatedly by the colonels who ran the Indian foundation in the 1970s and early 1980s. His tendency to salvage FUNAI as a legitimate agency for the defense of Indian rights is quite visible in his speech, although expressed in a critical manner. He keenly exposes the persistent use of official paperwork to disempower the Indians. Amid the tangle of endless laws authoritarianly created by nationals about Indians, the Indians remain helplessly at the mercy of Brazilians' good or bad intentions.

Although critical of the Brazilian government regarding indigenous policy and treatment, Terena has held onto his conviction that working from within the system is as valid as, and perhaps more productive than, confrontation from outside. For this he has paid the price of mistrust from companions and supportive non-Indians who have accused him of co-optation. His discourse has elements both of criticism and hope in the potential effectiveness of FUNAI to defend indigenous interests. It contains much of his political agenda of being part of the system in order to change it, without relinquishing his involvement in the movement. Terena tries to use the nationals' weapons—education, for instance—to resist them.

Like Sampaio, Terena stresses the theme of different but equal. Nationals must recognize that the Indians are Brazilians too, as capable, or more so, of handling aspects of the dominant society, such as a second language and a university education when they have a chance. The double sense of brasilidade is quite clear if we compare the meaning attributed to it by the president of FUNAI in Sampaio's speech and Terena's. Obviously, they are not speaking of the same thing. Whereas the president implies the dissolution of Indianness, Terena affirms the opposite: Brazilian Indian yes, but still, and above all, Indian. Terena's apparent apology for the great Brazilian nation is a skillfully constructed trope. His declared patriotism fluidly melts into a severe criticism: Brazil will not measure up to its potential as a developed nation if its Indians continue to be treated as "a myth, as a thing that doesn't exist." Terena's Brazil and Deloria's United States display a striking resonance:

> A recognition of the major Indian contention—the sacredness of land— as reflected in a legal affirmation of the rights of Indian communities to hold their lands as national entities exempted from the arbitrary decisions of state and federal governments, will mark the maturing of America as a society. At present we are told that it is "greening." After nearly four centuries we would hope so.
> Having "greened," it is now time to mature. (Deloria 1973, xv)

Terena's 1984 appointment to the position of chief of staff for one of FUNAI's rare progressive—some would say grossly populist—presidents, a civilian in the military era, was received with ambivalence. But even those who were suspicious of Terena's authenticity granted that his and other Indians' appointments were historically important. For the first time Indians were working in the higher echelons of a public bureaucracy. For the first time Indians were in charge of the agency of which they are wards. However, this achievement can be viewed as a double-edged sword, for a new breed of "Indian" emerged, the *Índio funcionário,* the civil servant, bureaucratic Indian, a category of seemingly self-interested job-hungry young men who would rather oppose the Indian movement than risk their newly acquired positions. Once again the authorities succeeded in the practice of divide and conquer. Nevertheless, some of these well-placed Indians never succumbed to the lure of co-optation. Terena remained in his position as long as it was politically feasible. Since then he has moved through various government bodies such as the Ministry of Culture, was an important leader in the organization of the indigenous events during the 1992 Rio Earth Summit, and created a radio program dedicated to the Indian issue.

As the political face of the country and of FUNAI changed in the mid-1980s, Indian leaders made a short-lived attempt to enter the domain of party politics in order to have access to the real center of power, that is, the National Congress. A rash of Indian candidates ran for the House of Representatives on the eve of the drawing-up of the 1988 Constitution. Among these candidates were Álvaro Sampaio and Marcos Terena. No Indian was elected. However, eight years later thirty Indians were elected in the 1996 municipal elections, one as mayor of the northernmost Brazilian town of

Oiapoque, another as vice mayor of São Gabriel da Cachoeira in Sampaio's homeland, and the others as representatives in various states of the country (Scharf 1996, 4).

The Symbolism of Contact

To say that indigenous societies are not static is to say the obvious. Even when viewed as peoples without history, it is widely recognized that the various mechanisms of their internal dynamics can and do result in considerable changes as generations come and go. Most observers now agree that when the West intruded, the Rest was already in motion. Nevertheless, it is impossible to minimize the impact of Europeans on indigenous peoples. The advent of the whites is an undeniable "founding event," to use an original phrase of Ricoeur's (1978, 40).

Interethnic contact has produced the figure of the Indian for nationals and that of the whites for Indians. The image and influence of whites have precipitated a whole range of symbolic elaborations among indigenous societies, from myths and millenarianism to political movements. Virtually no Indian society is left on the South American continent that is unaware of the Whiteman as an ethnic and political category. The image of the Whiteman, transformed into so many local versions, pervades the modes of thought and modes of being of most indigenous peoples. By penetrating Indian lives interethnic contact has contributed to the renewal of Indian traditions. And because tradition is constantly being reshaped—for a static tradition, as Gadamer (1975) says, is a dead tradition—the phenomenon of contact comes to feed into this process of ongoing transformation. Even amid the most malignant forms of domination, ranging from slavery, labor exploitation, punitive expeditions, and land usurpation to disease transmission, no Indian society has endured contact without exercising some sort of creative resistance. Absorption of the category of Whiteman is not limited to indigenous speech genres and modes of expression. In fact, it has the effect of creating states of mind and affect that predispose the Indians to interact with nationals in certain ways that in turn shape the character of contact. This pervasive presence is analogous to what Nandy (1983) referred to as the influence of the "intimate enemy."

At the root of the transformations triggered by interethnic contact is the passage from a political system characterized by the arts of persuasion to another defined by the use of coercion. Indians accustomed to conducting their lives on the basis of group consensus are apt to be shocked, if not altogether traumatized, by the imposition of the rule of force or threat of force brought to them by non-Indians, be they administrators, free-enterprise invaders, or missionaries. The enforcement of this politics of coercion is what gives the "middle ground" of contact its particular quality of domination and inequality.

The political field on which the three speeches presented were delivered is one of several in which the figure of the Whiteman looms large. For argument's sake let us assume that the symbolic realm of contact can be divided into three modes: mythic, historical, and political. Each would generate its own cultural allegories, its own discourse, its own praxis. The politics of contact is the most recent of these modes and should be understood as part of a larger symbolic universe that also contains myths and historical narratives that make use of the Whiteman as an underlying topos. Although each mode would have a genre, much blurring between them would defeat any attempt at rigid classifications.

What distinguishes these genres is not so much the symbols themselves as the uses made of them and the audiences to which they are addressed. For instance, regarding temporality, time is suspended in myths, oriented to the past in the case of "old times" narratives—or oriented to the future in the case of millenarianism—and concerned with a progressive present in the political arena of interethnic contact. Whereas in the mythic genre events are neutralized by the use of metaphor and allegory, and in the historical genre events are controlled by hindsight, in the political genre events are confronted by actions that are specifically addressed to the majority society. Unlike myths and historical narratives that are produced for internal consumption to be recounted around the household hearth or in the village plaza, political speeches delivered in lecture halls, church basements, or the National Congress require the actual presence of nationals. Without such listeners these speeches lose their purpose. Nationals' participation in the performative act of speech delivery provides the impetus for the speaker's choice of words, intonation, and presentation of self. Political speeches unfold in the context of what Goffman (1959) called impression management. As the audience reacts to the speaker, so the speaker reacts to the audience by making the adjustments necessary to engage the listeners. A genre that until recently was foreign to Brazilian Indians, the speech of protest has become their main vehicle for visibility as legitimate social agents in the country.

Most Indian leaders in Brazil operate both in the larger society and in indigenous communities. On the one hand, they are exposed to the traditional expressions of their own society; on the other, they pass on to their people their experiences in the interethnic camp. To what extent the ingredients of contact politics feed into the mythic and historical genres of the communities is yet to attract the anthropological attention it deserves. It would be surprising if the former did not influence the latter. One would expect events from the political field to be incorporated in an ongoing stream of interpretations that contribute to the dynamic character of specific indigenous traditions.

A well-studied case confirms these expectations. It is the case of the southern Yanomami in the Brazilian state of Roraima. According to the Yanomami's traditional theory of contact, metal tools brought into the Indian area caused the onset of lethal contagious diseases. Boxes full of trade goods, once opened up, released a scented smoke that seduced people while spreading its noxious miasma in the form of epidemics. The connection between epidemics, trade goods, and the Whiteman is unambiguous (Albert 1988). More recently, this theme of the deleterious effects of the metal tools has been validated by the heavy mortality rate the Yanomami have suffered from infectious diseases that followed the gold rush in the 1980s. The major author of the old myth's new version has been Davi Kopenawa, a young shaman who has traveled widely in Brazil, the United States, and Europe as a participant in the pan-Indian and environmentalist movements. Among other honors, he has been awarded the Global 500 prize. On his numerous trips Kopenawa has been exposed to a torrent of Western rhetoric on human rights and environmental concerns. The way he has processed this information, linking it with the "smoke of metal" myth to construct a "shamanic critique of the political economy of nature" (Albert 1993), is a good example of what the experience of an Indian leader in the world of interethnicity can do to transform traditional ideas. The dangerous metal previously associated with trade goods has come to typify mining activities. The fumes from machinery and the very notion of gold, an alluring metal that drives Westerners to insane acts, have gained an extraordinary destructive power because thousands of Yanomami are known to have died of malaria and other infectious diseases brought into the area by tens of thousands of placer miners. "After half a century of various transformations, this association [of metal with smoke] reappears in Davi's discourse as 'smoke of the gold' . . . 'smoke of mineral/metal' . . . and finally, 'disease of the mineral.' Its potency is so great that he sometimes uses the word *shawara* (epidemics) as a synonym for mineral (*booshikë*)" (p. 359). The immense craters dug by gold panners, the fumes of their machinery, the tampering with the dark depths of the earth, all cause noxious smoke to rise up to the sky and produce something remarkably similar to that which causes environmentalists to shudder—the hole in the ozone layer. These fumes, says Kopenawa, "this smoke-epidemic affects the 'whole world' [Kopenawa's rendering of the Yanomami expression *urihi pata*, great forest, universe]. . . . The wind carries it to the sky. When it gets there, its heat slowly burns up the sky and punctures it. The 'whole world' is then wounded as if in burning, like a plastic bag melting in the heat" (p. 360).

The Yanomami have slowly assimilated environmental rhetoric—"words of ecology," in Kopenawa's expression—which makes perfect sense in the face of health and ecological disasters brought about by the gold rush and in light of the traditional exegesis about non-Indians:

> Before we used to think: "we will protect the forest!" We thought that our shamanic spirits would protect us, that's all. These spirits were the first to possess "ecology." They chase away the evil spirits, prevent rain from falling endlessly, silence thunder . . . and, when the sky threatens to collapse, it is they who speak to "ecology." They protect the sky when it wants to change, when the world wants to darken. They are "ecology" and that is why they prevent these things from happening. We've always had these words, but you, whites, invented "ecology" and then these words were revealed and propagated all over. (p. 368)

Such a luminous example of what Bakhtin calls *assimilation!* "Our speech," he teaches us, "is filled with other's words, varying degrees of otherness or varying degrees of 'our-own-ness,' varying degrees of awareness and detachment" (1986, 89).

Parts or Whole?

Let us return to the issue of different modes in the symbolism of contact. If the division of a "totality" into portions is of considerable heuristic value for the purpose of describing, analyzing, and communicating our acquired knowledge to a readership, our language being what it is, especially in written form, carries a risk that such division might take on an aura of "reality," replacing the context that originated it. In fact, reification happens all the time. The hardening of our language of anthropology creates a reality of its own, follows its own path, and imposes its own rules and interpretations. If we say or write often enough that metal tools oozing lethal fumes is a myth and as such is a static exercise in bricolage, we end up fixing it in a rigid category, which is then quickly exhausted by analytical logic and sterilized by confining labels. Repetition "can give fictions or hypotheses the status of truth" (Torgovnick 1990, 96). Hence, once a myth, always a myth—and who would dare call it anything else, such as a manifestation of political or historical consciousness? Actually, in mythology as in other genres, there is already a universe of commentary about life, the world, time, space, stasis, and movement that transcends any attempt to slice up lived experience. In her analysis of Waiãpi oral tradition Gallois shows how myth can dissolve into "a discursive genre which is much closer to the 'historical' type" (1993a, 85). The rationale for separating spheres, be they myth, history, politics, geography, or whatever, is not in the indigenous discourses themselves but in our need to organize ethnographic material into familiar categories in order to make sense of it on our own and our readers' terms. Ironically, in our effort to capture totality, we compartmentalize and tend to forget that categorizations are only "as if" propositions. The indigenous way of thinking, as revealed in what we, not they, call myths, narratives, and so on, challenges the habits of compartmentalization that anthropology has inherited along with the scientific premises of Western rationalism and empiricism. Our difficulty is to perceive and express a holistic, undifferentiated, semantically blended universe of cross-cutting messages. But while we cannot reproduce the original context in which this blending occurs, it is not impossible to reach an intelligent and intelligible rendering of it. I see the rhetoric of the indigenous political movement as a passage from holistic thinking to compartmentalized thinking, a device that is necessary if the Indians are to make themselves effectively understood or heard by the larger population. This does not mean that they necessarily replace one mode of thinking with the other. Well, if they have learned to use our mode of expression without abandoning their own, why can't we do the same? If we try to blend the genres, we may find that under a rhetorical mode we have called "mythic" there is a sense of history that of course encompasses the political sphere of contact. How can we be so sure that all those myths of the Whiteman — of the beginning of agriculture, the building of the universe, the creation of disease and death — are not manifestations of an indigenous historical consciousness that we do not recognize as such because it comes in a package that does not fit into our mental containers? Conversely, much of what comes to us as historical fact may, under closer scrutiny, turn out to be as fictitious as we conceive myths to be. Just to pick an example from South American history, one may take the official history of the ·"Paraguayan War," at least as it is taught in Brazilian schools, to be an elaborate fiction about an episode that can also be told in a drastically different way. Far from being regarded as the villain of our schoolbooks, Paraguay can be read as the most heavily punished experiment in economic independence on the subcontinent (Galeano 1981, 204–14).

It would certainly be wrong to take myth for history if we transferred to the Indians our premise that history requires objectivity and the assumption of a realistic unfolding of sequential events, as opposed to mythic bricolage. If, however, we accept that language is bricolage, how can history or politics, or even science, not be bricolage, since it is human and everything human happens in some manifestation of language (Derrida 1970, 256)? If history, like myth, is a concretization of bricolage, or fiction, as Certeau argues (1986, 199–221), the categorical opposition of these two genres becomes artificial indeed.

Some may object, saying that because the category of "history" is a

Western concept and invention, it is not fair to use it for something other than what it is intended. Here again, the risk is of letting words crystallize, thus cutting down the possibility of a fresh gaze at new possibilities of conceiving otherness—or sameness, for that matter. We are entitled to organize the universe into categories that we can understand so long as we do not reify them. Heuristic value should not be taken for empirical fact. It is important to keep this in mind in view of the ever-present tendency of Western thinking to give supremacy to the former over the latter. If we need to separate some things as myths, others as history, and yet others as politics, it should be clear that we do so at our own risk and for our own benefit. We must recognize this separation for what it is, namely, an operational device rather than an ontological reality. To divide primitive mythic societies from historical societies is to add to the intellectual apparatus of domination, to build a sort of indigenist orientalism.

For centuries the Whiteman has been the Indians' most imposing "significant other." Far from being "peoples without history" with "totemic" minds, the Indians are and have always been engaged in interpretations and reinterpretations of contact in a truly kerygmatic way (Ricoeur 1978), as the post-gold rush Yanomami demonstrate. Their historical consciousness does not follow the path of a Western-style historicity, and if we are to adequately capture the expressions of this consciousness, we must change our habits of categorizing the world. We could benefit from influences outside the field of traditional anthropology, not the least significant of which are the Indians themselves.

So far, anthropologists have played the role of translators of indigenous universes to national audiences. But more and more we will have to face the issue of communicating with the people from whom we learn. The time is coming when our articles and books will have to be written with Indian readerships in mind. Will we know how to do it? Will we be believed? Will we know how to respond to their questioning or challenging interpretations, which necessarily will be different from ours? Will we resist the temptation to compete with them for the public's attention? And, perhaps most difficult of all, will we be able to restructure our language and conceptual framework in a way that does justice to the amazing wealth of imagination and aesthetic resourcefulness we find in the field? For example, we may question whether a Portuguese version of this chapter would be readable and/or acceptable to the Indian leaders about whom I write. And even if it were understood by them as an intellectual exercise, what about the ethical problems it raises? Is it, in other words, possible to avoid the tendency to objectify our subjects of study in our pursuit of anthropological understanding? The interpretive plea for ethnographic dialogue (Marcus and Fischer 1986) has had a modest effect so far, although some interesting attempts have been made in South American ethnography (Gallois and Carelli 1992; Rappaport 1994).

Most frequently, the "dialogue" of anthropologists with their native hosts has been less than harmonious because of the differential power that separates them, whether we want it or not. Briggs (1996) exposes some situations in which indigenous people resent having their voice muffled by the much more potent voice of the anthropologist. "What . . . [an] anthropologist writes about Hawaiians has more potential power than what Hawaiians write about themselves" (Trask, quoted in Briggs 1996, 437). Quite accurately, at least for much of South America, Briggs points out some limiting factors for this imbalance between native and anthropologist: "Both overt racism and limitations on access to higher education make it difficult in most cases for indigenous performers and scholars to compete with nonindigenous anthropologists and other professionals over the circulation of cultural forms" (p. 461). Indisputable as this analysis may be, it is, however, not sufficient to explain the ostracism that plagues those who inhabit the "periphery." The "center" tends to ignore the production of the periphery even when the latter's levels of education and professional quality are equal if not superior to the former's. There are then various degrees and contexts in which differential power in the dissemination of knowledge makes itself felt. Just as the voices of the periphery scholar are reduced to a virtually inaudible whisper, so are the voices of native peoples vis-à-vis their non-native counterparts.

Interethnic Indian: A Political Actor in Search of a Role

Brazilian Indians are increasingly using literacy as a weapon in their political actions. They recognize that orality has a limited efficacy in a world in which the hegemony of the West has been established via the extraordinary power of the written word. Indigenous peoples in the country are now matching their traditional ways of expression to such Western channels as writing (see, for instance, Pãrõkumu and Kẽhíri 1995; Diakuru and Kisibi 1996), video (T. Turner 1991a; Gallois and Carelli 1992; Carelli 1993), tape recording, radio, and television. But it seems that these new media are not displacing old modes of thought; rather, they are providing indigenous peoples with more effective means to conduct their struggle for recognition as legitimate Others.

What do Brazilian Indians do with these new media? There are two trends: one seeks equality through similarity with Brazilians; the other tries to achieve equality through equivalence. The first emphasizes the need to occupy spaces that have always been taken by nationals—the "FUNAI Indians" and those who go into party politics. The second tries to show that the Indian ways of being are as valid as those of nationals. The strength of the Indian ways derives precisely from their cultural differences, the Kayapó being the most outstanding example.

For instance, in contrast to the Shuar Indians, who have refused to enter directly into Ecuador's state machinery, some Indian leaders in Brazil have shown an inclination toward a career in national politics. Until recently, the degree of success was minimal and the results somewhat disastrous. Witness the career of the Shavante Mário Juruna. Elected by an urban constituency of Rio de Janeiro rather than his native Mato Grosso, Juruna was used by his party's leaders as a symbol of oppression under the military regime, the representative of a dubious Brazilianness emanating from the dispossessed, long-suffering, helpless Brazilian people, Indians included. When no national voices had the freedom to protest, Juruna, illiterate and uninformed about the complexity of national politics but protected by his Indianness—as ward of the state he is regarded as unimputable—was encouraged to bombard the government with caustic criticisms. When in 1983 he accused ministers of state of being thieves, he provoked a strong reaction that nearly led to his loss of office. As the country's political climate turned brighter, Juruna was no longer useful. Following his involvement in a senseless scandal involving accusations of bribery, he was gradually discarded from the political scene and failed to be reelected in 1986. Like a specter, for a long while he could still be seen wandering about the offices and hallways of the National Congress and of FUNAI headquarters in Brasília, until he fell into near oblivion (for more about his interethnic career see Juruna, Hohlfeldt, and Hoffmann 1982).

More realistic were UNI's first leaders, both at the national and regional levels; they opted for grassroots, unspectacular, long-term work at consciousness raising in the communities, emphasizing Indianness as a value to be preserved. Several of those leaders were pressured by the Catholic Church to avoid confrontation with the government, and as a result they were pushed into the background of the indigenous movement. As it turned out, UNI was a short-lived experience as a nationwide organization. Its command changed hands, its headquarters moved to the city of São Paulo, its ties with local communities were gradually severed, and by the late 1980s it ceased to exist. In turn, myriad local and regional indigenous organizations have cropped up, mostly in the 1990s and especially in the Amazon. For a total Indian population of about 280,000 in the whole country, more than one hundred indigenous organizations are legally registered, whereas non-Indian pro-Indian organizations operating in Brazil number thirty (C. Ricardo 1995, 1996a).

While regional leaders can combine militancy with community life, those who operate out of big cities are cut off from the daily routine of

5. House Representative Mário Juruna delivers a speech at the National Congress, Brasília, 1987. Photo courtesy of the Archive Coordination, House of Representatives, National Congress, Brasília.

6. Mário Juruna, the Brazilian flag, and his audience at the National Congress in Brasília. Photo by André Dusek, copyright 1984 André Dusek/AGIL.

the indigenous world. They travel regularly to the villages but, at least in some cases, are received as virtual outsiders, vague "kinsmen" who may be welcome for bringing news and perhaps some hope for solving local problems. Radio programs and television and newspaper interviews with these leaders are not infrequent, and their eloquence can move listeners, viewers, and readers, who, expecting to hear and read broken Portuguese, are often surprised by their articulateness.

In the ebb and flow of many failures and few successes the cost of political activism to Indian leaders can be extremely high. Alcoholism, marginalization at home and elsewhere, generalized distrust of the world, anguish, psychological confusion, and even assassinations are some of the burdens that make the life of most Indian leaders in Brazil a personal drama, sometimes tougher than they can take. Add to all this the ever-present possibility of manipulation and co-optation, instruments some nationals use to undermine indigenous integrity, and we may begin to grasp the extent of the predicament facing a critical Indian fighting against the current. Like actors in search of a role, Brazilian indigenous leaders keep struggling to gain a place in national society on equal terms, a place from which they can directly address the nation's authorities without the intermediacy and frequent misrepresentation of their guardian, the National Indian Foundation. Like actors on a gigantic stage, they strive to leave the shadow play of national irrelevance and be acknowledged by the public in their role as citizens of a double world—the Brazilian nation and their own societies.

Figures of Interethnic Speech

Returning to indigenous discourses about the Whiteman, the adage that "always the meaning of a text goes beyond its author" (Gadamer 1975, 264) could not be more appropriate. The peeling of layers of meaning contained in the three speeches presented here is an exercise in interpretation of the equivocality of symbols. The same symbol can be used for one purpose by one speaker and for the opposite purpose by another. The image of FUNAI and the notion of Brazilianness are examples of this equivocality. What emerges from the joint voices of the Indians is that their movement is a rebellion against political invisibility. In their collective cry to be seen and heard, and deemed deserving of respect and justice, the Indians summon the efficacy of certain symbols they know will strike home among Brazilians. But in so doing they are no different from government officials who, for instance, invoke the image of the flag, the sound of the national anthem, the idea of Union, or of brasilidade in an attempt to amass popular support and build legitimacy.

The multidimensional character of speeches such as those reproduced here emerges in both genre and style. The context is interethnic, the genre is political, and the styles vary from individual to individual, revealing a bit of the life history of each speaker. In the performative act of delivering a speech, Indians are turned into actors engaged with a specific audience. Who are the potential audiences for an Indian speaker performing a political act in an interethnic scenario? Most of the time, besides other Indians, they have been non-Indian sympathizers, be they anthropologists, lawyers, journalists, students, or members of other minorities. On other occasions the audience is composed of bureaucrats or politicians. For each of these various modalities of listeners a different rhetorical effort is needed, putting to test the speakers' stylistic versatility.

Speeches transformed into texts are a valuable tool for understanding the trajectories of Indian leaders along the road of interethnic contact. Because they are permanently available, texts can speak to us in different ways at different times, displaying a variety of angles through which their messages are refracted. A perceptive look at textualized speeches can give us some insights, preliminary as they may be, into which recondite corners of the speaker's personality have been most affected by the violence of prejudice, discrimination, and social injustice. For example, the tone of the speeches—some delivered in a tortured language, some in open confrontational style, some in cautious restraint, most of them desperate pleas for justice—tells us a great deal about the speakers.

Texts such as these can be the starting point for ethnographic encounters sufficiently dense as to reveal the intricacies inherent in the process of forging an interethnic being. But in addition to opening a door to the understanding of a certain human type—the "interethnic Indian"—such texts can lend themselves to some theoretical explorations in anthropology, with the potential to uncover dimensions that, until recently, had been left unexplored. The complexities of Indian-national relations in South America show that incursions into fields of thought traditionally outside the immediate range of anthropology can be not only timely but perhaps necessary, if we are to pursue our quest for a deeper understanding of what it is to be an Indian in this turn of millennium on the South American continent.

Part III
Speaking through the Indians

5
Seduced and Abandoned

Marginal, subdued, quaint, they go through history passively enduring a fate not of their doing. Thus regarded, Indians, the privileged Others of Brazilian consciousness, in their supposed passivity supply the perfect contrast for a nation that portrays itself as the dynamic country of the future while singing a destiny modulated in the national anthem as "eternally lying in a splendid crib." I thus invite the reader to follow me through the thicket of political symbolism that surrounds the representation of first contacts in Brazilian Indigenism. In this representation Indians appear to be forever hiding from interlopers, passively defending themselves with occasional attacks on the intruders but never engaged in the organized insurgence that history records for earlier centuries (Ellis 1965; Schwartz 1995; Vainfas 1995). By mimetically dressing Indians in passivity, as they appear in the national script, I hope to help convey the mood in which national society proceeds to bring newly contacted Indians under state control. By national society I mean the wide range of human components from state officials to affluent entrepreneurs and destitute squatters.

A quote from two of the most conspicuous heroes of contemporary Brazil, the Villas Bôas brothers, is an apt beginning for my discussion of how the country treats indigenous otherness. This passage refers to the first contact with the Suyá Indians of central Brazil in 1960 after a long campaign by the brothers to gain their trust:

> The Jurunas having been attracted [pacified, in 1950] and peace settled between them and the Txukahamãe [pacified in 1953], we now needed to conquer the Suiá. . . . One morning two Juruna Indians came to tell us there were Suiá canoes nearby. We prepared our boat, fueled its motor, and left with the two Jurunas. As they heard the engine, the "visitors" went up the Suiá-Missu River. When we reached its mouth we could just see them disappear along a left-hand tributary. . . . We got [to the high bank where two canoes were anchored]. On the bank, an Indian with an unfriendly look held a bow in readiness, gesturing for us to stay where

we were. We obeyed but behaved as indifferently as possible, turning our backs to him. More Indians came to the bank. They gestured violently for us to go away. We pretended not to understand and began to chat, as if ignoring their presence. With no choice, they lowered their bows and stood there staring at us. Very casually we pulled out a box full of gifts (mirrors, necklaces, knives, machetes, and axes) and placed it on the bank. We gestured to them to help themselves. Puzzled, they stood there, immobilized. One of them, bolder, came down the bank and walked to the box intent on picking it up. Before he did, we stepped forward and opened it. We gave him a knife, a machete and an axe. We called the others. They came down. We asked them to bring the women. . . . Shortly afterward they appeared on the river bank, each one bringing his woman, or rather dragging her along. We walked toward them and each one of us took hold of a woman, pulled her away from her husband's hands, and decorated her with a flashy necklace. Mirrors were a success among the women. Some screams and more women appeared. They looked suspicious, but curious about the mirrors and necklaces. Fraternizing was complete. (Villas Bôas and Villas Bôas 1994, 598–99)

Among the many layers of otherness that make Brazil a complex social entity, I focus on indigenous peoples who represent perhaps the most complex of the country's internal Others. As a national issue, the Indians act as a canvas on which Brazil paints its expressionist portrait with bold strokes that punctuate its unresolved perplexities. Its pathos as a nation— painstakingly trying to join the developed world while attempting to tuck its discriminatory skeletons in the democratic closet—is glaringly exposed by the spotlight within which officials perform the pantomime of Indian domestication. It is as if the Indian–non-Indian arena served as a convenient microcosm of the country—problems of citizenship, differential power, and use and abuse of authority appear as in a concentrated solution. Embedded in the imagery that accompanies the custom of taming wild Indians are questions of historical, political, and economic importance that have incited many a scholar to engage in endless attempts to understand or explain Brazil. The writers engaged in the herculean task of explicating why Brazil is what it is, a country that should develop and somehow never does, are too numerous to list here. A few references covering a wide range of fields, from social sciences to history, literature, and psychoanalysis, will have to suffice.[1]

Throughout the New World first colonial powers and then emerging nations dealt with native peoples in ways that differ in specifics (Seed 1992,

1. Azevedo 1996; L. Barbosa 1992; Birman, Novaes, and Crespo 1997; Bonfim 1993, 1996; Bosi 1992; Buarque de Holanda 1989; Candido 1967, 1993; J. Carvalho 1990, 1996; Da Matta 1979, 1985; Faoro 1991–93; Freyre 1992; Hess and DaMatta 1995; Leal 1993; D. Leite 1992; Martins 1994; Morse 1988; C. Prado 1942; Ribeiro 1995; Salles 1996; Schwartzman 1982; O. Souza 1994; Ventura 1991.

1995) but present a remarkable uniformity of result: the relentless subjugation of Indians to the new political order. What seems special about the Brazilian case is the double bind the state set for itself, that is, the coexistence of a humane ideology toward its indigenous minorities with a strong commitment to reach modernity via development, which is considered incompatible with indigenous ways of life. Janus faced, the Brazilian state opens its arms to the Indians and then stifles them in a choking embrace.

Most revealing of this choking embrace is the "pacification" venture carried out by the Brazilian state in its attempt to domesticate wayward Indians. I have chosen this type of event precisely because it reveals a great deal of what goes unsaid about the Brazilian nation. In the actions and gestures of the pacification agents one finds the marks of an ambivalent national ethos that considers the Indians obstacles to the much-desired development while projecting an image of humane concern for its indigenous peoples. In a nutshell, Brazil's pacification system contains some of the most pervasive historical, political, and economic issues that have haunted the country since its colonial days. What follows is an analysis of the imagery used in the process of submitting indigenous peoples to state control and what it reveals of this ambiguity. But a more detailed commentary on the place of the Indians in the national ethos will wait until the conclusion.

The Weapons of Seduction

The image of the benign state, protector of and provider for the Indians, is encapsulated in certain personalities elevated to the status of national heroes. The conquest of the hinterland, supposedly a fearful human void, was for a long time one of the greatest sources of heroism, supplying the required features of romance and daring. But behind feats of bravery and self-denial has always been a clear vision of the need to take possession of land and resources, not to mention people. This was true of the infamous seventeenth-century bandeirante conquerors (Morse 1965; Monteiro 1994) as well as of contemporary explorers:

> A truly unknown world . . . enveloped the central region of the Brazilian territory where the population was widely scattered. But it was not just the empty expanses gleaming with legend and mystery which fired the imagination and excited the enthusiasm of everyone as the Roncador-Xingu expedition got started. More realistically, one also saw in all that a profusion of truly formidable resources and conditions regarded as indispensable for the complete development of the country in the future. (Villas Bôas and Villas Bôas 1994, 41)

In taking possession of its immense territory, Brazil did not produce a Custer. Instead, it created icons of benevolent paternalism. The Villas Bôas brothers are the most famous *sertanistas*—a word one might freely translate as 'Indian tamers' and that one finds associated with bandeirantes and Indian slave hunters (Ellis 1965, 50)—since the founder of modern Brazilian Indigenism, Marshall Cândido Mariano da Silva Rondon. The brothers began their indigenist life as members of the Roncador-Xingu expedition, which was part of the government's project to open up the hinterland for colonization, under the auspices of the Central Brazil Foundation, which was created during World War II in the administration of Getúlio Vargas. For decades the Villas Bôas brothers were engaged in a campaign to create a sort of sanctuary for the indigenous peoples who inhabited the upper Xingu region. In 1961 President of Jânio Quadros created the Xingu National Park, to which the government trotted foreign diplomats and royalty to gaze at the magnanimous treatment Brazil dispensed to its indigenous population. Protected by the absence of colonization and the authority of the indigenist brothers, the Xingu park was for decades the Villas Bôases' paradise in which the Indians, on permanent display, became "metaphors of themselves," in the words of anthropologist Viveiros de Castro (quoted in Bastos 1983, 46).

Turning Custer upside down, men like the Villas Bôases, officially charged with the benevolent conquest of Indians in Brazil, used seduction rather than weaponry to tame entire populations that had resisted contact with Euro-Brazilians. The system, officially inaugurated by the army officer Rondon at the turn of the century, was first called *pacification* (Souza Lima 1995) and then renamed *attraction,* but, apart from the innovation of aircraft flying low over terrified Indians as attested by aerial photographs of Krenakarore-Panará Indians in the late 1960s (Arnt, Pinto, and Pinto 1998), it has kept its main features: surreptitious approaches to campgrounds or villages in scouting sorties by groups of men suggestively called *penetration teams* (CEDI 1985a, 28); the hanging of trinkets on tree branches to lure the Indians during a phase known as *namoro,* or courting; the unrelenting pursuit in hide-and-seek fashion; and, finally, many trinkets later, the triumph over the stubborn will of the Indians to remain secluded. That magic moment was usually sealed with the proverbial embrace of conqueror and conquered, often frozen in pictures taken by professional photographers who went along to capture on film generations of enraptured sertanistas. Each attraction campaign followed the same adventurous yet monotonous script, sometimes rehearsed for years on end, in which non-Indians chased Indians, Indian men appeared and disappeared from view, and—most revealing of all—Indian women always fled into the bush at the approach of the strangers; in the grand finale ecstatic Brazilians at long last reached the climax of attraction by putting their hands on the females of the tribe. Surrender was then complete.

7. *Sernatista* and "pacifier" Sydney Possuelo distributes gifts among the Zo'é Indians of the state of Pará. Photo by André Dusek, 1989.

By the time the Indians grow accustomed to the seemingly inexhaustible supply of goods from the apparently infinite generosity of the interlopers, the flow of free steel tools, beads, cooking pots, and other trinkets stops. Gratify one moment, withdraw the next is a typical way to create the double-bind effect (Bateson 1972), a virtually infallible strategy for disempowering someone. The effect on the recipient is usually a large dose of frustration and disorientation. The all-too-common begging that follows pacification may well result from the withdrawal the Indians are bound to feel when no more gifts turn up. The shock of realizing the high price they have to pay for that initial generosity comes too late to most Indians, for a successful pacification is but the first step in forcing the contacted group into an irreversible condition of dependence on the national society and one from which it will never again escape. The pattern has been repeated so often, and so strong is the expectation that Indians cannot resist the temptations of Western goods, that in 1975, speaking of the Waimiri-Atroari's refusal to submit, Orlando Villas Bôas predicted, to the *Jornal de Brasília,* that sooner or later these Indians would come to the attraction teams because "they will miss the gifts from the whites" (1975).

Seducing Indians into submission with trade goods is not a recent invention. We find the first hints of it in Pero Vaz de Caminha's 1500 letter to the king of Portugal: "And Nicolau Coelho signaled to them to put down their bows. And they did. . . . He only threw to them a red cap, a linen hood he wore on his head, and a black hat. And one of them threw back a feather headdress" (1963, 30). It is more explicit in Vespucci's 1504 letter to Soderini: "We returned thence to the ships, leaving ashore for them where they could see them many bells, mirrors, and other things. And when we were out at sea, they descended from the hill, and came for the things which we had left them, showing great surprise at them" (Vespucio 1951, 330). And let's not forget the Jesuits: "There was nothing original about Rondon's methods—the offering of presents, an attitude of nonaggression, and so on—since many of these date back to the Jesuits in the colonial period" (Souza Lima 1991, 253).

The humanitarian and careful attitude of the pioneer pacification teams decreased steadily as the Indian Protection Service (SPI) was replaced by the National Indian Foundation (FUNAI) and the early positivist thrust that animated Rondon and his followers (Ribeiro 1962) was gradually forgotten. In the late 1960s and 1970s members of attraction teams transmitted venereal diseases and other illnesses to recently contacted Indians. Some team leaders complained that men with tuberculosis were sent by FUNAI to work on the front line of isolated Indian groups. Accusations of initiating prostitution and homosexuality among newly contacted Indians were directed at members of these attraction teams. Only killings of Indians, although rumored, have not been established as fact in the history of pacification. One particular sertanista, Antonio Cotrim, aware of the implications of bringing Indians into permanent contact with the dominant society, resigned, saying that he "no longer wanted to play the role of undertaker for the Indians" (*Veja* 1972, 21). Behind this statement is the conviction that the protectionist agency, rather than defending the Indians from violations of their rights by nationals, has in fact done the opposite: protected the interests of the nationals against the Indians.

Why all the theatrical display at a high cost in money, time, and health (the Villas Bôas brothers said they each caught two hundred cases of malaria [1994, 18]) for a handful of Indians who could have been left to fend for themselves when farmers, lumberjacks, miners, cattle ranchers, or road builders came along? The fifteen hundred trails the Villas Bôas brothers opened in the jungle, the thousand kilometers of river they navigated, the forty-three towns they sowed in their wake, the nineteen landing strips they tore open (four of which have grown into military bases), and first contacts they made with five thousand Indians surely could have been achieved in a more direct and pragmatic way. What are the roots of their "adventure, unparalleled in the history of the country, with shades of fiction" (S. Souza 1994, 18)? By the way, the word *aventura*, 'adventure' in Portuguese, also has the connotation of a sexual affair, as in the prototypical title *As aventuras de Don Juan*.

Adventure accompanies virtually all occurrences of pacification-attraction in Brazil's hinterland. How to properly carry it out has been spelled out in a rather regimented and bureaucratic way by the Department of Isolated Indians created by FUNAI in the 1980s (which is ironic, because so few "isolated" Indians are left). In its guidelines (or the "operational manual," as it is called), known as the System of Protection of the Isolated Indian (SPII), FUNAI instructs future sertanistas on procedures—truly a "ritual of pacification" (Pechincha n.d.)—that cover a wide range of concerns, from the philosophy of attraction to the most minute practical details. For example, contact with isolated groups is justified by the inexorable advance of national society on their territories, forcing the Indians to "constant flights from roads, dams, ranches, and gold mining sites. If nothing is done, these groups will necessarily disappear." The attraction teams are thus charged with establishing first contact with these Indians and then preparing the way for the reorganization of their economy, providing them with "assistance in the process of acculturation, capable of protecting and orienting them through the difficult paths to civilization" (FUNAI 1987–88, 23). All this should be carried out by people with "emotional discipline, calm, and tranquility," qualities that must accompany "knowledge and commitment to the Indian cause" (p. 29). Team leaders are urged to "develop in the crew a sense of companionship, solidarity, and esprit de corps" (p. 39). FUNAI emphasizes the careful observance of a meticulous check list of the tools every team must take into the bush: "To find out in the middle of the jungle that one forgot to bring a sewing needle or a disposable hypodermic needle—when there is no longer the possibility of getting them—may produce a passing discomfort, or may cause a tragedy" (p. 54). Security measures against "the Indians' unpredictable behavior" include certain precautions, such as the erection of a panopticon, that is, a "surveilling tower, a scheme for night lighting against attacks, the use of fireworks" (pp. 53, 56). The list of personal equipment includes uniforms, bermudas, shorts, t-shirts, and long socks "for the expeditionaries . . . an opportunity to create symbols and identifications" (p. 55). One should not forget one's "tooth brush, soap, nail clip, bath towel" and beware of new shoes and inadequate clothes: "Watch out for brand new jeans, they usually cause a rash on the inner part of the upper thigh" (pp. 63, 56). The manual lists more than 230 items that the sertanistas should pack in pursuit of isolated Indians. Thus equipped, military-like, off they go to their jungle adventure. Symptomatically, the manual is almost silent about how these teams should or should not behave once they come face to face with the Indians. FUNAI provides instructions on how to record the "economic potential of the area being researched" (p. 35); the existence of ranches, gold sites, and the like; the "best time for penetration in the region" (p. 36); orders to protect the land, goods, and health of the Indians and to avoid providing trade goods in excess and contaminating the Indians with contagious diseases. But all these regulations lack specific provisions that spell out how all this should be accomplished. The Indians are as hidden in the manual as they are in the bush.

With contact established and the namoro-courting phase a success, sertanistas still should not assume that the worst is over and the Indians are no longer dangerous. "Today's trade good exchanges, the arrival of women and children which is always regarded as a good sign, may mean a strategy of the Indians for tomorrow's attack" (pp. 68–69). In other words, the sertanistas—and presumably the Indians too—live in a permanent state of tension and anxiety until the process of indigenous dependence is fully established, which may take weeks, months, or even years. An anonymous statement on the last page of the manual chronicles the constant strain:

> "Nobody will ever imagine what moral strength a man needs to dominate the unbearable nervous irritation caused by his feeling himself incessantly besieged, watched and studied in his smallest acts by people he cannot see, of whom he doesn't even know the numbers, whom he doesn't want to harm or chase away, but rather please and attract, and yet who are just waiting for the right moment to assault and kill." (p. 71)

As one assumes this dramatic passage to have been written by a sertanista, one also wonders what an equivalent account by an Indian during first contact would be like.

Obviously, it takes a certain type of personality to do what Rondon, the Villas Bôas brothers, and many other sertanistas did and go on doing. But I'm not so much interested in adventurous characters as in the channels that stamp their deeds as a service to the nation. What these channels are and how they came about is what I will now try to describe.

Positivism, Brazilian Style

In the late nineteenth century the era of Comtean Positivism reached its peak in Brazil. The Positivist movement was prominent in the campaign to end slavery and responsible for the fall of the monarchy and rise of the republican regime (I. Lins 1967; J. Carvalho 1990; Viveiros 1958; Souza Lima 1991, 1995; Gagliardi 1989). An evolutionary humanism pervaded the members of the Positivist Apostolate in Brazil whose motto is to this day printed on the national flag—ORDER AND PROGRESS. What was left out of the flag was the word *love,* which, with the other two, made up the triad of key Positivist concepts. Love for humanity should be extended to the "fetishist hordes," as Positivists called indigenous societies. Their hopes were to catapult the Indians from their fetishist stage directly to the Positivist-scientific stage, skipping the intermediary, and undesirable, metaphysical phase, as proposed in Comte's doctrine. It would thus be necessary "to seduce the Indians into this evolution" (J. Leite 1989, 268).

Yet the same Positivist doctrine imported from France infused the Argentine spirit in its unrelenting wars to exterminate or forcefully integrate indigenous peoples. The humanism that characterized Brazilian-style Positivism was thus the result of more than the simple delivery of a foreign creed. Mixed with native ingredients, it produced a flavor that was perhaps unique to Brazil. I will try to identify some of these ingredients later.

The army was an important stronghold of Brazilian Positivism. In its ranks was a young officer who was destined to become the hero of the hinterlands and the champion of the Indians—Cândido Mariano da Silva Rondon. From 1890 to 1919 Rondon built his career and reputation as a hero and, according to some, a saint (Souza Lima 1990) during a number of expeditions to open up the backlands for control by the central government by means of a network of telegraph lines. These expeditions were reported in spectacular descriptions of wilderness, complete with menacing Indians and, particularly to Rondon, fascinating jaguars (Viveiros 1958). In his passage through savanna and jungle Rondon made first contact with many indigenous peoples. The most famous of Rondon's pacifications were those of the Bororo and the Nambiquara of Goiás and Mato Grosso. His famous adage—"Die if need be, but never kill"—became a canon for dozens of sertanistas long after Vespucci had inaugurated it—"Twenty three of us Christians, having held a council, resolved to go with them, in good array, and with firm intent, if necessary it should be, to die [like brave men]" (Vespucio 1951, 318). Rondon's intrepid incursions into wilderness, their resulting detailed reports on geography and ethnography, and their explicit quest for order and control are reminiscent of nineteenth-century naturalists' reports as the Europeans hiked over mountain, river, and jungle in the name of scientific advancement (Pratt 1992). The major difference was that Rondon's calling did not come from science but from political ideals. Embracing the conviction that the Brazilian nation, a "collective individual," needed to be put under the state's guardianship (Reis 1988, 194), Rondon, the engineer, assumed the military destiny of becoming an " 'empirical builder' of the nation," thus putting into practice the teachings of his military education, which nourished "the idea of salvation through progress" (Souza Lima 1991, 240–47). The taming of wild Indians, first through economic dependence by means of pacification, and then through education, was part of Rondon's idea of state control through progress:

> In sum, the task of the Indian education was twofold: to forge out of Indians Brazilians who could populate the interior and guard the frontier, and to "Brazilianize" immigrants (the Indians) who would then

no longer constitute a threat to the nation. The SPI [Indian Protection Service] would help to mediate this transition from "hostile Indian" to "national worker." (Souza Lima 1991, 254)

Rondon's, then, was a project of gently leveling out ethnic differences by patiently waiting for the Indians to come of age as full Brazilians. Curiously enough, although deeply involved in the republican project, he seemed to dissociate progress from modernity. Reacting against a proposal to exterminate the Kaingang Indians, he affirmed: "We can never agree with such atrocity, even if we die crushed by the whole mass of those interested in it, by the dissolving modernism of this century" (Magalhães 1942, 315).

Rondon was aware of being responsible for flinging open vast areas as yet unknown and exposing the lives of those peoples to the hazards of contact. But he was also convinced that his method of bringing the Indians into civilization was far more humane than the persecution and destruction promoted "not only by pioneers of extractive industries, but also by scientific explorers of railroad companies with the pretext that the Indians are irreducible to civilization" (quoted in Gagliardi 1989, 166). His Positivist doctrine dictated that the Indians be preserved so they could evolve in peace and reach the point of choosing "civilization" of their own free will. His influence in that phase of indigenist policy was so strong that generations of "indigenists" proceeded to contact isolated peoples with the same spirit of protecting the Indians for later assimilation.

In 1910 Rondon created SPI in the wake of a bitter polemic regarding whether the Indians should be protected or exterminated (Magalhães 1942). European colonization was moving quickly in the southern states, and conflicts with Indians were constant. But the political climate of the moment and Rondon's carefully built reputation (Souza Lima 1995) tipped the scales in favor of official protection. The Indians were then declared wards of the state, and their lands became the property of the Union but reserved for their exclusive use.

In the Positivists' proposal for the first republican constitution indigenous societies appeared as "Brazilian American States" and, although labeled fetishist hordes, they were treated as nations. But this proposal was defeated, and those in power since have systematically refused to consider Indian peoples as nations. Indeed, from the moment the Portuguese took possession of the land that was to become Brazil, the Indians, in addition to suffering great losses from epidemics, warfare, and slavery, were subjected to various forms of paternalism, whether in the guise of protection or of submission. First, they endured a soulless phase as Europeans puzzled over whether the natives were human; then, by the magical stroke of a 1537 papal bull the Indians gained souls and were thus available for religious conversion. In the seventeenth century the Portuguese crown recognized Indian communities as "sovereign," but that seems to have been a political move to legalize "just wars" and their inescapable outcome, slavery (Carneiro da Cunha 1987, 58–63).

We reach the twentieth century and meet the 1916 Civil Code, which defined who in the country had full citizenship and who deserved the ambiguous status of relative incapacity. As we saw in Chapter 1, in this category of "relatively incapable" were grouped minors aged sixteen to twenty-one, married women, prodigal sons, and the Indians. In later decades the state emancipated married women and promoted sixteen-year-olds to relative adulthood with the right to vote but kept the Indians as legally incapable to take on the responsibility of full citizenship. After being made to appear like women—to be seduced into the glamor of civilization—the Indians were turned into hopeless children, lost in ignorance, living under the wing of the state, which had turned into a protective father figure who kept them in a sort of civil suspended animation and from time to time threatened to withdraw protection with attempts at false emancipation.

SPI lasted fifty-seven years, during which many a sertanista hero was begotten in the unrelenting search for recalcitrant wild Indians who needed to be tamed so that Brazilian society could expand in peace. But the original heroic tenor set by Rondon quickly softened, and the agency became riddled with dishonest bureaucrats. In 1967 the SPI was shut down amid a scandal of corruption and violations of indigenous rights. Serious accusations of crimes against people and property were never brought to legal conclusion in part because of a fire that conveniently destroyed the SPI files. SPI was replaced by the National Indian Foundation—FUNAI—which inherited from its predecessor its ideology, vices, and even some employees.

As frontier expansion steadily progressed, with Brazilians occupying virtually every corner of the country, the heroism of the sertanistas in search of isolated Indians rapidly declined and was replaced by a nationwide ineptitude in upholding indigenous rights to land, health, and education. What FUNAI has done to perfection, following in the footsteps of the late SPI, is to bring indigenous peoples into total dependence on either the state or religious missions. In fact, from the beginning of Rondon's incursions into the unexplored wild west, despite his good intentions, the Indians he sucked into contact experienced the dramatic change from being seduced with tons of trade goods to being abandoned in hopeless dependence on those same goods and Western medicines to cope with the most damaging aftermath of conquest, Western diseases. With their territories cut drastically, their numbers decreasing, and without the training necessary to face the surrounding national society, the Indians were reduced to pawns who provided the justification for a growing bureaucracy and the flow of public funding. The pacification-attraction system was so obviously a conquest gambit that the figure of sertanista was regarded as a grave digger of Indians. Today, the System of Protection of the Isolated Indian (SPII), FUNAI's niche for "Isolated Indians," is a pathetic nook in the agency to which a former FUNAI president was relegated after he fell from political grace.

Until the 1988 Constitution, to be an Indian in Brazil was a temporary condition that would inevitably be extinguished with the "harmonious integration of the Indians into national communion," as the 1973 Indian Statute put it, echoing the Positivists. The abuses the Indians have suffered for decades for being in the insulting position of being designated the relatively incapable wards of the state, which means being at the mercy of often unscrupulous characters, deserve a book of their own. As sympathetic non-Indians have pointed out, the state has been an unfaithful guardian for the Indians. Instead of helping Indians in dealing with things Western, the state curtails many of their rights in the name of a wardship, which often is no more than a smoke screen for the exercise of power and corruption. For example, to be a ward of the state does not prevent Indians from traveling in Brazil or abroad, but at certain moments of diplomatic embarrassment for breach of human rights, Brazilian authorities, clearly abusing their power, have denied Indians like Mário Juruna their right to get a passport (see Chapter 3).

To liken dominated peoples to the weak segments of Western society, such as women and children, in a metonymic trope of patriarchal mastery, is not a Brazilian invention. The African continent, for instance, is prodigal in examples of this kind. If, say the Comaroffs, "romantic piety made the dark continent into a woman despoiled, it also infantilized it" (1991, 117). What makes the Brazilian case somewhat unusual is its style of conquest. To my knowledge no other New World country tried to resolve its "Indian problem" by luring Indians into dependence with lavish distributions of gifts. Also, a specific Brazilian accent exists in the interplay between state and private initiatives regarding indigenous policy and practice. Adding an extra layer of complexity, a newcomer has entered the interethnic stage and is gaining strength as a lead actor, namely, nongovernmental organizations (NGOs) dedicated to the defense of indigenous rights. NGOs have acquired so much power that they have sometimes been dubbed "neogovernmental organizations." As private entities often supported by public—that is, government—money, the NGOs seem to be en route to becoming parallel states regarding resources, influence, and bargaining power, producing yet another version of indigenous otherness, as we will see in Chapter 10.

State against Society?

In one of his apologies for the Villas Bôas brothers Darcy Ribeiro comments on their courage, saying that they "risked their lives to attract various indigenous groups into civilization," and adding, "a sad thing for the Indians, but not so bad, for their pacification was carried out by the Villas Bôas who were intent on defending them, guaranteeing their survival in a better way than that of other peoples called into our society" (1994, 11). Ribeiro alludes to the counterpoint between state policy and private action regarding the Indians. What he fails to point out is that state and private roles may be played in different keys, their tunes may use separate scales, but they are essentially in harmony, if not unison, when it comes to controlling indigenous peoples and their natural resources. It is banal to say that the state protects the interests of its economically dominant society, but the division of ideological labor by society and state is subtle. It is the difference between the politics of rape and the politics of seduction.

In a world without NGOs the Indian agency long posed as defender of the Indians despite the poor track record as a guardian. New World countries such as the United States and Argentina had no qualms about acknowledging their official policies and setting their armies against Indian nations. The Argentine Conquest of the Desert, the military campaign to wipe out indigenous peoples on the southern plains (Walther 1980), for instance, was no exercise in humanism, not even as a rhetoric. But in Brazil one may criticize the state ad nauseam for not doing its constitutional job of properly defending the Indians' interests, but few would accuse it of official warfare against them. The country may not put much effort and money into protecting the Indians, but neither does it explicitly send troops to crush them. True, clear evidence exists that the army used force to subdue the Waimiri-Atroari in the 1970s, but this evidence is kept in semisecrecy and has never become public fact. In contrast, the worst atrocities have been publicized and attributed to private initiative. In their 1994 book the Villas Bôas brothers justify their yearslong chase after the Txicão Indians as a measure necessary to stop the latters' attacks on the passive Xingu villagers; once the brothers conquered the Txicão, the Villas Bôases removed the Txicão from their lands and relocated them in the Xingu park, supposedly to protect them from encroaching "violent and lawless" miners (Villas Bôas and Villas Bôas 1994, 592). It was a skillful move: subdue the Txicão, bring them under direct and immediate control, and free their lands for national occupancy, all in the name of Indian protection against evil invaders (see Ribeiro 1970, 185–86). Like the Txicão, other peoples such as the Txukahamãe, the Suyá, and the Panará (Krenakarore) were subdued and transferred to the park, often forced to live in proximity to former enemies, under state supervision. Only in October 1995 did the Panará manage to return to their homeland after years of unhappiness in the Xingu park (Cohen 1996; Arnt, Pinto, and Pinto 1998).

Another story in the Villas Bôas book echoes episodes reported by Rondon and his associates (Magalhães 1942, 321–22) and brings out more clearly the contrast between the "loving care" of the state and the explicit cruelty of private individuals: "One time the owner of a famed rubber property . . . gave a party and invited the Jurunas who lived nearby. Disaster and treason: the manioc flour was laced with arsenic. Practically all those Jurunas at the party died. . . . Because of such cruelty, the Indians decided to abandon their villages and head upriver" (p. 596). The Juruna Indians lost their traditional lands and were moved into the seemingly inexhaustible Xingu park.

Turning to Darcy Ribeiro again, we find a moving description of the extermination of the Oti, a Shavante subgroup that used to live in the state of São Paulo. After they lost their territory to cattle ranchers and were on the verge of starvation, the Oti began to hunt cattle. In retaliation the ranchers hunted Indians as if they were cattle. In 1903 the Oti were reduced to eight people — four children, three women, and one man who was then shot to death. "Soon afterward the women approached a group of farm workers, grabbing their hands to indicate they wanted protection. One of the workers imagined it might be a maneuver from the feared Kaingang. Panic broke out and immediately one of the Indian women was shot dead. In 1908, the Oti were seen for the last time: they were only two women sitting by the roadside hiding their faces in their hands" (1970, 88).

The Indian Protection Service was created early in this century, but despite the benevolent gestures of some of its personnel who were charged with keeping the Indians alive, one of the lowest points in indigenous depopulation occurred between 1900 and 1957 when eighty-seven groups were estimated to have become extinct (Ribeiro 1970, 250). This figure is not surprising when one ponders the effects of forced contact of entire peoples totally vulnerable to contagious diseases and unprepared to cope with deprivation of land and other basic resources. If we consider that the native peoples encountered attraction teams that included Brazil-nut gatherers, rubber entrepreneurs, and even men carrying infectious diseases, what is surprising is how many Indian groups survived this fatal attraction and reached the end of the twentieth century. Yes, they submitted to the state, but they became increasingly aware not only of their predicament but also of their rights.

Nevertheless, the official discourse about Indians takes pains to separate benign state policy from rapacious private initiative, and on the surface they do look distinct. Legislation guarantees many rights to the Indians, both in their special status within the Brazilian nation and as full members of their societies. But even at the rhetorical level we are periodically startled by blatant statements of government representatives who forecast the end of indigenous peoples in the near future, leaving to interpretation whether their disappearance will be the result of assimilation or not. Two notable pronouncements, mentioned in Chapters 1 and 2, were made by a former minister of the army, General Leônidas Pires Gonçalves, who, on an Indian Day (April 19) in the 1980s declared to the press that the Indians should not be protected because their cultures are not respectable. Then, in the 1990s, political scientist and former minister of science and technology Hélio Jaguaribe stated that Brazil will have no more Indians by the end of the twenty-first century.

What appeared to be contradictory in the official indigenist rhetoric was so only in appearance. If, on the one hand, the state brought upon itself the duty to defend Indian lives and cultures against the greed and brutality of the dominant society, it also proposed the termination in due course of indigenous special status. By declaring Indianness to be a transitory condition, the government expected to convert Indians to Brazilianness and thus proceeded to push the Indians into integration. As full citizens, the native peoples would then lose the right to exclusive usufruct of their lands. The pseudo-contradiction resolved itself in the long-term project of eliminating Indianness. Attempts at forced emancipation during the military regime were aborted because of public protests against the obvious maneuver of state officials, pressured by the strong lobby of private economic interests, to turn indigenous territories into marketable commodities.

But with the 1988 Constitution that apparent contradiction became real, for now the major law of the country says the Indians have the right to be what they are forever. To be an Indian is now a legal state, not simply a passing condition. Discourses defending the end of the Indians can no longer find legal support in the centuries-old assimilationist policy that was superseded by the new constitution.

Yet economic pressure on Indian lands continues. How long the state can maintain the posture of defending Indian rights against the stream of development projects that inundates the whole country and overflows into indigenous territories is a matter of much concern to Indians and their allies. The new constitution also opened a channel for them to air their grievances, the indigenous division within the attorney general's office. As defenders of the Union's interests, which include the lands occupied by indigenous peoples, the office's actions are constantly colliding with both private and public operations involving Indian rights. We now have a full-fledged contradiction within the state machine itself. The dialectical spiral that results is sure to occupy future observers.

The Indians in a Benevolent State of Cordial Men

Possession by seduction—what more alluring image could one find to conquer one's inferiors? How could one devise an appeal that would be more beguiling to win over a reluctant foe? Under the guise of unlimited generosity in the distribution of trade goods the conqueror lures the Indian into a trap of economic dependence from which there is no way out. Under the guise of protection from private assault the state corners the Indian in a political blind alley—the guarantee of exclusive use of territory in exchange for the surrender of full citizenship. The Brazilian state, in the self-ascribed role of protector-provider, thus ensures its rights to exercise total control over Indian persons and land.

While pondering the place of the Indian question in Brazil's awareness of itself and others, I was pulled, despite myself, toward a theme that has absorbed a number of scholars concerned with making sense of Brazil. I am referring to the problematic created around the image of the "cordial man." To make my point more clearly, even at the risk of a lengthy digression, I should say a little more about this cordial man, by no means an obvious or well-known phrase outside Brazil. I hope to thus establish its association with the undertaking of "taming" the Indians.

In 1936 historian Sérgio Buarque de Holanda revived the notion of the Brazilian as cordial man (are women left out, perhaps because they might be the objects of men's cordiality, just as Indians are the object of sertanista seduction?). The term had been used before, by writer Ribeiro Couto, to define Brazilian national character. Buarque de Holanda stresses that *cordial* derives from the Latin word for heart and does not simply mean good natured or gentle—he refers to an overemphasis on affect, causing the blurring of two domains that Western rationality keeps separate, family and state, with important consequences for the political and economic development of the nation (1989, 144—46). Following Weber's analysis of patrimonialism (1978, 1006–69), Buarque de Holanda (and later Faoro 1991–93 and Schwartzman 1982, among others) traces the roots of the cordial man to the patriarchal mode of rural life that persists:

> Smoothness of manners, hospitality, generosity, virtues that are so praised by visiting foreigners, in fact represent a defining feature of Brazilian character, at least in so far as it remains active and impregnates the ancestral influence of patterns of human conviviality as they occur in the patriarchal and rural milieu. (1989, 106–7)

This type of cordiality includes a strong dislike for formal aspects of civil life, such as the careful observance of social etiquette by the Japanese. Rules that create and safeguard citizenship would thus be disregarded in favor of individual privileges (Da Matta 1979). The mélange of private and public spheres carries over into the impersonal civil domain of certain highly personal habits developed in the hierarchical context of family life, such as "the prolonged reverence to a superior," "the desire to establish intimacy," or the need to befriend people engaged in business in order to ensure success in commercial transactions (Buarque de Holanda 1989, 108–109). It is the putting into practice of "representational patterns which make 'favors' and 'rights' interchangeable concepts" (Reis 1988, 201). In a São Paulo election campaign a politician from the most industrialized state in the country was the epitome of the cordial man when he said, "I'll be a friend, a brother, a father in government. When I'm unable to offer you something you'll have a friendly shoulder to cry your sorrows over" (*Folha de São Paulo* 1996c). A murky side of the cordial man syndrome is often exposed when family interests are associated with political power. In May 1997 Orleir Cameli, the governor of the state of Acre in Amazonia, was exposed in a scandalous case of multiple corruption involving the purchase of public goods (hospital equipment, schools, etc.) in illegal operations, including drug traffic, that favored his father, brothers, and sons. "Regarding Cameli it is as follows: one doesn't know where his family's business ends and the government's begins" (M. Carvalho 1997).

Those most skillful at the game of individual privileges enjoy all the advantages of citizenship and none of its duties. The result is a society so entangled in inequality as to be incompatible with the principles of the modern industrial world that stress the social value of the individual (Dumont 1985). A society of cordial men would, in other words, be the antithesis of Weber's bureaucratic rationality. "In principle, the modern organization of the civil service separates the bureau from the private domicile of the official, and, in general, bureaucracy segregates official activity as something distinct from the sphere of private life" (Gerth and Mills 1958, 197).

Buarque de Holanda inaugurated a widespread concern in the social sciences for this trait taken to be central to the Brazilian ethos. But the idea had been popular in nineteenth-century literature. The *favor* system was interpreted as a given in Brazil's formation (Schwarz 1992, 16). The question is why Brazilians needed to invent the cordial man. The idea behind this concern seems to be the following: in the natural course of things Brazil would join the concert of developed nations, but it has not. Its failure to do so is what needs explanation. Brazil's chronic underdevelopment persists despite all expectations. What, then, prevents full development? The attempts to answer this vexing question have been myriad and include external causes such as U.S. imperialism and the unequal exchange of the world system (Emmanuel 1972), but these do not seem to be sufficient or satisfactory. Thus I had to consider internal factors, such as how the cordial man came to be the main feature of the national ethos, the cornerstone for both collective assets and liabilities. While *cordiality* is an ambiguous attribute, taking economic development as a desired goal is in no way ambiguous. According to Buarque de Holanda, as the country reaches increasingly higher levels of industrialization, or, in Weberian terms, gets closer to the ideal type of rationality, the cordial man will gradually be superseded by individualistic relationships. Authors like Martins (1994) argue that so long as private and public domains are kept blurred for the benefit of a rapacious elite, the country will continue to trudge along the trail of underdevelopment.

One might see in the figure of the cordial man aspects associated with the typical Latin American *caudillo,* a powerful and authoritarian father figure who presides uncontested over the entire country, as if it were his big family. Such a figure is also common in Brazilian history, but that does not exhaust the full meaning of the notion of the cordial man. As Brazilian intellectuals strive to identify what is responsible for the political, economic, and social distortions of the country, they venture well beyond the strict realm of politics and attempt to grasp essentials at the man-in-the-street, capillary level of personal relations.

The origin of the patrimonial character of the Brazilian nation is attributed to the Portuguese or Iberian tradition. Depending on the analyst's inclination, Portugal comes out as the villain that transferred to Brazil its backward sociopolitical system (Bonfim 1996; Faoro 1991–93, 1994) or as the magnanimous ancestor that passed on to its colony the virtues of miscegenation, racial tolerance, and social malleability (Freyre 1992, 1953; Morse 1988). From its origin as a rhetorical device— "cordiality will be the Brazilian contribution to civilization" (Buarque de Holanda 1989, 106)— the cordial man has grown into a pervasive ideological tool that finds a suitable training ground in the interethnic arena of Brazilian contact.

The image of the cordial man may be too simple a formula for portraying an entire and highly diversified nation such as Brazil, and Buarque de Holanda himself uses it with caution. It has a family resemblance to Louis Dumont's blanket characterization of societies according to their holistic or individualistic ideologies (1977, 1986). Yet, no matter how limited I find this portrayal of the Brazilian national character, I can't help evoking a Weberian patrimonialism as I write about the attitude of state officials toward indigenous people. "The problem with national stereotypes," says Mexican writer Carlos Fuentes, "is that they contain a grain of truth, even if constant repetition has driven this grain underground" (1992, 17). Contrast should help bring this out more clearly.

In other countries the Indian question is handled in the most impersonal and detached of ways (treaties, by-laws, decrees, warfare). But in Brazil the master metaphors for the subjugation of Indians are attraction, courting, embraces, gifts—in a word, seduction, displayed in images that verge on the libidinous. In other countries the predominant image is often that of a rational Western machine whose logic is incompatible with the anachronistic irrationality of Indian thinking, in an expression of vulgar Levybruhlianism (which takes Lévy-Bruhl's prelogic primitive mentality too literally; Lévy-Bruhl [1910] 1985) that seems to resist the passage of time. But in Brazil sentimentality is the main trope: conqueror and conquered locked in a culminating embrace, the Indians calling the vague figure of the central government *Papai Grande,* Big Dad, and its indigenist delegates *Nosso Pai,* Our Father (as in the case of the Villas Bôas brothers in the Xingu park). What demonstration could be more revealing of the blurring of domestic and state genres? Whereas in other countries the Indians are considered inferior but autonomous in their inferiority, in Brazil they are nearly inert inferiors, "relatively incapable," dependent on the superior Brazilians who make decisions in their name and trace their destiny without consulting them. But none of this is free of ambiguity. The Indians may be seen as a nuisance (they occupy precious land, sit on precious resources, or cause enormous headaches to the state whenever charges of mistreatment reach the international press), but they also represent rich symbolic capital. They are good not only for internal consumption (the untiring cliché of the nation as a mixture of the three races, the noble and pure Indian among them) but also as an export commodity when Brazil wants to show the world how ethnically tolerant it is.

Although the notion of cordiality, an artifact of the fat times of rural hegemony, is hardly an apt chronotope for the country as a whole, in its "Indian slot" Brazil displays the cordial man with a vengeance. In this sense official indigenous policy seems to work as cue in a script that appears to be steadily falling into a dead file. If, as Buarque de Holanda says, the cordial man is doomed, bound to be killed by economic development, the Indian represents perhaps its last breath.

In the meantime the image of Brazil as a community of cordial men displaying their hyperbolic sexuality continues to be enacted in the interethnic pantomime performed behind the scenes of national society: the Whiteman, the seducer, meets Indian, the seduced. Whiteman leaves Indian consumed with diseases and a desire for commodities. Seduction turns into contempt, contempt turns into dependence, dependence turns into submission. Indians, women, and children come full circle as evidences of Whiteman's sexual and political prowess. Whereas married women were freed from legal shackles (at least in the letter of the law), and minors had their minority time span reduced, indigenous peoples, together with absentee children, continue to be the beguiled receptors of officialdom's dubious favors. In the farce of pacification—or, in more modern parlance, attraction—the Indians seem to represent the last chance for the guardians of the nation to exercise their undisputed power with cordiality before history definitively snatches the cordial man away. In the realm of Indigenism, as anywhere else in the country, the hypocrisy behind the cultivation of the image of Brazilians as cordial men is but a way to mask sheer violence in the guise of humanism, a humanism inspired in European ideas of equality, fraternity, and liberty but that in fact turned them into "ideas out of place" (Schwarz 1992).

Gendered conquest—powerful intruding *men* winning over female-like Indians—is nothing new in the Americas. But while we find direct and literal references to Europeans' treating Indian men as effeminates in a strategy of domination, what we see in the submission of Brazilian Indians is that the feminization of the Indians never leaves the realm of metaphor. Unlike the Indian as child, commonly verbalized by nationals, the Indian as woman never occurs in explicit discourse. Quite the opposite—the most common stereotype has been of the Indian male as brave, wildly savage, or disgracefully dumb but never as a woman to be sexually used and abused. The sexual violence involved in the conquest of Brazilian Indians by the national state can only be read between the lines as a symbolic statement that is never made literal. The trinkets, the embraces, the hide-and-seek of the pacification-attraction activity are elements in a scenario of pretenses in which the implicit message is domination by nationals of Indians of either sex. Indian tamers use the old say-it-with-flowers technique perhaps because that is the most established way of convincing an adamantly disinterested object of desire to surrender to one's pursuit. It is a matter of analogy rather than of literalness: Indian is to nation-state as woman is to man. The sexual innuendo inherent in the Brazilian-style pacification is a suitable trope for political submission, but most likely its practitioners are not fully aware of its load of gendered implications. Nowhere in their written or oral statements do people like the Villas Bôas brothers associate Indian males with women, Western or otherwise. Nor do they acknowledge that there ever was homosexuality among indigenous peoples, a far cry from the numerous references to the northern berdache, the master image onto which Europeans forged the notion that Indian equals woman on the North American continent (Trexler 1995). Nevertheless, one cannot overemphasize the sexual connotations of conquest, for, as Torgovnick concludes in her analysis of the Tarzan fiction, "when the West confronts the primitive, power and sex—geo-politics and gender politics—almost immediately come into play" (1990, 57).

In this rather subliminal fashion, reminiscent of Proust's involuntary memories, the Indian question works as a magnifying glass under which the nation's fabric shows its knots, broken lines, and convoluted texture, the result of the uneven warp and weft of the historical process of trying to weave odd threads together in a single social design.

Compared to other situations of first contact with native peoples—where private adventurers did not hesitate to kill when their lives or economic interests were at risk (see, for instance, the situation of the New Guinea Highlands in the 1930s as reported in Connolly and Anderson 1988)—the Brazilian approach to uncontacted indigenous groups as an official enterprise seems to be much more responsible and benevolent. But this apparent benevolence has not been sufficient to counteract the immense damage that pacification has brought to all Indian groups. Contagious diseases are the most immediate effects of first contact, for rarely are pacification-penetration teams in perfectly good health when they "embrace" the Indians. In fact, they are often the first pathogenic agents to contaminate them. Furthermore, unthinkable as it may seem, they usually take no preventative measures against epidemics, such as vaccination campaigns. Loss of territory comes next, for a demographically reduced population attracts invasions, for now it looks like too much land for so few Indians. Then cultural demoralization follows the bombardment of prejudice and negative stereotypes launched upon Indian survivors by their invaders. In a number of cases the final outcome of pacification is the extinction of entire societies either because of physical death or uprootedness, two forms of social obliteration.

Rondon lived long enough—he died in 1958 at the age of ninety-three—to witness the outcome of the "rites of conquest" (Cleland 1992) he and others performed. He had to acknowledge that his guiding premise of attracting Indians to civilization had not turned out to be as humane as he had expected.

> He became convinced that we should no longer nationalize the Indians, for, he affirmed, it "creates serious problems and maladjustments." Rather [we should] preserve tribal cultures by taking their specific economic patterns as a basis for new productive activities which, without being revolutionary, might provide them with the necessary means for their integration into the economic life of the regions where they live. Not that the old General had abandoned his positivist principles and his evolutionist outlook on cultures, but he pondered that every culture, no matter what its basic values are, constitutes a legitimate way of actualizing and expressing human nature. Moreover, unlike what he had defended earlier, giving up a tribal culture and adopting civilization, rather than constituting "progress," represented a form of impoverishment, the sacrifice of a more genuine way of being human. (Schaden 1960, 455)

Rondon died a disillusioned man in regard to the fate of pacified Indians.

6
The Specter of Nations
within the Nation

In 1980 different groups of Indians in different parts of Brazil created the União das Nações Indígenas (Union of Indian Nations). It followed a trend that had begun less than a decade earlier—a growing awareness by the myriad small indigenous societies in Brazil that they need to articulate their claims in a more concentrated manner than the occasional regional gatherings in which they had engaged. They chose the term *nations* to call the country's attention to the existence within the Brazilian polity of fully constituted societies with specific problems that required specific solutions. Although the name of the organization is seemingly innocuous, it provoked the wrath of many an official of both the military regime (1964–1985) and the civilian governments that followed. This chapter addresses the problems that emerge when minorities such as indigenous societies claim self-determination within a nation-state that has an authoritarian tradition like Brazil's. I begin by describing how the pan-Indian movement came about in Brazil, how the national government has reacted to it, and what these reactions reveal about the nature of the Brazilian state. In attempting to make sense of the intricacies of the diverse uses of the concept of nation, I insert a discussion of this concept both in terms of academic definitions and of political practices. Some revealing correspondences emerge, supporting the conviction that between the ivory tower and the real world are more bridges than meet the eye.

Birth and Growth of the Indian Movement

The Catholic Church was the prime mover in launching a supralocal indigenous political movement in the early 1970s. The Indigenist Missionary Council (Conselho Indigenista Missionário)—CIMI—was created in 1972 as a militant branch of the National Conference of Bishops of Brazil (Conferência Nacional dos Bispos do Brasil)—CNBB. It grew out of the deep engagement of members of the Catholic Church in liberation theology, along the lines that inspired the urban Christian Base Communities (Comunidades Eclesiais de Base) as well as the rural Land Pastoral Committee (Comissão Pastoral da Terra).

Two years later CIMI organized the first in a long series of "indigenous assemblies." By providing or substantially covering transportation, food, and lodging expenses, the missionaries brought together for the first time representatives of several indigenous groups to participate in informal gatherings. Assemblies were organized in various parts of the country from the early 1970s until well into the 1980s. The first took place in April 1974 in the state of Mato Grosso and was attended by seventeen Indians. The second, in May 1975, was called by the Munduruku Indians of the Cururu Mission in the northern state of Pará and was attended by sixty Indians.

The thrust of the meetings was to expose the Indian representatives to the interethnic experience of other groups so they could bring the information to their people back home. The initial phase was one of discovery. According to CIMI's report on the first indigenous assembly, Captain Aídji, whose Portuguese name was Eugênio, a Bororo from the Salesian Mission in Merure, told the group:

> It has been very good to get to know various friends and tribes I had never heard of before. The meeting is good for us to get to know different tribes. There are many differences—language, custom, food. Hunting and fishing is the same. Arrow cane is the same, but the arrows are different. Different traditions, entertainment. For example, we, Bororo, communicate by whistling. . . . It is good to get together and know each other. Many don't know we exist over to the east. (CIMI 1974, p. 3)

The Indians listened to each other recount not only aspects of their respective cultures but also the familiar litany of abuses and plunder by Brazilians, whether they were the result of private or official initiatives. The astounding similarities in the way group after group suffered at the hands of the dominant society struck a resonant chord in the listeners' consciousness. The sense that the same troubles also plagued other Indians they had never seen before generated a sense of solidarity and confidence that they were not alone in their plight after all. Now they could count on each other in fighting for a better life. A new world of generalized injustice opened up to them, creating an esprit de corps that persisted well after the meetings ended. Unlike later phases of the movement, when Indian leaders spoke directly to Brazilian audiences, the speeches delivered in those early meetings were addressed to other Indians in a direct exchange of misfortunes. CIMI's bulletins record the following testimonies: "My brothers, I call you brothers because I'm an Indian. I'm a brother of the same color, the same massacre" (Sampré, the Sherente also called José Carlos). "I came to hear about the Indian's life. We have no land. We have houses, game, but they are taking away our land" (Txuãeri, the Tapirapé also named José). "Down there where I live they are destroying the forest. They are selling the wood. I mean, food we used to have, we have no more. . . . Down there the Indian is tied up and beaten up" (Cláudio Nenito, Guarani).

CIMI organized, or helped organize, numerous assemblies, particularly in the north, northeast, and central west, with increasing numbers of participants. As indigenous awareness expanded beyond strictly local problems, the regional assemblies became national in scope. Consequently, they began to attract the attention of authorities, particularly officials of the National Indian Foundation (FUNAI) who opposed CIMI's organizing efforts outright. The thirteenth indigenous assembly of April 1979 gathered Indians from various regions in the northeastern state of Sergipe. The report of this assembly conveys both the combative CIMI style and the tense political climate of the day:

> October 11 was approaching. Newspapers all over Brazil, radio and television announced the upcoming nationwide Indigenous Assembly on the Isle of São Pedro, Porto da Folha (northeastern state of Sergipe).
>
> On the 9th, D. José Brandão, bishop of Propriá, one of the great defenders of the Shokó Indians in their struggle to repossess their land, receives a visit from Dr. Romildo Leite, FUNAI's attorney. If the Assembly took place on the Isle of São Pedro he [Leite] would withdraw from the Shokó case. Fortunately, neither the bishop nor CIMI were charged with such decision. The Indians were the promoters of the meeting and only they could alter the program.
>
> Meanwhile, the head of FUNAI's Third Regional Delegacy in Recife sent a radio message to all posts prohibiting the participation of Indians under his jurisdiction. In Palmeira dos Índios, Delegate Francisco Eudes and Dr. Luis de Patrício [from FUNAI's headquarters in Brasília] were there personally to forbid the Shukuru-Kariri and the Shokó-Kariri to participate in the Assembly.
>
> But this repression did not work. On the eleventh at dawn, the Kaimbé Indians from Maçarará, Euclides da Cunha (state of Bahia), and the Truká Indians from the Isle of Assunção, Cabrobó (state of Pernambuco) were already on the Isle of São Pedro.
>
> Meanwhile, in the early hours of the eleventh, the remaining Indians were being expected at the bus station in Aracaju [Sergipe's capital city]. At one in the morning, Tupiniquim and Guarani arrived from the [eastern] state of Espírito Santo. They camped right there, turning the very uncomfortable benches of the waiting hall into makeshift beds.
>
> [At daybreak] the Indians from Mato Grosso arrived with Father

Thomaz Lisboa. They were Kayoá, Guarani, Tapirapé, Kayabi, Shavante, Bakairi, Iranshe, Rikbaktsa, Nambiquara. . . . The Bakairi had walked for forty-eight hours besides the seven-day bus ride.

As night fell, the Indians approached the banks of [the San Francisco River]. The Shokó were waiting. Everything was ready, within the limitations of their poverty, to receive the representatives of the various Indian nations of Brazil. And how well they did it!

But the night also brings darkness. Colonel Hércio Gomes, head of the Security and Information division of the Ministry of the Interior, and his underlings, FUNAI's anthropologists Delvair Melatti and Sidney Possuelo, insisted on boarding the boat that would take Indians, missionaries, and journalists to the Isle of São Pedro. Despite his insistence, that authentic representative of repression did not succeed [in boarding the boat].

It was in this climate that the Assembly began. The Indians' cry of pain was heard. The extreme poverty of the Shokó was the obvious pitch of that cry. The Indians knew very well how to grasp the pain. They understood why during those days their lodgings would not be houses but the magnificent trees of the Shokó land. To this day there are no houses on the Isle. The Brittos [a family of landowners], usurpers of the Indian lands, destroyed them all.

Even so, the meeting of brethren turned into a feast. During the day, under the tamarind tree, the problems were brought up. At night, at the same place, all peoples' representatives showed their cultures. There are no words to express the pleasure and beauty of the feast.

On the twelfth, the session had hardly begun and a stranger tried to enter the Assembly. It was the spy-Colonel and those he commanded. The Indians reacted immediately. It was only after an argument between them that the Indians allowed them to stay. "To hear what we have to say to this FUNAI."

At Pão de Açucar (state of Alagoas), twelve kilometres away, a van . . . with four Federal Police agents was receiving and recording the messages from the Colonel's "recorder." Everything was ready for an intervention on the Isle, they said. The electronic spying and the weaponry mounted by [the agents of] repression betrayed the false rapprochement of the present regime. (Santos 1980, 3–4)

Like this Sergipe meeting, other Indian assemblies were disrupted or threatened with disruption by FUNAI or federal police agents during the military regime.

As CIMI continued to promote meeting after meeting in various parts of the country, an independent group of young Indians who attended school in Brasília proposed in April 1980 the creation of a nationwide indigenous organization they called UNIND (União das Nações Indígenas). These students belonged to groups such as the Terena, Shavante, Bororo, Patashó, and Tushá. Their intention was to "bring together the Indians' efforts to help them fight for an indigenist policy for the Indian's own benefit" (CEDI 1981, 38). Less than two months later an Indian assembly in the town of Campo Grande (state of Mato Grosso do Sul) ended with the founding of UNI, another version of the União das Nações Indígenas, which would "promote the Indians' autonomy and self-determination, reclaim and guarantee the inviolability of their lands, and assist the Indians in knowing their rights by drawing and putting into practice cultural and community development projects" (p. 38). One month went by, and representatives of fifteen "Indian nations" attended yet another meeting, a conference titled Creation of the Brazilian Indigenous Federation. The participants pledged allegiance to UNI, now considered "the outcome of the fusion of UNIND, created in April by Indian students in Brasília, and the project for the federation of indigenous groups of Mato Grosso do Sul which had been called by Terena chief Domingos Marcos" (p. 38). The invention and reinvention of UNI by different promoters attest to the ripeness and even urgency of the idea of a pan-Indian organization.

In the twelve years of its existence UNI went through several leadership crises, changed format from a pyramidal presidential system to an encompassing organization of national and regional coordinators, made and broke alliances with the Catholic Church, with non-Indian nongovernmental organizations (NGOs), and with the Alliance of the Peoples of the Forest, an organization that included non-Indian rubber tappers in Amazonia (CEDI 1991a, 408–12). UNI had its low and high points on the national political scene; not the least of its achievements was its successful challenge to the open hostility of a strong militarized state that rejected the idea of having nations within the nation and, as a further aggravation, organized in a union.

During the 1987–1988 Constitutional Assembly, UNI, backed by several non-Indian organizations—including the Brazilian Anthropological Association (ABA) and the National Association of Geologists (CONAGE) —was largely responsible for the effective indigenist lobby that brought the Indians some palpable gains, such as the deletion of the integrationist principle that had long prevailed. During the Constitutional Assembly UNI and CIMI had a falling out, symptomatically enough, around the term Indian nations. UNI and its allies, aware of the antagonism that the term generated, and fearing that to insist on it might jeopardize more important concerns, omitted it from their "peoples' amendment" and used "peoples" instead. But CIMI held onto the position that it was essential to keep the phrase Indian nations, even if it incurred the fury of the most conservative sectors of the country, as it in fact did, risking the success of the entire

8. Indians perform ceremonial dance for their constitutional rights in full view of Brasília at dusk. Photo by André Dusek, copyright 1987 André Dusek/AGIL.

indigenist lobby, as we will see shortly. The split that ensued was never mended.

UNI's eventual demise was to be expected. It never resolved the problem of its limited representation among the indigenous population in the country nor the top-heavy distortion in its management. It never succeeded in mastering the ethnic reality of indigenous Brazil with its multitude of small, scattered, and often politically detached societies. As Carlos Alberto Ricardo writes:

> The case of National UNI . . . illustrates the difficulties the Indians have in building stable and permanent forms for representing their interests in Brazil, given its so profoundly diverse and dispersed base. Founded in 1979 [sic], at a meeting sponsored by the state government of Mato Grosso and with no direct connection to the various so-called Assemblies of Indigenous Leaders stimulated by CIMI in the 1970s, UNI efficiently played the role of symbolic reference of generic Indianness in the context of the democratization process Brazilian society was going through up until the time when the new Federal Constitution was being drawn up (1986–88). To this purpose it took advantage of a series of alliances with non-Indians which included, among others, several support[ive] non-governmental organizations, CIMI itself, congressmen of various politi-

9. Kayapó men line up outside the National Congress in Brasília during a crucial meeting of the Constitutional Assembly. Payakan is the seventh from left. Photo by André Dusek, copyright 1988 André Dusek/AGIL.

cal parties, professional associations such as Conage (National Association of Geologists) and ABA (Brazilian Anthropological Association). At that time, the "Indian scene" in Brasília comprised representatives of about half the indigenous peoples in the country whose presence was made possible by the support they received from their non-Indian allies. However, in the forefront of those who closely followed the decisive moments of the voting on indigenous rights at the National Congress was an expressive and aggressive group of Kayapó, the only ethnic group who arrived at the country's capital by their own means collected either from controlling key connections with FUNAI's bureaucracy, or from the sale of mahogany and fees charged to miners who pan gold on their lands. (1996a, 91)

One gets the impression that the budding Indian movement, including UNI, directly reflected the organizational form in which official indigenist policy was carried out. Just as official policy flows from the top down, that is, from nationals to Indians, so outside efforts seeded the indigenous political consciousness. First, we have CIMI's fundamental role in overcoming one of the biggest barriers to consciousness raising, that is, isolation and lack of material means to travel. By helping to bring together dozens of Indians to discuss problems that recurred across the country, CIMI gave them the opportunity to share their experiences and organize agendas in common. The "cosmopolitanization" that resulted from CIMI's pedagogical experiment triggered future indigenous initiatives. After CIMI's pioneering, we have the founding of a pan-Indian organization, also stimulated by sympathetic Brazilians, which turned out to be an important platform from which to launch the Indian issue into national politics. More recently, nongovernmental organizations, both national and foreign, have similarly precipitated political action by Indians. In all these efforts the impetus has come from outside of indigenous communities.

There are many reasons that this is so and that Brazilian Indians took so long to begin organizing themselves interethnically. The gigantic size of the country aggravates already acute physical and financial difficulties in transportation and communication between remote Indian areas; the extensive dispersal of indigenous peoples through virtually all states of the Union is another factor, as is the fragmentation of Indian societies by language, custom, and degree of interethnic contact. Perhaps the most significant factor is the form in which the state has carried out its indigenist policy. Officially, and often in actual practice, the government is in total command of the affairs of indigenous communities. It is responsible for the political isolation of most Indian peoples, often through policelike control of indigenous circulation in and out of the reserves, and through lack of education. Lacking access to proper schooling, the Indians have not learned sufficient Portuguese to steer their way through the national society. Many representatives at the CIMI assemblies complained bitterly of their inability to speak well to other Indians, while several monolingual leaders had to have their speeches translated. Keeping the Indians illiterate is one way of retaining control over them (Ramos 1984a).

If we replace *Aboriginal* and *Aboriginality* with *Indian* and *Indianness* in the passage that follows, we will see that Brazilian Indians are not alone in this matter. Australia's "Aboriginal people are not free to construct their Aboriginality as they please. Others have a close interest in the process of ethnogenesis, not least the state" (Jones and Hill-Burnett, quoted in Beckett 1988a, 4). In addition, "formation of the Australian state [was] a crucial ingredient in the politics of Aboriginality" (1988b, 193). We will see shortly how true that also is of the Brazilian situation.

In contrast to indigenous movements in other Latin American countries, such as Ecuador and Peru, the first Brazilian Indian organization was neither local nor regional but national (for a useful comparison see Jackson 1991 and 1993 on Amazonian Colombia). The attempt to create regional UNI chapters failed to bridge the gap between headquarters (whether in Brasília or São Paulo) and the grassroots. Whatever concerted action there might have been at the beginning between the national UNI and the regional UNIs did not last long, and the national organization came to lead a life of its own. Thus no intermediate organizations existed to coordinate actions and translate the policy and procedures of national UNI to the local communities. No confederation existed that would have allowed the smaller organizations to nest within a broader unit. The problem of legitimacy that plagued UNI derived mostly from this skewed arrangement.

The lessons of the UNI experience have led to the opposite extreme. Now Brazil has no fewer than 109 indigenous organizations, ranging from the local (for instance, AITECA, the Indigenous Association of the Terena of Cachoeirinha) and regional (APIR, the Association of the Indigenous Peoples of Roraima) to "common interest" associations such as UNAMI, the National Union of Indigenous Women. A national entity, the Council for the Articulation of Indigenous Peoples and Organizations in Brazil (CAPOIB), aims to coordinate all the others but apparently has no decision-making powers. In the late 1980s as many as eighteen organizations were formed in the Brazilian Uaupés region alone. They are interlocal and bring together clusters of communities from a single microregion or river, as, for example, the Association of the Union of the Tiquié River Indigenous Community (AUCIRT), the Union of the Indigenous Community of the Iauareté District (UCIDI), and the Association of the Xié River Indigenous Communities (ACIRX). "Most of these organizations were created in 1987–88 in reaction to the turbulent interchanges, often considered illegitimate by the indigenous communities, of representatives who in the name of these communities negotiated with federal authorities and, in some regions, with mining companies" (CEDI 1991a, 104). They were responding to the pact between Álvaro Sampaio's faction and the military in charge of the Calha Norte Project, as well as the Paranapanema mining company.

Whereas the UNI model seemed to reflect the non-Indian part of the politics of contact—initial impetus from non-Indians, vertical management—the pattern of multiplying entities appears to correspond mimetically to the social reality of indigenous Brazil, that is, a proliferation of small societies living relatively independent lives with few common concerns apart from the underlying predicament of being Indian in a country that strongly favors cultural homogeneity. But, although it has gone from one extreme to the other, the Brazilian Indian movement is much more than a mere reaction to external conditions and stimuli. In the trial-and-error process of searching for a political vocation the Brazilian pan-Indian movement has made some experiments that cannot be attributed exclusively to external influence. The current trend of converting culture and ethnicity into political capital has no doubt been influenced by the emphasis by some outside agents of Indigenism, such as anthropologists who have placed value on cultural diversity. Nevertheless, the Indians have molded these concepts to serve their own goals, thus surprising and even shocking many a friend of the Indians (T. Turner 1991a; Albert 1997). The multiplication of indigenous organizations may be a symptom of the fragmentation that paradoxically accompanies today's "globalization" in an unprecedented rush toward commodification (Albert 1997), but it should not be reduced to a mere act of mimicry of the West's latest fad.

Officialdom Reacts

Returning to the muddled concept of Indian nations, perhaps the best demonstration of how indigestible the elite finds it is the incident involving CIMI during the 1987–1988 Constitutional Assembly.

For a whole week CIMI was under a vicious attack launched by a major national daily, O Estado de São Paulo, otherwise known as Estadão. The paper ran a series called "The Indians in the New Constitution" from August 9 to 14, 1987, and used such headlines as "Conspiracy Against Brazil," "CIMI Does Not Live by Indians Alone," "CIMI and Its 'Tin Brothers,'" "Indians, the Way to Minerals," and "CIMI Proposes the Division of Brazil." The first of the six articles mentioned a document signed by forty-seven thousand Austrians who "intended to amend the Brazilian Constitution with the pretext of saving the Indians." The newspaper claimed to have authenticated documents that proved CIMI's connection to an international plot, via a certain "World Council of Christian Churches," to divide Brazil, exploit its minerals, and "restrict the exercise of Brazilian sovereignty over indigenous lands in Amazonia" (Correio Braziliense 1987a). The unusual magnitude of the campaign made clear how far powerful interest groups, especially those in the economy's mineral sector, were prepared to go to ensure their right to exploit wealth from Indian lands. The assault by the media was aimed at the Catholic Church as a roundabout way of counteracting the high visibility and relative success the indigenist lobby was having at the National Congress. Because advocating an anti-Indian policy would have been politically incorrect (already an issue at the time), the newspaper, backed by other journalists, a multitude of conservative members of Congress, government officials, and businesspeople, chose to set the state against the church. Actually, the originality of the move has been questioned, with the hint that it might have been a gambit tested elsewhere, perhaps with similar success. "It is worth remembering that the campaign is similar to that launched by the intelligence agencies in Venezuela through the media in 1984. There are passages in the Estadão articles that were plagiarized from Caracas newspapers, duly 'adapted' to the Brazilian case" (CEDI 1991a, 20).

The repercussions of such publicity were enormous and nearly ruined the Indian cause at the Constitutional Assembly. One ultraconservative member of Congress, the late Roberto Cardoso Alves, issued a document calling for a parliamentary committee of investigation "to determine the charges about an international conspiracy involving restrictions to national sovereignty on the Amazon region, under the pretext of preserving the cultures and ethnicity of Indians (*silvícolas*), the environment, and mineral resources in that region's subsoil" (*Correio Braziliense* 1987a). Another politician, House Representative Nilson Gibson, in a "long and fiery speech . . . summoned Brazilians to defend the Country (*Pátria*) and the Constitutional Assembly with a public burning of the 'infamous Austrian amendment by means of which foreign citizens would interfere in our destinies.' . . . In concluding, Nilson Gibson clamored that other Constitutional congressmen unite 'as a single body in the integral defense of Brazil's interests' " (*Correio Braziliense* 1987b). Representative José Dutra, from the state of Amazonas, "speaking as . . . a descendant of Indians and representing a region where the issue is most important, denounced that national sovereignty 'is being violated in a mean, brutal way by international, alien forces that want to restrain at all costs the process of economic development of our Country' " (*Correio Braziliense* 1987b).

Once the storm subsided and CIMI pulled itself together, news began to trickle out revealing that *Estadão*'s "authenticated documents" were nothing but fraudulent papers referring to nonexistent organizations, such as the World Council of Christian Churches (not to be confused with the respected World Council of Churches). The highly respected president of the bishops' conference (CNBB), D. Luciano Mendes de Almeida, met with Paulo Brossard, then the minister of justice, to show him proof that the documents with accusations against CIMI were forged. Journalists overheard the exchange between bishop and minister:

> At a certain point of the conversation, the minister lost control. Several rooms away one could hear his complaints to the CNBB president.
> — Very nice, Father. Since when is Brazil a plurinational nation? Not even Anchieta, our great Father Anchieta would do this. This is something absolutely foreign to Brazilian constitutional law, shouted Brossard, referring to the charges published in *O Estado de São Paulo,* supposedly uncovering Church attempts to turn Brazil into a country of multinationalities. . . .
> — These Austrians, who have never set foot here, don't know a word of Portuguese, and now present themselves as protectors of the Indians. Could it be that, by now, after five centuries, we will have another reality? What will be the future consequences of this?
>
> The minister's screams were interrupted by the president of CNBB's remarks in a low, patient, almost inaudible voice. Brossard insisted: "It's obvious that there is an organization at work trying to interfere in Bra-

zilian sovereignty. There is no lack of such organizations, as I can tell by the letters I receive every day from all over the world in the same vein. Can this be the work of the Divine Holy Ghost, Father? (*Correio Braziliense* 1987c)

This tumultuous exchange between the representatives of state and church, reminiscent of Brazilian politics of the eighteenth and nineteenth centuries when "the ecclesiastic bureaucracy was a constant source of potential conflicts with the State" (J. Carvalho 1996, 167), exposes in no ambiguous terms the "essential tension," to borrow Kuhn's expression (1977), between two of the strongest forces in Brazilian politics in general and in interethnic politics in particular.

The crux of the matter came down to CIMI's having consistently used the term Indian nations in its uncompromising defense of indigenous rights to their land resources. The telltale fear of flustered Minister Brossard, that Brazil might turn into a country of "multinationalities," leaves few doubts.

The case of CIMI versus *Estadão* is a glaring example of the agonistic battles fought for the idea of nation. The caustic campaign that the economic and military establishment sustained against the Catholic Church in the name of national sovereignty actually provided the church with an opportunity to show that its two-thousand-year experience has not been for nothing. In its strict defense of the designation Indian nations CIMI challenged the establishment and exhibited an enviable self-assurance, the result of a long tradition of ideological crusades. The tug-of-war between church and state about embryonic indigenous nationalism nearly sank the Indian lobby and left a trail of unsettled resentment in all the sectors involved — state, church, and NGOs, including the Indian organization UNI.

The Nature of the Brazilian State

Why, we may now ask, is the idea of Indian nations so problematic in Brazil? Why does it so offend state authorities?

When in 1980 the name Union of Indian Nations was first heard in Brazil, the government reacted immediately. Repression took various forms. One was the withdrawal of scholarships from Indians who studied in Brasília and the expressed order to send them back to their home areas. Some returned, others stayed in the capital city. With legal aid they later managed to recover their scholarships.

In a letter stamped "Confidential" to the Minister of the Interior, Mário Andreazza, and dated November 24, 1980, the strong man of the day, General Golbery do Couto e Silva, then chief of staff, wrote that the president of the republic had been informed that an entity to be named Union of Indian Nations was about to be formed (in fact, it had been created seven months earlier) and ordered that "profound studies" be carried out to examine the convenience and legality of such an entity, considering that the Indians were relatively incapable and as such were wards of the state. Referring to a note issued by the National Information Service's Central Agency, supposedly reporting the results of this "research" to the chief of staff, Couto e Silva declared in the same letter:

> These studies having been concluded and the inconvenience and juridical unfeasibility of the proposed entity having been determined . . . I hurry to transmit to Your Excellency, by order of the President of the Republic, the instruction that FUNAI abstain from any action or support that might stimulate the constitution of the so-called "Union of Indian Nations." (Juruna, Hohlfeldt, and Hoffmann 1982, 208–9)

The "profound studies" by the National Intelligence Service (SNI), the notorious agency that promoted repression of civil society during the military regime, mentioned the "grave inconvenience of indigenous nations being brought together under an entity whose organization is already being undertaken with the 'protection' of people reputedly dedicated to set the Indians against the indigenist policy defined by the Government." SNI also recommended an immediate revision of the 1973 Indian Statute in order to curb "situations as absurd as" the formation of a pan-Indian organization by "relatively incapable" Indians. This also would prevent an "obviously integrated" Indian from raising controversial issues in the press because this individual is unwilling to give up his "penal irresponsibility but wanting to leave the country to join a 'tribunal' abroad" (p. 210), a clear reference to the celebrated case of Mário Juruna at the Fourth Russell Tribunal (see Chapter 3). It is worth noting that, whether because of a Freudian slip or sheer inattention, the author of the SNI document referred to indigenous peoples as "indigenous nations." Perhaps because the major objection in that context was to the formation of a "union," the decried phrase seemed to go unnoticed. But, as often as not, official wrath targets the term nations itself.

A matter so ominous as to occupy the attention of the National Intelligence Service and top-level state executives certainly deserves to be looked into more closely. The question seems to hinge on the contradiction generated by the persistence of cultural differences within a state designed to level out such differences. The origin of this contradiction is perhaps to be found in the specific way in which the Brazilian republic was constituted.

After sixty-seven years of monarchy Brazil became a republic by means of an 1889 military coup in which the population took virtually no part.

> The Brazilian Republic was born amidst the agitation of speculators. . . .
> There was simply no concern for the public. What prevailed was a preda-

tory mentality, the spirit of capitalism without Protestant ethic. . . . The central point of the debate [around difficulties in installing the republican regime] hinged on private and public, individual and community. (J. Carvalho 1990, 30)

In fact, in a very short time Brazil, as an emerging nation, rehearsed the two political configurations Dumont (1971) has pointed out as characteristic of two modern European states—France and Germany—namely, the emphasis on the nation as a collection of individuals or, distinctly, as a collective individual. Torn between a liberal and a positivist ideology, the new republic put a much greater emphasis on the workings of the state than on civil society. Reis, inspired by Dumont's analysis, elegantly spells out the options open to Brazil at its birth as a republic:

> At the beginning, competition was in terms of positivism versus liberalism. The Army, as actor in the coup that ousted the Emperor, struggled to impose a unitary State form so as to maximize the chances of organizing society "from the top down." What they preached as a limited decentralization was in fact an enlightened despotism, perceived as the ideal strategy to organize society. . . .
> The most active defenders of liberalism were São Paulo coffee growers, the most dynamic exporting region of the period. . . . They fought for a wide decentralization of power through federalism and perceived private initiatives as the most adequate to promote the construction of nationality. (1988, 192)

Although the first republican constitution of 1891 had a liberal flavor, soon the balance of power tipped so drastically that Positivists *and* liberals found themselves advocating "a representation of the nation predominantly as a collective individual. . . . The collection of individuals proposed by liberalism had to be replaced by a collective individual, an organic national whole under State tutelage" (pp. 193, 194). And so it was and has been ever since. The 1964 military coup reinforced this authoritarian option. "Once again there was the insistence on the idea of strengthening the collective individual, the Fatherland (*Pátria*). We should all accept the necessary sacrifices toward the construction of 'Great Brazil' ('*Brasil Grande*')" (p. 197).

Such an ideological context has no room for hyphenated identities. There are no Japanese-Brazilians, no Italian-Brazilians, no African-Brazilians, no Native-Brazilians. There are only Brazilians at various stages of national accommodation (Ramos 1995c). The ultimate goal is to render sociocultural differences into "harmonious communion" with the national majority, as consistently advocated by indigenous legislation. From this perspective social diversity is not regarded as an enemy to be physically wiped out (as in Argentina) but rather as an immaturity to be outgrown.

No wonder Indian nations are unwelcome by state representatives. And not only the term nations but *peoples* is taboo in official circles. Peoples implies self-determination and autonomy, which make the word as unacceptable as nations. In fact, the change from "indigenous populations" to "indigenous peoples" in the text of Convention 169 of the International Labor Organization led Brazil to abstain from voting on it (Cordeiro 1993, 114). Perhaps the overwhelming political and symbolic power of the famous phrase "We the people" rings alarm in the ears of Brazilian authorities. If people always means what it means in the U.S. Constitution, beware! These authorities seem determined not to test the performative capacity of words to create reality (Austin 1962, 4–11). For them, people, nation, state, and sovereignty are all part of an inviolable package. To circumvent such truculent semantics of power, diluted terms like *populations* and *societies* have been proposed as substitutes (Cordeiro 1993, 117; M. Santilli 1996).

Of Indians and Kings
Alcida Rita Ramos

Originally published in the weekly column of the Brazilian Anthropological Association in *Jornal de Brasília,* April 15, 1983, p. 4.

While the king and queen of Sweden visited Brasília ten days ago, 450 representatives of more than fifty Indian nations convened in the capital city for the largest national meeting of their history. In bleak counterpoint to the pomp and circumstance of regal protocol, the Indians, having been denied adequate accommodations, roughed it at an improvised camping ground unfit to shelter them from the chilly and interminable rain that poured all night long. It even crossed some minds that the exaggerated police patrolling that filled the city had something to do with the Indian meeting under the pretext of protecting their Majesties and entourage. However, the Second National Meeting of Indigenous Peoples in Brazil was conducted in perfect orderliness, notwithstanding the tension created by nervous policemen at the bus station and by preventative security measures taken by officials of FUNAI and the Ministry of the Interior.

What brought so many Indians to Brasília was the need to make themselves visible and present at the headquarters of the federal government, this same government that, last year alone, perpetrated no less than six Executive and Legislative acts that directly affected the rights of indigenous peoples. From the proposal for the new Civil Code, which seeks to categorize Indians as "absolutely incapable," to the law project by Deputy Fagundes (PDS/Roraima) that aims at compulsorily "emancipating them," these official measures place at risk the very survival of the Indians as members of constituted societies. It is needless to stress that such acts have been taken in total disregard for the Indians' will. It was precisely to express their will by repudiating these acts that they came en masse to the National Congress.

If we compare this Second Meeting with the First that took place in June 1982, also in Brasília, we can see some substantial changes. There were 220 indigenous representatives at the First Meeting, as compared to the 450 of the Second. In 1982, they were lodged at the headquarters of CONTAG (Rural Workers Confederacy) where they held their assemblies and made their decisions, all done with minimal political visibility. In 1984, precariously camped at the Boy Scouts camping ground, they occupied rooms at the House of Representatives, while they made the headlines of the major newspapers in the country for nearly a week. What does this mean? What consequences do these changes have for the Indian cause and its future? I believe they point toward an irreversible maturation process in the awareness of indigenous populations at a political moment of the country when the channels for venting grievances are kept to a minimum. Furthermore, the more oppressive state and federal government measures are, the more strongly indigenous peoples will react in the defense of their own rights. The Indian movement has not stopped; quite the opposite: it shows itself to be increasingly autonomous, less patronized by whites, even by those who espouse the Indian cause as their own political agenda. The movement is expanding into an orderly and aware national association, despite all the legal, political, and strategic hurdles put in its way. Overcoming immense difficulties of access to means of transportation, communication, and other public resources, indigenous communities will continue to send their representatives to other meetings like this, whenever their rights are drastically threatened as they are now.

While the Swedish royal couple were treated with excessive diplomatic zeal, representatives of indigenous nations in the country received—as usual—a minimum of official attention. Obviously, it is not simply a matter of "the house saint that doesn't work miracles." The problem is that, because they are not officially recognized as nations, our indigenous societies have not earned the minimal respect owed to peoples who are different from us. It is as though Brazil were doing them a favor in conceding that these nations go on existing, forgetting that Brazil became a nation at the expense of other nations, taking away their lands, lives, and even their right to define themselves as indigenous. A little more of domestic diplomacy would do no one any harm.

Given the genesis of the Brazilian state, how could nations and peoples, thus interpreted, ever be tolerated, even as a rhetorical gesture? For Indian nations and peoples are anathema to the idea of a national collective individual; the specter of their conditions of possibility can only precipitate a head-on collision with the trustee-state. If state guardianship is a sort of tacit reality for the majority population, a rather subliminal discomfort, for the Indians it is a tangible fact, overtly established in the juridical figure of relative incapacity and its attendant state wardship.

Once more we come around to denuding Brazil as we peep through its indigenist keyhole. As we saw in Chapter 5 in regard to the pyrotechnics of pacification, the Indian issue has the capacity to expose the underbelly of Brazilian ethos, showing all its blemishes and refusing retouches. Whatever subtlety may exist in the state's treatment of common citizenry (labor movements, for instance, were repressed *but* in the name of public order rather than as an acknowledgment of nervousness by the state), such discretion is starkly absent when dealing with the subject of Indians.

An obvious comparison comes to mind. The contrast between a collective individual and a collection of individuals is also the contrast between the indigenous policy of Brazil and that of the United States. Whereas official Brazil, by viewing its Indians as irresponsible children, treats them with seduction and paternalism, the United States, liberal nation-state par excellence, had no problem recognizing Native Americans as constituting Indian nations. Needless to say, the North American state has shown itself to be no more benevolent for that. The U.S. government signed treaties with indigenous nations that invariably were broken; the United States declared war on its native peoples, and disrespect for Indian lives and customs was a constant element in the formation of the nation and in the configuration of its nationalism. The presence of indigenous *domestic dependent nations* "within the heart of the United States continues to challenge the premises and constrain the ambitions of American nationalism" (Strong and Van Winkle 1993, 18). In the end, no amount of liberalism, Positivism, or any other state organization can exempt New World nation-states from the crimes committed against those whose main historical blunder was to have arrived on the continent first.

Practice in Theory

If using the term nations is so onerous, why not simply drop it and adopt another concept, such as ethnic groups (*etnias*) when one wishes to refer to indigenous peoples within the national boundaries? Why do some defenders of the Indian cause, such as CIMI, insist on Indian nations even if this means infuriating nationalists who fear that national sovereignty is endangered by foreign greed in concert with the alleged domino effect of indigenous separatism? Because, I dare say, the concept of ethnic group has neither the political strength nor the ideological wallop that nations does. Ethnic groups are regarded as social excrescences that history forced upon the country and that must be leveled out and diluted into mainstream nationality. Running counter to this ethnic pasteurization, the indigenous as well as the indigenist movements need a banner worthy of their struggle for the recognition of the Indians' right to their ethnic differences. As a politically insipid term, *ethnic* has been relegated to the realm of culture. And as a rule culture is regarded as politically innocuous. Instead, the expression Indian nations has the force of a political tool. Borrowed from the modern Western world, nation is about the only semantic vehicle that aptly conveys the quest for legitimate social and cultural specificity.

The discussion of the various practical uses to which the term nation is put does not occur in an vacuum. Behind the ideological battles fought for it in Brazilian Indigenism is a long chronicle of its development, both in politics and in the academy. One major current proposes that nation and state are inextricably entwined. To Mauss, for instance, nation, properly used, is the European prototype of the Western nation-state, namely, "a society materially and morally integrated, with a stable, permanent central power, with defined boundaries, with a relative moral, mental, and cultural unity of its inhabitants which, consequently, conform to the state and its laws" (1956, 20). In a similar vein Weber declares: "A nation is a community which normally tends to produce a state of its own" (Gerth and Mills 1958, 176). As spelled out in more detail later, Brazilian officialdom is a pragmatic example of this conviction.

Another view of nation disengages it from state. A representative of this trend is Anthony Smith, who, in studying nationalism, distinguishes three terms — tribe, ethnicity, and nation — and who says that nation should not be confused either with the nation-state or with the "state-nation." Nations, says Smith, "are 'ethnie' which are economically integrated around a common system of labour with complementarity of roles, and whose members possess equal rights as citizens of the unmediated political community" (1983, 187). An example that comes to mind is the situation of indigenous peoples in the United States, where they are regarded as "domestic dependent nations." That also seems to fit the way CIMI regards Brazilian Indian nations.

A third path toward nation is traced by Benedict Anderson for whom nation is an imagined political community in the sense that its members "never know most of their fellow-members, meet them, or even hear of them, yet in the minds of each lives the image of their communion" (1991, 6). As we shall see later, the actions of certain indigenist NGOs in Brazil come close to being an exercise in creating Andersonian indigenous imagined communities.

Far from being consensual, in theory or in practice, the concept of nation has become a sort of laboratory in which political ideas and attitudes are constantly tested. Indeed, if there is a recurring feature in the definitions of nation, it is indefinition. Some examples are illustrative. Says Weber: "In so far as there is at all a common object lying behind the obviously ambiguous term 'nation,' it is apparently located in the field of politics" (Gerth and Mills 1958, 176). Nation, remarks Hobsbawm, "like a mollusk, once extracted from the hard shell of the 'Nation-state,' emerges as a distinctly vacillating form" (1991, 213). "There are, after all, many states which are not nations, and vice versa. Some writers, while recognizing this, confound the matter by using 'nation' to refer to what is here termed the 'nation-state'" (Grillo 1980, 6). "As I perceive it, the distinctive character of the national State is to be found precisely in the explicit reciprocity between State and nation, which makes a clear conceptual distinction between these two terms very difficult" (Reis 1988, 187).

If the concept of nation is slippery in its Western application, it becomes utterly opaque when used to designate non-Western political units. "*Nation*, when used to designate American native groups, is a hybrid form. . . . The term nation applies to Indians who only have in common the fact of being tropical forest peoples . . . living in adjoining territories, and being members of a federation for indigenous rights" (Jackson 1993, 219–20). Behind the indigenous quest for "nationhood" is an intense desire to be visible in the eyes of the majority society. What their nations often amount to is a politicized way of referring to culture. Indian cultures are becoming precious assets in the struggle to gain ethnic respectability (Jackson 1989, 1991; T. Turner 1991a; Fisher 1994). The opacity of meaning inherent in the idea of Indian nations is, like the Melanesian *kastom*, an "essential feature . . . which can never be questioned, lest the notion should lose its ideological properties" (Babadzan 1988, 205).

Perhaps the thorniest problem with the term nation is the multiplicity of meanings accumulated around it. There is, as it were, a "cumulative intention" (Ricoeur 1978, 60), an overload on the word that, because of an excess of meaning, ends up meaning nothing. The surplus meanings that impregnate the word nation lend themselves splendidly to ideological manipulations and serve as a mooring for clashing postures, as, for instance, between "developmentalists" and "humanists." To the former, Indian nation signals the danger of encouraging Indians to be against development and national sovereignty. To the latter, nation is a modern concept, an icon of legitimate difference, that one can use to defend both rights of citizenship and universal human rights. On the other hand, recent analyses have stressed the effect that uprooted human masses, sucked into the uncertainty of global migrations, have had on the destiny of nation in its modern conception. Bhabba, for example, states that the "nation fills the void left in the uprooting of communities and kin, and turns that loss into the language of metaphor." Furthermore, "the nation turns from being the symbol of modernity into becoming the symptom of an ethnography of the 'contemporary' within culture." It "becomes a liminal form of social representation, a space that is *internally* marked by cultural difference and the heterogeneous histories of contending peoples, antagonistic authorities, and tense cultural locations" (1990, 291, 298, 299).

Whether nation, as the outcome of ethnic politicization, resolves itself into state form (Grillo 1980, 7), once a collectivity is recognized as a nation, its ethnic identity (or majority's identity) becomes canonized. While the West promotes the concept of nation as something unitary and even universal, it also proposes that each nation is expected to be different from all others in its cultural content. "We speak of differences in 'national character,' and each European country entertains stereotypes about its neighbors" (Dumont 1986, 114). In this context internal differences are at best tolerated, hardly ever celebrated.

Nation, "a bloated category" as Geertz might say (1995, 23), is one of those words that have been smuggled into Brazilian indigenist rhetoric. In the United States the use of Indian nations served as a sort of password for the expropriation of territories by the nascent North American state, by means of the signing and breaching of treaties and declarations of war with the owners of those territories; as "defeated nations" Indian peoples had to surrender their lands to the victors. In Brazil the term indigenous nations in its recent sense grew out of the awareness that Indian cultures/ethnies, regarded as half-baked products of immature minds, had not enjoyed a minimum stature deserving of political credit. By thus reducing the Indians to the eternal condition of children, the Brazilian state killed two birds with one stone: it conquered them and spared itself a diplomatic burlesque show.

By now firmly set in the vocabulary of interethnic contact, the indigenous nation has been stripped of its conceptual complexities and used as a bad translation, an impoverished rendition similar to so many others that accompany the diffusion of certain concepts in contexts of poor communication. What come to mind are the simplifications that circulate in the dimness surrounding Indian peoples whose command of Portuguese is too limited to express complex areas of their own lives, and where they render, for example, their elaborate rituals as mere "games" (*brincadeiras*), thus unintentionally replicating regional patronizing. After all, "is not ethnocentrism always betrayed by the haste with which it is satisfied by certain translations or certain domestic equivalents?" (Derrida 1976, 123).

Theory in Practice

Amid the vast intellectual production around the word nation that abounds with conceptions and counterconceptions, it is possible to detect some correspondences between academic definitions of nation and specific kinds of praxis in Brazilian Indigenism. In pointing this out, I am not implying that the agents of interethnic politics necessarily and self-consciously searched sociological sources to sustain their positions, but I find the remarkable convergence between the virtuality of intellectual conception and the reality of actual practice worth noting.

Within the specific historical formation of Brazilian society regarding indigenous peoples, we can draw some connections between the main academic trends discussed earlier and the postures of certain political agents of Indigenism. In the first place, as already noted, we have Maussian or Weberian politicians who link nation to state in the magical phrase "national sovereignty." Second, we have the church proposing that nation does not rhyme with state and therefore that defending the idea that "we are peoples, we are nations" is just fine (CIMI 1987). And, third, we have NGOs that advocate self-determination of indigenous ethnic groups but a self-determination based on cultural politics rather than state politics. For their part the Indians, at least some, appear to use the term Indian nations much as nineteenth-century "Indianists" (José de Alencar, for instance, discussed in Chapter 2) appropriated indigenous symbols to mark off Brazilianness vis-à-vis Europe, that is, as a metaphor of alterity, a mere instrument with which to shape nationalism. The difference between today's Indigenous attitude and last century's Indianist ideals is that the former aspire to ethnicism rather than nationalism. As the term Indian nations circulates among its various users, whether intentionally or not, a wide gray area of incommunication sprawls across the entire field of interethnic relations.

If we find academic agreement about nation to be quite meager, what we see when we move to the political field of Indigenism is a veritable war of interpretations. We have already seen numerous examples of these semantic battles and more are to come.

Controlling the Collective Individual

In taking Indian nations to be a threat to national sovereignty, state authorities protest use of the phrase by non-Indian activists as a symbol of legitimate indigenous collectivities. To present Indian cases to international forums is to put the Brazilian state on the spot, which adds even more fuel to the already burning issue of Indian nations within the nation.

In its repudiation of the term Indian nations the statist faction of Brazilian nationalism is most explicit in the military discourse of national security, but it also blooms in the rhetoric of some civilian professionals. Recall political scientist Hélio Jaguaribe and his diatribe about the ignominious obsolescence that Indians represent to the country's future (Chapters 1 and 5). Not only did Jaguaribe object to the "idea of congealing man in the primeval state of his evolution" as something "cruel and hypocritical" but he also declared that "independent indigenous nations are dangerous" and that "national unity can be threatened if Brazilian underdevelopment is to persist, that is, if the Indians remain as Indians" (*Jornal da Ciência Hoje* 1994). Here the credo of national unity—the nation as a collective individual—is once more professed with the added twist that Brazil must get rid of its primeval human vestiges, lest it enter the third millennium sunk in underdevelopment. Like a contagious disease, the Indians' alleged backwardness must be eradicated if Brazil is to grow into a fully developed nation. The logic that guided the distinguished political scientist in bringing together threats to national unity, underdevelopment, and Indians has a name—racism. One only hopes that the November 1996 granting to Hélio Jaguaribe of the "National Order of Scientific Merit for his relevant contributions to Science and Technology" by the president of the republic, sociologist Fernando Henrique Cardoso, was based on more edifying subsidies to the aggrandizement of the nation than his dubious legacy to the Indian cause.

Indeed, one need not belong to the armed forces to say what lawyer Breno B. de Almeida Alves said at a 1991 meeting on human rights:

> If we examine the postulates of the modern State, we first have, as is well known, a territory; the Indians already have language, customs, and also a form of government. There is then the question of nation. If we add all this together, we will give them conditions to practically have a State within another State. . . . Nation . . . is the same as State. We will then have a very serious problem, for this expression "indigenous nation" began to be used by congressmen who spoke at the Committee meetings about "indigenous nation"; some legal diplomats . . . speak of indigenous nation. And this means great danger to us, for the Indians can actually seize this concept, once they know about it, and request independence of their "nation" based on the postulates of the modern State. (quoted in Cançado Trindade 1992, 237)

How could Indian nations become independent states if the lands they occupy are not even their own property? What are these "postulates of the modern State" that do not include total dominion over a clearly constituted territory? Furthermore, what would be the chances of indigenous peoples'—who live in small dispersed villages with nonhierarchical societies and nonmarket economies—bridging the gap between the politics of persuasion—with capillary dissemination of power throughout the community—and the politics of coercion—with a centralized apparatus for the use of force—before their guardian nation-state intervened? One can only conclude that a considerable amount of bad faith exists in these conspiratorial readings of the phrase Indian nations. Or perhaps it reflects the need to be in a permanent state (how multivocal can words be?) of alert against a potential internal enemy, the inevitable consequence of the guardian state's predicament of keeping its collective individual under constant surveillance.

Nevertheless, as Smith declares, the "object of nationalist devotion is the 'nation,' not the State—even when the two happen to coincide after independence in a mono-ethnic state" (1983, 178). But, given the authoritarian nature of the Brazilian state, it is not so much a devotion to nation qua organized civil society as it is a concern with the internal homogeneity of the country's population that moves officials to contest the designation of indigenous nations, lest they pass from word to action.

Pulled from its historical and multivocal context, the term Indian nation loses the implication both of state organization and of nationalism, for it is a concept that does not refer to nation-state, patriotism, national pride, or imagined communities stitched together either by a widespread "popular culture" (Rowe and Schelling 1991) or by some sort of "print capitalism" (Anderson 1991). In short, it is a nation without nation.

Sensing this slippage of meaning that in fact unbinds indigenous peoples from a nationalist destiny (although in the Australian case Beckett takes Aboriginality to be a type of nationalism [1988a, 2, 7]), the guardians of Brazilian nationalism attribute the danger represented by the phrase Indian nations not directly to the Indians but to domestic subversive forces or to foreign greed. The power of such forces would emanate from their capacity to manipulate the purported moral innocence and political naïveté of the Indians.

At the end of the second millennium one notes a new drift in the guardian state toward liberalism, which entails the transfer of social responsibilities from the state to the private sector. In September 1995, during an official visit to Europe, President Fernando Henrique Cardoso attempted to offset potential criticisms of his indigenist policy by European NGOs by making an appeal for them to turn into "neo-governmental organizations" (Folha de São Paulo 1995). Even if it is taken as a witticism or a rhetorically defensive gesture, this statement signals what may be a real trend of the Brazilian state toward private managerial indigenist policy. So far less noticeable than in other Latin American countries (Favre 1996, 119–24), the handing over of state obligations to private initiative is evidenced in Brazil in such cases as the Waimiri-Atroari health and education programs in what has been called "entrepreneurial Indigenism" (Baines 1993).

In Search of the Universal Collective

Back in 1980 NGOs could say:

> The rise of an indigenous counsciousness and still embryonic forms of organization at the national level must be emphasized. This conscious-ness is demonstrated by the founding in 1980 of associations comprised of Indians who no longer speak in the name of a tribe or local group, but about the historical rights of indigenous populations as a whole and who demand to no longer be treated as "controllable masses," as children or mentally retarded. They want to be treated as members of sovereign nations. (CEDI 1981, 1)

Since then nongovernmental organizations have been much more cautions in evoking the haunting specter of Indian nations. But the phrase is by no means defunct.

Although NGOs and Indian organizations have not hoisted the ban-ner of an indigenous nationalism, they come close, probably unknowingly, to some aspects of the concept of imagined communities. When Ander-son proposes that nationalism results from a collectivity's process of self-awareness, he emphasizes the need to recognize the imagined dimension of the sentiment of belonging to a nation. What feeds this imagining is what he calls "print capitalism," the broad and accessible dissemination of information acknowledged by all readers as a common denominator, even though these readers are not acquainted with all other readers. Apart from any disagreements one may have about Anderson's success in prop-erly demonstrating his perceptive insight, and the criticisms he received for privileging an alleged hegemony of writing to the detriment of the power of orality in popular culture (Rowe and Schelling 1991), one is convinced that the compound that cements community components into a nation is laid by indirect, insidious, and tentacular means. Hence one deduces that the exis-tence of nation and nationalism requires a good measure of anonymity and impersonality, even though informed by a consensual knowledge of what it is to be anonymous and impersonal. In other words, one needs to have the ideological figure of the *individual:* "the nation, in the precise modern sense of the term, and nationalism, as distinct from mere patriotism, are historically conjoined with individualism as a value" (Dumont 1986, 10).

In this sense, Indian nations, or, in the more politically palatable phrase, indigenous societies, cannot be mistaken for nations, because their communities are neither collective individuals nor collections of individu-als. Nor are they imagined but *lived,* that is, the connection between their members is not made by totally impersonal means such as the press, tele-vision, or mass-marketed literature, or by an individualistic ideology but by means of the possibility of face-to-face contact between all members, who have a common set of traditions and beliefs. Here impersonality and anonymity are neither nourished nor desired. Instead of print capitalism or popular culture, we would have a sort of *consensual orality*.

Against this traditional background, pro-Indian NGOs seem to be determined to build a bridge between ethnic holism and the Western individualism responsible for the formulation of universal human rights. One glimpses a trend toward the creation of an imagined field of indigenous common destiny. It occurs in the scenario of a pan-Indian movement, particularly in the promotion of national conventions of indigenous leaders, in the circulation of films and videos through Indian villages and even widely separated societies (Gallois and Carelli 1992; T. Turner 1991a), and in the growing tendency to create indigenous entities for the defense of human rights. Both church and lay organizations have been crucial agents in the construction of this imagined domain. Being imagined, however, does not automatically turn this field of contact politics into the proposition of a potential nation, for it gathers together such a diversity of languages, customs, and traditions that it amounts to little more than a patchwork conveniently sown together for the specific purpose of defending Indian rights. It would be a kind of political bricolage, a strategic device limited to managing gains and losses on the battlefield of interethnic relations. External agents tend to induce the rise of a collective indigenous imagination where either none exists or it has different, nonpolitical contours. In such a context the idea of nation as "a community of people" (Seton-Watson 1977, 1) becomes the suitable model for outlining communities in the process of being politically awakened. Let us briefly examine the case of the Yanomami to better understand the details of this process.

About twenty thousand Yanomami live in both Brazil and Venezuela; this human population is sufficiently large to inhibit face-to-face contact among all its members. Although virtually the entire Yanomami territory is covered with a vast network of trails and streams that connects all villages, this connection is like the links in a continuous chain—the last link has little to do with the first (Ramos 1996a). Lacking a global means of communication, the Yanomami make contact in portions, as concentric circles of densities of information that vary as one leaves the known and enters the imagined. But who is included in this *imagined*? They are communities distant enough to discourage direct contact but close enough for other Yanomami to know the details of their lives, personal names, and the like. Individuals maintain a system of symbolic relationships with these communities; the imaginary is the propelling force. I am referring to the symbolic system of animal doubles, alter egos, and individual totemism, as Durkheim would say, and as studied by Yanomami ethnographers (Lizot 1984; Albert 1985; Ramos 1995b). By means of this belief complex, communities that are far apart in space are inextricably bound to each other with little involvement otherwise. Each village cluster has an animal double that lives in another remote village cluster. This sort of metaphysical trade-off sets the limits of the relevant social universe. Thus each community has a stock of other communities with which it maintains imagined relationships, but the stock is never large enough to include all twenty-thousand Yanomami.

It is we, the outsiders, who have the opportunity to perceive this cultural matrix as a whole, where the pattern repeats itself in clusters, eventually embracing the entire Yanomami territory. It is also we, as external agents, who, eager to guarantee the Yanomami's proper land rights, stir their imagination in the direction of an imagined unity by displaying photographs, videos, and other devices meant to arouse a common consciousness. *Yanomami* is a word invented by outsiders to encompass a totality that so far has been of little interest to most Yanomami. Although they are perfectly aware of the family and linguistic resemblances among the various subgroups, they still prefer to talk about themselves and others as Sanumá, Shiriana, Shamatari, Yanomam, and so on.

Since the mid-1980s a ruthless gold rush has brought Yanomami people from all corners of their indigenous territory into contact with each other. As devastating epidemics raged through the forest, hundreds of Indians had to be removed to the town of Boa Vista for treatment (Ramos 1995a, 1995b). At the Casa do Índio, a combination of hospital and hostel, Yanomami men and women endured being tossed together with total strangers (who therefore were potential enemies) whose languages they could understand, which made them all the more suspicious. The Casa do Índio has thus been a laboratory for a pan-Yanomami consciousness. The result has not been encouraging to those who hope to see a great Yanomami "nation" rise up from the harmonious realization of a collective self. For the heterogenous Yanomami patients at Casa do Índio meet each other, get to know each other, often hate each other, ward each other off, and go on preserving the distance they have always had between them, oblivious of any quest for political unity.

Even so, the military has nominally cited the Yanomami as a paradigmatic example of the danger that Indian nations represent. In proposing the Calha Norte Project (see Chapter 8), the military argued against the demarcation of a continuous Yanomami Indian area because, with the Indians living on both sides of the international border, it might lead outside operators to gather up all Indians from both countries into a "Yanomami State." "Statists" that they are, the designers of the project made a classic presupposition in the realm of nationalism: when a people has a common language, customs, and traditions associated with a territory, they are a nation, and when a nation exists, so does a state. This position presumes as fact an "aspiration of the colonised population for self-government of the new political community whose boundaries were established by the coloniser" (Smith 1983, 176). Whether consciously or not, these military men lend substance to a fiction. In turn, their opponents, the "ethnicists," "see the nation as a large, politicized ethnic group, defined by common culture and alleged descent" (p. 176).

We might say, as Clastres (1978) did about the extinct Tupinambá, that the structure of indigenous societies in Brazil is incompatible with a state form of government, that Indian nations, in and of themselves, have no potential, and probably no desire, to turn into states or promote an indigenous nationalism. In the political economy of interethnic affairs the absence of minimal conditions—societies demographically minute, stripped of territorial ownership, politically divested of power, socially decentralized—precludes the rise of ethnic separatism, as feared by the guardians of the Brazilian state. It is highly unlikely that all Indians—or all Yanomami, for that matter—would unite in an indigenous nationalism against the majority population. Consider, for instance, the intense "ethnic soldiering," in Whitehead's expression (1990), of the first centuries of Brazil as a colony, when different Tupinambá subgroups battled each other as allies of the Portuguese, the French, or the Dutch. In more recent times the failure of the only indigenous venture in the realm of centralization, the Union of Indian Nations, surely tells us something of what Clastres characterized as the rejection of the One in favor of the Multiple.

The concept of ethnie may not be sufficiently visible and potent to propel the Indian cause to the level of great national problematics, such as the case of trade unions, entrepreneurial organizations, or nationwide landless peasant movements. But nation, conceptually troublesome and politically explosive as it is in the Brazilian context, in certain historical conjunctures seems to do more harm than good, such as the fracas in the Constitutional Assembly in the 1980s. Overflowing with meaning, the concept of nation ends up emptying itself out, especially when it becomes a political metaphor, as indigenous nations is. If, on the one hand, the plainness of ethnie keeps the plight of indigenous peoples in a political semiobscurity, on the other hand, the complexity of nation threatens to obscure the issue with a dazzling light that exposes the Indian movement to all sorts of opportunism. Such is the dilemma that entangles the Indians in a semantic labyrinth constructed by a world reluctant to recognize, much less respect, nuances of cultural diversity.

7

Development Does Not Rhyme
with Indian, or Does It?

The trap of development could not be better sketched than in the following vignette by Andrés Nuningo Sesén, a Huambisa Indian from Peru:

> In my homeland I used to calmly wake up in the morning. I didn't have to worry about clothing because my house was isolated, surrounded by my gardens and the forest. I would quietly admire the immense nature of the Santiago River while my wife lit the fire. I would bathe in the river and at daybreak go off in the canoe to bring some *cunchis* or catch some *mojarras*. Without worrying about time, I would return home. My wife would joyfully welcome me, cook the fish, and give me my *cuñushca* as I warmed myself by the fire. We would chat, my wife, my children and I till we had no more to say. Then she would go to the garden and my son and I to the forest. While walking in the bush I would teach my son about nature, about our history, everything according to my taste and the teachings of our ancestors. We would hunt and cheerfully go back home with the game. My wife would happily welcome us, having just bathed and combed her hair, with her new *tarache*. We would eat until we were full. I would rest if I wished, otherwise, I would visit my neighbors and make crafts; soon my relatives would arrive and we would drink *masato*, tell tales and, if everything was all right, we would end up dancing all night.
>
> Now with development things have changed. There are morning hours for labor. We work the rice fields till late and return home with nothing. My wife, grumpy, *con las justas,* gives me a dish of *yuca* with salt. We hardly talk, my son goes to school where they teach him things about Lima. After harvest, a thousand squabbles to earn a pittance. Everything goes to the truck driver, to the shopkeepers. All I take home are some little cans of tuna fish, a few packages of noodles, but what is worst is that this type of agriculture eats up communal land and soon there will be none left. I can see all my fellow countrymen rummaging all the garbage dumps in Lima.

When I was in Bogotá I wanted to know how the millionaires lived and they told me that the millionaires have their isolated houses amidst beautiful landscapes; they calmly get up in the morning to admire the landscape, bathe and return with breakfast ready waiting for them, and as there is no hurry, they chat leisurely with their wives and children. The children go to a select school where they learn according to their fathers' tastes. The man strolls through his property and shoots at some birds or goes fishing, and on his return he finds the table set and the lady well groomed for lunch. He sleeps after the meal or does some painting or any other hobby such as carpentry. Then he goes out for a drink with friends and, if they want, they can dance as much as they feel like.

Then I ask myself: Does this all mean that I and all my fellow countrymen will end up in the garbage dumps so that one or two millionaires can have the life we used to have? What is this about development? (1991)

This Peruvian Huambisa is not the only one baffled by development, as the vast literature dedicated to both its virtues and evils attests. Is it totally incompatible with tribal ways of living, or can development be extended to non-Western societies without causing social and cultural havoc? Is it fair to impose it on indigenous peoples, or is it unfair to leave them out of its benefits?

At one end of the spectrum we have the critical position that perceives development as a particular cultural product of a particular type of society, a product that does not travel well cross-culturally. Perrot's commentary on the 1986 United Nations' declaration on the right to development is worth examining. The declaration defines development as "an economic, social, cultural, and political global process which aims at continuously improving the well-being of a whole population and all its individuals, on the basis of their active, free, and meaningful participation in development and their equitable sharing of the benefits that may result." Perrot compares this definition to "a pilotless airplane, one does not know where it came from nor where it will land." The vagueness and circularity of the definition omits the vast arena of conflicting interests that characterize development issues. Perrot continues:

> The impression of irreality that oozes out of the various [Declaration] articles, an irreality accentuated by the frequent use of tautology, says more about the rhetorical constraints in writing a text intended to be approved by the United Nations member-states than about the way in which a group, an individual, or a state will be able to exercise this right to development. The performative value of the Declaration is limited to its incantatory and declamatory character. (1991, 7)

Because development is a cultural artifact, a feature of the Western industrial world, it requires a certain background to make it both intelligible and desirable. To equate the right to self-determination with the right to development, as the declaration implies, is at the very least ethnocentric. A "founding myth of the modern West," development should be seen, Perrot emphasizes, as

> a set of practices based on a specific worldview associated with the history of industrialized nations according to the following principles: the atomized individual as the "social" reference unit; domestication and exploitation of natural resources without regard for their renewal; profit; world market; economic Rationality; Cartesian thinking; a linear, objective concept of time; a mythification of science and technique. (1991, 6)

Furthermore, "development appears as the broadest and most encompassing, dispossessing, and expropriating enterprise to the benefit of dominant minorities there ever was. In this sense, 'good' development cannot exist." Therefore, "to speak of auto-centered development or ethnodevelopment is a contradiction in terms" (pp. 5, 6).

At the other end of the spectrum we have the World Bank's position, according to which development is not only inevitable but can be beneficial to indigenous peoples if some protective measures are taken:

> It is not Bank policy to prevent the development of areas presently occupied by such peoples. However, the proposed Bank policy would assist projects within areas used or occupied by such tribal people, only if it is satisfied that (a) best efforts have been made to obtain the voluntary, full and conscionable agreement (i.e., under prevailing circumstance and customary laws) of the tribal people or that of their advocates, and (b) that the project design and implementation strategy are appropriate to meet the special needs and wishes of such peoples. Assuming that tribal people will either acculturate or they will disappear, there are two basic design options: the Bank can assist the Government either with acculturation, or with protection in order to avoid harm. (1981, 1)

This World Bank document makes no secret that development hurts "tribal" peoples, but, lamentably, it cannot be avoided. All one can do is try to make it hurt as little as possible. "Mitigation of the destructive effects of development on tribal populations will require implementation of measures toward" the observance of certain requirements that in fact amount to, in Perrot's words, a contradiction in terms. For how does the bank expect that "protection of tribal areas, resources and economic potential; . . . ensuring their cultural integrity and the maintenance of their cultures to the extent they so desire" will be achieved in face of such massively intrusive development projects as road construction, hydroelectric plants, mining operations, or colonization schemes? Moreover, how serious can the bank be about "ensuring their cultural integrity" and the like, if it declares itself willing to help governments with the "acculturation, or with protection" of indigenous peoples affected by development? In short, the money lenders get to decide whether an indigenous way of life will survive or not. Leaving aside the arrogance of such proposition, what strikes the reader most is the ethical ambivalence of the bank's document. Caught between the need to be politically correct and the drive to expand capitalism, which is, after all, its raison d'être, the World Bank seeks to have the ethical cake and eat it too. It is a typical example of "a 'humanist' discourse within a 'managerial' framework" (Viveiros de Castro and Andrade 1988, 8). The bank is willing to put considerable sums of money in the hands of national governments for demarcation of Indian lands and other "protective" measures, but it will not refuse financing for the sake of indigenous well-being alone. For this to happen a project will have to first prove itself uneconomical.

Adding insult to injury, the bank's 1981 statement foresees the exploitation not only of indigenous natural resources but of their cultural resources as well. Once this is accomplished, they might as well "acculturate." Indigenous knowledge as commodity has become a recurring theme in Western economic calculations, and the World Bank's statement epitomizes it: "Tribal groups can make valuable contributions to the wider society, especially to the national society's knowledge of socioeconomic adaptations to fragile ecosystems. At the same time, tribal populations cannot continue to be left out of the mainstream of development" (p. 3). Is a trade-off implied in the juxtaposition of these two sentences? Give us your knowledge and we will give you development? No, it seems more like unequal exchange: you cannot escape development anyway, so you might as well be reasonable and let us have your ecological know-how. Behind the apparently enlightened effort by one of the icons of capitalism (Rich 1986) one perceives touches of the old imperialist habit of trading raw materials for industrialized goods.

The immediate question that comes to mind is why indigenous peoples must be engulfed by development. That the World Bank, the epitome of development, foresees the entire planet covered with development comes as no surprise. But NGOs seem to hold onto the inevitability of the spread of development as the major justification for their existence. Some go to the trouble of providing "field guides" for Indian protectors-developers (Beauclerk, Narby, and Townsend 1988).

Bodley, for one, questions this inevitability and adds: "The incorporation of tribal peoples into national economies with the loss of tribal self-sufficiency results from specific national policies. It is not a 'natural, inevitable process' that cannot be avoided" (1988, 412). He procee_ reject what he calls the inevitability argument:

> It is expressed clearly on page 1 of the policy, as follows: "Assuming that tribal cultures will either acculturate or disappear . . ." This phrase is strikingly reminiscent of the words of Herman Merivale . . . the English expert on colonial policy, who declared in the mid-nineteenth-century, "Native races must in every instance either perish, or be amalgamated with the general population of their country." Implicit in this is the notion that industrial civilization is superior and has a moral right to incorporate what it considers to be obsolete cultural systems. The World Bank explicitly states that "tribal populations cannot continue to be left out of the mainstream of development" . . . but we are not told why this is the case. . . . The real danger is that if the inevitability assumption becomes the basis of World Bank policy it will be self-fulfilling and will preclude the possibility of tribal independence. (p. 408)

Bodley summarizes the World Bank's assumptions in four main points:

1. All tribals will inevitably be developed.
2. Development will benefit tribal peoples.
3. Tribals will be allowed a choice.
4. Tribals must become ethnic minorities. (p. 407)

He strongly objects to the last assumption and charges: "Replacing tribal culture with ethnic identity by forcing development on unwilling recipients is in direct opposition to Article 21 of the U.N. Declaration on Racism and Racial Discrimination of 1978, and it clearly opposes the spirit of the U.N. 1948 Declaration of Human Rights" (p. 410).

An intermediate position, perhaps best represented in a series of articles by Sahlins (1988, 1992, 1993), grants native peoples a much more active role in their destinies vis-à-vis development than either Perrot or the World Bank is prepared to allow. "There is a sense of the people's passivity in the received anthropological concepts of 'diffusion,' 'cultural borrowing,' or the 'acculturation' of indigenous societies by expanding European regimes" (Sahlins 1992, 16). Yet, in the dialectics of political economy, what travels from center to periphery is bound to suffer a number of transformations unforeseen in the original plan. How peoples on the fringes of capitalism receive and react to development is something no amount of diplomatic or financial rhetoric is capable of quite controlling. "Around much of the world . . . the universalizing cultural project of the West does not succeed so well" (Sahlins 1993, 18). The twists and turns of cultural adaptation have, to paraphrase Pascal, reasons unknown to capitalist rationality. In the process of absorbing the shock waves of the world system, non-Western peoples who survive the biological onslaught of Western diseases have shown a great deal of imagination and cultural vitality. "At the bottom line, *kastom* Melanesians distinguish the social model of development from the objects produced according to that model. They do not believe in the moral virtues of the Western social model, development society is not for them. Nevertheless, the objects are there, fascinating. . . . But, and this is their wisdom, they do not look for these objects because they judge them to be necessary; they look for them as a useless luxury," as an exoticism (Bonnemaison 1991, 17). How else, asks Sahlins, "can the people respond to what has been inflicted on them except by devising on their own heritage, acting according to their own categories, logics, understandings?" (1993, 18). Confronted with imposed changes, indigenous peoples have found in their traditional cultures the inspiration they need to innovate, sometimes amid the most grueling conditions of deprivation. Furthermore, culture change, rather than being a sign of ethnic collapse, can be an instrument for them to exercise their "capacity to freely determine their choices" (Descola 1982, 221).

In this chapter I shall focus mainly on three questions. First, in the context of Brazil's last economic frontier, Amazonia, is it possible for Indian minorities to survive development's steamrolling expansion? Second, if they survive, will they become integrated into national economy? And, third, if integrated, can they retain their ethnic identity? In examining these issues one is led to the conclusion that, at least in the context of current national policies of development, incorporation of Indian peoples in the national, or world, economy is not necessarily incompatible with the maintenance of their cultural and ethnic identity, transformed as it may be, for it takes a lot more than a commodity market to wipe out millenarian traditions.

Five Hundred Years of "Development"

Among the country's population, surely Brazilian Indians have paid the highest price for developmental aggression. Given that the quest for economic expansion is much older than Europe's "New World," Brazil's Portuguese discoverers did not take long to get over their initial disappointment at failing to find mountains of gold and turn their eyes to the lush Atlantic forest that covered the shores of the new continent. Within a few months after that momentous April 21, 1500, the Portuguese inscribed indigenous peoples into the hard work of brazilwood extraction that channeled high profits to the crown; mining and agricultural labor came later, along with all the activities that went into the construction of the new colony.

For nearly five hundred years national expansion has consistently killed Indians in Brazil. From an estimated population of more than five million in 1500, they are now fewer than 300,000. What has produced such extermination is well known from the writings of Ribeiro (1970), Hemming

(1978), Moreira Neto (1988), Monteiro (1994), Schwartz (1995), and Vainfas (1995), among others. The deadly effects of recurring epidemics and the opening up of new economic frontiers—be they cattle ranching in various parts of the country, extraction of forest products such as rubber and other Amazonian products, agricultural activities such as sugar plantations in the northeast, or coffee in the south—have always resulted in the decimation and, in many cases, the total extinction of entire Indian groups. In the twentieth century alone, at least eighty-seven indigenous peoples have vanished (Ribeiro 1970, 238).

Refuge areas, which in the first centuries of colonization meant virtually the entire country (excluding the narrow coastal strip), have shrunk dramatically in the past two hundred years, leaving the Indians with increasingly less space in which to lead their lives unaffected by European colonization. As Europeans expanded the colony's boundaries, Indians fled farther inland. Wherever it went, European expansion left in its wake whole indigenous societies either exterminated or so decimated as to be socially unviable. On the coast most of the Tupi-speaking peoples were killed off during the first two centuries of Brazil's existence. In Amazonia groups that lived along the main rivers, such as the affluent Manao, were wiped out in the same span of two hundred years. But in the second half of the twentieth century development reached unprecedented proportions because of a policy of integrating the fringes of the nation, as Amazonia is regarded, into more effective state control.

The Roaring Seventies

During the military administrations of Emílio Médici and Ernesto Geisel in the 1970s, Amazonia was the target of large-scale economic schemes, such as road construction, settlement projects, mining, hydroelectric works, and cattle ranching. This is the region with the most Indian groups in the country. Many were suddenly exposed for the first time to Western diseases, loss of land, and social disruption. Thousands of workers in poor health entered the territory of populations with no immunity to even the common cold. The result was an alarmingly high rate of epidemic diseases such as measles and malaria. Previously uncontacted Indians had their first experience with civilization by means of massive decimation delivered to them by uncontrolled pathogenic transmission. Completely unprepared to deal with uncontacted Indians, workers brought along not only a devastating death rate but also prostitution and begging among people who just a few months earlier had been leading their traditional lives, oblivious to the approaching turmoil that would turn their existence upside down.

Médici's highway program directly affected more than 160 indigenous peoples, or more than 90 percent of their total number in Amazonia, as roads cut through Indian lands in preparation for the vertiginous advance of large-scale colonization (Goodland and Irwin 1975, 74). Less than twenty months after the Cuiabá-Santarém road construction teams arrived at Panará (Krenakarore) lands, the Panará's estimated population of four hundred was reduced to seventy-nine people (Heelas 1978, 25–27). The Parakanã were "pacified" while the Transamazon Highway was being built, which meant the death of 45 percent of their population in twelve months (Bourne 1978, 233). The Yanomami who were affected by the Perimetral Norte Highway in Roraima suffered in one year the loss of about 22 percent of the population of the four villages first exposed to road construction; 50 percent of the population of another four villages farther up the road died in a measles epidemic in 1978 as a direct consequence of the road (Ramos 1979).

Mining operations, which experienced a boom in the 1980s, produced disruptive effects even in the 1970s. Indians of the Aripuanã area in Rondônia and Mato Grosso bore the brunt of exploitation of cassiterite and other minerals abundant in their territory. The Cintas Largas, Suruí, and other groups of the region had their lands drastically reduced, while their populations plummeted in consequence of the spread of contagious diseases. Already in those early years the Yanomami were feeling the effect of incipient mining in the central Surucucus region in Roraima. No sooner had a mineral survey been done in the area than about five hundred miners began to illegally extract cassiterite. According to subsequent reports, the Indians were suffering with venereal diseases and tuberculosis (Albert and Zacquini 1979, 106). Following the removal of the miners, large-scale government-approved exploitation of minerals at Surucucus was being considered; a preliminary survey was conducted in 1975 (K. Taylor 1979, 65–66; Albert and Zacquini 1979, 107–108). In addition to the Surucucus and Aripuanã operations, at least three other major projects were mining in Amazonia, all of them benefiting from U.S. financing and technical assistance. These projects affected at least eight Indian groups (Pinto 1980).

Fiscal incentives by the Brazilian government in the mid-1970s encouraged a number of national and international companies to initiate large-scale agribusiness in the Amazon. These operations encroached upon the following indigenous groups: nine Apalaí and several Kayapó villages in the state of Pará; the Tembé–Urubu Kaapor Indian reserve in Maranhão; several Shavante villages; the northern groups of the Xingu park; the Tapirapé Indians; and the Araguaia Indian Park in Mato Grosso and Goiás (Davis 1977). Agribusiness projects also affected the Yanomami. In the Mucajaí River valley the Indians lost nearly half the area assigned them by the government to a large state agricultural scheme in Roraima (K. Taylor 1979). The villages in the Apiaú River area were totally uprooted as their land was taken over by a colonization project. Expelled from their territory, the Apiaú Yanomami dispersed, with some roaming about other villages while others moved to the newly created town of Alto Alegre.

One of the largest colonization enterprises in Amazonia was the Polonoroeste Project that straddled the states of Mato Grosso and Rondônia. The World Bank financed 35 percent of about U.S.$1.4 billion (CEDI 1982b, 25–26; Mindlin 1984, 1985, 1987, 1990; Junqueira and Mindlin 1987; Leonel 1990; Mindlin and Leonel 1991). Planned in the 1970s but begun in 1982, the Polonoroeste was designed to "rationalize" the settlement and productivity of the dense stream of migrants flowing into the area. Rondônia experienced a population increase in the order of 11 percent per year between 1970 and 1980 because of migrations from other parts of the country (Mueller 1980). The plan was to open and pave a network of roads and intensify agriculture by means of a massive colonization program, all backed up by mitigating measures, such as health care, land tenure legalization, ecological preservation, and protection of indigenous peoples (Mindlin 1990, 87). But the outcome has fallen far short of the original promises and expectations:

> Generalized deforestation tolerated and even encouraged by the National Indian Foundation (FUNAI) in collusion with logging enterprises; Indian lands invaded by big landowners or landless peasants; massacres of isolated Indians such at those of the Omeré River; clandestine mining in indigenous territories with the complicity of FUNAI agents such as that among the Cintas Largas; Indians killed by epidemics and lack of medical assistance; armed conflicts and murders. . . . These are but a few examples of what the Polonoroeste and Brazilian economic growth has meant to the Indians. (p. 87)

About thirty Indian groups—approximately eight thousand people in fifty-eight villages—lived in the area covered by Polonoroeste. Degree of contact with national society varied from group to group, but all suffered loss of land (CEDI 1982b). The Nambiquara were particularly disrupted by outsiders' occupation of the Guaporé valley. With the opening of the Cuiabá–Porto Velho road in the early 1960s, the invasion of Nambiquara lands was quick and devastating. From 1968 to 1979 no fewer than twenty-one companies established agribusiness enterprises in the valley. From an estimated population of 20,000 at the beginning of the twentieth century, the Nambiquara were reduced to 650 in 1980, 250 of whom lived in the valley (Carelli and Severiano n.d.). An alternative route to the Cuiabá–Porto Velho road, under construction in 1983, passed through the homeland of four groups that had been granted reserves and within a short distance of three others. Scarcely ten years after coming into permanent contact with national society, the Guaporé Nambiquara found themselves living in a "neon jungle" (D. Price 1981, 26).

The 1970s were the decade of the Brazilian economic miracle (Davis 1977), when the military regime attracted huge amounts of foreign funding for megaprojects in Amazonia. Severe droughts were devastating the northeast, and the chronic poverty of that region was treated as a mere consequence of bad climate. To solve the problem of peoples without water the Médici government promoted the exodus of thousands of northeastern families to the land of water—Amazonia. Creation of the short-lived *agrovilas* along the Transamazon Highway was part of this colonization project, which had the extra advantage of contributing to the National Integration Plan (Plano de Integração Nacional, PIN), a grandiose nationalist scheme for the geopolitical control of the Amazon. In addition to contributing to Brazil's gigantic foreign debt, the miracle decade left a trail of Indian casualties (Ramos 1980c, 1984b) and plenty of regional strife. "The net effect," says Nugent, "and in spite of intra-regional differences, is the creation of a Hobbesian playground in which, to no great surprise, the big, bad and ugly control the ball, and it requires an act of faith to distinguish the forces of law and order from the criminal fraternity" (1990, 13).

The Bright Golden Eighties

While agricultural ventures such as the Polonoroeste and the Plan for the Protection of Environment and Indigenous Communities (PMACI) continued to be financed by multilateral banks such as the World Bank and the Interamerican Development Bank (CEDI 1991a, 84–92), hydrolectric schemes and gold mining became the main development features of the 1980s. The mid-decade transition from military to civilian government made virtually no difference in the pace of colossal expropriation of indigenous natural resources. But whereas dam construction has been part of state policy, gold mining has been characterized by the massive and turbulent flow of private individuals to gold sites in various parts of Amazonia, particularly in Indian territories. Both hydroelectric dams and gold panning have had immensely disastrous effects on indigenous peoples.

In the 1970s a joint Brazil-Paraguay venture, the mammoth Itaipu Dam, "the biggest hydroelectric power plant in the world (!)" as official propaganda puts it, flooded fertile lands of both peasants and Indians in the southern state of Paraná, not to mention the submerging of the spectacular Sete Quedas Falls. Part of a dispute between Brazil and Argentina over impoverished Paraguay, the Itaipu Dam was as much an economic venture as a geopolitical investment by the military rulers of Brazil in the 1960s and 1970s. Hence, the bigger the better, even though other possibilities had been presented, including a series of small dams much less harmful in social and ecological terms (CPT n.d.). Itaipu was designed to generate 12,600 megawatts at a cost, calculated in 1979, of more than U.S.$10 billion (Aspelin and Coelho dos Santos 1981, 154). The estimated forty thousand people affected by the dam included thirteen Ñandeva-Guarani families whose 1,500-hectare territory was flooded; they were moved to a 231-hectare patch of land in the security area of the dam. They still face a long, drawn-out struggle for proper resettlement (CEDI 1982b, 60–62, 1983, 84–85; F. Ricardo 1991).

In the mid-1980s Eletrobrás, the state company in charge of the energy sector, devised the National Plan for Electric Power, which contemplated the building of more than 165 hydroelectric dams by the year 2010. An update foresees the hydroelectric project extended to the year 2015 (CEDI 1991a, 83). Many of these dams are designed for Amazonia. To put this plan into practice Eletrobrás will need an annual investment of about U.S.$5 to $7 billion, mainly financed by the World Bank. If all these projects come into being, twenty-eight power dams

> will affect forty-one indigenous areas in the next decades. [They] . . . will suffer the direct consequences of these dams—with flooding, construction, installations, power lines—or indirectly with changes in water level, fauna, and flooding of Indian trails affecting distances and means of transportation. Among these projects is the Xingu Hydroelectric Complex which is a veritable deluge; it includes six dams, five on the Xingu River and one on its tributary, the Iriri River, directly affecting, that is, flooding, parts of twelve indigenous territories (F. Ricardo 1991, 77–78)

Inevitably, "the Juruna, Arara, Kararaô, Xikrin, Asuriní, Araweté, and Parakanã will face a substantial escalation in the process of confinement and land expropriation, population decrease, political subjugation, and planned socio-cultural destruction that has affected them since the end of the sixteenth century" (Viveiros de Castro and Andrade 1988, 7). As it is, two large dams completed in the 1980s, namely, Tucuruí in the state of Pará and Balbina in the state of Amazonas, have already disrupted the lives of hundreds of Indians.

The Parakanã were perhaps the hardest hit. While their more isolated communities were being contacted for the first time by FUNAI, the Transamazon Highway cut through their lands in 1974 and in 1975, and construction began on the Tucuruí Dam, "the largest ever built in tropical forest" (Bunker 1985, 88). Flooding came in the early 1980s. Distress was made worse by the multiple displacements forced on these Indians, first to keep away from the road, then to keep away from the flood. Not surprisingly, in one year of contact with the road the population of the Paranati village, moved five times from 1971 to 1983, plummeted from an estimated two hundred to a low of eighty-two people, that is, a loss of 59 percent, before they began to recover demographically in the 1980s (CEDI 1985a, 20–28). The estimated total population of the three extant villages was about 350 in 1984. After an agreement was signed between FUNAI and the Vale do Rio Doce state company in charge of the Carajás Mining and Railroad Project, which also affected the Parakanã, World Bank funds were used for land demarcation and health services for these Indians. But the Parakanã were not the only people who lost their lands under the dam's water. About four thousand regional families had to be removed under uncertain circumstances regarding proper resettlement (Mougeot 1988, 238–40).

The huge Carajás industrial complex is in fact the greatest beneficiary of the power generated by the Tucuruí Dam. "Tucuruí . . . was installed without any consultation whatsoever, as an element of the Greater Carajás program—a large mining, metallurgic, and agricultural project with much support from transnational interests—because the government decided to attract private investments for the supply of subsidised electric power to metal (particularly aluminum) industries" (Coelho dos Santos and Nacke 1990, 58; see also Arnt and Schwartzman 1992, 215-28). The Carajás-Tucuruí scheme has also affected the Gaviões, Suruí, Guajajara, Amanayé, and Anambé Indians in the states of Pará and Maranhão where the hydroelectric-railroad-mining complex is located (Aspelin and Coelho dos Santos 1981, 50–93; CEDI 1982b, 43).

Balbina, the power dam built by Eletronorte, a branch of Eletrobrás, on Waimiri-Atroari land in the state of Amazonas, turned out to be a glaring engineering fiasco:

> Balbina is considered to have one of the worst results in the use of hydraulic resources in the country, both for the environment and for the production of electric power; it flooded 2,360 hectares, equivalent to the Tucuruí Reservoir, but only produces 250 MW as against 7,300 MW of Tucuruí. Moreover, the reservoir is shallow, with an average depth of 7.4 meters, and as little as four meters in a 800 square kilometer area. "There are more than fifteen hundred islands within the reservoir," says Inpa researcher Philip Fearnside, which prevents water circulation. At the same time, aquatic plants and rotten trees which were not removed exude an "acid broth" which may corrode the turbines. (F. Ricardo 1991, 77)

As a consequence of Balbina, the Waimiri-Atroari lost more than 10,000 square kilometers, or 10 percent, of their demarcated area and gained virtually nothing in return (Baines 1991a, 103).

As misfortune never comes alone, loss of territory for a useless dam came to the Waimiri-Atroari after a brutal phase of unrelenting harassment from the construction of the Manaus–Boa Vista Highway in the 1970s that cost many indigenous lives, and some nationals' as well, in massacres and epidemics. The Waimiri-Atroari, who probably numbered 2,000 in the nineteenth century, were reduced to 332 people in 1983 (Baines 1991a, 74–78). Like the Parakanã, they have had to cope with the devastating road-dam-mining triad. In the late 1970s the Paranapanema mining company took over about 526,000 hectares of Waimiri-Atroari territory, after FUNAI officials passed false information: "There has been no reported presence of Indians in the northeast part of the Waimiri-Atroari reserve" and there was "no knowledge of the existence of Indians in this sector of the reserve, nor that this region was one traversed by Indians" (Baines 1991b, 145). When the government decided on the demarcation of the Waimiri-Atroari Indian area, it excluded the portion expropriated by the mining company. As a matter of fact, in addition to Paranapanema, which has been effectively exploiting tin ore since the early 1980s, twelve other mining companies have applied for concessions in the area (Baines 1990, 35).

The Waimiri-Atroari Program was created in the 1970s to handle compensations from Eletronorte and Paranapanema. Part of these compensations is a toll charged the mining company for the loading trucks that cross the reserve. In late 1996 a group of 110 armed Waimiri-Atroari blocked the 45-kilometer access road from the Paranapanema cassiterite mine to the Manaus–Boa Vista Highway. They demanded a tax increase from U.S.$15,000 to $75,000 a month. About two hundred trucks pass through the Indian area every month, and U.S.$75,000 represents one truckload of cassiterite, that is, one half of 1 percent of the value in mineral production. The money is meant as indemnity for environmental degradation and pollution of the Alalaú River. According to a director of Paranapanema, the company extracts eight thousand tons of cassiterite every month. "This mineral is converted into four thousand tons of tin in the company's metallurgic plant in São Paulo. A ton of tin is worth 6,000 reais [approximately U.S.$58,000] in the international market. The gross profit from the mine would be around twenty-four million reais per month" (Muggiati 1996b). But then control of the money went to the largest stockholders of the company, Vale do Rio Doce, Petrobrás, and Banco do Brasil, at the time all state enterprises, and they did not agree to the Indians' demands. "The Indians warned they were prepared to blow up the access bridges . . . and take over the mine before it devoured the rest of their territory" (ISA 1996b, 10). FUNAI sent an envoy to the area to try to convince the Waimiri-Atroari to end the blockade and resume negotiations with the mining company. The Indians remained adamant. In the end the Waimiri-Atroari and Paranapanema settled for thirty thousand reais a month (roughly U.S.$30,000) plus one half of 1 percent of the gross monthly production. A contract was signed in November 1996 and the road reopened (Stephen Baines, personal communication).

Even more predatory and hence damaging to indigenous populations than industrial mining was the swift advance of hundreds of thousands of gold prospectors throughout the entire Amazon region in the 1980s, particularly in Indian areas.

> On the one hand, mining companies try to get a written legalization of research and exploitation [in Indian areas] as a condition for their capital investments. On the other, placer mining entrepreneurs foster invasions and intrusions by prospectors (*garimpeiros*) in several Indian areas, trying with a fait accompli to get there before the companies. Caught between the two types of invaders are the Indians, harassed and uninformed, subjected to co-optation maneuvers and forced to negotiate in extremely unequal conditions. (CEDI/CONAGE 1988, 1)

Placer mining (*garimpo*) activity, known in the Amazon since the 1930s, soared after a state survey in the mid-1970s, known as the RADAM-BRASIL Project, revealed the mineral wealth buried in Amazonia and especially after the dramatic rise of gold prices on the international market in 1980 (Schmink and Wood 1992, 500, 217; MacMillan 1995). From then on, gold was like a giant magnet, attracting multitudes from all parts of the country in the most chaotic form of frontier expansion. "By the middle of the decade the population of gold miners in Amazonia reached around half a million" (Schmink and Wood 1992, 220). Many indigenous groups were directly affected by garimpo activities, among them the Munduruku and Kayapó in the state of Pará, the Waiãpi in Amapá, the Waimiri-Atroari and Tukanoans in the state of Amazonas, the Nambiquara and various other groups in Mato Grosso and Rondônia, and the Makushi and Yanomami in Roraima.

In contrast to the relatively rare presence of large-scale industrial mining in Indian areas, the garimpos have invaded twenty-two indigenous territories. "The profoundly harmful effects of these activities (*garimpagem*) are already well known: violence, massive contamination, and generalized pollution" (W. Carvalho 1990, 43). According to Carvalho, the 600,000 garimpeiros who had moved to Amazonian mining sites in the 1960s provoked

> inumerable conflicts with mining companies and Indian populations; conflicts which sometimes degenerated into armed combats with numerous victims: garimpeiros, Indians, geologists, and mining engineers. One should add to this the serious ecological problems caused by the massive effluence of mercury into the rivers by the garimpeiros who use it to amalgamate gold without any precaution. (p. 44)

It should be stressed that placer mining in Indian areas is prohibited by law (1988 Constitution; 1973 Indian Statute), as it involves the exploitation of a surface resource that, like all other natural resources except subsoil, is set aside for the exclusive use of the Indians. This illegal activity has often had the complicity of state governors and even FUNAI because of its highly profitable results—about one hundred tons a year (p. 44).

In late 1983 a rich gold site was found in the Serra do Traíra in the territory of the Tukano-speaking Indians of the Upper Rio Negro–Uaupés region. The Tukanoans, who had hardly recovered from a traumatic phase of army control following their participation in coca traffic with Colombian dealers, and after accusations of involvement with the Colombian guerrilla known as M-19 (Wright 1990, 39), now confronted the invasion of two thousand garimpeiros supported by the governor of the state of Amazonas, Gilberto Mestrinho. The Indians organized a militia to expel the miners, which caused frequent conflicts and social turmoil. "The nine guards don't have a minimum of safety in confronting the garimpeiros who have a large quantity of guns, for they are many. . . . The worst of it is that . . . the white garimpeiros don't have the least civility, are arrogant and show much savagery when they quarrel with the Indians" (Gentil and Sampaio 1985, 69).

In 1985, as Paranapanema acquired concessions from another company, Gold Amazon, "conflicts at the Serra do Traíra between Tukano, gold prospectors and the mining company intensified, causing armed confrontation and creating a climate of tension and fear responsible for the [unconfirmed] rumor of a massacre of 60 Tukano Indians" (Wright 1990, 39; see also CEDI 1987a, 90–98). In desperation, as conflicts with the garimpeiros became unbearable, the Indians sided with the mining company, which, backed by the army and the company's militia, expelled the garimpeiros. The Indians signed a "gentlemen's agreement" with Paranapanema according to which the company could exploit minerals at Serra do Traíra in exchange for providing the Indians with technical mining skills, land demarcation, security, and health, education, and transportation facilities. As it turned out, the mining site of Serra do Traíra was left out of the Indian area, and Paranapanema lost interest in the site and left, opening the way for new garimpeiro invasions, which started again in 1993 (ISA 1996a, 147–48). Meanwhile, the military in charge of the Calha Norte Project cut up the Indians' lands into small patches—"indigenous agricultural colonies"—surrounded by "national forests" intended for commercial use. Having made a deal with both military and mining company for the sake of land demarcation, unsatisfactory as it might be, Tukano leaders such as Álvaro Sampaio—the same man who in 1980 gained prominence with his denunciations at the Russell Tribunal—engaged in conspicuous consumption and became totally alienated from the national Indian movement. Not much time passed before these Tukano leaders felt betrayed by both Paranapanema and the military, both of which failed to deliver the goods as promised (Buchillet 1990).

But the most blatant calamity in terms of human and ecological cost of garimpo operations has fallen on the Yanomami Indians in Roraima since a massive gold rush started in their territory in 1987. About seven thousand of the ten thousand Yanomami in Brazil, most of whom were previously uncontacted, were suddenly stormed by an overwhelming number of aggressive invaders. In three years the number of prospectors rose from an initial two thousand to more than forty-five thousand, five times the Yanomami population in Roraima. In the same period at least fifteen hundred Indians died of malaria and shootings, or more than 20 percent of that population (Ramos 1995a, 1995b). Thus most Yanomami had their first exposure to mass invasion through people with "a minimal level of education and in deplorable health conditions, most coming from a sizeable contingent of landless peasants (twenty million) and of the country's urban unemployed, an assorted lot of adventurers" (W. Carvalho 1990, 48; for more about the social background and organization of the garimpeiros, see Cleary 1990; Hecht and Cockburn 1990, 164–69; Monbiot 1991; MacMillan 1995).

It is not surprising that the garimpeiros' regard for the well-being of indigenous peoples was virtually nonexistent. This was also true of the pro-garimpeiro governor of Roraima, Romero Jucá, a former FUNAI president—"an old scalp hunter," in the words of the late senator Severo Gomes (1991, 163)—and the military that controlled the region and did nothing to prevent the invasion; in fact, the military encouraged it by enlarging the Paapiú airstrip the year before the gold rush broke out (Ramos 1995a, 1995b). Gruesome massacres of Yanomami were reported, beginning with the first slaughter at the Paapiú landing strip, where the invaders killed four important local men, dismembered their bodies, and displayed them for the other Yanomami, then the 1990 Olomai killings of both Indians and garimpeiros (Ramos 1995a, 1995b, 1996b), and the notorious 1993 Haximu carnage when sixteen Yanomami were brutally slain (Albert 1996, 203–207). A volley of protests from within Brazil and abroad eventually got the federal government to launch a vast operation to remove the garimpeiros in the early 1990s. For a while their numbers were reduced to a few hundred before they repeatedly reinvaded the area, as they continue to do to this day, in defiance of the official ban.

A large number of garimpeiros who were expelled from the Yanomami area moved on to other indigenous territories. The Makushi of the Roraima grasslands have struggled with a gold rush in the Raposa–Serra do Sol region that has in turn been the target of much resistance against its demarcation. In the 1990s the number of prospectors soared, intensifying the chronic violence of nationals against Indians, in addition to bringing epidemics of malaria and leishmaniasis (a parasitic disease transmitted by sand flies) and environmental destruction to that region (ISA 1996a, 162).

The Guaporé valley in Mato Grosso has been the stage for a massive invasion of Nambiquara lands and natural resources already grossly damaged by agribusiness in the 1960s and 1970s (D. Price 1977; Chimanovitch 1972). As Valente writes:

> In only three months, about 8,000 garimpeiros and 150 loggers invaded the Sararé reserve . . . and erected a town within the area of the Nambiquara Indians. The town—just fifteen km from the Indian village—has one hundred business establishments, including brothels, groceries, and repair shops; it is inhabited by some 6,000 of the 8,000 plus invaders. . . . To the south of the village, a thousand garimpeiro dredges make a roaring noise, according to the Indians, from dawn [to dusk]. . . .
>
> To the north and west of the village, 150 loggers have opened up roads and devastated the forest to get hardwood such as mahogany and cherry wood. . . . The latest [malaria epidemic] affected twenty-five percent of the village population and was brought under control a month ago. Since January, ten conflicts occurred between Indians and loggers. . . . Two months ago, the Indians tied up ten invaders and poured gasoline over them, threatening to burn them alive. They were prevented by FUNAI personnel. On November 16, the loggers attacked the village, wounding fourteen Indians with blows of revolver and shotgun butt. . . . To avoid risking a confrontation, the Nambiquara are entrapped in their own village, prevented from walking about the forest now taken over by garimpeiros and loggers. (1996, 8-1)

And so the story continues to repeat in an alarming time-space progression. The extermination of Indian lives and subsequent illegal expropriation of their lands have as long a history as Brazil itself. This trend has had a remarkable continuity throughout the centuries. If anything is new about the second half of the twentieth century, it is the scope, the speed, and virulence of the effect that national society is having on practically every indigenous people in the country. Whereas in the past a group under pressure would last some centuries before its final collapse, nowadays it takes only a few years or even months of frenzied intrusions to bring an Indian group to the brink of extinction. This is true despite a whole apparatus of state and private protection that FUNAI and numerous NGOs represent.

Yet "development" does not have to kill. Let us look at some examples of incipient, modest, and relatively successful indigenous experiments with the market economy.

Alluvial gold mining reached the northermost part of Yanomami territory in the late 1960s. A small number of prospectors contacted the Yanam subgroup, first in Brazil, then in Venezuela, and taught the Indians the basic manual techniques of gold extraction. One of these pioneer garimpeiros settled down among the Brazilian Yanam, married a local woman, had children, and learned the language with great fluency (Ramos, Lazarin, and Gomez 1987, 80–81). When two thousand garimpeiros took over an area to the south of their villages, the Yanam were encouraged to produce their own gold and sell it to the gold panners. Repeated malaria epidemics and other setbacks disturbed the Indians' lives, but they never felt the effect of the massive 1987–1990 gold rush that devastated the more central Yanomami communities. Small-scale hand-operated mining has entered the economy of the Yanam pretty much as an extension of slash-and-burn gardening, with mining sites and work following the same model, that is, a seasonal family activity. People keep what is often a minute amount of gold they have extracted in a little medicine vial decorated with a string of glass beads, as are the boxes used to wash the gold. Although they have the option of selling their gold in the town of Boa Vista assisted by FUNAI, the Yanam prefer to trade it directly with non-Indian garimpeiros in the area, aware they may be cheated on price and infected with contagious diseases. Nevertheless, the two hundred Yanam of the Ericó River have weathered some serious health and social crises—in 1985 they were further traumatized by the attack of a FUNAI post manager who went berserk, murdered two Indians, and wounded a third—and survived as a coherent group that has succeeded in incorporating new elements such as gold in its traditional way of life. The Yanam have long demanded an education program that can prepare them to cope with the snarls of interethnic commercial transactions, and they are one of the rare examples of relative stability among the chaos that has characterized the recent history of the Yanomami in Brazil.

A similar case of getting the best out of a potentially disastrous situation is that of the Tupi-speaking Waiãpi of Amapá. The 310 Brazilian Waiãpi (440 others live in French Guiana) had their first experience with gold panners in the 1970s when the federal government opened up the east-west Perimetral Norte Highway designed to reach the Pacific. The Waiãpi went through the usual epidemiological shock that immediately follows careless contact, experienced the paternalistic tactics of FUNAI, and were threatened with land usurpation. But they fared quite well in organizing against all these forces. In the mid-1980s they expelled the garimpeiros, began to extract their own gold, and devised an efficient way of patrolling the borders of their 573,000-hectare area. Aided by the Center for Indigenist Work (CTI), a São Paulo–based NGO, the Waiãpi carried out their own demarcation with funding from GTZ, a German government agency for technical cooperation. Like the Yanam subgroup of the Yanomami and the Makushi in Roraima, the Waiãpi consider gold a sort of savings account (W. Carvalho 1990, 49). It is their explicit intention to keep gold mining to a minimum, just enough so they can purchase commodities such as ammunition, pots and pans, flashlights, and cloth. They are in no hurry, for, as they say, gold does not rot, and "it is our land, nobody needs to rush, who's going to frighten us?" (Waiãpi chief Waiwai, quoted in Gallois 1996, 53).

Like the northern Yanomami, the Waiãpi fit gold panning into their regular cycle of economic and ritual activities. There is a time for gardening, another for fruit gathering, another for garimpo, another for village ritual life (Gallois 1996, 264). Trips to garimpo sites are comparable to seasonal trips to old distant gardens where resources are more abundant than in the current village of residence. Division of labor follows exactly the same lines as agricultural work—garimpo sites are managed by the family unit, which takes one to six trips a year to collect an average five to eight grams of gold during a week or a month (Gallois 1990, 1993b, 1996). Furthermore, the Waiãpi take advantage of their trips to garimpo sites to supervise the reserve's boundaries, which they are marking off with long-cycle fruit trees as well as the usual concrete markers (Gallois 1996, 269).

In view of the combination of relatively favorable circumstances and cultural wisdom, Dominique Gallois, the Waiãpi's activist ethnographer, concludes: "Amidst the panorama of social and environmental devastation that affects the majority of indigenous areas in the country, the Amapá Waiãpi represent, it seems, a privileged situation" (1996, 262). It is a situation that the Peruvian Huambisa, whose plaint opened this chapter, would long for. As a result of their successful management of such an unruly activity as placer mining, the Waiãpi are beginning to earn the respect they never had from the regional population (p. 271). But while the Indians are enjoying a new prosperity, they and their national allies have been under a defamatory campaign launched by local politicians and other anti-Indian characters who regard this Waiãpi experiment as harmful to the interests of nonindigenous gold prospectors.

In terms of using economic success to effect ethnic "rehabilitation" in the eyes of the regional population, the Gaviões in the state of Pará provide another notable example. They are a good illustration of an Indian group that has achieved economic incorporation in the national and international market economy without losing their ethnic identity. They also show that regional discrimination can be overcome, or drastically reoriented—the lazy, poor, backward Indians are now envied as rich Indians—and that indigenous achievements may be recognized, at least to a certain extent.

The Gaviões resisted permanent contact with outsiders for more than fifty years but were finally "pacified" in the 1950s. During the attraction (pacification) phase they lost about 70 percent of their population. When Brazilian anthropologist Roberto Da Matta visited them in 1961, one of their villages had eight people. No wonder Da Matta considered himself to be studying a virtually extinct society: "It was in that phase that the Gaviões disappeared as a group, from then on they were to be a mere collection of Indians totally dependent on the national society" (Laraia and Da Matta 1967, 101). But in the next fifteen years the Gaviões made a dramatic demographic recovery, from no more than 30 people to 108 in 1976 (Bourne 1978, 223). By that time FUNAI had moved one of their two villages twice because its traditional territory was to be flooded by the Tucuruí Dam. The other village had been bisected by the Marabá-Belém road: the FUNAI post stayed on one side, the Indians on the other (pp. 222–23).

Their area was rich in Brazil nuts, which gained a new place in their lives: once a foodstuff of minor importance, it became a market product of great value. Under FUNAI patronage the Gaviões had been constrained to sell their produce exclusively to the agency itself, thus obtaining less than 20 percent of its market value (Bourne 1978, 222; Brooks et al. 1973, 134–35), and sometimes as low as 11 percent. The huge FUNAI profit was never reinvested in the Gaviões area.

In 1975–1976 FUNAI, which was going through a somewhat "enlightened" phase under President Ismarth de Araújo Oliveira, launched a project for "community development" for the Gaviões. Then a student at the University of São Paulo, anthropologist Iara Ferraz was contracted to run the project, which was designed to provide the Gaviões with the material means that would allow them to control the marketing of their Brazil-nut production. The first step was to buy them a truck to transport the produce directly to Belém, the Pará state capital. With this little push the project succeeded in "eliminating the paternalistic character of the relations between FUNAI and the Indians" (*Jornal de Brasília* 1976b). In December 1976 Ferraz was dismissed by FUNAI for alleged improper behavior, but by that time the Gaviões had definitively taken control of their nut production. About a month later they got a loan from Banco do Brasil to cover transportation and other expenses (*Jornal de Brasília* 1977). In mid-1977 they expelled the FUNAI agent from their village (*O Estado de São Paulo* 1977) and were reported to have twenty non-Indian Brazilian employees (Bourne 1978, 222).

Having defined themselves as producers rather than a cheap labor force, the Gaviões proved their worth in the eyes of the regional population. Just before the Geisel administration's attempt to decree the emancipation of indigenous peoples (see Chapter 9), the same FUNAI president, General Ismarth Araújo de Oliveira, invited them to Brasília for a meeting in early 1977. The Gaviões declined for two reasons. One was that some years before they had received a similar invitation from the FUNAI office in Belém, which turned out to be a trick to send them to the Krenak Indian jail in the state of Minas Gerais. The other reason was that they were afraid of being emancipated by FUNAI. Now economically successful, they feared that if emancipated they might lose their lands.

No sooner had the Gaviões won the Brazil-nut battle than a new source of anxiety appeared in the form of a long transmission line from the Tucuruí hydroelectric plant that in 1980 cut through the immediate vicinity of their Mãe Maria village. A four-year judicial hassle with Eletronorte resulted in much smaller compensation than the Gaviões claimed originally. That same year found the Gaviões watching the construction of a railroad through their area as part of the gigantic Carajás mineral project toward which ran the transmission line. Again the Gaviões had to engage in negotiations around indemnity, this time with the Vale do Rio Doce state company in charge of the project. In 1982 compensation brought them a substantial amount of money (CEDI 1985a, 70–71).

The hard-won economic success of the Gaviões has been accompanied by a number of setbacks, including the repeated disputes with FUNAI over fair compensation, the destruction of an entire village by the railroad, and the invasion of colonists along the tracks. In 1987 the Gaviões blocked the railroad to pressure the authorities to remove 198 families that had been settled in their reserve five years before by the Getat state colonization program. A year later the colonists were removed (CEDI 1991a, 347–48). All things considered (I must agree with Gallois's evaluation of the Waiãpi situation), compared to the panorama of social and environmental devastation that affects the majority of indigenous areas in the country, the 333 Gaviões, with a demarcated area of 62,488 hectares, are an Indian people whose cultural and ethnic pride has been greatly enhanced by the prosperity they acquired from economic exchanges with national society.

The Pragmatic Nineties

But the symbol of indigenous cunning and affluence are the Kayapó of central Brazil. The way they have converted drawbacks—such as invasions by garimpeiros and loggers—into economic profit has had as much publicity as the way they have converted their cultural assets into instruments of power (T. Turner 1991a). No doubt, their assertiveness toward nationals from their earliest contacts is rooted in Kayapó society, which favors political fissioning and political shrewdness. But the arrival of outsiders in their universe, back in the nineteenth century, seems to have greatly intensified village splitting. The numerous raids the Kayapó launched against Brazilians were motivated by the need to acquire guns with which to escalate warfare against other indigenous groups. Before pacification the Kayapó were nationally famed for their attacks on Brazil-nut gatherers and colonists. But Kayapó assaults on intruders appear not to have been a defensive strategy but instead were for the purpose of acquiring goods: "warfare with Brazilians was, in other words, for the Kayapo essentially a form of circulation of commodities" (T. Turner 1992, 329). With pacification in the late 1950s the Kayapó "were ready to seize upon an easier way of acquiring more" (p. 330). The ease with which they accepted peaceful contact was part of such a strategy.

In the 1980s thousands of garimpeiros invaded Kayapó territory and established three garimpos in different parts of it, paying the Indians one-tenth of 1 percent of the gold they sold. Five years later the Kayapó took over the garimpo headquarters and tried to expel the garimpeiros but did not succeed. Instead, the Kayapó organized themselves as overseers of the gold operations—they have not extracted gold themselves—and make sure the invaders pay them a 12 percent tax on what is sold. They receive the money in cash and immediately take it by plane to a bank in the town of Redenção. In less than a month, October–November 1989, the Gorotire-Kayapó received U.S.$70,000 (CEDI 1991a, 311).

Logging also began on Kayapó land in the 1980s. In 1987, the most productive year, about 69 percent of all Brazilian mahogany exports came from Kayapó lands. Considering the high value of the wood, the Kayapó got no more than U.S.$40 per cubic meter, eleven times less than the export price. Even so, hundreds of thousands of dollars flooded the communities. The Kayapó purchased an airplane, expanded their agricultural production, bought houses in Redenção, and began to construct their national and international image.

In 1988 two Kayapó leaders, one of whom was Paulinho Payakan, had an interview with the president of the World Bank in Washington, D.C., where they argued against the construction of a series of dams on the Xingu River that was being planned by the Brazilian government. The dams would create a string of lakes where there are nineteen Indian areas (CEDI 1991a, 332). Upon their return to Brazil the two Indians were shocked to find themselves indicted for supposedly violating the Law of Foreigners, along with U.S. anthropologist Darrell Posey who had accompanied them in the United States. They were accused of harming the interests of the country. The case had wide press coverage, and the absurdity of framing Brazilian Indians as foreigners had two effects: it discredited the authorities who committed the faux pas and provided the Kayapó with a magnificent opportunity to show their political acumen. A profusion of photos invaded the news media showing an entire community of Kayapó men in shorts, black paint, and feathered headdresses dancing in protest outside the Belém court. They had been barred from entering because they were not "properly dressed," which added to the public interest in the story.

An NGO—The Rain Forest Foundation (Fundação Mata Virgem)—was created for the purpose of lobbying for the demarcation of Kayapó lands under the banner of environmental protection. Rock singer Sting was a major promoter of it (Sting and Dutilleux n.d.), and again the Kayapó made international news when Sting and Chief Raoni toured Europe to defend the rain forest and the demarcation of Kayapó lands.

Having amassed so much political and monetary capital, the Kayapó were ready for the next step, the monumental rally in 1989 in the town of Altamira to protest against the Xingu dams, where about "three thousand people, between Indians, ecologists, onlookers and journalists filled the gymnasium at Altamira" (CEDI 1991a, 333; see also T. Turner 1991b). The repercussions from the publicity were enormous, and the Kayapó have succeeded, at least for the time being, in halting the government plans for the Xingu dams. Nevertheless, media coverage missed much of the point, "because of the emphasis by the press and environmental activists on the symbolism of native participation to the detriment of analysis of the larger political and institutional context of the indigenous protest" (Fisher 1994, 222). Indeed, beyond the body painting, feather headdresses, dancing, and—the media quintessence of the Altamira meetings—the much publicized gesture of a Kayapó Indian woman's pressing the side of her machete against the face of an Eletronorte director, what the organizers of the meeting wanted was expressed by Payakan: an end to decisions about Amazonia without the Indians' participation. The "Whiteman who thinks he owns everything on the surface of the earth" is not to be trusted. If the nations represented at the meetings can help it, the Kararaô Dam will never materialize (CEDI 1991a:333).

After the World Bank, Sting, and Altamira, the image that environmentalists (despite the gold and mahogany operations they encourage) have of the Kayapó is that of warriors: "for a Kayapó to be an environmentalist today is in some senses similar to being a warrior in other times" (Fisher 1994, 229). This image has brought the Kayapó yet another source of earnings, albeit modest by their standards. The English-based cosmetics company, The Body Shop, selected the Kayapó as its symbol for its Tropical Rainforest line of natural products (Seidl 1990). With the slogan TRADE NOT AID, Body Shop director Anita Roddick defends the idea that "commercial production of ecologically non-destructive types . . . provides [indigenous communities] with a more reliable and less environmentally destructive source of funds" (T. Turner 1995, 114). Her negotiations with Payakan for the installation of a press for the production of Brazil-nut oil included the gift of an airplane to his community, and production began in the early 1990s. "The Kayapo thus became the first Indians in Amazonia to participate in the new wave of 'green capitalist' enterprises based on environmentally sustainable production" (p. 116). However, as with the mahogany business, the Kayapó do not seem to be getting their fair share of The Body Shop proceeds:

The Body Shop pays a good wage by regional standards. . . . By far the most important value the Kayapo contribute to The Body Shop, however, is not the oil and bead bracelets they produce, but their photographic images, and reportage about the projects in the media, which serve as free advertising for the company and for which it pays not a penny to the Kayapo. (pp. 116–17)

And so the twenty-five hundred to three thousand Kayapó enter the end of the century as the most economically prosperous, politically shrewd, and ethnically envied indigenous group in Brazil. Much of their political effort has been to expand their territory, originally demarcated at 3.28 million hectares (CEDI/PETI 1990, 67). Ethnically speaking, they could not be more "Kayapó" than they are now, having transformed their traditional culture into precious political and economic capital. Perhaps the measure of Kayapó success can be seen in the comment of a mining technician who, "with considerable irony," stated that "in Rio Branco it was the Indians who exploited the whites" (Schmink and Wood 1992, 267).

Frontiers Unbounded

Economic frontiers are not limited to the direct exploitation of natural resources. After centuries of encroachment by intruders eager to get their lands, forest products, mineral wealth, and other resources, the Indians are now plagued by new demands, no longer on the "nature" that surrounds them but on their cultural and physical essence. The "knowledge" frontier and the genetic frontier (see Cultural Survival 1991) are completing the plunder.

The supposed respect for indigenous wisdom in handling unruly ecosystems such as Amazonia's is in fact good old economic exploitation in humanist disguise. We have seen how the World Bank's avowal of admiration for indigenous knowledge is inserted in a clear context of taking advantage of such knowledge for the benefit of national and international development. The same declaration of esteem for indigenous acumen can be found in statements by Eletrobrás technocrats who regret the absence of writing among the Indians, a skill necessary to preserve the "valuable collection of knowledge accumulated by indigenous tribes. Especially with regard to the thousands of native biological species which exist in their ecosystems and with which they have lived for centuries" (quoted in Viveiros de Castro and Andrade 1988, 19).

Intellectual property rights are a concern totally absent in these and virtually all other development schemes. Considering that there is a 74 percent positive correlation between the modern therapeutic use of 120 active components extracted from plants and their traditional use by native peoples, "the employment of traditional knowledge (both indigenous and non-indigenous) increases the efficiency in the process of screening plants for medicinal properties in more than four hundred percent" (J. Santilli 1996, 19). Amazonia and its living beings, including the Indians, have become a haven for the pharmaceutical industry dependent on biodiversity.

> Brazil . . . is the richest country in the world in biodiversity (with thirty percent of all tropical forests, concentrating more than fifty percent of their species), with a rich sociocultural patrimony (there are about 200 indigenous peoples speaking about 170 different languages . . .). Moreover, ninety-eight percent of Indian lands are in Amazonia (mostly in tropical forest) where sixty percent of the indigenous population lives. Therefore, the correlation between indigenous peoples, tropical forest, and biodiversity is obvious. (p. 19)

The problem is that indigenous peoples are not effectively protected by national or international legislation against predatory exploitation of their traditional knowledge (pp. 17–20).

Indian knowledge, however, cannot be acquired by the mere transfusion of indigenous technical know-how. The much admired sustainability the Indians achieve in the use of their natural resources derives from much more than the simple identification of fauna and flora and descriptions of their use. Such knowledge is anchored in a whole dimension of worldviews and lifestyles that is virtually incompatible with the rapacity of industrial activities. What passes as "symbolic" manifestations of a quaint culture— food taboos, hunting restrictions, metaphysical reasons for a specific division of labor, agricultural or hunting rituals—can actually be at the heart of indigenous wisdom. This "esoteric" part of native knowledge is unlikely to be of any interest to developers. In other words, all those demonstrations of esteem for indigenous wisdom are but an exercise in paying lip service to political correctness.

A more ecologically concerned approach to the commodification of native knowledge argues that Indians and other "forest peoples" must develop some sort of economically feasible production in order to justify occupation of their lands. The argument is that market forces will sooner or later evict the inhabitants of territories that are deemed exploitable. With this in mind Jason Clay of the United States, a former NGO activist-turned-green-entrepreneur, has launched "Rainforest Harvest," mainly involving non-indigenous Amazon dwellers. What seems to be objectionable in such an effort is the failure to do what it proposes, that is, satisfy the market forces that a thriving production is at work in the jungle:

> The proportions of total product actually sourced from forest peoples in commodities marketed by Rain Forest Harvest schemes . . . have in some

instances been minuscule, the great bulk being made up of convention-
ally sourced items produced in the usual socially and environmentally
exploitative ways. The implicit or explicit claims of such schemes to constitute economically significant incentives to save the rainforest . . . are
mere hype. (T. Turner 1995, 115–16)

Indeed, it is hard to imagine that Amazon forest peoples would make it
as market champions on the basis of the "Rainforest crunch" that North
Americans occasionally nibble at cocktail parties.

On the indigenous side is a growing awareness that traditional knowledge, combined with new technologies, can increase the chances of ecological recovery and economic gain by Indian communities. In 1985 Ailton
Krenak, the last UNI coordinator, created the Nucleus of Indian Culture
"as a reference for our relatives in search of cultural and socio-economic
alternatives that affirm their cultural identity" (Krenak 1996, 5). Four
years later he launched the Program for Education and Research in Indigenous Communities, which taught law and applied biology to a small select
group of students from various Indian societies in the country. In the mid-
1990s the Nucleus was awarded grants from Austria and the London Gaia
Foundation to carry out pilot projects in the Amazon, the central savanna
region (*cerrado*), and the Atlantic rainforest. Two main reasons motivated
the founding of the Nucleus: "to turn the Indians into the masters of their
own territory, and provide the communities already in charge of it with an
adequate technology for its use. This means recovering the land through
the exercise of Indian rights, and restoring the habitat degraded by the expansion of civilization" (Garcia dos Santos 1991, 73). Fish farming and the
herding of wild animals, such as the large capivara rodent, were the main
economic projects. In subsequent years the Nucleus joined non-Indian rubber tappers in the state of Acre to produce a newly found marketable forest
commodity, vegetal leather, an entirely local initiative (Ginú 1995).

More straightforward and blunt than the knowledge frontier is the genetic frontier. The inhumanly ambitious Human Genome Project, designed
to map the entire human genetic layout, depends on taking biodiversity to
its ultimate consequences. Without getting into the question of its potential
benefits for the health of the human race, or potential political abuses, the
Human Genome Project raises disconcerting questions about how property rights are being handled by the huge scientific-commercial genetic
enterprise (Wilkie 1994). There is probably nothing wrong with collecting
blood from an Indian person in the most recondite corner of Amazonia
for the benefit of those who suffer from genetic diseases somewhere in
Europe or North America. But why should that Indian, most likely suffering from some sort of effect of Western invasion, do it for free? When the
U.S. National Institutes of Health patented the cellular lineage extracted

from the semi-isolated Hagahai of New Guinea as its property and justified doing so by saying that it "had not patented the native's blood, much less the Hagahai himself . . . but the cellular lineage derived from the HTLV found in him" (Lins da Silva 1996), the argument is, to say the very least, specious. The cellular lineage produced in a lab is to its human originator as a photograph is to a celebrity. How would the celebrity react to the unauthorized use of his or her picture for profit? The justification continues by saying that the natives are informed about the operation and agree to it. How would a most likely monolingual New Guinea native understand the language of the blood taker, let alone the language of avant-garde Western genetic science? Is the Columbus syndrome of instant cross-language understanding still alive and well in the West?

In 1996 Coriell Cell Repositories, a North American genetics firm, was advertising the sale of DNA samples from the Karitiana and Suruí Indians of Rondônia via the Internet and in scientific conventions for U.S.$500 per sample (Braga 1997). "Suppose some lab buys a cellular lineage from the Suruí, does the research, identifies a gene related to some disease and then patents it. This business can amount to astronomical sums" (Mansur 1996). The prospect is real enough, judging by the news that "Incyte Pharmaceuticals of California has requested the patent of 40,000 DNA sequences" (ISA 1994, 3). Again, Brazilian Indians and everyone else, including citizens of the United States (Wilkie 1994, 22–23), are at the mercy of the gene market, or "biopirates" (Gielow 1997), as no legislation can protect them from the "geneticidal" rapacity of the North American genetics industry.

A companion project to the Human Genome, the Human Genome Diversity Project came into existence "after a plea published in *Genomics* calling attention to the disappearance of indigenous peoples and their absorption by predominant genetic clusters" (ISA 1996c, 22). After natural resources, labor, knowledge, and now genes, what else is left of the Indians to be converted into commodities "before they disappear" from this Brave New World?

8

No Man's Land, Everybody's Business

Amazonia, the Invidious Void

Brazil possesses two-thirds of the 4.8 million square kilometers of Amazon forest (M. Santilli 1990, 111). It thus owns one of the largest concentrations of cultural diversity and biodiversity in the world. The indigenous population of the Brazilian rainforest and grasslands north of the equator represents 50 percent of the country's 280,000 Indians (C. Ricardo 1996b, xii). It is home to approximately 140,000 Indians in more than 140 societies, not counting 18 groups about which no demographic data are available, the still uncontacted, and the Indians who live in towns and cities (ISA 1996a, vi–xii). This native population, combined with the regional dwellers of Amazonia, amounts to a significant human occupation. Yet developers and particularly the military in Brazil insist that the Amazon constitutes a demographic void. Portraying the region as a vast emptiness is part of its attraction as a highly coveted object of economic desire. Acting as if Indians and other traditional peoples do not exist, state and private enterprises, both national and foreign, have caused much devastation to Amazonia, mainly in the twentieth century. From the areas of easier and older encroachment to the more remote and, until recently, fairly isolated corners of the region, Amazon populations in general and Indians in particular have been the involuntary and often unwilling actors in the long history of ransacking of and disrespect for both human lives and natural resources.

This chapter deals first with the trajectory of outsiders' occupation of Amazonian indigenous lands, placing special emphasis on the role of the military as an agent of order at the service of outside economic interests, and then focuses on a particularly revealing example of military action in the region, namely, the project known as Calha Norte, or North Watershed (*calha* also means gutter, ditch), the most explicit militarization scheme for the Amazon in the years immediately after the return to civilian rule in Brazil.

A Residue of Brazil

"Amazonia cannot continue to be considered the residue of the country. . . . Amazonia is sold by marketing and politics as an ideal locus for Brazil's unresolved problems." This phrasing, by journalist Lúcio Flávio Pinto (1989), neatly describes the predicament of Amazonia and its inhabitants. Historically, the region has been the site of the largest concentration of wasteful policies in the whole country; for centuries the waste of natural resources, human lives, social justice, public money, and time has been colossal. And those most victimized by this centuries-old trend are the indigenous populations.

By the middle of the eighteenth century Amazonia had been effectively occupied by Spaniards. As they searched for gold, Francisco de Orellana (in 1542) and Pedro de Ursúa-Lope de Aguirre (in 1561) were the first Europeans to encounter Indians such as the Omagua. The successive waves of European invasions decimated these peoples to virtual extinction (Sweet 1974). The military, missionaries, and backwoodsmen (*sertanistas*) in search of spices, drugs, and wood to feed Western Europe's craving for luxury (Neto 1979, 69) continued the expansion. Each of these agents, in their own way and for their own purposes, ensnared the Indians in activities that were totally alien to their traditions. The European occupation established in lowland Amazonia during the seventeenth and eighteenth centuries used as its bases the enormous Indian settlements (*reduções*) created by the Jesuits. In the midseventeenth century, colonists from Maranhão turned to Amazonia to hunt Indians as forced labor for sugar and tobacco plantations. Both colonists and missionaries went deeper and deeper into the Amazon forest competing for Indians, the former looking for prospective slaves, the latter purportedly to defend the natives but in fact engaged in their own hunt for prospective converts (Cardoso and Müller 1978, 21), in what Darcy Ribeiro once called the missionaries' "sacred fury" (1970, 32). By the early eighteenth century the few remnants of the once numerous Omagua Indians of the floodplains had taken refuge at the headwaters of the Amazon in Peru, whereas the Manao and Tapajós of the middle and lower Amazon no longer existed (Meggers 1971, 124, 131), having met the same fate as the coastal Tupinambá.

The rubber boom brought opulence to nineteenth-century Amazonia but also unleashed a new phase in the interminable drain of Indian lives and cultures caused by forced labor, torture, and contagious diseases (Taussig 1987). According to one estimate, the rubber era left thirty thousand dead and ten thousand permanently disabled (Cardoso and Müller 1978, 35). In addition, indigenous peoples especially in the northwestern Amazon, had deteriorated physically and socially, subjected to the "tyranny" of rubber tappers

> who came from everywhere in successive waves, either down the Upper Uaupés from Colombia, or up the Rio Negro from São Gabriel, but both with the same purpose of "getting Indians" and tak[ing] them by force to the rubber fields. Very few of these Indians managed to return to their villages, most of them perished of starvation, burning in fever, or simply exhausted from hard labor. (Ribeiro 1970, 32)

Meanwhile, missionary zeal in domesticating the Indians resulted in "the most clamorous failure: Indians ever more similar to poor whites, in the indigence of their houses, in the tatters they wore, in the unhealthy food [they ate]" (p. 32).

The great wealth generated by the rubber boom, rather than being channeled to the public good and lasting social improvements, was merely grabbed by private individuals for their mindless conspicuous consumption à la Herzog's *Fitzcarraldo*. The region entered the twentieth century poorer than before in terms of material wealth and social justice.

The pharaonic hydroelectric works of Tucuruí and Balbina were but two in a series of operations for which successive military governments used public money as incentives for private agribusiness in environmental areas notoriously unsuitable for large-scale monoculture and grazing. Other projects included the road network that chopped up long ribbons of rainforest, mammoth mining operations such as the Paranapanema tin mine in Amazonas, and the Great Carajás iron ore extraction in Pará and Maranhão. These projects have turned lush forest into unproductive deserts, such as the Paragominas region in the state of Pará that has been exhausted by inappropriate cattle ranching. In fact, many of these enterprises have boomeranged against the investors who benefited from the bonanza. "Several studies have shown that these pastures can never be sustained and that the end of lavish fiscal incentives and depletion of soils are halting the short-term profits of the cattle companies. More than 80% of the cattle ranches in the Paragominas area, for example, have been abandoned, and officials are now rejecting all new applications" (Goodland 1978, 3).

As in the rubber boom, none of these projects and activities has produced lasting benefits for the majority of Amazonian peoples, be they indigenous or not. Most megaprojects have resulted in resource depletion, human misery, and growing foreign debt. "The economic 'leap,'" says Lúcio Flávio Pinto, "by means of which mock planners thought of pushing Amazonia into contemporaneity created only a vacuum. The natives fell into it. The outsiders benefited by sucking out the riches of the region, especially its energy [hydroelectric and fuelwood]. It is necessary to replenish this loss if the region with its inhabitants, its specific knowledge, and its history is to have its say in this project" and reverse the process that has caused the uplands to be "crisscrossed by roads, strewn with gold panning pits, perforated by mining, devastated by ranches." Amazonia, he continues, "needs a more modulated rhythm. Why destroy the largest [culturally sovereign] indigenous nation in the country, the Yanomami, in order to extract from their lands gold that will feed drug traffic . . . and tin that will absurdly increase the durability of beer and pop cans that will just be thrown in the garbage?" (1989, 7).

The Mined Fields of Amazonia under National Security

Historically, Amazonia has been a paradise for Brazil's armed forces. Manaus, Belém, Santarém, and Macapá are Amazon towns that grew out of military outposts. As jungle bastions they ensured the definitive establishment of Portuguese domain over land and natural resources formally assigned to Spain in the 1494 Treaty of Tordesillas. As a matter of fact,

> until mid eighteenth century, the Amazon actually belonged to no one, or rather, it belonged to its autochthonous populations. . . . Paradoxically, it is in the period [between 1580 and 1640, when Portugal was part of the Spanish crown] that Portuguese colonists under Spanish orders took decisive steps to assure control over the mouth of the Amazon. (M. Santilli 1990,111)

Since then the armed forces have been the main "guardians" of Amazonia and a principal agent for making inroads into the region. A spectacular example of military action was the opening up of the interior of Mato Grosso by General Rondon at the turn of the twentieth century, supposedly to run a telegraph line from the hinterland to the main eastern cities. In a long drawn-out process he took possession of Brazil's western wilderness, but by the time he succeeded telegraph lines were rather obsolete as a means of fast communication. On his way westward Rondon contacted many indigenous villages and established a national reputation as a heroic figure who braved the hardships of the jungle and the dangers of wild Indians in the name of the Brazilian nation. He actively participated in the military coup that installed the republican regime and in 1910 took the initiative to create the first official agency for the protection of indigenous peoples.

Thus militarization of the Amazon and of the Indian issue is not new, but it has intensified substantially since the 1960s. "In 1966, the Federal Government began a more aggressive policy toward Amazonia because it was a vast underpopulated area, considered as a priority to national security, besides representing a frontier of resources for the country" (Neto

1979, 75). The image of Amazonia as a human wasteland was renewed, and the Transamazon Highway came to represent the "big leap into the void." Amerindians and regional populations, leading their traditional lives as usual, were virtually ignored, perhaps because they followed the experience of their long history, that a sustainable livelihood in the rainforest requires a sparse settlement pattern, the complete opposite of the military's agenda of "vivifying" the northern border with massive colonization.

The military regime (1964–1985) put Amazonia at the disposal of big capitalists. In the late 1960s the Suiá-Missu agribusiness, a joint venture of Brazilians from São Paulo and Italians, laid claim to an immense area in Mato Grosso—nine million hectares—that was part of the traditional Shavante territory. Following international protests against the displacement of these Indians, in 1969 General Costa Cavalcanti, then minister of the interior, affirmed that the "Indian has to stay in the minimum space possible" (Cardoso and Müller 1979, 156). The military justified the elephantine projects of the early 1970s in terms of the need to integrate Amazonia into the rest of the nation to safeguard state sovereignty. Rumors of foreign plans to internationalize Amazonia, periodically stirred up, nourished part of the rhetoric that defended large-scale development as geopolitical protection. The other part of official rhetoric addressed the extreme poverty of the northeast, exacerbated by a particularly severe drought, turning the region into a potential site for generalized social and political unrest. Surely, the military still remembered the painful experience of the Northeastern Peasant Leagues that thrived before the 1964 coup. Amazonian development was said to "provide water for the thirsty," and the Transamazon road network was displayed by President Emílio Médici as the miracle solution for suffering *nordestinos* when in fact it would simply spare the government the bother of facing up to the structural problems of the northeast.

Behind these justifications was the matter of state control of historically recalcitrant Amazonia. Among the various measures taken by the central government in Brasília were the creation of the National Integration Plan, Plano de Integração Nacional (PIN), which was funded from the national budget and by international financing agencies, and the RADAM-BRASIL Project, created to carry out basic surveys of the Amazon's natural resources—minerals, vegetation, soils—and their characteristics in terms of geomorphology and carrying capacity. The combination of new roads and news of mineral wealth precipitated such phenomena as the gold rush in Serra Pelada and the first big invasion of *garimpeiros* (prospectors) in search of cassiterite on Yanomami land. But those were a pale preview of what was to come ten years later. The 1980s saw a dramatic increase in mining activities in Amazonia. The Uaupés region, Rondônia, Roraima, Amapá, and Pará attracted millions of people—many of whom were landless—who followed the trails of gold discovery. In some cases, such as in the Uaupés region, mining companies dislodged the garimpeiros after encouraging them to invade indigenous lands. It was the decade of illegal *garimpo* (placer mining) explosion all over Amazonia on a scale that so impressed the National Congress that the new constitution legalized it in non-Indian areas. But illegal mining on indigenous lands continued, the most scandalous of its effects falling on the Yanomami in the late 1980s (Ramos 1995a, 1995b) as described in Chapter 7.

While the military ruled the country, the armed forces, although present in Amazonia, were no more prominent there than in the rest of the country. But when civilians took over the government during the so-called New Republic, military engagement in Amazonia was conspicuous. The Calha Norte Project, covering the immense area north of the Solimões and Amazon Rivers, was conceived in 1985 in total secrecy. It was never submitted to Congress and became public only in late 1986 when it was substantially funded. The public at large was oblivious of its existence, not to mention its essence, until it was leaked to the press (supposedly by CIMI). Indigenous leaders and national activists in the Indian cause were staggered by its implications.

The Calha Norte Project

In his statement (*exposição de motivos* No. 018/85, June 19, 1985) to President José Sarney, General Rubens Bayma Denys, secretary-general of the National Security Council, stated that a preliminary study of the northern border of Amazonia, done by his secretariat, had concluded that

> the immense demographic void of the region, the hostile and little known environment, the great length of the border strip, scarcely populated, as well as the susceptibility of Guyana and Suriname to Marxist ideological influence [are] aspects that render our national sovereignty vulnerable. Analysis of these and other economic, political, and social aspects leads to the conclusion that medium and long term comprehensive planning is necessary to guide government action, together with private initiative, to promote the occupation and development of the area in harmony with and in a way appropriate to national interests. . . . Moreover, it is to be expected that the integration of this geo-economic space to the rest of the Country will strengthen relations with our neighbors from which Brazil may emerge as a more trustworthy option than any other alignments.

Earlier, the document stated that the

> area is practically unexplored, corresponding to 14% of the National Territory and delimited by an extensive border zone inhabited almost solely

by Indians. By itself this last aspect adds a new magnitude to the general problem of the area, since the well-known possibility of border conflicts between some neighboring countries, together with the present-day conjuncture in the Caribbean, may lead to the projection of the East-West antagonism onto the northern part of South America. (*O Liberal* 1986, 16)

This insidious association of ideological cold war with the presence of indigenous peoples on the international border gained the status of reality and became a suitable justification for bringing all the Indian groups living within the 150-kilometer-wide strip between Brazil and its northern neighbors under the control of the National Security Council. The project that followed Denys's document states as one of its strategies:

> Immediate actions on the border strip through the implementation of SPECIAL PROJECTS with the effective participation of Navy, Foreign Affairs, Army, Air Force, and Interior (National Indian Foundation) ministries [in] the following areas, priority being on the first four and their routes of access:
>
> > The area characterized by the presence of Yanomami Indians, with a small population estimated as 7,500 Indians[1] living in dozens of scattered *malocas* [Indian houses], adjacent to a long stretch of 900 kilometers of border with Venezuela, where numerous groups of this same ethnic group reside. For a long time there have been pressures, both from nationals and from foreigners, for the creation—at the expense of the present Brazilian and Venezuelan territories—of a Yanomami State. (*O Liberal* 1986, 17)

The other three areas were the Upper Rio Negro, Eastern Roraima, and the Upper Solimões.

The government immediately poured large sums of money into the Calha Norte Project. Designed to be completed in five years (1986–1991), it was supposed to require less funding as it headed toward completion (even so, in 1989 it got nearly U.S.$50 million), which meant that the initial phase would require special effort in order to create an irreversible fait accompli. For the first two years the army ministry kept nearly half the budget, the navy 21 percent, Interior Ministry–National Indian Foundation (FUNAI) 19 percent, the air force 12 percent, and the Foreign Office (oddly enough, considering the proclaimed diplomatic commitment) a mere 3 percent (GIPCT 1987, 27). The money was to be spent in

> (a) intensification of bilateral relations with the neighboring countries, with special attention to commerce . . . (b) increase of Brazilian presence in the area . . . (c) enlargement and intensification of FUNAI's action

1. This number was probably based on a survey carried out by FUNAI in 1977. Two years later the military promoted its own survey of the Yanomami territory in Roraima and Amazonas and arrived at a figure of 9,910.

among the indigenous populations . . . (d) intensification of demarcation campaigns of the border . . . (e) enlargement of the road system . . . (f) acceleration in the production of energy . . . g) stimulus to the establishment of poles of economic development in the interior . . . (h) greater availability of basic social resources . . . and (i) increase in colonization. (*O Liberal* 1986, 16–17)

The geopolitical concerns of the Brazilian government are not recent. Many neighboring countries felt Brazil's expansionary power during the nineteenth century as they lost considerable portions of their territories, either to the furtive occupation of rubber tappers and other colonists or to the diplomatic shrewdness of Brazilian chancellors. In the late 1970s Brazil took the initiative to involve most of its northern and western neighbors in the Amazon Pact. After much reluctance Venezuela and Peru signed the Treaty for Amazonian Cooperation, overtly designed to stimulate economic development in the region but implicitly set up to neutralize the effects if Suriname and Guyana became "Cubanized" (Miyamoto 1989, 155; M. Santilli 1989). In fact, after some concentrated effort by the Brazilian Foreign Office, and the investment in loans and technical cooperation to Suriname (CEDI 1987b, 65), by 1983 that country had not only reduced its Cuban diplomatic representation but canceled all previously signed agreements with Cuba (Miyamoto 1989, 157). But the military had other reasons for turning its attention northward. Aside from the fear of Cuban influence in the region, Guyana and Venezuela were in conflict over the Essequibo area; French Guiana claimed part of Surinam territory; Guyana and Suriname disputed fifteen square kilometers; Venezuela and Colombia disagreed about maritime rights; and, last but not least, the Brazil-Colombia border had two big problems: guerrilla activity, and coca planting and drug trafficking (Miyamoto 1989, 154). Diplomatic cunning and military tactics joined forces.

> These North borders which at one point were regarded as "dead" and today are "alive" (according to the Foreign Office), and "hot" (according to the Armed Forces) take on a crucial importance in governmental strategics. Whereas the Treaty of Amazonian Cooperation was inserted in the framework of the Amazon regarded as a global geopolitical unit and thought of in diplomatic terms, the Calha Norte Project signifies the military consummation of the said treaty, enlarging it even more. (Miyamoto 1989, 158)

Military officials found in the Calha Norte Project the legitimacy they needed to dictate the form of development in the Amazon, control public investments and private activities, promote migrations into the region, and influence local state governments. At a 1989 dinner with politicians General Leônidas Pires, the army minister in the Sarney government, said, "All I have to do is press a button and the Armed Forces will occupy Amazonia" (Renan Antunes, quoted in CEDI 1991a, 93). From the beginning of the Calha Norte Project to the administration of Fernando Collor de Mello (1990–1992), the military ruled official Indian policy, "transforming the National Indian Foundation into a mere branch of the secretary-general of the National Security Council" (M. Santilli 1990, 113). During its first four years the Calha Norte Project caused a great deal of upheaval in indigenous affairs, as group after group in the Amazon experienced the threat the military policies posed to their lives and territories.

An interesting forerunner to the Calha Norte Project was the 1979 proposal by the late Hélio Campos, a member of Congress, retired air force officer, and former governor of Roraima, to move to the south all indigenous peoples living within the 150-kilometer-wide frontier belt, thus "interiorizing" the Indians and leaving the border strip free for military and economic purposes. For Campos it was not a matter of filling a void but of creating one. Had he had his way, nearly half the Indian population in Brazil would have been sent into areas riddled with land conflicts. In his main argument Campos hammered at the old canard that because the Indians were ignorant, they were easy prey for foreign usurpers posing as missionaries—so this was a national security matter. He followed the example of the Indian removal in the United States that resulted in the death of four thousand Cherokee during their removal west of the Mississippi. Campos made no secret of his real motivation for proposing a latter-day, Brazilian-style Trail of Tears. His project had a clear destination, namely, the Yanomami area where the RADAMBRASIL survey had detected a wealth of mineral deposits. Since publication of the survey in 1975 Roraima governors and members of Congress had made repeated attempts to displace the Indians from the uplands in order to install mining operations. Thus the Calha Norte Project was a systematic concerted effort to achieve something that had been on the horizon for quite a while.

Goose Steps in the Jungle

The belt of Brazil's northern border, which is the 150 kilometers wide and more than 6,500 kilometers long, is home to 63,000 Indians from 54 different ethnic groups occupying 83 Indian areas, most of them officially recognized as such (CEDI 1991b, 93).

Before they began construction or restoration of the planned nineteen military outposts and the approximately thirteen air bases, Calha Norte engineers concentrated their energies on defining Indian lands. Starting from the extreme west of the area affected by the project, they worked eastward, applying the same cookie-cutter approach, regardless of the Indians' cultural differences and degrees of contact. The results, in terms of reaction to the government proposal and the relationships between Indians and military, were different in each case. Let us take a close look at the cases of the Tikuna, Tukano, and Yanomami.

Since 1978 the Tikuna Indians of the upper Solimões River, one of the largest indigenous groups in Brazil with twenty-three thousand people, had been pressuring the federal government to demarcate the lands they traditionally occupy. In 1987 members of the National Security Council approached the Tikuna with a proposal to create a series of "Indian colonies," separated from each other by "national forests." These national forests, far from representing a concern for ecological conservation, were in fact "designed for profit and economic exploitation" of both renewable and nonrenewable resources (Oliveira Filho 1992, 30). The Indians' immediate response was that they needed time to discuss the matter before they could give a definitive answer. The military took this as a rejection of its proposal and withdrew: whatever trouble the Tikuna were to face, they could not count on the government's aid or protection (Oliveira Filho 1996, 308). They were on their own. In March 1988 a group of Tikuna was gunned down by twenty men paid by a local logger and cocaine dealer. Fourteen Indians were killed and twenty-three wounded (Oliveira Filho and Souza Lima 1990). The killers were arrested and released.

Three days after the massacre Romero Jucá Filho, FUNAI's president, declared: "Incidents such as this will certainly come to an end with the establishment of the Calha Norte project in the region. The Calha Norte guarantees financial, technical and human resources for the effective demarcation of the indigenous lands in the border area" (*O Liberal*, Belém, March 31, 1988, quoted in *Magüta* 1988, 78).

A month later the governor of the state of Amazonas, Amazonino Mendes, declared: "If we go deep into the matter, we will find that certain federal agencies were involved in expropriations and then covering things up; they were also bankrupt, failed to act in time, and did not provide convincing explanations for the occurrence" (*A Notícia*, Manaus, April 7, 1988, quoted in *Magüta* 1988, 76).

A wave of hostility against the Indians swept the local town of Benjamin Constant in reaction to police investigations and the wide publicity. Anthropologists and other nationals working among the Tikuna were prohibited by FUNAI to go into any Indian area in Brazil. Jucá ordered the ban from Brasília in a May 5 telex to Manaus: "From this date FUNAI prohibits the Center of Documentation and Research of the Upper Solimões . . . to enter all the Indian areas in the country due to their behavior in the Tikuna area being incompatible with the guidelines of the Brazilian government's indigenist policy" (Magüta 1988).

In October 1989 the government returned to the upper Solimões, now no longer with a proposal but with the decision to disregard all earlier proposals and demarcate two discontinuous "colonies" for the Tikuna, reducing their original territory by 47 percent and omitting three communities. The Indians' indignation can be measured in the statements by Pedro Mendes Gabriel, the executive secretary of the General Council of the Tikuna Tribe (Conselho Geral da Tribo Tikuna, CGTT):

> It is demagogy, it is a crime against the lives of the Tikuna Indians to say they accept the demarcation of their lands in the form of colonies. There is no justification for this because, in several petitions, meetings, audiences with federal authorities, we Tikuna at no time stated that we accepted colonies. . . . FUNAI was negligent, Saden [National Security Secretariat] was negligent, and the rest of the institutions that handle the matter of demarcation of Indian lands paid no attention when we expected to have definite solutions and explanations about the demarcation of our lands as colonies. We Tikuna feel this aggression in our very skin, this disrespect of the government toward the Tikuna peoples. (CIMI Norte 1989, 17)

The Calha Norte Project proceeded to select small areas where the concentration of Indians was smaller and squatter families were numerous. Tension built during the two years that went by before squatters were removed and compensated for the material losses involved in their removal from the Indian area. "The region was transformed in a virtual pressure cooker, with conflicts aggravated by the government's decreasing credibility and inaction as well as by the uncertainty regarding the rights of the parts involved" (Oliveira Filho 1996, 308). The Tikuna massacre occurred in this climate.

Only in 1993, when the project had been halted, did the government allocate to the Tikuna six of their areas, including fifty villages and an estimated population of twenty-one thousand people. The two major areas— Évare I and Évare II—together have nearly 725,000 hectares and the rest about 500,000 hectares, whereas seven others are being set aside for the Tikuna (Oliveira Filho 1996, 307).

Turning to the Uaupés region, in January 1988 an interministerial decision granted a number of different indigenous groups the "permanent possession" of three Indian colonies in the Pari-Cachoeira area; two national forests surrounded these three colonies, and the forests were to be "preferentially used" by the Indians but were intended for economic exploitation by outsiders as well. These three colonies meant a 58 percent reduction in traditional Indian lands officially recognized by FUNAI in

1986. Further reductions trimmed another 14 percent of indigenous lands (Buchillet 1990).

It must be pointed out that the military associated the notion of "Indian colony" with the status of "acculturated Indian," a category created by decree (No. 94.946, September 1987) a few months before the new constitution precluded any such distinction. The decree set out the difference between "nonacculturated" and "acculturated"—disturbingly evocative of the colonial classifications of "wild" and "tame" Indians—and guaranteed "Indian areas" to nonacculturated Indians and provided "Indian colonies" for acculturated Indians. Whereas Indian areas were intended for the exclusive use of their indigenous inhabitants, Indian colonies were to be open to colonization by non-Indians. Under this definition the invasion of Indian colonies would have been legal (Teixeira de Carvalho and Carneiro da Cunha 1987, 90). Although totally unconstitutional, this classification device was maintained by FUNAI, which had become a mere executive branch of the National Security Council (Oliveira Filho 1992), until the 1988 Constitution was ratified. It was applied to the Uaupés population with the rationale that the Tukanoans already spoke Portuguese and were conversant with national society. Never mind that included in this land partition were most of the Maku, an Indian population little influenced by contact with outsiders. The Calha Norte Project contemplated only one independent Maku "Indian area" of 48,000 hectares in the Iauaretê region. In November 1989 a new interministerial document changed "Indian colonies" to "Indian areas" but maintained the land fragmentation (Buchillet 1990). In a curious contradiction the same decree that confirmed Pari-Cachoeira I, II, and III as Tukanoan (and Maku) areas, designated them as "Indian areas," "due to the degree of contact" of these Indians.

All this tampering with concepts was obviously done in anticipation of and in an attempt to make moot pro-Indian decisions by the Constitutional Assembly. The military was running against time in its effort to reach a point of no return in the policy of Indian land demarcation. By co-opting leaders such as Álvaro Sampaio, the Calha Norte also provoked serious cleavages among the Tukanoans, dividing those who were negotiating with the military and those who resisted any interference with their land rights. Collaboration with the military included pro–Calha Norte propaganda on television, with Tukanoans exalting the great future of the Amazon thanks to the project.

Members of the Federation of Rio Negro Indigenous Organizations (Federação das Organizações Indígenas do Rio Negro, FOIRN), the faction that accepted the Calha Norte Project and collaborated with the military's plans, gambled on the benefits promised by the military (land demarcation, infrastructure for health, education, and economic development) in exchange for the eviction of garimpeiros and subsequent installation of the Paranapanema mining company. FOIRN members incurred heavy criticism and censure from other regional and national indigenous organizations and non-Indian NGOs, only to learn a few months later that the military was breaking its promises.

> The three "hospital-boats" acquired by the Calha Norte Project are already abandoned at the São Gabriel da Cachoeira harbor, two of them badly damaged. The health posts that were actually built cannot operate for lack of equipment, medicines and qualified personnel. . . . Of the much proclaimed "progress" Calha Norte was supposedly bringing to the North Amazon region, it is clear that there was little benefit, if at all, to the Indians, and only in the form of development projects that are ecologically predatory (cattle raising, logging, etc.), and of aid structures that are materially spectacular but technically unfeasible, designed to make the Indians sedentary in minuscule parcels of their former territories now transformed into Indian Colonies. (Buchillet 1990, 135)

As a result of this co-optation, Sampaio and companions incurred a long list of debts—airfares and hotel bills for trips to the capital to meet with government officials—with the Paranapanema mining company, which supported the pro–Calha Norte lobby in Brasília. "Paranapanema left the region, thus deactivating their security system and other benefits which were the basis of the alliance between the Indians and the company as a means to rid themselves of the torment of invasions and conflicts with garimpeiros" (C. Ricardo 1991, 103). Now they owed the company airfares, hotel bills, and other expenses, which the company had kept careful track of to use as political fuel against those Indians (p. 103). In 1991 Benedito Fernandes Machado, a former Calha Norte partisan, filed a suit at the United Nations against the military command of Amazonia and the Union. He and other Tukano leaders sought the moral condemnation of the Brazilian government and army for damages inflicted on the Tukano community (CEDI 1991a, 128).

The Calha Norte cookie-cutter continued eastward and reached Yanomami lands—a traditional territory of nearly 9.5 million hectares, according to FUNAI's own 1985 evaluation. In the Yanomami case the military had no way to justify the creation of Indian colonies, as the Yanomami cannot, by any stretch of the imagination, be classified as "acculturated Indians." So the Calha Norte designers divided Yanomami lands into nineteen disconnected "Indian areas" in two national forests and one national park. From September to November 1988 a deluge of resolutions and decrees by FUNAI and President Sarney established and then amended the status of Indian rights of access to these national forests. First, the Yanomami were robbed of 13 percent of their lands, although they retained exclusive rights to the resources of the national forests. Next, those rights were withdrawn. Within two months the Yanomami had suffered a net loss of about 70 percent of their traditional territory (Albert 1990).

Plans for a military presence on Yanomami lands included the construction of four army garrisons and seven air force airstrips. The justification for this apparatus initially was to better supervise the border zone and control colonization in the area. The deception behind this rhetoric was exposed when the armed forces failed to prevent or control the disorderly activities of more than forty thousand garimpeiros who in August 1987 began the most violent gold rush in modern times, invading Yanomami territory both inside and outside the nineteen "Indian areas."

In June 1989, after nearly two years of bleak news from the area regarding the Yanomami's health and environmental damage caused by the massive garimpeiro invasion, a group that included members of Congress, church members, representatives of Brazilian scientific associations, and NGOs went to Roraima to gather firsthand information (Ramos 1991). On that occasion the group contacted the military commanders of the Second Special Frontier Battalion (Batalhão Especial de Fronteiras, BEF), and of the Sixth Engineering and Construction Battalion (Batalhão de Engenharia e Construções, BEC). The statements by the BEF commander, Colonel Lima Mendes, the army officer in charge of the local part of the Calha Norte Project, left no room for doubt about the real reason for the military presence in the Yanomami area. He estimated that 50,000 garimpeiros were in the jungle and 80,000 to 100,000 were in town. That being so, he added, it would be impossible to remove the miners by force. Therefore it was absolutely necessary to reach a "negotiated solution" with them and the government of Roraima. Romero Jucá, who by that time had left the presidency of FUNAI to become Roraima's governor (appointed by President Sarney), strongly backed gold panning in the area; he wanted to bring the mining operations under his government's control and stop the smuggling of more than 80 percent of the gold extracted. He also wanted to show that some Yanomami actually preferred to have the garimpeiros on their land. The undeniable fact, continued Lima Mendes, was that the quantity of gold was very "rewarding" and therefore a solution had to be found so that extraction could continue.

In answer to questions posed by the fact-finding delegation the colonel acknowledged that the army was there to ensure "internal security" by which he meant "to do the groundwork for community development; Surucucus is a development pole for the settlement of populations." When it was pointed out that Surucucus was an Indian area, indeed the most densely populated Yanomami region in Brazil, he simply replied: "This doesn't concern me; it is up to the government to decide" (Ramos 1991, 1995a, 1995b).

The large Yanomami population stood in stark contradiction to the much cherished notion of empty Amazonian spaces. How to justify colonization where the land was already occupied? The astronomical Yanomami mortality rate during the peak of the gold rush was a sign that a demographic void was being created. Garimpeiros and malaria were doing their work. How better to turn a region "where numerous groups of this same ethnic group reside" (as General Denys asserted) into a void but to let loose a swarm of malaria carriers among them?

Three telltale events exposed the military as a spearhead for economic interest groups. One was the enlargement of the airstrip at Paapiú, originally a small landing strip for one-engine aircraft used by Protestant missionaries and later by FUNAI personnel. At no time was there a plan to build an army garrison at Paapiú, but the air force increased its presence while ordering the destruction of a Yanomami communal house because it happened to stand within 100 meters of the edge of the runway, now declared a national security zone. The following year this airstrip became the hub of gold-mining operations on Yanomami land. Because the military never made explicit its tacit encouragement of illegal gold mining in Indian areas, we can only infer the purpose of improving the landing conditions in a location expected to be rich in gold.

Another indication was the total inaction of the armed forces during the invasion of Brazilian garimpeiros in Venezuelan territory. Considering the great emphasis the Calha Norte Project put on the maintenance of good relations with Brazil's northern neighbors, it is intriguing that Venezuela's formal complaints were ignored even after repressive action by the Venezuelan National Guard against Brazilian intruders and their mining equipment. Commander Lima Mendes explained that the invasion of Brazilian garimpeiros in Venezuela was not the responsibility of the Brazilian Army: "If our people invade Venezuela, it is their problem; if their people invade Brazil, the problem is ours." This simple-minded system appears rather odd in face of the elaborate descriptions of the Calha Norte's diplomatic intentions.

A third and particularly revealing fact was the participation of the military (both BEF and BEC) on a committee created by the Roraima government to control the settlement of garimpeiros in Yanomami territory. Governor Jucá's Meridian 62 Project was designed to organize gold-panning operations within the "Indian areas" as defined by the nineteen demarcation decrees. The remainder of the area—the national forests—would be managed by the Roraima state company (CODESAIMA), which would then subcontract other companies to exploit the gold deposits. Royalties would be transferred to FUNAI, which was to pass them on to the Yanomami. Roraima's governor would have the task of supervising and controlling the whole set of operations. Thus the triad of private interests, local government, and military was explicitly laid out.

It should be pointed out that practically the entire Yanomami area in Brazil became an object of desire after the results of the RADAMBRASIL Project were made public. Ten mining companies filed requests to explore for various minerals in areas amounting to about 230,000 hectares (CEDI/CONAGE 1988, 57–58). Difficult access to the area, oscillations in market prices for gold and cassiterite, and the moral visibility of the Yanomami on the international circuit of human rights helped cool these companies' enthusiasm for immediate investment in the region, keeping them on standby.

It would not be improper to mention the hypothesis, actually raised quite frequently, that the military installation on Yanomami territory served as a beachhead for the garimpeiro avalanche that nearly killed off the Yanomami in Brazil. The gold rush would in turn create politically favorable conditions for the entry of large-scale industrial mining, which would play the role of "rational" agent capable of bringing order to the chaos left by the garimpo adventure. In 1993, after the controversy about Yanomami land had subsided, a top-level national security executive made a revealing statement that seems to confirm the hypothesis:

> The chief-minister of the Secretariat for Strategic Affairs (SAE) [successor to the National Security Council], Admiral Mário César Flores, proposes the entry of mining companies in the Yanomami reserve. According to him, this is the best way to control garimpeiro activity because the companies would be "more responsible" in their relations with the Indians and the environment. (Martins 1993)

The political clout of big mining enterprises cannot be overemphasized. The 1988 Constitution prohibits placer mining in Indian areas, but industrial mining can be done if approved by the National Congress after consultation with the indigenous communities concerned. These communities may express their opinion, but they have no veto power. Ultimately, the mining companies derive most of the benefit from military action and from the trail of disease and death left in the wake of garimpo activities among the Yanomami.

The gold rush is still costing the Yanomami lives, the total number of which is yet to be properly reported. Researchers, medical personnel, and Catholic missionaries were expelled from the area by FUNAI and the military precisely as waves of adventurers flew freely into Yanomami territory. For the first three years after the garimpeiro invasion began, no independent sources witnessed the devastation in any extensive, let alone intensive, way. Journalists made short visits to some mining areas, bringing back images of malnutrition, Yanomami bodies rotting on trails, patronizing gold miners distributing medicines and canned foods. Accusations of genocide poured in against the federal government from Brazil and abroad. The crisis reached such catastrophic proportions that the judiciary issued a restraining order in late 1989 that commanded the executive to put a stop to it. Two months later the government made plans to remove the garimpeiros and install an emergency medical program. Both the Ministry of Health and FUNAI were involved in the effort to curb the malaria epidemics that constantly raged throughout the countryside as the result of the influx of large numbers of miners and that were wiping out whole Yanomami communities. In desperation government authorities appealed to the anthropology and medical experts they had banned from the area. Before the garimpeiro invasions malaria was at most endemic in some localities. Paapiú, for example, had been entirely free of it. Between 1983 and 1987 the detailed medical records kept during a series of visits by the Committee for the Creation of the Yanomami Park (CCPY) and Médecins du Monde (a French medical NGO) medical teams show only three or four cases of malaria, all contracted by individuals who had traveled to other regions.

The Yanomami case brought to one political arena an odd collection of characters with the most conflicting postures and interests: the savage capitalism of gold entrepreneurs; destitute masses of uprooted squatters; Yanomami cultural diversity; a local government openly in favor of garimpo activities; a federal government swaying like a pendulum between meeting private demands and maintaining the illusion of democracy; a local judiciary at the service of economic powers; and a federal judiciary at the service of justice. The state was devouring itself.

What in fact happened was that at the very end of the Sarney administration (January 1990), rather than removing the garimpeiros, as ordered by a court, the authorities—the minister of justice, the governor of Roraima, the chief of federal police, and the Department of Mineral Resources— made a pact with the miners' leaders. The authorities simply offered to open other Yanomami areas in the so-called national forests to the garimpeiros and did this before the astonished eyes of a legion of national and international journalists who had flown to Roraima's capital of Boa Vista to report on the Yanomami decimation. As one of the reporters said, the miners were receiving the gift of leaving destroyed forest areas to enter virgin ones. Although public reaction was swift and angry, the authorities played ping-pong, making decisions in favor of the Indians one day, in favor of the garimpeiros the next, and keeping reporters busy for weeks. The government released approximately U.S.$1.5 million for an eviction operation that never actually took place. What happened to that money is not known, a common occurrence in the history of Amazonia—and of Brazil, for that matter. The Collor administration dynamited the clandestine landing strips in an attempt to stop the garimpeiro invasion. Finally, in 1991, after nearly a quarter of a century of pleading, Collor himself signed the decree establishing the large continuous territory of Yanomami Indian land.

The Yanomami, once an exotic and fierce people, became a symbol of indigenous peoples threatened with extinction. Propelled into the international media spotlight by a series of campaigns for the demarcation of their territory, the Yanomami assumed the involuntary role of icon for pro-Indian and environmental NGOs. "In this fin-de-siècle, Brazil and the world watch through TV and newspapers the genocide of one of the largest indigenous peoples in the Amazon forest" (CEDI 1991c, 172). Although they were unaware that they represented the opposition to dehumanizing economic development, the Yanomami have occupied prominent places in the field of human rights, involving agencies such as the United Nations, Organization of American States, and International Labor Organization (pp. 178–93). This national and international visibility has halted the headlong economic and political aggression against them. Thus, the very strategy designed to conquer the Yanomami by exploiting their epidemiological vulnerability was turned around in their favor. They have gone through excruciating agonies of disease and death, but the public knowledge of their agony has saved them from extinction.

Calha Norte was not the only project on the military agenda for Amazonia. In 1988 the Secretariat for National Defense (SADEN), the military organism that replaced the National Security Council, created the Program for the Development of the Western Amazon Border (PROFFAO). Its purpose was to build a regional infrastructure that would encourage large investments along the border with Peru and Bolivia. The military expected to link the region to the rest of the country and to neighboring nations by means of road systems, hydroelectric schemes, and the "rationalization" of extractive activities, as well as "land distribution, Indians and garimpeiros" (CEDI 1989, 26). Unlike the Calha Norte Project, which was entirely devised by the military and the president of the republic, the West Amazon Program needed congressional approval, according to the new constitution. But unfavorable political circumstances have so far relegated this program to wishful thinking by the military.

To appease public indignation against environmental and ethnic destruction in the Amazon, the Sarney government devised the Nossa Natureza (Our Nature) Project, and the military promptly seized control of it. The declared objective of the project, much advertised on television, was to curb fiscal incentives for agribusiness and mining activities in Amazonia as a way to slow the rate of deforestation. However, because the World Bank and other international financing agencies conditioned their funding of potentially harmful projects on protective measures by the receiving countries, the Brazilian government reacted with the strongly nationalist argument that Amazonia was a matter of national sovereignty and therefore its sole responsibility. The wolf was guarding the sheep. The House of Representatives in Brasília created the Parliamentary Inquiry Committee (CPI) to scrutinize Nossa Natureza, but the committee fizzled out, "and the Nossa Natureza Project died of administrative-political lethargy before it was actually born" (Brigagão 1996, 29).

The military agenda for Amazonia seems inexhaustible. In 1980 General Meira Mattos spelled out his concern for the internationalization of the Amazon in a strategy he called Pan Amazonia and included all seven countries that share the Amazon forest. In his view "it would be dangerous to leave the vast Amazon basin unpopulated and underdeveloped when there are areas going through serious problems with overpopulation—Bangladesh, Indochina, Japan. . . . It would not be desirable for the Amazonian countries to lose their sovereignty over this unexploited region with the pretext of incapacity to exploit it" (quoted in Rios 1993, 56). Again, the idea was to fill up with nationals a region that was regarded as demographically empty. Regional and indigenous populations remained geopolitically invisible.

In 1996, amid an interminable corruption scandal involving military authorities, members of Congress, private companies, and Raytheon, the North American missile manufacturer, the administration of Fernando Henrique Cardoso launched the U.S.$1.4 billion Amazonia Surveillance System (SIVAM). It was originally conceived during the Sarney years (1985–1990) and officially created but never implemented by the Collor administration (Brigagão 1996, 52). A grandiose project that will operate with state-of-the-art technology, SIVAM is designed to carry out not just national but "ecological security" by monitoring deforestation, human settlement, drug trafficking, weather, air and water pollution, and what goes on in indigenous areas (p. 29). In other words, it will be the ultimate step toward total military control of the Amazon. There are, however, some skeptical voices in the military itself. Comparing SIVAM to fantasies in Arnold Schwarzenegger movies, Thaumaturgo Sotero Vaz, the humorous general who criticized "beer-loving anthropologists" (Chapter 1), is displeased with the climate of corruption surrounding the approval and financing of the project and adds that "the Federal Police, with or without SIVAM, has no structure to combat drug trafficking" (p. 72). His complaint expresses a common opinion—that the hypersophisticated aerial apparatus will have no counterpart at the ground level, where things usually happen.

But Senator Romeu Tuma, a former federal police chief, has no qualms about declaring his intention to take advantage of the SIVAM scandal to resurrect Calha Norte. "The Project is abandoned, without funding. Yet it remains fundamental to the Country's security. Due to its configuration, it could lead to an internal division of labor complementing SIVAM in the job of air control" (quoted in ISA 1996a, 107). Brigadier Mauro Gandra, a former air force minister ousted during the SIVAM scandal, ventured a peculiar air-to-ground analogy: "Calha Norte is a bulldozer whereas SIVAM is a television" (p. 107). A special congressional committee was created in 1995 to draw up a strategy to revitalize the Calha Norte Project after it declined and became a mere appendage to the Secretariat for Strategic Affairs (SAE) (Brigagão 1996, 27). Actually, the

> only things that prospered in the region in three and a half years of military tutelage were the loot[ing] of minerals, disrespect for human rights, and forest devastation. Examples are many and little by little the world is getting to know them: there is the Yanomami genocide, the Balbina reservoir which drowned a forest the size of Greater São Paulo, while fifty thousand garimpeiros throw tons of mercury into the rivers, contaminating the Amazon basin. (CEDI 1991b, 93)

A Political Economy of Waste

Wasting away as a result of various waves of development fever, Amazonia, the world's enchanted *ecosystemic cornucopia* (Brigagão 1996, 41), has become a wasteland of mismanaged resources (Pinto 1980). While private enterprise has rapaciously depleted these resources, the actions of the state have contributed nothing to generate wealth and stability for the region. Amazonia has been treated "as an empty frontier from which profits could be rapidly and wastefully extracted with little regard for, or sustained economic participation by, existing socioeconomic or environmental systems." Reckless misuse of Amazonian resources has so disrupted "ecological and human systems as to limit the possibility of future modes of production to respond to new opportunities for either economic exchange or social reproduction" (Bunker 1985, 77).

The decimation of indigenous populations and loss of indigenous lands have been the constant companions of this ecological abuse of Amazonia. Fearnside (1989, 9) estimates that until 1988 nearly 590,000 square kilometers of forests and savannas had been cut down, representing nearly 12 percent of the total area of Amazonia in Brazil. If Calha Norte had been successful, Indian lands would have been further reduced by 12 million hectares of national forest, not to mention 10 million hectares reserved for "special use" by the armed forces (CEDI 1989, 10).

If all this nature devastation and human affliction had at least resulted in an improvement in the country's economic situation, or in better living conditions for the rural and urban poor, one might consider that such sacrifice had a positive side. But this is not the case. The sad conclusion is that the hardships inflicted on the Indian and regional populations of Amazonia amount to precious little benefit for the nation. Dennis Mahar of the World Bank makes the devastating assessment that, "despite the case of intense development, Amazonia still accounts for only an insignificant 3% of the national income" (1989, 46).

Despite the rhetoric that exalts indigenous ecological knowledge and wisdom, development assaults on Amazonia have systematically ignored the experience of Indian peoples who have been occupying and exploiting the forest for centuries. Long-standing native practices of agriculture, hunting, and gathering have no doubt transformed the environment, and yet, as can be easily verified, they have not destroyed it. The irony of this is that the very Indian peoples who have proved themselves so competent in their treatment of the forest are so often disparaged as obtuse and backward by those who have proved themselves so wanting in their ability to handle Amazonia. Consider the following:

> It happened at noon on 22 February 89, at the barracks of the 5th BEF in São Gabriel da Cachoeira (AM), Calha Norte's military capital. A group of Indian-soldiers recruited from the Baré, Tukano, Wanano, Tiriano, and Piratapuia nations, armed with shovels and hoes, prepared to work on the road that links one barracks to another. An officer makes fun of the troop: "They are good labor force, but have no brains. If I tell them to open a trench and don't order them to stop, they can go on digging a hole right through Amazonia." (CEDI 1991b, 93)

An olive-green quip just to illustrate the arrogance and disrespect to which indigenous peoples are exposed when put directly in the hands of Amazonia's overseers.

9

Legal Weapons of Conquest

A certain strain of schizophrenia runs through official Brazilian Indian policy. On the one hand, legislators in general have been fairly sensitive to cultural and ethnic differences and produced a substantial amount of legal protection for indigenous peoples. On the other hand, executive agents, be they FUNAI administrators, state governors, or even ministers and presidents of the republic, have consistently attempted to undermine the effects of pro-Indian laws, including the Constitution. Here I shall present three of these attempts: the emancipation decree, the criteria of Indianness, and a 1996 decree that changes the decision-making process regarding the demarcation of Indian lands.

Dawes Act, Brazilian Style

To most of us the word *emancipation* means the acquisition of a new status of freedom from a previously subordinated and essentially undesirable condition. When emancipated, slaves and minors stop being slaves and minors and become citizens no longer under the control of their masters and guardians. In late 1978 some Brazilian Indian groups were on the verge of becoming "emancipated" from their condition of wards of the state by means of a decree prepared by Maurício Rangel Reis, the minister of the interior to whom the National Indian Foundation (FUNAI) then reported.

In contrast to slaves and minors, one cannot expect ethnic groups such as Indian peoples to stop being Indians by force of a decree. Yet that was what Minister Rangel Reis committed to do during his term in office (1974–1979). Even before he became minister, he had revealed his intention to put a stop to the official guardianship of the Indians within a short time. A week before taking office he stated that "the policy of the new government is to absorb the Indians into civilized society and to abandon—as quickly as possible—the idea of Indian reserves" (*Jornal do Brasil* 1974). From then on Rangel Reis took the issue of Indian emancipation as one of his main goals. He predicted that "within the next thirty years at the most all Indians living in Brazil will be perfectly integrated in our society" (*Jornal de Brasília* 1976a). His policy culminated in the ill-conceived "decree of emancipation," an attempt to alter the Indian Statute to give FUNAI the power to terminate indigenous special status.

During the second half of 1978 the Brazilian press, enjoying its first phase of seemingly genuine freedom since the military coup of 1964, was engaged in a campaign against the emancipation decree. This campaign was extended abroad, and the Brazilian authorities were showered with international protests. It worked and the decree was shelved.

What would have been the consequences of emancipation for the Indians at that point in the history of Brazilian Indigenism? The first and foremost problem was land. According to the 1967 federal Constitution and its 1988 successor, the Indians have the exclusive right to "possess" (but not "own"), use, and exploit the land they inhabit, although this land remains the inalienable property of the Brazilian state. Furthermore, the Indian Statute, Law No. 6001 of December 1973, declares in Article 25 that the right of Indian groups to permanent possession of their territory does not depend on its physical demarcation. Therefore, so long as the Indians are legally recognized as Indians, the law protects the inalienability of their lands. The legal provision for indigenous special status took the form of wardship, a mechanism operating in the New World since the eighteenth century (Bennet 1978, 7).

Although being wards of the state puts the Indians in a position that is highly vulnerable to paternalistic abuses, it is nevertheless one way to protect them from exploitation by a much more powerful society, which has shown little tolerance for indigenous peoples and no desire to coexist with them on equal terms. An alternative would be to confer upon the Indians the right to maintain their lifestyles while remaining the legal collective owners of their lands, in recognition of their historical position as the country's first inhabitants. But for Brazilian legislators such a possibility does not really exist.

The emancipation decree was a clear maneuver to untie Indian lands from the strings of state wardship. By coercing Indians into formal integration the state was finally eliminating "an obstacle to the country's development," as a former FUNAI president, General Oscar Jeronymo Bandeira de Mello, used to say in the 1970s. For if the Indians were no longer Indians, their lands would be open to the market. It would be yet another repetition of the New World pattern epitomized by the U.S. Dawes General Allotment (Severalty) Act of the nineteenth century. This act resulted in "the individual allotment of Indian lands as a first step toward the adoption of 'the habits of civilized life' by the Indians of the United States. When the Dawes Act passed in 1887, U.S. Indians owned approximately 140 million acres of land. Over the next 45 years, more than 90 million acres passed from Indian to white hands" (Davis 1978, 1; see also Eggan 1978). In the 1960s Canadian Indians were threatened with two attempts to force their "emancipation" from special constitutional status and to establish that their lands would no longer be federal lands. Both attempts failed. Not only did Canadian Indians keep their territories but they steadily moved toward self-determination (Sanders 1978).

Responding to pressures from economic groups with a strong interest in exploiting resources located in Indian areas, the Brazilian government conceived the emancipation decree, taking care to keep this interest undeclared and insisting on a seemingly democratic treatment of indigenous minorities. In his insidiously hypocritical rhetoric Minister Rangel Reis claimed that he was only concerned with the welfare of the Indians. The government's intention, he declared, was "in the long run to allow the Indians to become politicians, generals, and even presidents of the Republic" (*Jornal de Brasília* 1978; see also *Time* 1978). But to anyone minimally informed about the history of interethnic contact, and about the strong bent of the Brazilian state to oversee the country's affairs in general, it was clear that the emancipation decree would put the Indians in an impossible position: not allowed to continue with their traditional way of life and not properly equipped to cope with national society. The blast of criticism that poured over the government came as no surprise.

In August 1978 Brazilian anthropologists made a strong and united statement about the emancipation decree:

> We are now witnessing the last and perhaps the most overwhelming wave of expansion westward and northward. This expansion is being carried out primarily by large business corporations. This is then a particularly inappropriate time to leave the Indians without protection. To emancipate them *now* is to abandon them unarmed to forces that are infinitely more powerful and that will, sooner or later, take their lands away from them for a token price by means of land speculation or the creation of chronic indebtedness. Without their lands, the Indians will then be swallowed up as cheap labor. Too many Brazilians are already subjected to these conditions and there is no reason why their numbers should be increased. . . . To emancipate indigenous groups now in the name of equality among citizens is to "wash one's hands" of what will happen. . . . It is argued . . . [that there is] a disproportion between the number of Indians and the area they occupy, forgetting that right beside them are land properties many times larger, the owners of which are many times fewer than their Indian neighbors. (Comissão Pró-Índio 1979b, 18–19)

After the public outcry that greeted the minister's stated intention to implement his emancipation policy, another draft of the decree was written, declaring that even after emancipation the Indians would, if they wished, retain the permanent and exclusive right of possession and usufruct of their lands, which would continue to be inalienable whether demarcated or not (*Jornal do Brasil* 1978). Now it sounded as if emancipation was not so bad after all and that the Indians would perhaps have the best of two worlds, that is, they would be free of government paternalism and still enjoy official protection from land grabbers. The question was then raised: if his purpose is not to take over the lands, why should the minister go to the trouble of emancipating Indians and expose himself to so much criticism?

Soon the promise of land protection for emancipated Indians was proved to be legally meaningless. A statement by a São Paulo lawyer made it clear that "by means of emancipation, the Indian stops being Indian from a legal point of view and, as a consequence, he is freed from the condition of ward of the state and also loses the privileges granted him by law, including the right to land possession" (Dallari 1978, 80). Legal contradictions of this sort, plus national and international pressure, led President Ernesto Geisel to abandon the idea of emancipating the Indians. For the time being, the government would let the matter rest.

Articles 9, 10, and 11 of the 1973 Indian Statute establish that once Indian individuals or communities have acquired sufficient knowledge and familiarity with the national society, they can request their emancipation. But because no Indian individual or community had ever done so (other than a short-lived attempt by the Xokleng of Santa Catarina who requested emancipation and almost immediately withdrew it), the Geisel administration decided not to wait for voluntary emancipations that might never come. This was the decade of the megaprojects in Amazonia, when the interior of the country was being taken over both by private and state-sponsored economic operations. In the three drafts of the emancipation decree were two articles that would have given the National Indian Foundation the ultimate power to decide whether an Indian individual or community was to be relieved of official wardship, which amounted to forced emancipation and the consequent eviction of the Indians from much coveted lands. Otherwise, there would be no reason to legislate a procedure already contemplated in the Indian Statute.

As in Canada, an impressive outcome of the minister's efforts was the sudden growth of political awareness on the part of the Indians themselves. Leaders of several groups from all over the country organized meetings to discuss the problem, thus accelerating the experience they had slowly accumulated with the CIMI-supported Indian assemblies. The prospect of a full-fledged Pan-Indian movement became very real. In fact, two years later the Union of Indian Nations came into existence.

Two major issues were constant in indigenous statements. One was the ever-present loss of land. The other was their total and unqualified rejection of the emancipation decree. All anthropologists, other advocates of indigenous rights, and, more important, the Indians themselves saw through the declared good intentions of the government, perceiving quite clearly that behind its apparently enlightened proposition powerful political and economic forces were at work. This awareness was evident in a document addressed to the president of the republic by thirteen different indigenous peoples:

> Just as public opinion has condemned this emancipation, so do we also, in the name of the Brazilian Indian Community, repudiate this emancipation. Let it be removed from your office and let our claims be taken into consideration. . . . Let it be recognized that the Indian is the legitimate heir and owner of his land and let the reserves be recognized as the collective property of the Indian communities. . . . If pretty words solved our problems, today we would not be in this situation which is so different from that guaranteed by the Indian Statute. The emancipation desired by the minister will only bring detribalization to the Indian communities, and therefore, the collective and individual destruction of their members. (Comissão Pró-Índio 1979c, 28–29)

Turning Indians virtually overnight into ordinary Brazilian citizens would have had other consequences. They would have lost protection for their specific ways of life, curtailing their freedom to act according to their traditions. Such common practices as polygamy, infanticide, nakedness, the use of hallucinogens, some mortuary rites, modes of social control, and many other cultural features would have automatically fallen under the sanctions contained in the national civil and penal codes. It is doubtful that cultures would be respected without official protection. Most likely, un-Brazilian customs would be summarily outlawed. The obvious consequences would be many. One such example is provided by the Salesian missionaries in the Upper Rio Negro area who until not so long ago forced acculturation upon the local Indians, particularly by means of physically and culturally constricting boarding schools. For about fifty years priests and nuns hammered the same message: what the Indians do as Indians is never any good, and it has to be changed—they *must* be civilized (Reichel-Dolmatoff 1972, 1996). Another example is the tragic story of a Guajajara Indian from the state of Maranhão who was persuaded to accompany members of the military police to a neighboring town. He was jailed and tortured almost to death like a political prisoner of the military regime. His crime? He belonged to a culture that makes ritual use of marijuana (CIMI 1978).

   In their 1978 manifesto opposing emancipation Brazilian anthropologists put the issue of Indian cultural rights succinctly and emphatically: *"They have not only the right to be 'like us' but also the right to be themselves."* Diversity does not imply inequality. The democratic treatment of diverse societies does not require the blending of all in one single way of life, but . . . a recognition of the value of different ways of life" (Comissão Pró-Índio 1979b, 18).

A year later, while the emancipation muddle was still being digested, there was another attempt to change the Indian Statute, this time by a legislator, Hélio Campos, a member of Congress from Roraima, which at that time was still a federal territory. He proposed that Indian areas be excluded from the 150-kilometer-wide frontier zone with the justification that "the border areas of the country, by their geographical condition, are vulnerable to all sorts of alien abuse." Although his proposal included the entire international boundary, from its northern border with French Guiana to the southern border with Argentina, the target was the northern Amazon where "there are Indian areas located in the border zone. And the Indian of that region, given his socio-cultural condition, has become an easy prey to foreign groups who, disguised as false evangelical missions, spread ideas that are contrary to our interests, besides affronting National Security" (quoted in Ramos 1980a, 12). The argument of false missionaries was nothing but a smoke screen. The plan itself was like using a cannonball to kill a small bird. To justify his interest in the mineral wealth of Yanomami lands Campos conceived of a law that would have affected all indigenous groups that live on the huge arch that runs from Amapá in the extreme north to Rio Grande do Sul in the extreme south of the country. In fact, a 1955 law, reenacted in 1979, prohibited foreigners from making any kind of transaction involving rural land.

Since the days of empire the country's border strip has been the dominion of the central government. Accordion-like, it contracted or expanded as the Brazilian state grew more or less apprehensive about sovereignty — from 65 kilometers in 1850, to 100 in 1934, back to 66 in 1945, and, from 1955 on, 150 kilometers (Rios 1993, 54–55). International borders have increasingly become the country's Achilles heel. The 1988 Constitution declares that the 150-kilometer belt is fundamental for the defense of national territory and should remain the exclusive property of the Union. It is therefore unavailable to "traditional forms of acquisition, such as buying, selling or donation, or to unconventional ways, such as occupation and *usucapião* [prescription; acquisition of rights through continuous use]" (Rios 1993, 55). This being the case, keeping the boundaries under direct state control and having them *occupied* by indigenous peoples whose lands are also the Union's property are not legally incompatible moves. Thus the efforts, mostly by the military, to clear the border region, particularly in the Amazon, of Indian populations actually have nothing to do with national security.

A True-False Test for Indianness

Less than two years after the emancipation fiasco two retired air force colonels, João Carlos Nobre da Veiga, FUNAI's president, and Ivan Zanoni Hausen, director of FUNAI's Community Planning Department, devised the "criteria of Indianness." In January 1981 Zanoni created a committee of three FUNAI employees to prepare a list of more than sixty items meant to be traits of Indianness. It amounted to a ludicrous check list to be applied to individuals whom the agency deemed unworthy of its protection. Among the items were such things as whether the candidate for Indianness displayed "primitive mentality" (pace Lévy-Bruhl [1923] 1966), "undesirable cultural, psychic, and biological characteristics," "representative cultural traits," enigmatic "social characteristics to be defined," or "qualitative physical features" such as the Mongolian spot (regardless of the candidate's age![1]), nose shape or profile, and amount of body hair. Included in the test was whether the candidate dressed, ate, and performed like an Indian. The criteria also included "concepts pointed out by national society," namely, social marginalization, preservation and influence of regional stereotypes, and six other items that are simply reworded repetitions of the same thing. Zanoni also proposed "blood criteria," which consisted of taking blood samples from Indians to check the presence or absence of such genes as the Diego Factor, said to be most frequent among American Indians in general but, symptomatically enough of such generalizations, is conspicuously absent among the icons of Indianness, the Yanomami. The idea behind this rather racist exercise was to rate people on a scale of zero to one hundred. Those who made fifty points or fewer failed the Indianness test and would be discharged as FUNAI's wards.

The consternation this move aroused in Indians with a long history of interethnic contact can be perceived in an interchange that took place in September 1981 between a man (José Saraiva) from the Tingui-Botó of the northeastern state of Alagoas and Colonel Zanoni at FUNAI's headquarters in Brasília. The five hundred Tingui-Botó had been "discovered" in February of that year, living on two hectares of land surrounded by big ranches where they worked for a few cents a day. They still spoke some of their traditional language and were concerned about maintaining their ancestral and secretive Ouricuri ritual away from the eyes of scoffing regional neighbors (CEDI 1982a, 51–52). In the interview, recorded and then transcribed by the Conselho Indigenista Missionário (CIMI) in

---

1. Indian and Asian babies are usually born with a dark spot on their lower back that disappears in the first years of life.

its December 1981 issue of the monthly journal *Porantim* (also published
in CEDI 1982a, 82–83), Zanoni exhibits an unusual degree of arrogance,
even by FUNAI standards. "What's up?" he began, "have you been waiting long? Sit down and speak up because I'm leaving." Saraiva replied by
cautiously signaling that Zanoni should do the speaking—to explain why
FUNAI was dragging its heels in recognizing Saraiva's people as indigenous and demarcating their land. He insisted on showing the colonel some
material evidence of his Indianness. Zanoni steered the conversation away
from these cultural displays and insisted that their Indian status had yet to
be proved. "Someone's got to explain . . . to you that you people are half-
Indian, you're remnants. . . . When we look at you . . . we know you have
Indian blood, but you also have African blood." Perplexed, Saraiva simply
muttered a puzzled "African." Zanoni continued, echoing the old Brazilian
refrain that he too has Indian blood. The rest of the conversation revolved
around Zanoni's amazing theory of miscegenation:

> ZANONI: Zé, you know it isn't FUNAI's fault. Because you, for a long
> time . . . Let's sit down. . . . You, for a long time, you've always been iden-
> tified as *caboclos* [roughly, "mixed-blood" Indians]. I learned in school
> that whoever has half white blood with black is mulatto.
> SARAIVA: Mulatto.
> ZANONI: Those who have Indian and white blood are caboclos. And
> those who have half Indian and half black are *cafusos*. Didn't we learn
> this? Now, there comes a day when someone comes along and says: No,
> those who have such and such of Indians are Indian. Of course! If I say
> that I have German blood, I have a twenty whatever of German. But I'm
> not German. I'm not German at all. I'm no longer German. Now, I have
> German blood, as I have French blood, Portuguese blood from Azores,
> and Indian blood. Well, Saraiva, just think. An American, in the United
> States, he's got the answer. He said this: Indian is only that who is half
> Indian or more. Then you're half-Indian. What does half-Indian mean?
> Here you have the Indian, right? And here you have the white. If white
> marries Indian, then we call you pure caboclo. Over there in the United
> States, he's Indian. Because it's written that it's half blood. Now, this
> here is white. Therefore, this other will be half-Indian. But if he mar-
> ries a white person, he'll no longer be, because then there won't be half
> blood, but a quarter.
> SARAIVA: A quarter.
> ZANONI: Now, if this one here marries an Indian again, then he'll feed
> the blood again, and the result is Indian. Something like that. But here in
> Brazil there's nothing written about this. The day we have a law saying
> this . . . there won't be these bad fights any more. Well, then, what is an
> Indian remnant? An Indian remnant is someone who has Indian blood,
> like I am a remnant. I'm a German remnant. Like a boy whose father is

Japanese is a Japanese remnant. One has to know how far blood goes. Then he comes up to you, the anthropologist, and asks, José Saraiva, who are your parents? Then you say, My father was Indian, my mother, white. Your grandmother? Well, my mother's father was black and she was Indian, but her father . . . Get it?

SARAIVA: I'd like you to really . . . see our traditions, if with . . .

ZANONI: But look, the problem with tradition is that it brings up something else. What's your tradition? Your tradition is stronger precisely because of the trait. If you're on Indian land, those people, even blacks with kinky hair, take up Indian culture, three hundred years ago blacks entered the area because of Palmares [a slave revolt]. Then we'll reach the conclusion that FUNAI will say no. Even though in culture you go on being Indian. . . .

SARAIVA: But that's what I've come to ask. . . .

ZANONI: Well then, rest assured, my boy. Now, one thing, . . . you were wrong in coming here without talking to your delegate.

SARAIVA: Colonel . . . Colonel Zanoni, I know I was wrong. But you . . .

ZANONI: Whether you're Indian or not, it is the expert report that's going to say. [About] everybody. Indian is that who's Indian, who assumes his condition. Now, this has nothing to do with the land problem. This is a much tougher business. . . .

SARAIVA: Would you mind taking a look at a little of our culture? At our ritual? Right here in front of you?

ZANONI: Not now, because I have an appointment, as I told you. This afternoon I have a meeting at the Ministry of the Interior. Now I have guests for lunch at home. I can't. I would prefer to be honored by you when I visit your village.

In hindsight it is easy to laugh at Zanoni's pathetic obtuseness. But at the time the comical side of the criteria of Indianness was superseded by a real fear that FUNAI's colonels might be determined to carry out their grotesque true-false act. It was safer to take the thing seriously. Outraged Indians, missionaries, anthropologists, lawyers, and journalists bombarded FUNAI in the press, in rallies, and in professional meetings with accusations of racism.

Another consequence of compulsory termination of special status would have been the elimination of Indian leaders who had been active in the emergent pan-Indian movement, such as Mário Juruna, Álvaro Sampaio, and Marcos Terena. Ending state wardship for Indians older than twenty-one, who spoke Portuguese, were familiar with national society, and had a profession amounted to punishing those who were most politically aware and assertive; they could then "be arrested and charged with any kind of penal or criminal process, including the National Security Law" (CEDI 1982a, 81).

The criteria of Indianness were eventually dropped, but not before they were tried on some Indians in the northeast, as the Zanoni interview testifies, and on the Ocoí Guarani whose land had been flooded by the Itaipu Dam. As a result, some of these Guarani were denied the right to relocate. In December 1981 they went to Brasília to prove to the new president of FUNAI, Colonel Paulo Moreira Leal, a former member of the National Security Council, how Indian they were in their broken Portuguese and physical "traits." Leal promised to revise the criteria of Indianness as it had been applied to them. The FUNAI agent who had done it was accused of having spoken to a single person about the legitimacy of the Indians' ethnic claim. This person was a land speculator who wanted the Indians expelled from the area in order to get the land compensation (CEDI 1982b, 87). In any case, the phase of Indianness criteria was over.

The practical effects of these attempts to turn the Indian Statute against the Indians lingered for a while. In 1981 Marcos Terena, an airplane pilot and college student in Brasília, complained bitterly about the pressure the government was putting on Indians to relinquish their special status. Because he flew FUNAI airplanes from time to time, he sought permanent employment with the agency, but Colonel Nobre da Veiga, its previous president, proposed a trade-off: employment for emancipation. "Why," Terena asked, "to be a pilot of the Indian Protection Agency, do I need to stop being Indian?" He continued, "I accept 'progressive and harmonious' integration to the national communion, as stated by the Indian Statute. It is inevitable. But I only admit to integration if it is based on a profound respect for the ethnic aspects and communal characteristics of each nation." To him the utmost offense is to be the object of laws and regulations without so much as a cursory consultation. "During last year's Indian Week we asked . . . Colonel Zanoni to participate in the events. The Colonel responded with a pile of papers and, blasé, asked us to accommodate to what was already programmed. There were films, posters, exhibits, everything just perfect. Only one thing was missing: the Indian." Loathing the Indians' demands, Zanoni fired back: "We are raising vipers to bite us" (Terena 1981, 90).

Guarding the Guardian

The slow political transition from military to civilian rule in the country brought about a particularly critical period of instability at FUNAI. The postmilitary New Republic moved the agency from the Ministry of the Interior to the Ministry of Justice, disregarding suggestions by the Indians' allies that indigenous policy be handled by a special secretariat directly under the presidency. FUNAI also went through an unusually acute administrative crisis. Between July 1983 and May 1986 the agency had eight presidents, some lasting five, four, and even just two months (CEDI 1987b, 27–29). Its first civilian president of the decade, an economist, fired four colonels, including Zanoni. The civilian president had to cope with the announcement of a mining decree that authorized mining companies to enter Indian areas. He in turn was fired for his "disastrous performance as a negotiator" during a Kayapó rebellion on the northern border of the Xingu park (p. 28). His next two successors had to cope with the commotion generated by the implementation of the mining decree, which turned out to be a rehearsal for what was eventually included in the 1988 Constitution.

The government's 1983 mining proposal would have altered the Indian Statute to permit "research and extraction of minerals deemed to be strategic, necessary to national security and development" in Indian areas. Indigenous support groups and sympathetic members of Congress protested that the proposed decree was unconstitutional—the 1967 Constitution precluded such activities in indigenous territories. "The Brazilian state should not be so docile in submitting itself to the lobby of companies that have already filed 300 requests for mineral exploration in indigenous areas" (Gomes 1984).

A State Against Its Indians
Alcida Rita Ramos

Originally published in the weekly column of the Brazilian Anthropological Association in *Jornal de Brasília,* December 3, 1983, p. 4.

They killed Marçal Guarani, the venerable indigenous leader who represented Brazilian Indians, who participated, during the pope's visit to Brazil [in 1982], in an international convention on multinational mining companies and Indian lands, who always stood out for his courage and determination to denounce crimes and abuses against Indians. They killed him as he performed his duties as a FUNAI nurse, a few days after he rejected a bribe of five million cruzeiros to remove his people from a village coveted by landholders in Mato Grosso do Sul. He is the eleventh Indian assassinated this year for defending the rights of his people.

It would seem that 1983 is the year chosen for exterminating indigenous peoples from the country. While at the local level—in Mato Grosso do Sul, Bahia, Paraíba, and other states—Indians are assassinated with impunity, at the federal level a profusion of anti-Indian decrees and laws is signed. There have been no less than six of these federal acts this year, each one carrying a deadly dose of poison against the Indians. From February to November this legal assault kept expanding. First, there was a decree signed by the minister of the interior, the minister ex-officio of land tenure, and by the president of the republic that removes from FUNAI the responsibility for demarcating indigenous lands and passes it on to a work group that includes "other federal and state organisms judged to be convenient." And one knows only too well how intent state governors are in taking away indigenous lands. This decree is tailor-made to satisfy these intentions. In May federal deputy Mozarildo Cavalcanti (PDS/Roraima) introduced a bill proposing the opening up of placer mining (*garimpo*) in the heart of Yanomami territory, one of the largest indigenous nations in the country with little contact with the outside world. According to the project, the Yanomami would be employed as labor in the garimpos. Given the vulnerability of these Indians, such a project would literally decree the death of the Yanomami at Surucucus.

In September an interministerial preliminary statement was approved that allowed military and federal police to intervene in cases of conflict or tension in Indian areas. Both FUNAI and "interested private people" could request police intervention. It goes without saying that this measure legalizes suppression of any organized and demanding movement by indigenous peoples. One can only note that the much touted relaxation of the military rulers' political control is quite selective: it exists for Brazilians (albeit only some) but not for Indians.

While the Civil Code shackles Indians to an absolute incapacity, the project by Deputy João Batista Fagundes (PDS/Roraima) denies Indians official protection. None of these proposals reflects the actual needs of the Indians, who, by the way, are never consulted.

What sort of a country is this that declares its pride for Cândido Mariano da Silva Rondon and his benevolence toward indigenous peoples but produces a flood of laws and decrees aimed at putting an end to the Indians; concedes restoration of civilian rights to some Brazilians but represses the Indians'; lets pass the death of eleven Indians without a single gesture toward punishing the killers? The year 1983, rather than bringing about the celebration of the Indian Statute's tenth anniversary, has become one of the most sinister years for indigenous peoples. We mourn Marçal Guarani as one more victim, not only of his killer's bullets but also of the volley of legal shots fired at the Indians by the powers that be.

In those uncertain years Brasília became a focal point for gatherings of Indians who came to the capital to pressure FUNAI. The Shavante in particular made several shows of force, especially after their leader Mário Juruna was elected to the National Congress in 1982. In April 1984 during a large assembly in Brasília the Indians provoked a conspicuously defensive reaction from federal authorities:

10. Indian rally outside the National Congress during the Constitutional Assembly. Photo by Beto Ricardo/ISA, 1988.

The scenes reminded one of a university campus in the sixties on a student rally day: shock troops, policemen armed with billy clubs and revolvers, federal agents, and German shepherds ready to go. This was how FUNAI employees found the Indian tutoring agency yesterday morning. On the other side of town, the same scenes: the Ministry of the Interior was surrounded by policemen. Both Minister Andreazza and FUNAI's president, fearing the invasion of 450 Indian leaders gathered in Brasília, requested that the Secretariat of Public Security take precautions against the Indians. . . . Shavante Chief Aniceto showed his sorrow: "This is how they welcome us. We have never received a FUNAI chief with armed warriors. This is coming to an end. FUNAI is coming to an end. It's no longer a tutor [guardian], now it attacks us with disrespect. We aren't enemies. All we want is the guarantee of our lands." (CEDI 1985b, 20)

Two years earlier a group of Shavante men, clubs in hand, had threatened to throw FUNAI president Nobre da Veiga out of a window if he persisted in ignoring their claim for land demarcation.

The rush of Indians to Brasília continued until 1986 when Romero Jucá, an economist and the sixth FUNAI president during the New Republic (1984–1986), cut off all expenses for Indians' bed and board in the capital, refused to receive indigenous delegations, and kept journalists at arm's length. This was during the initial phase of the Calha Norte Project when Indian policy was being conducted with an iron hand. Jucá repre-

11–12. Indians in full attire mingle with journalists and members of Congress during the Constitutional Assembly, 1988. Photos courtesy of the Archive Coordination, House of Representatives, National Congress, Brasília.

sented a two-year respite in FUNAI's turbulent turnover rate. When he left the agency in 1988 to become governor of Roraima during the Yanomami gold rush, the agency was again plagued with presidential turnover: four presidents in one year (CEDI 1991d, 42).

The 1987–1988 Constitutional Assembly was another intense moment in Brazil's Indigenism. The indigenous lobby, gathering together a multitude of Indian support organizations, professional associations, the Union of Indian Nations (UNI), and a massive Kayapó presence, was stronger than that of most civil society movements, such as the black movement or the movement for agrarian reform. Wide media coverage kept the Indian issue at a high level of visibility, which in itself was a double-edged sword. It both furthered the indigenous cause among members of Congress and provoked the tremendous reaction that culminated in the slanderous campaign against CIMI that was launched by a major São Paulo newspaper (see Chapter 6). There was no shortage of theatrical touches. Dressed in a white suit, Ailton Krenak, UNI's national coordinator, took to the podium in the House plenary room to protest the setbacks generated by the anti-Indian campaign. As he spoke, he slowly and solemnly smeared his face with black paint, mourning the constitutional losses that seemed to be looming for the Indians:

> I hope I'm not attacking you members of the House with my protest. . . . Today we are the target of an aggression which aims at hurting our faith in its essence, our confidence that there still is some dignity, that it is still possible to build a society that knows how to respect the weaker, knows how to respect those with no money to pay for a relentless defamation campaign, knows how to respect peoples who have always lived against the grain of wealth, peoples who live in thatched houses, who sleep on floor mats and who must not be identified as Brazil's enemies, enemies of the nation's interests who are a risk to development. Indigenous peoples have watered with their blood every single one of Brazil's eight million square kilometers. You are witnesses to this. (CEDI 1991a, 23)

Krenak's gesture and words caused an enormous flap in the media, as did the spectacle of dozens of colorfully clad Kayapó conspicuously occupying the front rows of congressional rooms and the timely display to a crowd of stunned members of Congress of a huge map prepared by CEDI (Centro Ecumênico de Documentação e Informação) and professional geologists showing the distribution of proposed mining sites in Amazonia. It resembled the blueprint for some gigantic scheme for land speculation. The political weight of these three events was decisive in the vote on the new constitution regarding indigenous matters.

The new constitution brought both gains and losses to the Indians, although the overall result was judged quite positive (M. Santilli 1991, 13).

13. UNI's president, Ailton Krenak, smears black paint on his face as he addresses members of Congress. Photo by Luis Antonio Ribeiro/AJB, 1987.

14. Kayapó and other Indians occupy a Congress room during the Constitutional Assembly. Photo by Beto Ricardo/ISA, 1988.

The major loss was rights to subsoil. Usufruct is now limited to surface re-sources—soil, rivers, and lakes. Moreover, the usual objects of development projects, such as hydroelectric dams and industrial mining, are open to non-Indians if approved by the National Congress, "after the affected communi-ties are heard, their participation in the yield being guaranteed, in the form of the law" (Article 231, paragraph 3). It was the frustrated 1983 mining decree come true, despite the new safety measure of congressional approval.

Perhaps the greatest improvement over the 1967 Constitution was the end of required and inevitable integration of Indians into national society. "Indigenous societies are no longer considered to be disappearing cultures whose inevitable and desirable destiny would be their incorporation into the so-called 'national communion.' To the contrary, indigenous rights to cultural alterity have been fully assured" (Gaiger 1989, 8).

Another victory was the recognition that Indians are capable of repre-senting themselves in disputes, no longer dependent on FUNAI as their guardian. Article 232 spells this out: "The Indians, their communities and organizations are legitimate parts in due process to defend their rights and interests, with the intervention of the Public Ministry in all acts of the process." This amounts to the virtual obsolescence of state wardship, re-quiring necessary, but not yet approved, adjustments to the Indian Statute,

15. Members of the Constitutional Assembly examine map of Amazonia covered with mining projects. Photo by André Dusek, copyright 1988 André Dusek/AGIL.

which defines wardship, and the Civil Code, which defines the Indians' "relative incapacity." As a consequence, the new constitutional rights leave the Indians free to organize themselves in associations without the specter of repressive measures such as those that haunted the creation of UNI (see Chapter 6). The result has been a proliferation of indigenous organizations, especially in the Amazon.

To some extent the 1988 Constitution reduced the military power concentrated in the Calha Norte Project launched two years earlier. For instance, the proposed "Indian colonies" for "acculturated Indians" disappeared, as the new constitution makes no distinction between Indians along the lines of contact experience. But a delayed reaction to the new Indian constitutional rights occurred, and during it the effects of the Calha Norte continued to be felt. Furthermore, supplementary legislation, such as the new Indian statute, has not been forthcoming, which can have a paralyzing effect with regard to some aspects of indigenous rights.

Deconstructing the Constitution

In 1993 House representative and lawyer Nelson Jobim signed a report requested by the governor of Pará proposing the reduction of Indian lands in his state. Jobim's report was favorable to the governor and against the Union's interests. His law firm was paid for this service, although Jobim broke the Brazilian Bar Association's rule that a member of Congress cannot act as an advocate against public interests.

Three years later, as President Fernando Henrique Cardoso's minister of justice, Jobim satisfied an "old obsession" (Ricardo and Marés 1996a, 64), namely, to change Decree 22 of 1991, which spelled out the norms for demarcation of Indian lands. Issued by ousted President Fernando Collor de Mello, Decree 22 followed the new constitution both in letter and spirit, granting the Indians their *original* right to exclusive usufruct of the lands they traditionally occupy. Jobim modified the decree based on the misconceived argument that to demarcate indigenous territories by presidential decree was undemocratic because it prevented non-Indians from defending their rights to these lands. He replaced Decree 22 with another decree, 1775, signed by Cardoso in early 1996. The new mandate opens the demarcation process to contestation by anyone who feels inconvenienced, including state governors, colonists, landholders, agribusiness companies, *garimpeiros* (prospectors), and so on. Decree 1775 had been announced many months earlier. It generated strong protests from indigenous organizations, lawyers, anthropologists, missionaries, members of Congress, European governments, and NGOs. Public Ministry attorneys issued long legal analyses demonstrating the fallacy of Jobim's argument. CIMI lawyers did the same. Members of Congress exposed the motivation behind the decree as a maneuver to comply with old demands by landholders, loggers, miners, and other anti-Indian interest groups (Viana and Suplicy 1995), and critics accused the president of buying political support with anti-Indian measures (Ricardo and Marés 1996b, 78; see also Viana and Suplicy 1995). In mid-1995 the president, Jobim, and other state officials met with various pro-Indian groups that were unanimously opposed to the decree, pointing out the high risks of harming the Indians, encouraging invasions, and generating conflicts in the countryside. They listened "democratically" to all these arguments and proceeded to declare the unconstitutionality of Decree 22. With Decree 1775, not only the 154 lands to be demarcated but all the 170 that had been officially defined were opened to revision retroactively. The only exception was the 221 areas (including the Yanomami's) already registered in a notary public's office. In September Cardoso's otherwise successful trip to Germany was marred by questions about Decree 1775. The German Parliament threatened to cut its participation in a program financed by the Group of Seven countries to protect the Amazon rainforest (Rossi 1995).

Cardoso and Jobim's main justification was based on a dispute raised by Agropecuária Sattin S/A, a cattle-ranching enterprise operating in Mato

16. Blind Justice crowned with feather headdress presides over indigenous rally against Decree 1775. Photo by Wilson Pedrosa/AE, 1996.

Grosso do Sul that reclaimed the 9,000 hectares occupied by 230 Kaiowá-Guarani in the area known as Sete Cerros, after 70 of the company's employees were evicted by FUNAI (*Folha de São Paulo* 1996a). The company filed a suit in the Federal Supreme Court claiming that its owners were entitled to defend their property rights regardless of indigenous occupancy. At a meeting with anthropologists in early August 1995 the president and his justice minister argued that there was a high probability that the Supreme Court would rule in favor of the company and, as a consequence, would not only open up the issue of the alleged unconstitutionality of the current procedure but nullify all demarcations, *including the Yanomami area* (the president's emphasis). The president expressed concern for his public image if such a thing were to happen. The Supreme Court was thus transformed into a bogeyman haunting the legitimacy of indigenous territorial rights. To prevent the court from handing down a negative verdict, the executive had to act quickly, or "even the Yanomami area will be in danger." A member of the Supreme Court was overheard expressing his unhappiness that words had been put in the court's mouth. But, fulfilling the wishes of Minister Jobim and a legion of anti-Indian interest groups, Decree 1775 was signed on January 9, 1996. Two days later Jobim sent a letter to the governor of Pará, informing him that fourteen Indian areas were now open to administrative contestation (O. Neto 1996, under the headline "Jobim Teaches How to Alter Indian Land").

A new wave of protests both in Brazil and abroad flooded the press. Amnesty International said that the new decree was a recipe to disaster because it opened Indian areas to invasion and possible massacres. Dalmo Dallari, a São Paulo lawyer, criticized Minister Jobim by affirming that "the Indians' rights are in the Constitution. The minister of Justice should be the first one to respect them." Members of indigenous organizations protested by walking out of Congress during a debate with Jobim (*Folha de São Paulo* 1996b).

To appease public opinion Jobim had taken the precaution of installing a new FUNAI president. Soon after his meeting with the anthropologists, also attended by NGO activist and former House representative Márcio Santilli, Jobim appointed Santilli head of FUNAI and made him responsible for putting Decree 1775 into practice. Santilli stayed in office for six months. In his attempt to cut the privileges of people such as a demanding Shavante faction, he incurred in the latter's wrath and was given the same treatment former President Nobre da Veiga had suffered in 1980. In a widely publicized commotion the Shavante held Santilli hostage for several hours in the garage of FUNAI headquarters before letting him go, demanding his dismissal. In an interview with Beto Ricardo (1996b, 40–48), Santilli indicated that the Shavante's aggressive act was the visible manifestation of the unruly FUNAI power structure controlled by a long-entrenched circle of corrupted bureaucrats who use the faithful Shavante bloc as frontline insurgents. Along with the central administration's chronic withholding of funds, the humiliation of this fracas was decisive in Santilli's decision to leave FUNAI. He left two weeks before Jobim went to Europe to ineffectually defend the decree to prospective investors and before the full consequences of the new decree had been felt.

Santilli was replaced by Julio Gaiger, a former NGO activist, ex-CIMI lawyer, and a consultant to Congress and later to Jobim's ministry (ISA 1996c, 7). In early 1995, while serving in Congress, Gaiger issued an elaborate analysis contesting the applicability of what became known as *contraditório*—the right to "contradict" a state decision—to the case of Indian land demarcation. He argued that the constitutional provision guaranteeing the right of the accused to contradict an accusation is a "procedural" rather than a "processual" measure, generating a political rather than a legal argument. He concluded that the demarcation procedure had no legal conflict that might justify the need to activate the contraditório. Nevertheless, by August 1995 the draft of Decree 1775 was traced to Gaiger, at the time a consultant to Minister Jobim. As such, Gaiger became especially appropriate for the job of president of FUNAI. Soon after he took office, he fired anthropologist Isa Rogedo, among the FUNAI employees most actively committed to defending Indian lands. Gaiger's justification was reported as having been Rogedo's rebellious attitude toward Jobim's policies. Despite his shrewdness, Gaiger was not immune to Shavante raids. In April 1997 a small group of Indians painted in red and wearing feather headdresses took over Gaiger's office for about three days, forcing him to move temporarily to the justice ministry's building. The Indians wanted Gaiger fired because he allegedly planned to close down twenty FUNAI regional offices (*Folha de São Paulo* 1997, 1; Gondim 1997; Sá 1997), thus threatening to jeopardize their access to FUNAI benefits at the local level. On April 11 at 4:30 in the morning a group of federal police stormed into the FUNAI building and removed the Shavante at gunpoint in full view of TV cameras, which were mysteriously present at such an ungodly hour. The case was widely commented on and certainly epitomized the irony of Indians' being forcefully ejected from the agency that exists to protect them.

But the case is not so simple. Shavante truculence has been a familiar feature in Brazilian Indigenism. Their constant demands for special treatment, reinforced by the empowering election of Mário Juruna in the early 1980s, have been met with a strong paternalism on FUNAI's part, thanks to its prodigal endowments of material resources to their villages. An organic clientelism has developed between the Shavante, or at least some factions, and their FUNAI allies that has been converted into significant political clout for the Indians. If one compares Shavante with Kayapó tactics, one is impressed by the latter's independence of the Indian agency. Kayapó demands are more often for principles and policies than for material advantage. For all the negative publicity generated by the Shavante "invasion" of FUNAI headquarters, Gaiger, unlike Santilli, held onto his post for a while longer, no doubt on the strength of the minister's backing. In July 1997 he resigned.

Returning to Decree 1775, it brought to Gaiger's desk from April to June 1996 a pile of more than eight hundred requests, about half of which were considered for examination. Of these, FUNAI and the justice minister agreed to revise eight, including the much disputed Raposa–Serra do Sol Indian area in the grasslands of northeastern Roraima.

Raposa–Serra do Sol is the traditional area of a number of indigenous peoples—Makushi, Wapishana, Ingarikó, Taurepang, and Patamona—with a total population of about twelve thousand Indians living in ninety-four villages. A proposal to demarcate its nearly 1.7 million hectares was sent to the Ministry of Justice in 1993. There was no response until Decree 1775 encouraged a barrage of requests from Roraima to reduce and fragment the area. Roraima was the country's leading state in number of post–Decree 1775 petitions, with a total of 664, most of them contesting Raposa–Serra do Sol (Farias 1996). On Christmas Eve Jobim rejected the petitions but on his own initiative ordered FUNAI to revise the proposal to demarcate the area to exclude from it five garimpo settlements recently established within the Indian area. He argued that these non-Indian villages were a fait accompli just like the town of Normandia, excluded from the original proposal (Internet message from Instituto Socioambiental, Brasília, January 23, 1997). The prospect seems to be a fragmented cluster of Indian areas, a solution that pleases neither Indians nor nationals. Whereas the Indians are dissatisfied with the alternative to a continuous uninterrupted single area, the ranchers, garimpeiros, and other non-Indian invaders are unhappy because they would like to have the Indians confined to house and backyard units, and also because they would be surrounded by indigenous land with no prospect of expanding (M. Santilli 1997, 10).

In Roraima government officials, members of Congress, and a substantial portion of the population have consistently discriminated against the state's indigenous population, whether in open conflicts such as assassinations, the burning down of indigenous houses and gardens (Ramos 1991), or as encouragement for invasions of Indian lands. Roraima's governors have promoted migrations, land titles, garimpeiro settlements, road construction, and even a hydroelectric dam within the Raposa–Serra do Sol indigenous area. Perhaps the epitome of Roraima's anti-Indian sentiment is the album by a band quaintly named *Pipoquinha de Normandia* (Little Popcorn of Normandia—Normandia is one of several regional settlements that have encroached on Makushi land since the late 1970s). The album's title is *Macuxi Esperto* (Smart Makushi), and its signature "song" is called "Continuous Area, No Way." In this song the singers claim they are not prejudiced against Indians, but they voice their resentment about Indians who are politicians and even doctors. While Indians amuse themselves burning bridges and stealing the landowners' cattle, the album trills, they have the nerve to demand land demarcation for themselves (Muggiati 1996a). The song's refrain is also revealing:

> *Área contínua, não* (Continuous area, no way)
> *Área contínua, não* (Continuous area, no way)
> *O índio tá querendo* (What the Indian wants)
> *É ser nosso patrão* (Is to be our boss)

The album, put on the market by Amazon Records in February 1996, was seized by a federal judge who also prohibited its playing on the radio. The Federal Attorney's Office in Roraima banned the tune as discriminatory, punishable by law 7.716 of 1989, according to which it is forbidden "to practice, induce, or incite through social channels of communication or by publication of any nature discrimination or prejudice based on race, color, religion, ethnic descent, or origin." A Makushi leader, insulted by the reference to Indians as thieves, lamented: "This music shows that Roraima's population has no commitment to the Indian cause" (Muggiati 1996a).

Such is the interethnic climate that many an Indian people normally confront without the added aggravation of a self-serving, cumbersome, ministerial tactic such as Decree 1775 to deconstruct the Constitution.

A certain dose of irony is not lacking in this "contradictory" affair. At the height of social unrest in rural Brazil and after repeated massacres of landless peasants by police forces, President Fernando Henrique Cardoso decided to hasten the process of land distribution with a decree as "unconstitutional" as Decree 22 that was replaced by 1775. By means of a "summary procedure" he sent to Congress his decree of land disappropriation for the purpose of "agrarian reform," as the excruciatingly slow process of rural settlement has been called. Defenders of landholders in Congress protested, accusing the president of ignoring the "contradictory," the same legal device that was invoked to revise Indian lands. The government's double standard—paying heed to the "contradictory" to the detriment of the Indians and bypassing it when it worked against landholders—produced the odd result of bringing together pro- and anti-Indian arguments, but for exactly the opposite reasons. Cardoso's summary procedure was unanimously approved by the Senate in December 1996.

Closing the circle, Jobim was nominated to the Federal Supreme Court in 1997, thus assuring that this new judge will help fulfill the Jobim-Cardoso prophecy that the court might rule against Indian land claims.

10
The Hyperreal Indian

An Affair to Remember

On May 9, 1990, 123 Tukano men, women, and children were expelled from their land in the upper Uaupés region by twenty-eight soldiers of the Brazilian Army. The Indians were panning for gold in the Pari Cachoeira III Indian Area, one of the "Indian colonies" assigned to them by the Calha Norte Project a year earlier. Claiming the Indians were involved in gold smuggling and, as an extension, with drug traffic and even Colombian guerrillas, the soldiers forced the Indians from their homes at gunpoint and made them walk for days along heavily flooded paths carrying all their belongings to the villages of relatives. According to the military, the Indians had been living outside the Indian area, even though cement posts showed that a demarcation had taken place. To crown the expulsion the soldiers burned down the Indians' houses and destroyed their gold-panning equipment.

I had heard outraged accounts of this story from colleagues in Brasília before I got the details from Álvaro Sampaio and two other Tukano men who had come down to the capital city three weeks after the incident to demand that federal authorities correct the injustice done to the Pari Cachoeira families. They filed a petition, addressed to Carlos Tinoco, then the army minister, at the attorney general's office in early June.

The three Tukanoans also told me about the reception they had from a member of the non-Indian support organization they first approached to ask for help. The negative response from this white man, who was there to assist Indians in coping with breaches of human rights, aroused my interest in analyzing the changes that have occurred in nongovernmental organizations (NGOs) dedicated to the Indian cause. NGOs proliferated in various countries in the 1970s and 1980s. As the term reflects, they are nonprofit organizations that are independent of specific governments. In fact, they are an attempt by civil society to minimize the effects of predation on peoples

267

and resources as a result of both private and public development policies. Some NGOs have acquired considerable political power and as a consequence have become strong lobbyists with both national states and international organizations, such as the World Bank and the United Nations. They exist to pressure governments to obey the laws that protect the most fragile segments of national societies. Unlike minority support groups before them, today's NGOs are distinguished by their international suprastate forums and networks and in many cases by the amount of human and financial resources they manage. In recent years their influence has grown so strong that some critics, including President Fernando Henrique Cardoso, suggest that the acronym NGO should stand for "neogovernment organization" (see Chapter 6). Thirty pro-Indian organizations are active in Brazil; the vast majority were created after the aborted emancipation decree of 1978 (ISA 1996a, 94).

But let us return to the three frustrated Tukanoans. The Indians, who were now denouncing an arbitrary act by the military, two or three years before had come under intense criticism from and even total rejection by both Brazilian indigenists and other Indians for making agreements with a mining company and with the military in charge of the Calha Norte Project. The Paranapanema mining company offered to evict thousands of illegal *garimpeiros* (prospectors) from indigenous territory in exchange for the right to mine gold on an industrial scale on the Indians' land. The military, allied with Paranapanema, promised the Indians schools, hospitals, and funding for economic development projects in exchange for a massive reduction of their traditional lands in the Uaupés region.

After long years of lobbying in endless hallways in Congress, ministries, and other government quarters to get his people's lands properly demarcated, Álvaro Sampaio, backed by a Tukano faction usually referred to as the Machado family, finally decided to accept the military's offer and allow the territory to be cut up in small parcels. At the least, Sampaio and his supporters reasoned, the Indians would gain something from the military and protection and royalties from the mining company. They publicized their new alliances by being photographed with top officials of the National Security Council and by appearing in television ads that glorified the Calha Norte Project.

The deal cost Sampaio and his group a long and bitter ostracism by the indigenist community. It was a calculated risk, and they took it, fully aware of the repercussions of their agreements with the very sectors that epitomized "the enemy" to Indians and sympathetic Brazilians.

Two years later these same Tukanoans felt betrayed by both the mining company and the military. Paranapanema abandoned the area, arguing that the region's mineral reserves were not worth the investment and leaving the Indians at the mercy of new garimpeiro invasions. The military, claiming its funds had been devoured by inflation, failed to come through with the promised hospitals, schools, and economic projects and instead erected military outposts throughout the area. The Indians were left with the bitter feeling that their co-optation had been for nothing, particularly after the incident at Pari Cachoeira III. Their ethical immolation at the stake of the indigenous-indigenist movement had served no real purpose. After all, except for a short spree of conspicuous consumption, what they had done—debasing themselves in the eyes of their peers—had been for the cause of Tukano well-being and the tranquility of a demarcated territory, unsatisfactory as the bargain might have been.

The three Tukanoans proceeded to tell me that their encounter with the NGO man in Brasília had been like a police interrogation. They said he asked them how many Indians were involved in guerrilla activities, drug trafficking, and gold smuggling. Had their traditional trails through the forest to Colombia (where many of their relatives live) been enlarged to facilitate drug traffic? They said he even called into question the legitimacy of their claims about the official status of Pari Cachoeira III and told them that by bringing their complaints to the capital they were jeopardizing their case, because they were "poking the beast with a short stick"— that is, they were pushing their luck too far by nagging the powerful in government about the Tukanoans' petty problems. They had their dealings with Paranapanema and the military "thrown on their faces." In the end they were told that the NGO in question could do nothing for them until all its members could meet to discuss the case.

Disappointed and disoriented, Sampaio and his companions looked for old acquaintances from their "co-opted" days. They contacted Senator Romeu Tuma, then director of the federal police, whom they had met during their negotiations with the Calha Norte military (the Tukanoans had helped Tuma burn up their traditional coca—*ipadu*—crop and handed their shotguns over to him); they turned to journalists and anthropologists, including an ethnographer dedicated to the defense of their lands whom they had banned from the area during their interlude with the powerful. With this anthropologist's help they reached the attorney general's office, which the 1988 Constitution charged with assisting Indians in their legal claims.

The incident—as reported to me by the three Indians, the anthropologist, and an angry journalist—combined with my own experience in indigenist activism, prompted me to reflect upon the way the indigenist scene in Brazil has changed since the mid-1980s. It is not my intention to pass judgment on non-Indians or Indians or to pursue an exhaustive analysis of the case; I do not, for instance, have the NGO man's version of it. What I want to do is take that event in Brasília in the late 1980s as a compelling social drama sufficiently laden with meaning to allow us to examine sociological, political, and symbolic dimensions that might otherwise be overlooked in the dim light of semiawareness. I focus exclusively on secular, pro-Indian, nongovernment organizations. I do not include feminist, environmentalist, or any other kind of NGO. The specificity of the Indian issue is such that in some important ways it sets indigenist NGOs apart from the others. Also excluded here are official indigenism as practiced by the National Indian Foundation (FUNAI) and the activities of the Catholic Church, embodied in the Catholic Indigenous Missionary Council (CIMI), important as they may be in the construction of Brazil's Indigenism. My focus is thus concentrated on the trajectory of lay associations from rather amorphous and humble beginnings to a formalistic maturity and what happened to the figure of the Indian when support groups came of age as bureaucratic bodies.

The End of "Communitas"

For all intents and purposes, the contemporary phase of civil activism began in 1978 for Brazilian Indigenism. It was triggered by the emancipation decree, an attempt to terminate the Indians' special status and thus exempt the state from the duty of protecting them as well as their traditions and their lands (see Chapter 9). Drafted during the military administration of Ernesto Geisel, the emancipation decree worked as a catalyst in bringing to the table a wide range of professionals, such as anthropologists, lawyers, journalists, artists, and church people. Taking turns as solo and choir in monopolizing the media on the politically hot stage of Indigenism, these non-Indian actors alternated with Indian leaders, who seemed to appear on the national stage as if by magic. It was the heroic moment of contemporary Indigenism. Nurtured by the success of their protests that led to the shelving of the emancipation bill, the Indians founded the Union of Indian Nations (UNI) in 1980, while their sympathizers organized a plethora of Indian support groups. Nearly every state capital in the country had its Associação Nacional de Apoio ao Índio (National Indian Support Association, ANAI) or its Comissão Pró-Índio (Pro-Indian Committee, CPI). But, like the androids in *Blade Runner*, they seemed programmed for short lives. With a few exceptions, such as the São Paulo CPI and the Acre and Porto Alegre ANAIs, none of the support groups created at that time survived the end of Indigenism's heroic moment.

Initially, the climate was one of *communitas*, to use Victor Turner's sometimes convenient expression (1969), when excruciatingly long meetings took place in church basements or in the homes of enthusiastic militants. That phase, however, was predictably short, as befits communitas, that realm of antistructure that stands out for its ephemeral liminality. The esprit de corps of the activists was like ideological parentheses, at once uniting them and setting them apart from the rest of the world. But it began to fade with the first signs of internal strife and later with the quest for a more structured organization that would give the indigenist movement a more solid sociological shape.

Signs that the interests of Indians and non-Indians were diverging were perceptible as early as 1982. By then the Indian movement had become pan-Indian, reaching out to all regions of the country and to most indigenous groups. During the first national meeting of Indian leaders held in Brasília in 1982, most of the anthropologists and other activists who attended the meeting rebelled against the Indians when they invited Colonel Paulo Moreira Leal, president of FUNAI and a member of the National Security Council, to speak. Because opposition to the military regime was growing fast, some Brazilians were offended by the Indians' decision to honor a colonel in the National Security Council. Those Brazilians who had helped to raise money for the conference and to organize it claimed the right to tell the Indians what was right and wrong, who were the good guys and the bad guys. Several said they felt betrayed by the Indian leaders who trampled on the nationals' political principles. The reaction could be read—and was by some observers—as saying, "We nationals help you Indians, and in turn you Indians must do what we nationals think is correct." The attitude reflected a common practice in those days: to use the Indian issue as a way to criticize the military government. The Indian question was never as politically hot as, say, the workers' movement in São Paulo or the Northeastern Peasant Leagues. At the time Indian issues were among the few political issues one dared raise without being censored and suffering other curtailments in freedom of expression.

But until 1985, with the advent of what came to be known as "New Republic," the non-Indian indigenist movement—as distinct from the Indians' movement—managed to maintain an appearance of unity by suppressing internal differences, such as those between church members, lawyers, anthropologists, and journalists. They were still united against a common enemy, the military. During civilian Tancredo de Almeida Neves's presidential campaign from November 1984 to March 1985 the long-held dream of indigenist activists—to participate in the creation of an official Indian policy—seemed about to come true. Activists even expected that they would become part of government. But Neves's death and the rise to power of the administration of José Sarney demonstrated within a few months that nothing was really new about the New Republic. The indigenists had to endure the bitter taste of a crumbled utopia (Fundação Nacional Pró-Memória 1988). By the first half of 1985 it was clear that the military era of indigenism was anything but over. In fact, the militarization of Amazonia and of Indian affairs intensified as the 1980s unfolded. The common enemy was alive and well in its usual olive-green splendor.

Profound political frustration notwithstanding, the chimera of power had brought the first discord to the indigenist movement. Not even the awareness that Indian support groups would continue to oppose the tenacious military was enough to stifle competition and squabbles among some of these organizations. During the Constitutional Assembly of 1987–1988 prolonged lobbying by indigenist groups marred the picture of peaceful unity. A bitter argument developed between São Paulo indigenists, including the head of UNI, and CIMI about the use of the officially cursed term *nations* to define indigenous societies. CIMI's insistence on using that term prompted anti-Indian interest groups to begin a long and ferocious defamatory campaign against the Catholic Church (see Chapter 6). But by then there was no longer an esprit de corps that might prompt all concerned to join ranks against the attacks on the church. Since then CIMI has become a virtual enemy of some lay support groups. Meanwhile the Indian support organizations were going their separate ways.

But what interests me here is not the discord between support groups but their transformation from informal gatherings to professional entities. As we look at indigenist NGOs in Brazil, and perhaps elsewhere, we see them taking the same route to bureaucratization. This process discloses a curious transformation in the relationships between support groups, something akin to changing from organic unity to regimented uniformity. It is a process that, paraphrasing Weber, we might call the routinization of heroism.

En Route to the Office

The moment of disillusionment with the New Republic was also when indigenist organizations that survived the heroic phase began to consolidate their administrative structures. Professionalism in work relations and financial commitments to international funding agencies created the need for an organization appropriate for the management of an unprecedented amount of resources, in terms of both money and personnel. New employees often had no experience or special commitment to the Indians, but their technical skills were indispensable in getting the new bureaucratic machine to work smoothly. Passion was no longer enough to run an NGO; now one needed competence most of all. Indians were conspicuously absent from the administration of most pro-Indian organizations. And Survival International in London replaced its anthropological staff with high-tech experts. One is tempted to evoke the reaction of an employee of the U.S. Bureau of Indian Affairs as he lambasted affirmative action for bringing "incompetent" Indians to work in the federal agency. In his view the BIA should have maintained its emphasis on technical skills, thus favoring European Americans, Japanese-Americans, and African-Americans—in other words, anyone but Indians, who may know a lot about Indianness but don't know anything about running a *bureau* (Feraca 1990, 271–89).

Computerized information replaced personal contacts and created a network of foreign agencies that turned complex live issues into instantly digested shorthand messages. The need to rally support for indigenous rights from various quarters of public opinion produced a sort of international lingua franca of Indigenism that deleted subtleties and homogenized messy political disputes. The indigenist panorama today has little to remind us of the solidarity, excitement, and civic idealism of the seemingly remote days of the late 1970s and early 1980s.

The Tukano episode in Brasília is a potent floodlight for illuminating two different theses, one by a classic of sociology, Max Weber, the other by an enfant terrible of postmodernity, Jean Baudrillard. In a here-and-now fashion that event highlights the outcome of the passage from political bricolage to technical professionalism. Let me take it step by step.

Weber tells us how crucial the creation of the *Kontor*, or bureau—that is, the office—was in the history of bureaucracy from the Middle Ages on. The rise of bureaucracy made possible the emergence of new specializations, attitudes, and situations and with them a new ethical outlook. The office, says Weber, is a "vocation" expressed in "the devotion to impersonal and functional goals" (1978, 957–59). Granted, Weber had in mind medieval despotic regimes rather than a harmless handful of well-meaning people such as those involved in late twentieth-century makeshift indigenism in Brazil. But what is striking is that in both cases personalism played a prominent role. In medieval Europe, as in early 1980s Brazil, the options remained basically—bureaucracy or dilettantism (p. 223). In fact, choice practically disappeared when the first support groups became NGOs with their emphasis on efficiency, thus driving away the lingering dilettantes.

Although efficiency is the hallmark of the Weberian definition of bureaucracy, today's popular image of it is quite the opposite. One speaks of it as red tape, a mass of tangled papers that clogs the flow of administration and, as a consequence, the channels for the exercise of full citizenship. "To feed the bureaucratic machine" means to waste precious resources with little benefit other than perpetuating the bureau system. But it is not loss of efficiency that plagues bureaucracies. When that happens, they are no longer bureaucracies but some sort of perverse *bureaucratitis*. In a number of cases the rules of the bureaucracy take priority over everything else. Although a bureau exists as a means to achieve some goal that is different from its own existence, the running of it creates such a complex web of rights and duties that it is not uncommon to find that much of the effort goes to administration at the expense of the goal to be achieved. Taking the Indian support NGOs as an example, the contrast between the old and the new formats is apparent. Whereas in the old days of "heroic" indigenism the goal of defending indigenous rights was paramount and the means were improvised, flexible, and pragmatic, now the main concern is often with the means, such as fund-raising, accounting, salaries, high-tech equipment, report writing, and, in some cases, publishing. These activities may all be important, and the NGOs may do them efficiently, but flesh-and-blood Indians have often been edged off stage.

The path to bureaucratization may be as inevitable for NGOs as for other organizations in the West, but in the case of indigenous support groups, given their raison d'être, that is, the defense of indigenous peoples in their rights to be different, the uncomfortable coexistence of disjoined means and ends is particularly evident. Because the logic of the bureau is alien to Indian societies, gross misunderstandings between Indians and friends of the Indians are not infrequent. What is to be done about the Indians' otherness that is so resistant to domestication by the bureau's logic? How is it possible to control that otherness and render it compatible with the "impersonal and functional goals" of bureaucratic organization? How can anyone overcome the disjunction between the organizational impetus of the NGOs and the need to act in the interstices of indigenous and nonindigenous polities? The Weberian vocation of the office seems especially inappropriate for dealing with the interethnic question for the simple reason that the Weberian "rationality" it cherishes is at odds with both the ethos of most indigenous cultures and the "irrationality" of most relationships involving Indians and non-Indians. How to rationally administer irrationality is the ultimate challenge for indigenist NGOs.

In pursuing their Weberian destiny of bureaucratization while dealing with Indian rights NGOs seem to have found a way out of the dilemma by creating a bureaucratizable Indian. Flesh-and-blood Indians would either have to be kept at arm's length or have their wild otherness—a potential source of disorder—filtered and tamed and be transformed in model Indians.

Bureaucratization may have meant greater efficiency—hardly if ever completely, as befits Weberian ideal types—but at the cost of a wide and still widening gap between NGOs and the social world and worldview of the Indians. The gap may become an abyss, and as such it may bring the NGOs into question. It seems paradoxical that the explicit commitment of the private indigenist machine is to the flesh-and-blood Indian, but its working

tool is the model Indian. The real Indian must be given the status of a remote source of ideological raw material to justify the NGOs' commitment.

Indeed, the real Indian is getting further and further away and is becoming increasingly unintelligible to the technical and administrative rationale of the NGO office. It is as if two opposing forces were in tension—
the real needs of real Indians embedded in the irrationality of contorted
and controversial relationships in the interethnic arena, and the office mys-
tique generated by the need for resource management required for the
self-maintenance of the office.

Caught in this tug-of-war, the NGOs seem to have forged for themselves an ontological autonomy vis-à-vis that which was both their origin
and their purpose, namely, the rights of real Indians, regardless of their
ideological and cultural ideosyncrasies. Furthermore, in their oscillation
between the ethics of human rights and the impersonality of bureaucratic
practice, NGOs run the risk of falling prey to a nebulous social and symbolic field in which individual morality becomes confused with the basic
guiding principles of being advocates for the Indians as subjugated peoples.
As in the case of Payakan, the Kayapó Indian accused of raping a white
woman, discussed in Chapter 1, the individual act became an excuse to
voice anti-Indian sentiments and an opportunity to denigrate the Indian
cause as a whole. Such a confusion was apparent in the incident involving
the three Tukanoans in Brasília. It is as though by practicing condemnable
acts, these real Indians dishonored the NGOs, even if those acts were motivated by the desire to meet the needs of their people. By reprimanding the
three individuals, that friend of the Indians was also withdrawing support
to the 123 dislodged Tukanoans deep in the Uaupés jungle.

From the time that the workplace of alternative indigenist action was
our kitchens and living rooms to today's computerized offices, the Westerner's Indian cause has been pursuing its Weberian destiny to a point
where it risks imploding in a Baudrillardian simulacrum.

> It is no longer a question of imitation, nor of reduplication, nor even of
> parody. It is rather a question of substituting signs of the real for the real
> itself, that is, an operation to deter every real process by its operational
> double, a metastable, programmatic, perfect descriptive machine which
> provides all the signs of the real and short-circuits all its vicissitudes.
> Never again will the real have to be produced. (Baudrillard 1983, 4)

The simulacrum results from the perhaps totally unconscious construction
of a simulation of the real Indian, the model that by anticipation replaces
the lived experience of indigenous peoples. It is a model that molds the Indians' interests to the organization's shape and needs. Again, the treatment

of the Tukanoans in Brasília reveals a tendency that has been around the indigenist circuit for a while, that is, the fabrication of the perfect Indian whose virtues, sufferings, and untiring stoicism have won him the right to be defended by the professionals of indigenous rights. That Indian is more real than the real Indian. He is the hyperreal Indian.

From Generic to Domesticated Indian

The domesticated Indian is the Indian of many a support organization. My comments are not intended to invalidate the effectiveness of NGOs in defending the human rights of indigenous peoples. A clear example of the results of perseverance in face of official reluctance and private antagonism are the efforts of the Pro-Yanomami Committee (CCPY), engaged since 1979 in the defense of Yanomami land rights and instrumental in securing the official demarcation of Yanomami territory in 1991. What my comments are meant to do is point out the dangerous course that at least some NGOs have taken. Whereas older support groups changed their approach in order to, in their view, better serve the cause of human rights, new ones have appeared with an already established bureaucratic agenda. But for most, particularly the well established, defending Indians has become a sort of business enterprise, complete with market competition and publicity.

From Darcy Ribeiro's frustrated 1970 prophecy that all Indians would lose their ethnic identity and become part of a generic Indian, that ethnically hollow prisoner of the interethnic war, to the golden years of hard work to raise a pan-Indian awareness and then to the bureaucratization of private indigenism, Indians have been the target of a peculiar ethic on the part of their non-Indian allies. As in the Indianist phase of Brazilian literature, when nineteenth-century writers such as José de Alencar conjured up an Indian character that was to become part of the nationalist dream, the contemporary version of the friends of the Indians also portrays the Indian with a generous dash of romanticism. In fact, Indians are required to display, if not redeeming exoticism, at least an invincible integrity of principles: as Marshall Cândido Mariano da Silva Rondon, the hero of official indigenism, would say, die if need be but never surrender to greedy demands put on your lands, never succumb to the bribes of the powerful, never capitulate to corruption, always denounce injustice. The more stoic and resistant to temptation, the more deserving the Indian will be of Western solidarity. Co-optation was not made for Indians, so, like good guardians, let us make sure to keep it from their reach.

Virtuous principles, ideological purity, willingness to die heroically for cherished ideals—they are nothing more than fantasies. Indigenist activists who cultivate such an image of the Indian do not seem to realize that by demanding it they are in fact creating a perfect model of the honorable in-corruptible Westerner. The contrast between the martyred Indian and the Indian who has sold out mimics the difference between the honest West-erner and the corrupt Westerner.

Ribeiro's generic Indian was the intellectual creation of a prophesied catastrophe. It depicted an amorphous mass of uprooted individuals with no specific identity wandering about the fringes of Brazilian society carrying the weight of a demoralizing stigma that both discriminated against them for being Indian and for pretending to be otherwise. As an idea, the generic Indian did not take off for lack of social and historical resonance. Like a hologram in search of an operator, it collapsed in the void of its fiction.

In turn, the hyperreal Indian, this unobscured object of defense for a number of NGOs, is an appropriate working hypothesis for the profes-sional activist. The model Indian, the projection of an illusion, has become the NGOs' ethical hologram. On that day in May at a Brasília NGO office the man in attendance expected to see a true three-dimensional image of three Indians, but in came three real, problematical, and embarrassing Tukanoans who upset the routine of the office. Strange occurrences such as this may occur repeatedly, punctuating the absurdity of an oxymoronic ethics: NGO defender evicts Indians who interrupt his work in defense of the INDIAN! The NGO could not meet the Indians' plea for help until the non-Indian directors got together to decide whether to take up the case. They had to weigh the pros and cons of a potentially harmful association with such volatile agents of contact politics.

The formalistic personas of present-day NGOs are one more manifes-tation of what C. Wright Mills called "managerial demiurge" in referring to the bureaucratization of fields such as academia (1956). Managerial demi-urge also illustrates how means can take priority over ends, in a replay of the bridge-on-the-River-Kwai syndrome. After all, what are the painstakingly built works for, if not to be enjoyed in their own right, even if one forgets the original reason for their existence? It becomes a sort of blind alley, an obstructed ethical road where "the hypersimilitude would amount to the assassination of the original, and therefore, to pure nonsense" (Baudrillard 1981, 162). Rigid structures are created for the management of often con-siderable resources that make possible the production and maintenance of the simulacrum of the Indians: dependent, distressed, victims of the system, unaware of bourgeois evils, honorable in their actions and intentions, and preferably exotic (that is perhaps why the Yanomami are so popular among NGOs). The Indians thus created are like clones made in the image of what the Westerners would like to be. Over and above the real Indian, the model Indian comes to exist as if in a fourth dimension, a being with whom one en-joys having close encounters of whatever kind. Flesh-and-blood Indians are not immune to simulation. Brazil is not lacking in examples of indigenous personalities who play up their hyperreal role on the interethnic stage while transporting NGO rhetoric to their communities, if they still live in them.

Model Indians are what justify funding and personnel for their defense, for otherwise how would it be possible to convince financing agencies to contribute to the protection of recalcitrant Indians who manage their own alliances with whomever they choose, including some of the most hardened opponents of the Indian cause? Because most Brazilian NGOs operate with funding from foreign NGOs or governments, they are accountable to agencies for which Brazilian Indians evoke the objects of paradise lost, ecological disasters, and the guilt of developed countries. Foreign agencies would have difficulty accepting that their money was being spent on Indians who were involved in objectionable compromises. Caught between the Euro-American imagination and the demands of real Indians, Brazilian NGOs find themselves in a corner that has forced them to opt for institutional security as the surest way to please their financial sources and thus get things done smoothly. In so doing they are compelled to keep clear of ignoble savages in their real-life dealings. In such a context it is not surprising that NGOs have developed a selection process that favors well-behaved Indians who are more apt to reinforce the Western image of the suffering, helpless, and noble savage. UNI, the indigenous NGO that ceased to exist in 1992, closely followed the pattern of non-Indian NGOs in that it was concerned with fund-raising, development projects conceived and planned in its São Paulo office, and a tendency to adopt the simulacrum of the model Indian. Like many other NGOs, UNI showed a special inclination to cherish the Yanomami as the epitome of the defenseless "pure" Indian in search of protectors.

Environmental NGOs differ greatly in outlook regarding Indians. For instance, some see them as predators and thus exclude them from ecologically protected areas, even using eviction to do so. Others naturalize Indians, reducing them to yet another endangered species or to the role of custodian of nature. Indigenist NGOs contest both positions and focus instead on the ethical and political responsibility of civil society and the state to defend the historical rights of indigenous peoples to traditional land and ethnic autonomy. They are less interested in the Indians' place in nature than in their misplace in the Western world. In fact, this difference in perspective has led to a mild antagonism between indigenist and environmentalist NGOs.

I am excluding from the category of NGO a number of indigenist associations that are arranged along lines that are different from the bureaucratic template. They have no "office," no full-time personnel, no managerial agenda. Furthermore, their undertakings are designed to bring together

Indians with similar experiences and grievances. They are concerned with local people who face specific problems in specific contexts rather than with the generalized simulacrum that is the object of urban indigenism. Such associations still retain much of the old verve. They are run by people who have had prolonged firsthand contact with indigenous peoples from various regions of the country and are familiar with the diversity and contradictions of village life. The real Indian is not lost on them. But chances are that they too will follow the path of routinization and bureaucratization if they are to survive, given that factors such as competition for funds favor large-scale, impersonal, technical, and efficiency-oriented organizations. Such efficiency, however, refers more to the way a NGO is run than to its accomplishment of adequate projects *in the field*. Bureaucratization is likely to be structurally inevitable. If this is so, the figure of the hyperreal Indian is bound to spread (in what Baudrillard calls "epidemics of value" [1990, 13]) in a mounting process of conformity and uniformity until indigenous grievances and NGO responses become virtually undifferentiated.

Obviously, this is not an individual process, as adhering to it is not the fault, or perhaps even the choice, of any particular NGO. If it is structurally unavoidable, NGOs can hardly escape it. The system in which the NGOs are situated operates in such a way as to generate an increasing complexity that may eventually lead to its involution. It is symptomatic of this trend toward overelaboration that NGOs are being created with the sole purpose of administering the finances of other NGOs, as in a corporate dream or science fiction nightmare. Whether this trend will continue in the direction of ever-increasing managerial sophistication, or whether it will degenerate into a machine gone berserk, a postmodern sorcerer's apprentice, is yet to be known. What seems clear is that looking into the eye of the flesh-and-blood Indian is not on the agenda of these new managerial NGOs of the fourth kind.

Intimate Enemy or Remote Friend?

We can hardly blame the three Tukanoans if, after being so ungenerously treated by the Brasília NGO, they repeated bandit Salvatore Giuliano's famous words: "God protect me from my friends." But no, they continued their pilgrimage through offices, corridors, and living rooms, seeking help from a variety of people, including those to whom these Tukanoans had been anything but friendly. Such are the meanders of interethnicity, the turbulent flow of conflicting interests, forever creating oppositions that wind up contradicting each other.

Here proximity and distance show themselves to be categories even more relative than we usually take them to be. For *colonized* peoples, such as the East Indians once ruled by the British, colonizers have become what Nandy (1983) calls the "intimate enemy" who, hated as they may still be, are now so ingrained in postcolonial Indian self-awareness as to be constitutive of a new national personality. But for *nationalized* peoples such as Amerindians, the sympathetic non-Indian is a "remote friend" who takes on the role of defender but who rarely has a deep existential, intellectual, or social intimacy with the Indians. Model Indians rather than the Indians themselves are the working object for the militant indigenist.

Relations between Indians and professional non-Indian indigenists, who are expected to be well informed about Indian affairs, are not close enough to permit the crossing of interethnic barriers. Collaboration between Indians and indigenists is possible, but it is never a Durkheimian "mechanical solidarity," for it never happens between people sharing a universe of sameness. On the other hand, an organic collaboration would also be unlikely, for it would first have to put the non-Indians through the test of dealing directly with the real Indian. Because the functional interdependence of differences that characterize organic solidarity presupposes the interaction of elements that are distinct but of the same order, the indigenists would have to abandon the hyperreal Indian or, conversely, create a hyperreal indigenist, a probability that apparently has not yet materialized. What seems to be real enough, however, is the tendency for unequal power-laden relations to develop, according to which defended Indians become subalterns to their non-Indian defenders. It is increasingly common to hear Indian leaders rebel against the management of support groups, either lay or religious, demanding that Indians' voices be heard instead of some well-meaning ventriloquist's.

There are, to be sure, many points of convergence between members of NGOs and Indians, or the term *Indian support NGOs* would be empty indeed. After all, non-Indians can do some things on behalf of Indians without hurting the latter's sensitivities about representation. Writing documents, lobbying in Congress, fund-raising, denouncing injustices, and launching campaigns in the country or abroad are some activities most Indians cannot yet carry out themselves and that do not necessarily generate overempowerment of friendly Westerners. However, the reverse, although true, is not true in the same way. Indigenist NGOs owe their existence to the abuse of Indians by national societies at large, the Indians' lack of preparedness to combat these abuses, and usually their lack of access to proper channels through which to vent their grievances. If by some unimaginable miracle all Indian claims and needs were satisfactorily met by the state as the accountable body for indigenous affairs, the NGOs' mission would come to an end and so would they as organizations. In this sense NGOs depend on Indians for their survival. But the NGOs' dependence is not on the Indians who pick fights, accept bribes, deceive, go out of their minds in fits of frustration, or succumb to pressures. As mentioned earlier—and here comes the paradox that inhibits organic collaboration—the NGOs' bureaucratic machine is fed by agencies built around ethical standards that are part of the Western value system. These standards are in turn instilled in the national NGOs, requiring that their concern be with ethically correct Indians. Thus, if the NGOs depend on the Indian, it is not on the real Indian but on their model Indian.

Since 1988 a major slice of indigenous rights has escaped NGO hands and landed within the purview of the attorney general's office. Article 232 of the new constitution assigns to that office the duty to take on any indigenous claim filed against private or public individuals or groups. This article was included in the 1988 Constitution because of the untiring efforts of several NGOs and professional associations. Ironically, it has had the effect of emptying an important space that support groups had occupied, although they can still play the role of go-betweens for Indians and Public Ministry attorneys. Of course, as before the 1988 Constitution, NGO activities are not now limited to legal battles, but the courts undoubtedly are one of their most important platforms.

The collaboration between NGOs and idealized objects is not limited to Indigenism. The same seems to happen, for instance, with the women's movement in Brazilian cities (Teresa Caldeira, personal communication; see also Mohanty 1991 about the representations of women in other underdeveloped countries). It is even possible that an inescapable consequence of the defense-of-human-rights phenomenon is the generic human being that replaces the complex individual that falls out of bureaucratic control. It is as generic human beings that Indians are eligible for protection according to the precepts of the Universal Declaration of Human Rights. This may be the only feasible way to raise public awareness and bring national and international visibility to political actors such as minorities. One either creates a generic human being that is intelligible as a focus of public interest, or one risks having that focus blurred by the overwhelming profusion of cultural minutiae and baffling social differences that populate the world. To leave individual and ethnic specificities unabsorbed and ignored by the public in general and funding agencies in particular is to create an ethical and political tangle. The result is that the cause, too complicated to be handled in actual practice, ends up submerged by the impersonal dicta of ethnic groups wronged by the nation-state. From this perspective the effort and efficacy with which the NGOs have conducted their advocacy work must be duly acknowledged. By translating undigestible alterity into accepted humanity they render Indian needs understandable to Westerners.

Suspicion

I don't think it is an accident that few ethnographers are full-time professionals in indigenist politics, although a great many are activists for the cause. Anthropological training includes one basic principle that might well be an antidote to the virus of simulacrum, that is, a disposition to suspect, to distrust, established truths. The questioning we do as our working routine has, at least in part, vaccinated us against this Baudrillardian epidemic. On the other hand, our profession—here I am referring specifically to ethnography—puts us in prolonged and intimate contact with real concrete Indians, their virtues and vices, their complexities and ambiguities, but never a perfect model of themselves, never "frozen, cryonized, sterilized, protected *to death*" (Baudrillard 1983, 15).

In this respect my comments are addressed to what Baudrillard calls "anti-ethnology" (1983, 14), implying the ethical and political commitment of ethnographers to the peoples they study rather than to a scientific approach to indigenous cultures. The complicity often created between Indians and their ethnographers—and frequently misunderstood and resented by professionals in indigenism (with a small *i*)—comes from that common experience of ontologically discovering each other. It is upon the "reality" generated by this experience that we build our ethics regarding indigenous peoples rather than on an image idealized by an aseptic and formal distancing. If ethnographers are frequently the source of raw material for professional activism, it is because we are perceived as a phenomenon of first kind, more accessible than the Indians themselves. When we translate our lived experience among the Indians to the language of symbolic consumption of alterity, we make available abridged images of those Indians that will be vicariously lived by the industry of indigenist activism. Our proximity to real Indians turns us into their surrogates. It is as if the NGO universe has created a space, a vacant position to be filled, preferably by the model Indian—or, failing this, by the ethnographer as ersatz real Indian— or, if all else fails, by the real Indian.

Clearly, my comments do not entail an apology to professional indigenism, but neither do they imply condemnation. Unlike criticism, a critique such as this aims at clarifying certain issues that have been kept obscure or not addressed at all. In writing this I am, above all, concerned with the future of indigenist activism in Brazil and elsewhere. Despite the growth of the Indian movement in the country, and the increasingly audible voices of the Indians themselves, they still need outside support and assistance. If this task is to be carried out with full awareness, one must be on the alert for problems such as the constitution of an indigenist ethic, the distortions that the virus of simulation can impose on that ethic, and the change in priorities between means and ends that leads professionalization to risk the loss of sensitivity, spontaneity, and the sense of historical justice that accompanies the defense of indigenous rights. Obviously, one should not confuse political engagement with its bureaucratization. The latter may be a medium necessary for the exercise of the former, but it is wise to avoid subverting the very premises that legitimate indigenist action.

Anthropologists and indigenists were together in the heroic phase of contemporary Indigenism in Brazil. It seemed like an ideal partnership and a sensible and efficient division of labor: ethnographers would produce firsthand empirical information and analyses, and professional indigenists would feed the pertinent ethnographic accounts into the political circuit of interethnic contact. But episodes such as that involving the Tukanoans have made us, the ethnographers, rethink our association with professional indigenism. Such incidents have made us aware that our ethics do not always coincide with the NGOs'. The ethnographer's allegiance is ultimately to the Indians, real people going about their lives in a flow of ups and downs, and to the principles of anthropology, particularly the respect for cultural and individual diversity.

This analysis has made me stop to think how professional indigenism has come into existence, how it has developed, and where it seems to be going. In short, it has been an exercise in anthropological suspicion. The habit of constant reflection, a part of our habitus, as Bourdieu put it (1974, 191), makes it difficult for us and should actually preclude us from letting final and established truths crystallize in our minds. Our commitment is to make explicit what was not articulated before. It might be wise for all of us to ponder the question posed by Mexican writer Carlos Fuentes (1988, 173): "How to fight injustice without creating injustice?"

Conclusion

What Would We Do without Them?

My white side will die without understanding my Indian side.
    João Maria Tapixi Rodrigues, president of the
    Indigenous Council of North Paraná

My main purpose in writing this book has been to explore some of the "contact zones" (Pratt 1992, 6) covered by the politics of interethnicity where Brazilian Indigenism is engendered. It has emphasized the world of Brazilians rather than the world of Indians in the conviction that the differential power characteristic of interethnic contact becomes more evident when seen through the manifestations of the dominant society, be they economic projects, legislation, scientific knowledge, or philanthropy. Part of my purpose in writing the book in the form of essays focusing on specific problems and their repercussions on the national landscape was to expose the underside—or is it the id?—of the Brazilian nation. I wanted to explore the idea that Brazil is inconceivable without its Indians, not as human aggregates in their own right but as creatures of the national imagination and its manipulation. After what has been said in these chapters about the juggling act by the Brazilian nation-state to do away with the Indians and have the Indians too, we reach the point of attempting to answer the initial question posed in the introduction: Why have so few Indians attracted so much national attention? Like a Proustian madeleine, the Indian issue has the potency to expose what remains unsaid of Brazil's declared self-image. To again use a Freudian metaphor, it is as though the Indians represented a part of the country's unconscious—intractable but necessary to its constitution. As I see it, to study Indigenism is to put Brazil on the couch where, often unwittingly, it reveals itself. To study Indigenism, then, is to disclose the nation rather than the Indians themselves.

Some authors explicitly recognize this identification of Brazil with its Indians. In the words of Manoel Bonfim, an early twentieth-century Brazilian historian who is now being rediscovered and appreciated for his foresight, during the nineteenth-century Indianist literary movement, we "tried to identify ourselves with the *brasis* [the Indians] in the belief that the very essence of our Americanism was contained in them. All of this can be explained by the first conditions of our formation—such as the open and

284

cordial assimilation of the Indian." But there the resemblance with my position ends. Bonfim continues, "Hence the contrast: in the other neo-Iberian societies, even where romanticism had a clear expression, Indianism is not known. Why? Just think of the conditions under which their Indian was put: would there be any inspiration to sing about him?" (1996, 346).

Were there any conditions that Spanish American Indians submitted to and that Brazilian Indians were spared? Did the latter escape decimation and slavery whereas the former did not? Were Brazilian Indians so resistant to domination that they maintained their idyllic appeal despite the dominant society's yoke and pestilence? What is, after all, the ontological nature of this super-Indian sung by Indianist literati if not a figment of their nationalist imagination? For while they sang of the prowess of fictitious Indians from centuries past, novelists like Alencar and poets like Gonçalves Dias were contemporaries of defeated indigenous populations that somehow managed to survive through centuries of defilement. But of course those impoverished Guarani, Terena, Guaikuru, and others were not fit to be anybody's model of nationalism, or Americanism, as Bonfim prefers to say. Brazil needed the Indian but only the fictionalized Indian, the redeeming ectoplasm of troublesome flesh-and-blood Indians who needed to die in order to populate the conquerors' imagination. While, on the one hand, this constructed Indian

> has a great symbolic value in the ideology of [Brazilian] nationality, on the other, he has always been considered a hindrance to progress and development, both projects of the Brazilian Nation. . . . This ambiguity underscores the relationship between the state and indigenous societies which, from the beginning, has been characterized by protective legislation and, at the same time, by the systematic disrespect of such formal rights. (Viveiros de Castro and Andrade 1988, 12)

The great ambivalence the Brazilian nation shows toward Indians is in fact a reflection of the vacillation the nation displays about itself. The country's intellectual history is a sequence of ups and downs in terms of self-evaluation, the oscillation between self-praise and self-condemnation. Ideological constructs of Brazil take turns in describing the national character in bright colors or gloomy pessimism. Following the naturalist mode of the colonial days, when the vision of paradise (Buarque de Holanda 1992) competed with the failures and struggles to colonize the new land and conquer its inhabitants, the nineteenth century saw Brazilian national identity become definitively established. Political independence from Portugal was the result of an act by the heir to the Portuguese crown (pressured as he might have been by a Creole elite) in 1822, and the "1823 Constitutional Assembly was the first expression of Brazilian sovereignty" (Bonfim

1996, 68). Except for a few localized movements for independence by isolated groups of intellectuals, Brazil's coming of age as a nation did not emanate from the people at large, eager for a distinctive identity, but from the effort of a discontented elite (J Carvalho 1990).

From then on nationalism pervaded virtually all intellectual production, which began in earnest after 1808 when Brazil had its first printing press (Bonfim 1996, 283). But while the Romantics of the Indianist movement in the first half of the nineteenth century, in their struggle to build a real sense of Brazilianness, praised the magnificence of nature and native as icons of a glorious past and a prodigal future for Brazil, the intellectual mood turned sour in the second half of the 1800s and into the 1900s. Author after author attempted to draw the definitive outline of Brazilian national character. Blind patriotism alternated with vehement criticism. For some Brazil was an example of outstanding superiority: "To be Brazilian means to have distinction and advantage . . . no [other country] is more distinguished, more endowed with fundamental advantages, more enviable" (Afonso Celso, quoted in D. Leite 1992, 196). Peopled by supposedly gentle, warm, and sensitive beings, Brazil was even regarded as an example of racial tolerance: "Few in our country would feel repugnance or contempt for the Black or the Indian" (Torres [1914] 1982, 30—31). For others the Brazilian was a pitiful expression of insignificance: "Apathetic, lacking in ambition, disheartened." Brazil would do better to follow "the example of Anglo-German nations in order to correct its 'Latin feeblenesses' " (Silvio Romero, quoted in D. Leite 1992, 190), because its inhabitants were rather poor material for building a developed nation. Silvio Romero (1851–1914) is perhaps the best example of this self-contempt; to him the Portuguese, Indians, and blacks were incapable of producing a satisfactory society. His icon of national inferiority was the figure of the *mestiço*, the half-breed, the product of the unfortunate combination of Portuguese, black, and Indian, accentuated by a less-than-propitious environment and the craving to imitate foreign styles (D. Leite 1992, 185). Replacing the Indianists' quest for a distinctive Brazilian identity, the pessimism expressed by Romero, Moog, and others was at least in part derived from the prospect of the country's integration in Euro-American civilization. The inevitable comparison with developed nations precipitated a bleak assessment of Brazil and an inferiority complex that was to persist in varying degrees of explicitness. "In a radiant land a sad people lives" (P. Prado [1928] 1997, 53). "And Brazil continued to be intoxicated [with Portuguese influence], fed with dead lies, in an absolute surrender of everything that elevates thought and exalts the heart" (Bonfim 1996, 287). Brazil as the crucible of *métissage,* the result of the encounter of white, black, and Indian, reminiscent of the Colombian Three Potencies (Taussig 1997), remained a canvas on which different points of view were projected according to each author's ideological inclinations.

Much of the blame for the evils that plagued the new nation, both in its monarchic phase (1822–1889) and as a young republic, took the form of racism against Indians and blacks. Oliveira Viana refers to people of color as "this formless and swarming rabble of inferior mestiços" (quoted in D. Leite 1992, 227). Nina Rodrigues proposed as a solution to the peril represented by the mestiço races "to crush them under the pressure of an enormous immigration by a vigorous race which, in the struggle for life spoken of by Darwin, will annihilate them by means of assimilation" (quoted in D. Leite 1992, 218). Scholars attributed the capacity to reproduce vast numbers of these mestiços either to the "genetic excitement" of mulatto women (Nina Rodrigues, quoted in D. Leite 1992, 218) or to the "exacerbated sexuality" of Indian women (Freyre 1992, 100). With a generous dash of vulgarity Freyre depicts scenes dense with eroticism and wickedness as the

> European jumped on shore stumbling over naked Indian women; the [Jesuits] themselves needed to be careful on landing lest they got their feet stuck in flesh. Many [non-Jesuit] clergymen let themselves be contaminated by depravity. The women were the first to throw themselves at the white men, the most ardent among them rubbing themselves on these men's legs whom they took to be gods. (p. 93)

From these carnal excesses a society of Brazilian mestiços was born, overloaded with the racial prejudice the Portuguese first dedicated to Moors and Jews back on the Iberian Peninsula and carried over to Indians and blacks in the New World (Vainfas 1997, 238–39).

The drift of intellectual efforts at self-examination changed from impressionistic essays by a bookish elite to professional analyses by historians and social scientists, particularly after 1950 (D. Leite 1992, 310). But the quest to determine why Brazil lags behind in the march toward development has persisted as a constant concern of the Brazilian intelligentsia. The pendulum between nationalist pride and bitter condemnation goes on swinging through modern and postmodern times. While scholars such as Leal (1993), Faoro (1991–93, 1994), Furtado (1963), Viotti da Costa (1989), Schwartzman (1982), J. M. Carvalho (1987, 1990, 1996), Reis (1988), and Martins (1994), to mention a few, dedicate their professional efforts to critically analyzing the contradictions that riddle Brazil's past and present, other authors such as DaMatta (1979, 1985, 1986) and Ribeiro (1995), although they recognize the severe social distortions that plague the nation, nevertheless emphasize positive features in Brazilian social formation. An interesting gauge for the ambivalence that still vexes the Brazilian citizenry can be found in semantic discrepancies in the press and even in bumper stickers, as perceptively analyzed in Dias (1993). They constitute collective Freudian slips that betray an unspoken uncertainty about what it means to be Brazilian.

Whether stressing civic euphoria or collective malaise, much of what is said about Brazil refers to the Indian issue. Contemporary writer Osman Lins, discussing high culture, states that Brazil resembles an Indian compound—"in every Brazilian writer there is an Anchieta [the Jesuit poet of the early 1500s] who preaches his Gospel with joy and despair" (1979, 25). He regards Indian "culture" as "little evolved" and presumes that Indians "never offered flowers because they were most likely busy with urgent survival problems and, buried as they are in the forest, the refined taste for cultivating a garden perhaps never crossed their minds" (p. 27).

Either in disparaging remarks such as these, or in laudatory Edenic terms, the Indians are held responsible for some of the best qualities as well as for the worst vices of Brazilianness. A seemingly endless reservoir of pliable images, the Indians of the Brazilian imagination can project equally the noble savage of the Romantics, of contemporary environmentalists, or of many an NGO and the atavistic primitiveness that keeps Brazil locked in underdevelopment. The same Afonso Arinos de Melo Franco who, as we saw in Chapter 2, exalted the influence of the Tupinambá on the beginnings of the French Revolution (1976), decried the bent of both Indians and blacks toward frivolity and disrespect for legal order. Writing in 1936 against the populism of the day, he attributed the then (as now) disregard for legality to the "impulses of Afro-Indian cultural residues," an inheritance from "the 'embryonic stage' of both Indians and Blacks who based their world on force rather than on reason" (quoted in D. Leite 1992, 247). To him these were primitive subterranean forces that threatened to pull Brazil asunder. Brazil's short history makes the Indians' primeval-ness too close for comfort.

This 1930s fear of being dragged into eternal backwardness by inferior races is projected well into the 1990s. Remember political scientist Hélio Jaguaribe: "National unity can be threatened if Brazilian underdevelopment is to persist, that is, if the Indians remain as Indians." Blaming the Indians for Brazil's chronic underdevelopment is reminiscent of the widespread myth among Amazonian indigenous peoples about what we might call the "primordial blunder." The demiurge offered the Indians' ancestors the choice between a set of goods that included such items as shotguns, airplanes, radios, aluminum pots, and outboard motors and another set containing such things as bows and arrows, hammocks, clay pots, and dugout canoes. To their descendants' chagrin they selected the latter, after which the demiurge gave the modern goods to the Whiteman. Given the privilege of first choice, the forefathers committed a fatal blunder. The sense of regret and loss for something never actually gained seems to haunt not only the children of those original Indians but of Brazilians as well.

The double bind that pulls the country between a humane ideology and a quest for modernity is reflected in the schizophrenic treatment the nation dispenses to its ethnic minorities, particularly the Indians. Throughout this book we have seen indigenous peoples transformed into various currencies of the nation's symbolic capital, from suppliers of "Brazilian blood" to emblems of foreign cravings. No wonder Indigenism is a finely tuned instrument for measuring the country's political humor, a microcosm of the national climate. In times of civil crisis the Indian issue comes to the fore as an outlet for the grievances of society at large. No crisis, no special attention to the Indians. As a measure of the country's political temperature, the Indian issue and its immediate manager, the National Indian Foundation (FUNAI), reflect the anxiety of transition times such as the end of military rule (1984–1985), the drafting of the new constitution (1987–1988), the first elections in a quarter of a century (1989), and a presidential impeachment (1992). Probably no other branch of the nation's sensitive body is as politically jittery as official Indian policy. A careful study of the historical correspondence between critical moments in the nation's life and peaks of prominence of the Indian issue might be quite revealing of the nature of this microcosm.

Let me just mention a particularly heinous episode that shook the nation. Just after the 1997 official Day of the Indian (April 19), a middle-aged Patasho man from the state of Bahia was burned to death on the streets of Brasília by a group of upper-middle-class youngsters (the cruel irony of this is that one of the boys is the son of the federal judge who in 1989 issued a restraining order in favor of the Yanomami). The boys later claimed that they took the man for a mere beggar, not knowing he was an Indian, and that they did not know it was wrong to burn beggars, which turned out to be quite a common nightly sport in some urban centers of the country. The revulsion of the country at this gratuitous act of mindless cruelty was much greater because the victim was an Indian. The case reverberated through public opinion, which was already highly inflamed by scandals and unpopular measures imposed by the federal administration. A generalized sense of indignation encompassed issues that were troubling the citizenry. The case of the Patasho murder became conflated with the plight of landless peasants, discontent for rampant corruption among politicians, the demeaning treatment of civil servants by the administration of Fernando Henrique Cardoso, and its questionable privatizations of prestigious state companies. Significantly enough, the Patasho people politicized the tragedy by turning their companion's funeral into a vehement protest against FUNAI and against the landholders who have long invaded their

ESCOLA LACANIANA DE BRASÍLIA

- MESA REDONDA -

FEROCIDADE HUMANA

"UM DEBATE SOBRE A VIOLÊNCIA SOCIAL"

SIRON FRANCO - 1997

COMPONENTES DA MESA:

Dr. CLAUDIO CORTES PAIVA - PSIQUIATRA
Fundação Hospitalar do Distrito Federal / Fundação do Serviço Social

Prof. CLAUDIO MARTINS NEIVA MONTEIRO
2º Grau - História

Dr. JOSÉ JORGE DE CARVALHO - ANTROPÓLOGO
Universidade de Brasília - Deptº de Antropologia

Dra. JOSELITA RODOVALHO - PSICANALISTA
Analista Membro da Escola Lacaniana de Brasília

Dra. SILVIA TAVARES - ADVOGADA CRIMINALISTA
Membro da Comissão de Direitos Humanos da OAB/DF

COORDENADOR DA MESA:

Dr. JOSÉ NAZAR - PSICANALISTA
Analista Membro da Escola Lacaniana de Psicanálise do Rio de Janeiro

Apoio:
CEB - COMPANHIA ENERGÉTICA DE BRASÍLIA
ESCOLA LACANIANA DE PSICANÁLISE DO RIO DE JANEIRO

Agradecimento:
Pela colaboração de DÉA MARIA CAMPOS OLIVEIRA

Data:
19 DE SETEMBRO DE 1997

Horário: **20:00h**

Local:
ASSOCIAÇÃO MÉDICA DE BRASÍLIA
SEPS 713/913 Lote E

Informações:
ESCOLA LACANIANA DE BRASÍLIA
Fone: (061) 346-8308

Patrocínio:

ROMANO VERAS

HOB HOSPITAL OFTALMOLÓGICO DE BRASÍLIA
INSTITUTO DE OLHOS CANROBERT OLIVEIRA

ÓCULOS - JÓIAS E RELÓGIOS

17. Poster invites the public to a round table in Brasília on "Human Ferocity," the symbol of which is the sculpture by Siron Franco in memory of the Patasho Indian Galdino Jesús dos Santos, who was burnt to death in 1997.

lands. The slain Indian became a sort of immolated victim of the country's deep social injustices. Not the least relevant element of this gruesome story is that one of the most acclaimed artists in the country, painter Siron Franco, was commissioned to erect a monument for the Patasho on the precise spot where he was killed. Considering that hundreds of street children, homeless adults, landless peasants, and dispossessed in general have been brutally murdered in the last five years, this homage to a dead Indian stands out as a measure of the prominence Indians have in the minds of Brazilians.

Indigenism is a crossroads where many agents meet. Not the least of these agents are the Indians themselves, whether they are coming together as in the Patasho demonstrations of grief or turning the anthropologist's concept of culture into an empowering device, as practiced, for instance, by the Kayapó. Other obvious actors such as the state, the Catholic Church, and NGOs have well-defined profiles and clear agendas. Agents like the mass media take the Indian issue as something of peripheral interest, but journalists are greatly responsible for the formation of public opinion and for maintaining—or destroying—public interest in the subject. As we saw in Chapter 1, anthropologists, whether they intend it or not, bear the responsibility of translating otherness into intelligible texts. It is in their power to portray an indigenous people as respectable or despicable.

All these agents move about in the uncertain terrain of interethnic ambivalence, for the symbolic richness of Brazilian interethnicity resides precisely in the haziness that pervades this political field. The state passes laws that protect indigenous rights but breaks its own laws in actions that are blatantly anti-Indian. The Catholic Church—and here I mean progressive sectors of the church like the Indigenist Missionary Council (CIMI)—proposes to absorb indigenous customs through an intercultural "incarnation" but for the purpose of turning the Indians into Christians. Nongovernmental organizations advocate indigenous rights, but the Indians must be deserving of this advocacy by behaving according to non-Indian expectations. Journalists sway between sensationalism and social responsibility. Anthropologists try to be cross-culturally fair but can hardly avoid value-laden concepts. And so the unbearable ambivalence of being Indian creeps up from everywhere, creating a fertile medium for the propagation of as many "Indians" as there are agents willing to try their hands as bricklayers in building the amazingly multifaceted edifice of Indigenism. Images of both the Brazilian nation and of the Brazilian Indian pour copiously from writers' fictions, legislators' pens, missionaries' pieties, advocates' proposals, journalists' columns, anthropologists' analyses, and Indians' grievances, not to mention the myriad foreign observers who are as monological as the nationals. From this ideological Babel, one message comes dimly across the babble—how impossible it is to extricate the Indian from Brazil's self-consciousness.

Brazil, the crucible of three races, the land of both exalted and decried métissage. Brazil, forever the country of the future, the giant eternally lying in splendid crib, as sung in the national anthem. The land of illusionary racial democracy, tropical fantasies, paradisiacal beaches, and Amazonian green hell. Brazil, the champion of social inequality, the haven of impunity, the meeting ground of autocratic rule and liberalism. The home of the cordial man, warm hospitality, friendly informality, humor, diversity, inventiveness. Plural Brazil that denies its plurality, the multiethnic giant who pretends to be ethnically uniform. Brazil, killer and defender of Indians, of the Indian grandmother caught with a lasso in the depths of the jungle and whitened by the mists of memory. This is the complex Brazil that continues to nourish its unresolved love-hate relationship with its minorities, its ambivalence toward the Indian as a necessary evil, a convenient bone stuck in its throat, a perfect ideological alibi that goes on justifying its choking in a stifling inferiority complex.

At last we come around to squarely facing that first question of why so much attention to so few Indians. For Brazil and the Indians have their destinies inexorably intertwined. The country would be unthinkable without its constructed Indian. All this makes sense when the nation's eye reflects the likeness of its creation: Indian as counterpoint to Brazilian, as the utmost limit of human possibilities, as ancestor, as destiny. Indian as doomed, redeemer, pure, arcane. Indian as design, soul, purgatory. Indian as repressed past, minor, mirror, obstacle, blood. Indian as derision, false pride, part of nature, fleeting knowledge. Indian as hope, frustration, wisdom, antination. Indian as both Other and us.

References
Index

References

A Crítica. 1980. Causa indígena vira instrumento político. December 10, p. 3.

Agostinho, Pedro. 1982. Incapacidade civil relativa e tutela do índio. In *O Índio Perante o Direito*, edited by Sílvio Coelho dos Santos, pp. 61–88. Florianópolis, Brazil: Editora da Universidade Federal de Santa Catarina.

Ahmad, Aijaz. 1992. *In theory: Classes, nations, literatures*. London: Verso.

Alatas, Syed Hussein. 1977. *The myth of the lazy native: A study of the image of the Malays, Filipinos, and Javanese from the sixteenth to the twentieth century and its function in the ideology of colonial capitalism*. London: Frank Cass.

Albert, Bruce. 1985. Temps du sang, temps des cendres. Unpublished doctoral dissertation, Université de Paris X, Nanterre.

Albert, Bruce. 1988. La fumée du métal: Histoire et représentations du contact chez les Yanomami (Brésil). *L'Homme* 106–107, no. 28 (2–3): 87–119.

Albert, Bruce. 1990. Développement Amazonien et sécurité nationale: Les indiens Yanomami face au Projet Calha Norte. *Brésil: Indiens et developpement en Amazonie*, edited by Bruce Albert, special issue of *Ethnies: Revue de Survival International* (France), nos. 11–12: 116–27.

Albert, Bruce. 1992. Indian lands, environmental policy, and military geopolitics in the development of the Brazilian Amazon: The case of the Yanomami. *Development and Change* 23: 35–70.

Albert, Bruce. 1993. L'or cannibale et la chute du ciel: Une critique chamanique de l'économie politique de la nature (Yanomami, Brésil). *L'Homme* 126–128, no. 33: 349–78.

Albert, Bruce. 1996. O massacre dos Yanomami de Haximu. *Povos Indígenas no Brasil, 1991–1995*, pp. 203–207. São Paulo: Instituto Socioambiental.

Albert, Bruce. 1997. Territorialité, ethnopolitique et développement: à propos du mouvement indien en Amazonie brésilienne. *Cahiers des Amériques Latines* 23: 177–210.

Albert, Bruce, and Carlo Zacquini. 1979. Yanomami Indian Park: Proposal and justification. In *The Yanoama in Brazil, 1979*, edited by Alcida R. Ramos and Kenneth I Taylor. International Work Group for Indigenous Affairs Document 37, pp. 99–170. Copenhagen.

Almeida, Rubem Thomaz de. 1996. O caso Guarani: O que dizem os vivos sobre os que se matam? In *Povos Indígenas no Brasil, 1991–1995*. São Paulo: Instituto Socioambiental.

Amoroso, Marta Rosa. 1992. Corsários no caminho fluvial: Os Mura do rio

Madeira. In *História dos Índios no Brasil,* edited by Manuela Carneiro da Cunha, pp. 297–310. São Paulo: Companhia das Letras.

Anderson, Benedict. 1988. Afterword. In *Ethnicities and nations: Processes of interethnic relations in Latin America, Southeast Asia, and the Pacific,* edited by Remo Guidieri, Francesco Pellizzi, and Stanley J. Tambiah, pp. 404–406. Houston, Texas: Rothko Chapel.

Anderson, Benedict. 1991. *Imagined communities: Reflections on the origin and spread of nationalism.* Rev. ed. London: Verso.

Andrello, Geraldo. In press. Profetas e pregadores: A conversão taurepang à religião do Sétimo Dia. In *Religiões indígenas e cristianismo no Brasil: Perspectivas antropológicas,* edited by Robin Wright. Campinas: Universidade Estadual de Campinas (in press).

Araújo, Ricardo Benzaquen de. 1994. *Guerra e paz: Casa-grande e senzala e a obra de Gilberto Freyre nos anos 30.* Rio de Janeiro: Editora 34.

Arnt, Ricardo, and Stephan Schwartzman. 1992. *Um artifício orgânico: Transição na Amazônia e ambientalismo.* Rio de Janeiro: Rocco.

Arnt, Ricardo, Lúcio Flávio Pinto, and Raimundo Pinto. 1998. *Panará: A volta dos índios gigantes.* São Paulo: Instituto Socioambiental.

Arze Quintanilla, Oscar. 1990. Del indigenismo a la indianidad: cincuenta años de indigenismo continental. In *Indianismo e indigenismo en América,* edited by José Alcina Franch, pp. 18–33. Madrid: Alianza Editorial.

Aspelin, Paul, and Silvio Coelho dos Santos. 1981. *Indian areas threatened by hydroelectric projects in Brazil.* International Work Group for Indigenous Affairs Document 44. Copenhagen.

Austin, J. L. 1962. *How to do things with words.* 2d ed. Cambridge, Mass.: Harvard University Press.

Azevedo, Fernando de. 1996. *A cultura brasileira.* 6th ed. Brasília/Rio de Janeiro: Editora Universidade de Brasília/Editora Universidade Federal do Rio de Janeiro.

Babadzan, Alain. 1988. *Kastom* and nation building in the South Pacific. In *Ethnicities and nations: Processes of interethnic relations in Latin America, Southeast Asia, and the Pacific,* edited by Remo Guidieri, Francesco Pellizzi, and Stanley J. Tambiah, pp. 199–228. Houston: Rothko Chapel.

Baêta Neves, Luiz Felipe. 1978. *O combate dos soldados de Cristo na terra dos papagaios: Colonialismo e repressão cultural.* Rio de Janeiro: Forense-Universitária.

Baines, Stephen. 1990. Les Waimiri-Atroari et la compagnie Paranapanema: Cronique d'une expropriation officielle. In *Brésil: Indiens et développement en Amazonie,* edited by Bruce Albert, special issue of *Ethnies: Revue de Survival International* (France), nos. 11–12: 33–37.

Baines, Stephen. 1991a. *"É A FUNAI Que Sabe": A frente de atração Waimiri-Atroari.* Belém, Brazil: Museu Paraense Emílio Goeldi.

Baines, Stephen. 1991b. The Waimiri-Atroari and the Paranapanema Company. *Critique of Anthropology* 11 (2): 143–53.

Baines, Stephen. 1993. O território dos Waimiri-Atroari e o indigenismo empresarial. In *Ciências Sociais Hoje,* edited by Eli Diniz, J. S. Leite Lopes, and Reginaldo Prandi, pp. 219–43. São Paulo: Associação Nacional de Programas de Pós-Graduação em Ciências Sociais/Hucitec.

Bakhtin, M. M. 1986. *Speech genres and other late essays,* edited by Caryl Emerson and Michael Holquist. Austin: University of Texas Press.

Balandier, Georges. 1955. *Sociologie actuelle de l'Afrique noire: Dynamique des changements sociaux en Afrique centrale.* Paris: Presses Universitaires de France.

Barbosa, Lívia. 1992. *O jeitinho brasileiro.* Rio de Janeiro: Editora Campus.

Barbosa, Marco Antonio Rodrigues. 1989. A arbitrariedade do preconceito. *IstoÉ Senhor,* May 17, p. 1026.

Barreto, Luís Filipe. 1983. *Descobrimentos e renascimento: Formas de ser e pensar nos séculos XV e XVI.* Lisbon: Imprensa Nacional-Casa da Moeda.

Barros, João de. 1968. *O Caramuru: Aventuras prodigiosas dum português coloniza-dor do Brasil.* Adaptação em prosa do poema épico de Frei José de Santa Rita Durão. Lisbon: Livraria Sá da Costa Editora.

Barth, Fredrik. 1964. Herdsmen of Southwest Asia. In *Cultural and social anthro-pology,* edited by Peter Hammond, pp. 63–84. New York: Macmillan.

Bartolomé, Miguel Alberto. 1972. La situación de los indígenas en la Argentina: Área chaqueña y provincia de Misiones. In *La situación del indígena en América del Sur,* edited by Georg Grünberg, pp. 309–52. Montevideo: Biblioteca Cientí-fica/Tierra Nueva.

Bartra, Roger. 1994. *Wild Man in the looking glass: The mythic origins of European otherness.* Ann Arbor: University of Michigan Press.

Bartra, Roger. 1995. The imperial dilemma: Artificial wild men or supernatural devils? *Critique of Anthropology* 15 (3): 219–47.

Basso, Keith. 1979. *Portraits of "the Whiteman": Linguistic play and cultural symbols among the western Apache.* Cambridge, England: Cambridge University Press.

Bastos, Rafael de M. 1983. Sistemas políticos, de comunicação e articulação social no Alto Xingu. *Anuário Antropológico* 81: 43–58.

Bateson, Gregory. [1938] 1958. *Naven: A survey of the problems suggested by a com-posite picture of a culture of a New Guinea tribe drawn from three points of view.* Palo Alto, Calif.: Stanford University Press.

Bateson, Gregory. 1972. *Steps to an ecology of mind.* New York: Ballantine.

Baudrillard, Jean. 1981. *Simulacres et simulation.* Paris: Éditions Galilée.

Baudrillard, Jean. 1983. *Simulations.* New York: Semiotext(e).

Baudrillard, Jean. 1990. *La transparence du mal: Essai sur les phénomènes extrêmes.* Paris: Éditions Galilée.

Beauclerk, John, Jeremy Narby, and Janet Townsend. 1988. *Indigenous peoples: A field guide for development.* Oxford, England: Oxfam.

Beckett, Jeremy R. 1988a. Introduction. In *Past and present: The construction of Aboriginality,* edited by Jeremy R. Beckett, pp. 1–10. Canberra, Australia: Ab-original Studies Press.

Beckett, Jeremy R. 1988b. The past in the present; The present in the past: Con-structing a national Aboriginality. In *Past and present: The construction of Ab-originality,* edited by Jeremy R. Beckett, pp. 191–217. Canberra, Australia: Ab-original Studies Press.

Bennet, Gordon. 1978. Aboriginal rights in international law. Occasional Paper No. 37. Royal Anthropological Institute of Great Britain and Ireland/Survival International, London.

Berkhofer, R. F. Jr. 1978. *The white man's Indian: Images of the American Indian from Columbus to the present.* New York: Knopf.

Bestard, Joan, and Jesús Contreras. 1987. *Bárbaros, Paganos, Salvages y Primitivos: Una Introducción a la Antropología.* Barcelona: Barcanova.

Bettencourt, Lucia. 1992. Cartas brasileiras: Visão e revisão dos índios. In *Índios no Brasil,* edited by Luís Donisete B. Grupioni, pp. 39–46. São Paulo: Secretaria Municipal de Cultura.

Bhabba, Homi K. 1990. DissemiNation: Time, narrative, and the margins of the modern nation. In *Nation and narration,* edited by Homi K. Bhabba, pp. 291–322. London: Routledge.

Birman, Patrícia, Regina Novaes, and Samira Crespo, eds. 1997. *O mal à brasileira.* Rio de Janeiro: Editora Universidade Estadual do Rio de Janeiro.

Bodley, John H. 1975. *Victims of progress.* Menlo Park, Calif.: Benjamin/Cummings.

Bodley, John H. 1988. The World Bank tribal policy: Criticisms and recommendations. In *Tribal peoples and development issues: A global overview,* edited by John H. Bodley, pp. 406–13. Mountain View, Calif.: Mayfield.

Bonfim, Manoel. [1905] 1993. *A América Latina: Males de origem.* Rio de Janeiro: Topbooks.

Bonfim, Manoel. [1931] 1996. *O Brasil nação: Realidade da soberania brasileira.* 2d ed. Rio de Janeiro: Topbooks.

Bonnemaison, Joël. 1991. Le développement est un exotisme: Le détachement et la fascination d'une île Mélanésienne. In *La fiction et la feinte: Développement et peuples autochtones,* edited by Dominique Perrot, special issue of *Ethnies: Revue de Survival International* (France), no. 13: 12–17.

Bosi, Alfredo. 1989. Vieira, ou a cruz da desigualdade. *Novos Estudos* (Centro Brasileiro de Análise e Planejamento) 25: 28–49.

Bosi, Alfredo. 1992. *Dialética da colonização.* São Paulo: Companhia das Letras.

Bourdieu, Pierre. 1989. *O poder simbólico.* Lisbon: Difusão Européia do Livro.

Bourne, Richard. 1978. *Assault on the Amazon.* London: Victor Gollancz.

Braga, Paulo Henrique. 1997. A patente que veio do índio. *Folha de São Paulo,* June 1, sec. 5, p. 15

Brigagão, Clóvis. 1996. *Inteligência e marketing: O caso SIVAM.* Rio de Janeiro: Editora Record.

Briggs, Charles. 1996. The politics of discursive authority in research on the "invention of tradition." *Cultural Anthropology* 11 (4): 435–69.

Brooks, Edwin, René Fuerst, John Hemming, and Francis Huxley. 1973. Tribes of the Amazon basin in Brazil 1972. In *Report for the Aborigines Protection Society.* London: Charles Knight.

Buarque de Holanda, Sérgio. 1986. *O extremo oeste.* São Paulo: Brasiliense.

Buarque de Holanda, Sérgio. [1936] 1989. *Raízes do Brasil.* Rio de Janeiro: José Olympio.

Buarque de Holanda, Sérgio. [1959] 1992. *Visão do Paraíso.* São Paulo: Editora Brasiliense.

Buchillet, Dominique. 1990. Pari Cachoeira: Le laboratoire Tukano du projet Calha Norte. In *Brésil: Indiens et développement en Amazonie,* edited by Bruce Albert, special issue of *Ethnies: Revue de Survival International* (France) 11–12: 128–35.

Bunker, Stephen G. 1985. *Underdeveloping the Amazon: Extraction, unequal exchange, and the failure of the modern state.* Urbana: University of Illinois Press.

Caminha, Pero Vaz de. 1963. *Carta a El Rei D. Manuel,* edited by Leonardo Arroyo. São Paulo: Dominus Editora S.A.

Cançado Trindade, Antonio Augusto, ed. 1992. *A proteção dos direitos humanos nos planos nacional e internacional: Perspectivas brasileiras.* San José de Costa Rica/ Brasília: Instituto Interamericano de Derechos Humanos.

Candido, Antonio. 1967. *Literatura e sociedade: Estudos de teoria e história literária.* São Paulo: Companhia Editora Nacional.

Candido, Antonio. [1975] 1993. *Formação da literatura brasileira.* Belo Horizonte, Brazil: Editora Itatiaia Limitada.

Cardoso, Fernando Henrique and Geraldo Müller. 1978. *Amazônia: Expansão do capitalismo.* São Paulo: Brasiliense/Centro Brasileiro de Análise e Planejamento.

Cardoso de Oliveira, Roberto. 1960. *O processo de assimilação dos Terêna.* Rio de Janeiro: Museu Nacional.

Cardoso de Oliveira, Roberto. 1978. *Sociologia do Brasil Indígena.* Rio de Janeiro: Biblioteca Tempo Brasileiro.

Carelli, Vincent. 1993. Vídeo nas aldeias: Um encontro dos índios com sua imagem. *Tempo e Presença* (Publicação do CEDI) 15 (270): 35–40.

Carelli, Vincent and Milton Severiano. n.d. *Mão branca contra o povo cinza.* São Paulo: Brasil Debates.

Carneiro da Cunha, Manuela. 1987. *Os direitos do índio: Ensaios e documentos.* São Paulo: Editora Brasiliense.

Carneiro da Cunha, Manuela. 1992. Justiça para Paiakan, justiça para os índios. *Folha de São Paulo,* July 16, sec. 1, p. 3.

Carvalho, José Murilo de. 1987. *Os bestializados: O Rio de Janeiro e a República que não foi.* São Paulo: Companhia das Letras.

Carvalho, José Murilo de. 1990. *A formação das almas: O imaginário da República no Brasil.* São Paulo: Companhia das Letras.

Carvalho, José Murilo de. 1996. *A construção da ordem-Teatro de sombras.* Rio de Janeiro: Editora Unversidade Federal do Rio de Janeiro/Relume Dumará.

Carvalho, Mario Cesar. 1997. Cameli mistura família com estado. *Folha de São Paulo,* May 18, sec. 1, p. 14.

Carvalho, Wanderlino Teixeira de. 1990. Indiens et garimpeiros. In *Brésil: Indiens et développement en Amazonie,* edited by Bruce Albert, special issue of *Ethnies: Revue de Survival International* (France) 11–12: 43–49.

CEDI (Centro Ecumênico de Documentação e Informação). 1981. Surgimento das organizações indígenas. *Povos Indígenas no Brasil, 1980: Aconteceu Especial,* no. 6: 38–39.

CEDI (Centro Ecumênico de Documentação e Informação). 1982a. Emancipação e critérios de indianidade. In *Povos Indígenas no Brasil, 1981: Aconteceu Especial,* no. 10: 81–84.

CEDI (Centro Ecumênico de Documentação e Informação). 1982b. Os objetivos do Polonoroeste. *Povos Indígenas no Brasil, 1981: Aconteceu Especial,* no. 10: 25–26.

CEDI (Centro Ecumênico de Documentação e Informação). 1983. *Povos Indígenas no Brasil, 1982: Aconteceu Especial,* no. 12.

CEDI (Centro Ecumênico de Documentação e Informação). 1985a. *Sudeste do Pará*

(Tocantins). Monograph series no. 8. São Paulo: Centro Ecumênico de Documentação e Informação.

CEDI (Centro Ecumênico de Documentação e Informação). 1985b. Tropa de choque contra a presença de líderes indígenas. *Povos Indígenas no Brasil, 1984: Aconteceu Especial*, no. 15: 20.

CEDI (Centro Ecumênico de Documentação e Informação). 1987a. *Povos Indígenas no Brasil, 1985-1986: Aconteceu Especial*, no. 17.

CEDI (Centro Ecumênico de Documentação e Informação). 1987b. Calha Norte: O projeto especial para a ocupação das fronteiras. *Povos Indígenas no Brasil, 1985-1996: Aconteceu Especial*, no. 17: 64-69.

CEDI (Centro Ecumênico de Documentação e Informação). 1989. PROFFAO [Program for the Development of the Western Amazon Border]: O "Calha Sul." *Tempo e Presença* 244-45: 26-27.

CEDI (Centro Ecumênico de Documentação e Informação). 1991a. *Povos Indígenas no Brasil, 1987-1990: Aconteceu Especial*, no. 18.

CEDI (Centro Ecumênico de Documentação e Informação). 1991b. Projeto Calha Norte. *Povos Indígenas no Brasil, 1987-1990: Aconteceu Especial*, no. 18: 93-95.

CEDI (Centro Ecumênico de Documentação e Informação). 1991c. Cronologia de um genocídio documentado. *Povos Indígenas no Brasil, 1987-1990: Aconteceu Especial*, no. 18: 172-93.

CEDI (Centro Ecumênico de Documentação e Informação). 1991d. FUNAI: A galeria da crise permanente II. *Povos Indígenas no Brasil, 1987—1990: Aconteceu Especial*, no. 18: 41-43.

CEDI/CONAGE (National Association of Geologists). 1988. *Empresas de Mineração e Terras Indígenas na Amazônia*. São Paulo: Centro Ecumênico de Documentação e Informação.

CEDI/PETI (Projeto Estudo sobre Terras Indígenas no Brasil). 1990. *Terras indígenas no Brasil*. São Paulo: Centro Ecumênico de Documentação e Informação.

Certeau, Michel de. 1986. *Heterologies*. Minneapolis: University of Minnesota Press.

Chimanovitch, Mario. 1972. Fome e morte rondam os nhambiquaras. *Jornal do Brasil* September 12, p. 18.

CIMI (Conselho Indigenista Missionário). 1974. 1ª Assembléia de Chefes Indígenas. April 17-19. Diamantino, Mato Grosso, Brazil. Mimeo.

CIMI (Conselho Indigenista Missionário). 1978. *Boletim*, no. 50.

CIMI (Conselho Indigenista Missionário). 1979. Encarnação e inculturação. *Porantim* 2 (12): 10-11.

CIMI (Conselho Indigenista Missionário). 1987. *Somos povos somos nações: Subsídios didáticos sobre a questão indígena*. Brasília: CIMI-Conferência Nacional dos Bispos do Brasil.

CIMI (Conselho Indigenista Missionário). 1994. *A violência contra os povos indígenas no Brasil em 1993*. Brasília: CIMI-Conferência Nacional dos Bispos do Brasil.

CIMI Norte. 1989. Informativo Calha Norte. CIMI Norte I, no. 4, Manaus, Brazil.

Clastres, Pierre. 1978. *A sociedade contra o estado*. Rio de Janeiro: Francisco Alves.

Cleary, David. 1990. *Anatomy of the Amazon gold rush*. London: Macmillan.

Cleland, Charles E. 1992. *Rites of conquest: The history and culture of Michigan's Native Americans*. Ann Arbor: University of Michigan Press.

Coelho dos Santos, Silvio and Aneliese Nacke. 1990. Peuples indigènes et développement hydro-électrique. In *Brésil: Indiens et développement en Amazonie*, edited by Bruce Albert, special issue of *Ethnies: Revue de Survival International* (France) 11-12: 56-63.

Cohen, Marleine. 1996. O caminho de volta: A saga dos gigantes Panará. *Povos Indígenas no Brasil, 1991-1995*, pp. 601-13. São Paulo: Instituto Socioambiental.

Colby, Gerard with Charlotte Dennett. 1995. *Thy will be done–The conquest of the Amazon: Nelson Rockefeller and evangelism in the age of oil*. New York: Harper-Collins.

Comaroff, Jean and John Comaroff. 1991. *Of revelation and revolution*. Vol. 1. Chicago: University of Chicago Press.

Comissão Pró-Índio. 1979a. *A questão da emancipação*. São Paulo: Cadernos da Comissão Pró-Índio, No. 1.

Comissão Pró-Índio. 1979b. Antropólogos manifestam-se contra projeto de emancipação de grupos indígenas. In *A questão da emancipação*, Cadernos da Comissão Pró-Índio/SP No. 1, pp. 17-20. São Paulo: Global Editora.

Comissão Pró-Índio. 1979c. Depoimentos e exigências da Assembléia de Chefes Indígenas. In *A questão da emancipação*, Cadernos da Comissão Pró-Índio/SP No. 1, pp. 27-29. São Paulo: Global Editora.

Comissão Pró-Índio. 1981. *A questão da terra*. São Paulo: Cadernos da Comissão Pró-Índio, No. 2.

Comissão Pró-Índio. 1982. *Índios: Direitos históricos*. São Paulo: Cadernos da Comissão Pró-Índio, No. 3.

Comissão Pró-Índio. 1985. *A questão da mineração em terra indígena*. São Paulo: Cadernos da Comissão Pró-Índio, No. 4.

Conklin, Beth and Laura Graham. 1995. The shifting middle ground: Amazonian Indians and ecopolitics. *American Anthropologist* 97 (4): 695-710.

Connolly, Bob and Robin Anderson. 1988. *First contact: New Guinea's Highlanders encounter the outside world*. London: Penguin.

Cook, Noble David and W. George Lovell. 1991. *"Secret Judgments of God": Old World disease in colonial Spanish America*. Norman: University of Oklahoma Press.

Cordeiro, Enio. 1993. Política indigenista brasileira e promoção internacional dos direitos das populações indígenas. Brasília: Ministério das Relações Exteriores. Manuscript.

Correio Braziliense. 1981. Juruna diz que Funai está tentando derrubá-lo. January 31, p. 5.

Correio Braziliense. 1987a. Brossard e Funai querem Cimi investigado. August 13, p. 13.

Correio Braziliense. 1987b. Na Constituinte, surgem as propostas de consenso. August 16, p. 16.

Correio Braziliense. 1987c. Brossard grita com bispo por causa do Cimi. August 28, p. 15.

CPT (Comissão Pastoral da Terra). n.d. O Mausoléu do Faraó. Manuscript.

Cultural Survival Quarterly. 1991. Intellectual property rights: The politics of ownership, special issue of *Cultural Survival Quarterly* 15 (3).

Dallari, Dalmo. 1978. O índio, sua capacidade jurídica e suas terras. In *A questão da emancipação*, Cadernos da Comissão Pró-Índio/SP No. 1, pp. 77–82. São Paulo: Global Editora.

Dallari, Dalmo. 1983. Índios, cidadania e direitos. In *O índio e a cidadania*, Comissão Pró-Índio/SP, pp. 52–58. São Paulo: Brasiliense.

Da Matta, Roberto. 1979. *Carnavais, malandros, e heróis: Para uma sociologia do dilema brasileiro*. Rio de Janeiro: Zahar Editores.

Da Matta, Roberto. 1985. *A casa e a rua*. São Paulo: Editora Brasiliense.

Da Matta, Roberto. 1986. *O que faz o Brasil, Brasil?* Rio de Janeiro: Rocco.

Davis, Shelton. 1977. *Victims of the miracle: Development and the Indians of Brazil*. New York: Cambridge University Press.

Davis, Shelton. 1978. Emancipation: A Dawes Act for Brazilian Indians. *Newsletter* of the Anthropology Resource Center (Boston) 2 (4): 1.

Deloria, Vine Jr. 1973. Foreword. In *One hundred million acres*, Kirke Kickingbird and Karen Ducheneaux, pp. vii–xv. New York: Macmillan.

Derrida, Jacques. 1970. Structure, sign, and play in the discourse of human sciences. In *The languages of criticism and the sciences of man*, edited by Richard Macksey and Eugenio Donato, pp. 247–65. Baltimore, Md.: Johns Hopkins University Press.

Derrida, Jacques. 1976. *Of grammatology*. Baltimore, Md.: Johns Hopkins University Press.

Descola, Philippe. 1982. Ethnicité et développement économique: Le cas de la Federation des Centres Shuar. In *Indianité, ethnocide, indigénisme en Amérique Latine*, edited by F. Morin, pp. 221–27. Toulouse: Éditions du Centre Nationale de Recherche Scientifique (CNRS).

Diakuru and Kisibi. 1996. *A Mitologia Sagrada dos Desana-Wari Dihputiro Põrã*. São Gabriel da Cachoeira, Amazonas: União Nacional Indígena do Rio Tiquié/ Federação das Organizações Indígenas do Rio Negro.

Diamond, Stanley. [1974] 1981. *In search of the primitive: A critique of civilization*. New Brunswick, N.J.: Transaction.

Diário do Congresso Nacional. 1980a. Câmara dos Deputados, November 8, pp. 13905–906.

Diário do Congresso Nacional. 1980b. Câmara dos Deputados, November 14, p. 14178.

Diário do Congresso Nacional. 1980c. Câmara dos Deputados, November 14, pp. 14427–428.

Dias, Luiz Francisco. 1993. Ser brasileiro hoje. In *Discurso fundador: A formação do país e a construção da identidade nacional*, edited by Eni P. Orlandi, pp. 81–88. Campinas, São Paulo: Pontes.

Dimenstein, Gilberto. 1992. PC, Collor e o estupro. *Folha de São Paulo*, June 21, sec. 1, p. 2.

Domínguez, Virginia R. and Catherine M. Lewis, eds. 1995. *Questioning otherness: An interdisciplinary exchange*. Papers from the 1995 Distinguished International Lecture Series. Iowa International Papers Occasional Papers 30–37. Iowa City: Center for International and Comparative Studies with the University of Iowa Libraries.

Dumont, Louis. 1971. Religion, politics, and society in the individualistic universe. *Proceedings of the Royal Anthropological Institute for 1970*: 33–41.

Dumont, Louis. 1977. *From Mandeville to Marx: The genesis and triumph of economic ideology.* Chicago: University of Chicago Press.

Dumont, Louis. 1986. *Essays on individualism: Modern ideology in anthropological perspective.* Chicago: University of Chicago Press.

Eggan, Fred. 1978. Beyond the bicentennial: The future of the American Indian in the perspective of the past. *Journal of Anthropological Research* 34 (2): 161–80.

Ellis, Myriam. 1965. The bandeiras in the geographical expansion of Brazil. In *The bandeirantes: The historical role of the Brazilian pathfinders,* edited by Richard Morse, pp. 48–63. New York: Knopf.

Emmanuel, Arghiri. 1972. *Unequal exchange: A study in the imperialism of trade.* New York: Monthly Review Press.

Evans-Pritchard, E. E. 1976. *Witchcraft, oracles, and magic among the Azande.* Abridged ed. Oxford, England: Oxford University Press.

Fabian, Johannes. 1983. *Time and the Other: How anthropology makes its object.* New York: Columbia University Press.

Faoro, Raymundo. [1957] 1991–93. *Os donos do poder.* 9th ed. (2 vols.). São Paulo: Editora Globo.

Faoro, Raymundo. 1994. *Existe um pensamento político brasileiro?* São Paulo: Editora Ática.

Farage, Nádia and Manuela Carneiro da Cunha. 1987. Caráter da tutela dos índios: Origens e metamorfoses. In *Os direitos do índio: Ensaios e documentos,* edited by Carneiro da Cunha, pp. 103–17. São Paulo: Editora Brasiliense.

Farias, Orlando. 1996. Roraima encolha 90%. *Jornal do Brasil.* April 19, p. 7.

Favre, Henri. 1996. *L'Indigénisme.* Paris: Presses Universitaires de France.

Fearnside, Philip. 1989. Como frear o desmatamento. *Tempo e Presença* 244–245: 8–11.

Feraca, Stephen E. 1990. Inside BIA: Or, "We're getting rid of all these honkies." In *The invented Indian,* edited by James A. Clifton, pp. 271–89. New Brunswick, N.J.: Transaction.

Fernandes, Rubem César. 1980. Um exército de anjos: As raízes da Missão Novas Tribos. *Religião e Sociedade* 5: 129–65.

Figoli, Leonardo. 1982. Identidade étnica e regional: Trajeto constitutivo de uma identidade social. Master's thesis in anthropology, Departamento de Ciências Sociais, University of Brasília.

Fisher, William. 1994. Megadevelopment, environmentalism, and resistance: The institutional context of Kayapó indigenous politics in central Brazil. *Human Organization* 53 (3): 220–32.

Fisher, William. 1995. Native Amazonians and the making of the Amazon wilderness: From discourse of riches and sloth to underdevelopment. In *Creating the countryside: The politics of rural and environmental discourse,* edited by Melanie E. Dupuis and Peter Vandergeest, pp. 166–203. Philadelphia: Temple University Press.

Folha de São Paulo. 1991. Amazônia pode virar Vietnã, diz general. July 23, sec. 1, p. 7.

Folha de São Paulo. 1992a. Antropólogo duvida da acusação a Caiapó. June 9, sec. 1, p. 10.

Folha de São Paulo. 1992b. Eles beberam o meu sangue. June 11, sec. 1, p. 15.

Folha de São Paulo. 1992c. Paiakan e a Justiça. Editorial. June 13, sec. 1, p.2.

Folha de São Paulo. 1992d. Estudante quer indenização. June 16, sec. 1, p. 10.

Folha de São Paulo. 1992e. Irekran não pode ser processada. June 20, sec. 1, p. 14.

Folha de São Paulo. 1995. Tucano faz apelo a ONGs. September 15, p. 5.

Folha de São Paulo. 1996a. Agropecuária apresenta primeira contestação de terras indígenas. January 13, sec. 1, p. 7.

Folha de São Paulo. 1996b. Índios deixam debate na Câmara em protesto contra decreto federal. January 25, sec. 1, p. 11.

Folha de São Paulo. 1996c. Ombro amigo. July 20, sec. 1, p. 4.

Folha de São Paulo. 1997. Xavantes invadem sede da Funai. April 9, sec. 1, pp. 1, 5.

Forde, Daryll. 1949. *Habitat, economy, and society.* New York: Dutton.

Freyre, Gilberto. 1953. *Um brasileiro em terras portuguêsas.* Rio de Janeiro: Livraria José Olympio Editora.

Freyre, Gilberto. [1933] 1992. *Casa grande e senzala.* 29th ed. Rio de Janeiro: Record.

Fuentes, Carlos. 1988. *Myself with others.* New York: Farrar, Straus, & Giroux.

Fuentes, Carlos. 1992. *El espejo enterrado.* Mexico: Fondo de Cultura Económica.

FUNAI (National Indian Foundation). 1987–1988. Departamento de índios isolados: Sistema de proteção ao índio isolado. Fundação Nacional do Indio, Brasília. Mimeo.

Fundação Nacional Pró-Memória. 1988. *Atas indigenistas.* Brasília: Secretaria do Patrimônio Histórico e Artístico Nacional/Fundação Nacional Pró-Memória.

Furtado, Celso. 1963. *Formação Econômica do Brasil.* Brasília: Editora Universidade de Brasília.

Gadamer, Hans-Georg. 1975. *Truth and method.* New York: Crossroad.

Gagliardi, José M. 1989. *O indígena e a República.* São Paulo: Hucitec.

Gaiger, Júlio M. G. 1989. *Direitos indígenas na Constituição Brasileira de 1988.* Brasília: Conselho Indigenista Missionário.

Galeano, Eduardo. 1981. *As veias abertas da América Latina.* Rio de Janeiro: Paz e Terra.

Gallois, Dominique. 1990. L'or et la boue: Cosmologie et orpaillage Waiãpi. In *Brésil: Indiens et développement en Amazonie,* edited by Bruce Albert, special issue of *Ethnies: Revue de Survival International* (France), nos. 11–12: 50–55.

Gallois, Dominique. 1993a. *Mari revisitada: A reintegração da Fortaleza de Macapá na tradição oral dos Waiãpi.* São Paulo: Núcleo de História Indígena e do Indigenismo/Universidade de São Paulo/Fundação de Amparo à Pesquisa do Estado de São Paulo.

Gallois, Dominique. 1993b. "Jane Karakuri," o ouro dos Waiãpi: A experiência de um garimpo indígena. In *Sociedades indígenas e transformações ambientais,* edited by Antonio Carlos Magalhães, pp. 25–46. Belém, Brazil: Núcleo de Meio Ambiente, Universidade Federal do Pará.

Gallois, Dominique. 1996. Controle territorial e diversificação do extrativismo na

Área Indígena Waiãpi. *Povos Indígenas no Brasil, 1991-1995:* 263-71. São Paulo: Instituto Socioambiental.

Gallois, Dominique and Vincent Carelli. 1992. "Vídeo nas aldeias": A experiência Waiãpi. *Cadernos de Campo* 2 (2): 25-36.

Gallois, Dominique and Luis Donisete Grupioni. In press. O índio na Missão Novas Tribos. In *Religiões indígenas e cristianismo no Brasil. Perspectivas antropológicas,* edited by Robin Wright. Campinas, Brazil: Universidade Estadual de Campinas.

Galvão, Eduardo. 1979. *Encontro de sociedades: Índios e brancos no Brasil.* Rio de Janeiro: Paz e Terra.

Gambini, Roberto. 1988. *O espelho índio: Os Jesuítas e a destruição da alma indígena.* Rio de Janeiro: Espaço e Tempo.

Garcia dos Santos, Laymert. 1991. O sonho de Sibupá. *Povos Indígenas no Brasil, 1987—1990. Aconteceu Especial,* no. 18: 73-74. São Paulo: Centro Ecumênico de Documentação e Informação.

Geertz, Clifford. 1984. Distinguished lecture: Anti-antirelativism. *American Anthropologist* 86 (2): 263-78.

Geertz, Clifford. 1995. *After the fact.* Cambridge, Mass.: Harvard University Press.

Gentil, Gabriel dos Santos and Álvaro Fernandes Sampaio. 1985. Febre do ouro no Alto Rio Negro. *Povos Indígenas no Brasil, 1984: Aconteceu Especial,* no. 15: 68-69. São Paulo: Centro Ecumênico de Documentação e Informação.

Gerth, H. H and C. Wright Mills, eds. 1958. *From Max Weber: Essays in sociology.* New York: Galaxy.

Gielow, Igor. 1997. Biopiratas agem livremente na Amazônia. *Folha de São Paulo,* July 13, sec. 1, p. 18.

Ginú, Chico. 1995. The experience of the Alto Juruá Extractive Reserve with vegetal leather: Engaging forest product markets for the survival of ecosystems and cultures. In *Local heritage in the changing tropics: Innovative strategies for natural resource management and control,* edited by Greg Dicum, pp. 105-12. Bulletin series of the Yale School of Forestry and Environmental Studies. New Haven, Conn.: Yale University.

GIPCT (Grupo Interdisciplinar de Política Científica e Tecnológica). 1987. Projeto Calha Norte: Autoritarismo e sigilo na Nova República. *Série Documentos do GIPCT.* Belém, Pará, Brazil: Universidade Federal do Pará.

Giucci, Guillermo. 1993. *Sem fé, lei ou rei: Brasil, 1500-1532.* Rio de Janeiro: Rocco.

Gnerre, Mauricio and Juan Bottasso. 1986. Del indigenismo a las organizaciones indígenas. In *Del indigenismo a las organizations indígenas,* pp. 7-27. Quito, Ecuador: Ediciones Abya Yala.

Goffman, Erving. 1959. *The presentation of self in everyday life.* New York: Doubleday Anchor.

Goffman, Erving. 1961. *Asylums: Essays on the social situation of mental patients and other inmates.* Middlesex, England: Penguin.

Gomes, Laurentino and Paulo Silber. 1992. A explosão do instinto selvagem: Paiakan, o cacique-símbolo da pureza ecológica, estupra e tortura uma adolescente. *Veja,* June 10, pp. 68-73.

Gomes, Mércio and Paulo de Bessa Antunes. 1995. O suicídio dos guaranis e os direitos humanos. *Folha de São Paulo,* December 19, sec. 1, p. 3.

Gomes, Severo. 1984. Entre Custer e Rondon. *Folha de São Paulo,* October 4, sec. 1, p. 3.

Gomes, Severo. 1991. Paapiú—Campo de extermínio. *Povos Indígenas no Brasil 1987-1990: Aconteceu Especial,* no. 18: 163. São Paulo: Centro Ecumênico de Documentação e Informação.

Gondim, Abnor. 1992a. Paiakan pode ser preso a qualquer momento. *Folha de São Paulo,* June 10, sec. 1, p. 14.

Gondim, Abnor. 1992b. Professora consentiu em relação, diz Paiakan. *Folha de São Paulo,* June 11, sec. 1, p. 15.

Gondim, Abnor. 1992c. Juiz admite revogar prisão de Paiakan. *Folha de São Paulo,* June 15, sec. 1, p. 14.

Gondim, Abnor. 1992d. Juiz permite que líder caiapó fique em aldeia. *Folha de São Paulo,* June 22, sec. 1, p. 15.

Gondim, Abnor. 1994. Paiakan recebe sentença hoje no PA. *Folha de São Paulo,* November 28, sec. 3, p. 1.

Gondim, Abnor. 1996. Revisão atinge só 3 áreas indígenas. *Folha de São Paulo,* November 5, sec. 1, p. 15.

Gondim, Abnor. 1997. PF prende índios que ocupavam a Funai. Tribo afirma ter sido vítima de violência. *Folha de São Paulo,* April 12, sec. 1, p. 12.

González, José Marín. 1989. Los protestantes y los indígenas: Estado y misiones en la selva peruana. In *Las religiones amerindias 500 años después,* edited by P. Juan Bottasso, pp. 271-304. Quito, Ecuador: Ediciones Abya-Yala.

Goodland, Robert. 1978. A plea for Amazonian diversity. *Newsletter* of the Anthropology Resource Center (Boston) 2 (4): 3.

Goodland, Robert and H. S. Irwin. 1975. *Amazon jungle: Green hell to red desert?* Amsterdam: Elsevier Scientific.

Goody, Jack, ed. 1968. *Literacy in traditional societies.* Cambridge, England: Cambridge University Press.

Grillo, R. D., ed. 1980. *"Nation" and "state" in Europe: Anthropological perspectives.* London: Academic.

Gutkoski, Cris. 1994. Justiça absolve Paiakan de estupro. *Folha de São Paulo,* November 29, sec. 3, p. 1.

Habermas, Jürgen. 1989. *Identidades nacionales y postnacionales.* Madrid: Tecnos.

Hecht, Susanna and Alexander Cockburn. 1990. *The fate of the forest: Developers, destroyers, and defenders of the Amazon.* New York: HarperPerennial.

Heelas, Richard. 1978. An historical outline of the Panará (Kreen-Akarore) tribe of central Brazil. *Survival International Review* 3 (2): 25-27.

Hemming, John. 1978. *Red gold: The conquest of the Brazilian Indians.* London: Macmillan.

Herzfeld, Michael. 1997. *Cultural intimacy: Social poetics in the nation-state.* London: Routledge.

Hess, David J. and Roberto A. Da Matta, eds. 1995. *The Brazilian puzzle: Culture on the borderlands of the Western world.* New York: Columbia University Press.

Hill, Jonathan, ed. 1988. *Rethinking history and myth: Indigenous South American perspectives on the past.* Urbana: University of Illinois Press.

Hobsbawm, Eric J. 1991. *Nações e nacionalismo desde 1780.* Rio de Janeiro: Paz e Terra.

Holmberg, Alan. 1960. *Nomads of the long bow: The Siriono of eastern Bolivia.* Chicago: University of Chicago Press.

Hsu, Francis L. K. 1964. Rethinking the concept "primitive." *Current Anthropology* 5 (3): 169–78.

Hulme, Peter. 1986. *Colonial encounters: Europe and the native Caribbean, 1492–1797.* London: Methuen.

Huxley, Francis. 1956. *Affable savages.* New York: Capricorn.

Hvalkof, Soren and Peter Aaby, eds. 1981. *Is God an American? An anthropological perspective on the missionary work of the Summer Institute of Linguistics.* Copenhagen: International Work Group for Indigenous Affairs/Survival International.

ISA (Socio-Environmental Institute). 1994. Pirataria avança sobre genes indígenas. *Parabólicas,* Bulletin of the Instituto Socioambiental, 2 (1): 3.

ISA (Socio-Environmental Institute). 1996a. *Povos Indígenas no Brasil, 1991–1995.* São Paulo: Instituto Socioambiental.

ISA (Socio-Environmental Institute). 1996b. Waimiri-Atroari bloqueiam caminho da Paranapanema. *Parabólicas,* Bulletin of the Instituto Socioambiental, 23 (3): 10.

ISA (Socio-Environmental Institute). 1996c. Gaiger: O homem de confiança de Jobim na FUNAI. *Parabólicas,* Bulletin of the Instituto Socioambiental, 17 (3): 7.

Ismaelillo and Robin Wright, eds. 1982. *Native peoples in struggle: Cases from the Fourth Russell Tribunal and other international forums.* Bombay, N.Y.: Anthropology Resource Center and Emergency Response International Network.

Jackson, Jean. 1989. Is there a way to talk about making culture without making enemies? *Dialectical Anthropology* 14: 127–43.

Jackson, Jean. 1991. Being and becoming an Indian in the Vaupés. In *Nation-states and Indians in Latin America,* edited by Greg Urban and Joel Sherzer, pp. 131–55. Austin: University of Texas Press.

Jackson, Jean. 1993. El concepto de "Nación Indigena": Algunos ejemplos en las Américas. In *La Construcción de Las Américas,* edited by C. A. Uribe Tobón, pp. 219–41. Bogotá: Universidad de los Andes.

Jaguaribe, Hélio. 1994. O jardim antropológico de neolíticos. *Folha de São Paulo,* September 2, sec. 1, p. 3.

Jobim, Nelson. 1996. Uso de passaportes e dupla nacionalidade. *Folha de São Paulo,* October 23, sec. 1, p. 3.

Jornal da Ciência Hoje. 1994. Jaguaribe e o destino dos índios. September 16, p. 3.

Jornal de Brasília. 1975. Antropólogos defendem paralisação na BR-174. January 9, p. 7.

Jornal de Brasília. 1976a. Indígenas serão emancipados. June 30, p. 10.

Jornal de Brasília. 1976b. Antropóloga demitida aumenta insatisfação. December 3, p. 11.

Jornal de Brasília. 1977. Gaviões recebem crédito do BB. January 27, p. 10.

308   References

Jornal de Brasília. 1978. Geisel verá lei da emancipação. October 19, p. 7.

Jornal do Brasil. 1974. Novo Ministro quer fim das reservas indígenas. March 9, p. 1.

Jornal do Brasil. 1978. Decreto permite emancipação do índio isolado ou em comunidade. November 9, p. 8.

Júnior, Policarpo. 1992. À espera da guerra (interview with Thaumaturgo Sotero Vaz). *Veja*, January 22, pp. 7–9.

Junqueira, Carmen and Betty Mindlin. 1987. The Aripuanã Park and the Polonoroeste programme. International Work Group for Indigenous Affairs Document 59. Copenhagen.

Juruna, Mário, Antonio Hohlfeldt, and Assis Hoffmann. 1982. *O Gravador do Juruna*. Porto Alegre, Brazil: Mercado Aberto Editora e Propaganda.

Kickingbird, Kirke and Karen Ducheneaux. 1973. *One hundred million acres*. New York: Macmillan.

Krenak, Ailton. 1996. Preface. In *Nucleus of Indian culture/Indian Research Center*, edited by Ailton Krenak, pp. 4–5. São Paulo: Núcleo de Cultura Indígena.

Kuhn, Thomas. 1977. *The essential tension: Selected studies in scientific tradition and change*. Chicago: University of Chicago Press.

Kuklick, Henrika. 1991. *The savage within: The social history of British anthropology, 1885–1945*. Cambridge, England: Cambridge University Press.

Kuper, Adam. 1988. *The invention of primitive society*. London: Routledge.

Laraia, Roques de Barros. 1993. *Los indios de Brasil*. Madrid: Editorial Mapfre.

Laraia, Roque de Barros and Roberto Da Matta. 1967. *Índios e castanheiros*. São Paulo: Difusão Européia do Livro.

Leal, Victor Nunes. [1949] 1993. *Coronelismo, enxada e voto*. 6th ed. São Paulo: Editora Alfa-Omega.

Le Goff, Jacques. 1977. *La civilisation de l'occident médiéval*. Paris: Arthaud.

Le Goff, Jacques. 1980. *Para um novo conceito de Idade Média: Tempo, trabalho e cultura no Ocidente*. Lisbon: Editorial Estampa.

Leite, Dante Moreira. 1992. *O caráter nacional brasileiro: História de uma ideologia*, 5th ed. São Paulo: Editora Ática.

Leite, Jurandyr C. F. 1989. Proteção e incorporação: A questão indígena no pensamento político do positivismo ortodoxo. *Revista de Antropologia* 30–32: 255–75.

Leite, Serafim, S.J. 1993. *Breve história da Companhia de Jesus no Brasil, 1549–1760*. Braga, Portugal: Livraria A.I.

Lemaire, Ria. 1989. Rereading *Iracema*: The problem of the representation of women in the construction of a national Brazilian identity. *Luso-Brazilian Review* 26: 59–73.

Leonel, Mauro. 1990. Dernier cercle: Les indiens isolés du Polonoroeste. In *Brésil: Indiens et développement en Amazonie*, edited by Bruce Albert, special issue of *Ethnies: Revue de Survival International* (France), nos. 11–12: 97–100.

Lévi-Strauss, Claude. 1969. *The elementary structures of kinship*. Boston: Beacon.

Lévy-Bruhl, Lucien. [1910] 1985. *How natives think*. Princeton, N.J.: Princeton University Press.

Lévy-Bruhl, Lucien. [1923] 1966. *Primitive mentality*. Boston: Beacon.

Lins, Ivan. 1967. *História do Positivismo no Brasil*. São Paulo: Companhia Editora Nacional.

Lins, Osman. 1979. *Evangelho na taba: Outros problemas inculturais brasileiros*. São Paulo: Summus Editorial.

Lins da Silva, Carlos Eduardo. 1996. Estados Unidos patenteiam vírus de índio e são acusados de vampirismo. *Folha de São Paulo,* June 16, sec. 5, p. 13.

Lizot, Jacques. 1984. *Les Yanõmami Centraux*. Paris: Éditions de L'École des Hautes Études en Sciences Sociales.

Machado, Josué. 1994. PC e os índios. *Folha de São Paulo,* May 28, sec. 1, p. 11.

MacMillan, Gordon. 1995. *At the end of the rainbow? Gold, land, and people in the Brazilian Amazon.* London: Earthscan.

Magalhães, Amilcar Botelho de. 1942. *Impressões da Commissão Rondon.* São Paulo: Companhia Editora Nacional.

Magüta 1988. *A lágrima Ticuna é uma só.* Benjamin Constant, Amazonas: *Magüta* (Centro de Documentação e Pesquisa do Alto Solimões).

Mahar, Dennis. 1989. *Government policies and deforestation in Brazil's Amazon region.* Washington, D.C.: World Bank.

Mannoni, Octave. 1990. *Prospero and Caliban: The psychology of colonization.* Ann Arbor: University of Michigan Press.

Mansur, Alexandre. 1996. Empresa americana vende DNA de índios. *Jornal do Brasil,* August 18, p. 20.

Marchant, Alexander. 1942. From Barter to Slavery: The Economic Relations of Portuguese and Indians in the Settlement of Brazil, 1500–1580. The Johns Hopkins University Studies in Historical and Political Science, Vol. 60. Baltimore: The Johns Hopkins Press.

Marcus, George and Michael Fischer. 1986. *Anthropology as cultural critique: An experimental moment in the human sciences.* Chicago: University of Chicago Press.

Marés, Carlos Frederico. 1983. A cidadania e os índios. In *O índio e a cidadania.* Comissão Pró-Índio/SP, pp. 44–51. São Paulo: Brasiliense.

Martins, Américo. 1993. Flores propõe mineradoras na reserva. *Folha de São Paulo,* October 3, sec. 6, p. 5.

Martins, José de Souza. 1994. *O poder do atraso.* São Paulo: Hucitec.

Mauss, Marcel. 1956. La nation. *L'Année Sociologique,* troisième série (1953–1954): 5–68.

Maybury-Lewis, David. 1965. *The savage and the innocent.* Boston: Beacon.

Maybury-Lewis, David. 1974. *Akwè-Shavante society.* London: Oxford University Press.

Maybury-Lewis, David, ed. 1984. *The prospects for plural societies.* Washington, D.C.: Proceedings of the American Ethnological Society.

McCallum, Cecilia. 1994. The *Veja* Payakan: The media, modernism, and the image of the Indian in Brazil. *Commission on Visual Anthropology Newsletter* 2/94: 2–8.

McGrane, Bernard. 1989. *Beyond anthropology: Society and the Other.* New York: Columbia University Press.

Meggers, Betty. 1971. *Amazonia: Man and culture in a counterfeit paradise.* Chicago: Aldine.

Meliá, Bartolomeu and Liane Maria Nagel. 1995. *Guaraníes y Jesuítas en tiempo de las misiones: Una bibliografía didáctica.* Asunción, Paraguay/Santo Angelo,

Brazil: Centro de Estudios Paraguayos "Antonio Guasch"/Centro de Cultura Missioneira.

Mello e Souza, Laura. 1987. *O diabo e a Terra de Santa Cruz*. São Paulo: Companhia das Letras.

Melo Franco, Afonso Arinos de. [1937] 1976. *O índio brasileiro e a Revolução Francesa. (As origens brasileiras da teoria da bondade natural)*. Rio de Janeiro/ Brasília: Livraria José Olympio Editora/Instituto Nacional do Livro.

Mendes de Almeida, Candido. 1876. Notas sobre a historia patria. *Revista Trimestral do Instituto Historico Geographico e Ethnographico do Brasil* 34 (2): 5–24.

Mills, C. Wright. 1956. *White collar: The American middle class*. New York: Galaxy.

Mindlin, Betty. 1984. Avaliação do Programa Polonoroeste. *Povos Indígenas no Brasil, 1983: Aconteceu Especial*, no. 14: 167–70. São Paulo: Centro Ecumênico de Documentação e Informação.

Mindlin, Betty. 1985. Avaliação do Polonoroeste: Uma proposta. *Povos Indígenas no Brasil, 1984: Aconteceu Especial*, no. 15: 221–24. São Paulo: Centro Ecumênico de Documentação e Informação.

Mindlin, Betty. 1987. Polonoroeste, 1985. *Povos Indígenas no Brasil, 1985–1986: Aconteceu Especial*, no. 17: 71–74. São Paulo: Centro Ecumênico de Documentação e Informação.

Mindlin, Betty. 1990. Le projet Polonoroeste et les Indiens. *Brésil: Indiens et développement en Amazonie*, edited by Bruce Albert, special issue of *Ethnies: Revue de Survival International* (France), nos. 11–12: 87–96.

Mindlin, Betty and Mauro Leonel. 1991. O que o Polonoroeste deve aos índios? *Povos Indígenas no Brasil, 1987–1990: Aconteceu Especial*, no. 18: 90–92. São Paulo: Centro Ecumênico de Documentação e Informação.

Miyamoto, Shiguenoli. 1989. Diplomacia e militarismo: O Projeto Calha Norte e a ocupação do espaço amazônico. *Revista Brasileira de Ciência Política* 1 (1): 145–63.

Mohanty, Chandra Talpade. 1991. Under Western eyes: Feminist scholarship and colonial discourses. In *Third-world women and the politics of feminism*, edited by Chandra T. Mohanty, Ann Russo, and Lourdes Torres, pp. 51–80. Bloomington: Indiana University Press.

Monbiot, George. 1991. *Amazon watershed: The new environmental investigation*. London: Michael Joseph.

Monteiro, John Manuel. 1992. Os Guarani e a história do Brasil meridional: Séculos XVI–XVII. In *História dos índios no Brasil*, edited by Manuela Carneiro da Cunha, pp. 475–98. São Paulo: Companhia das Letras.

Monteiro, John Manuel. 1994. *Negros da terra: Índios e bandeirantes nas origens de São Paulo*. São Paulo: Companhia das Letras.

Montero, Paula. 1996. A universalidade da Missão e a particularidade das culturas. In *Entre o mito e a história: O V centenário do descobrimento da América*, edited by Paula Montero, pp. 31–135. Petrópolis, Brazil: Vozes.

Montserrat, Ruth Maria F. 1992. Línguas indígenas no Brasil contemporâneo. In *Índios no Brasil*, edited by Luís Donisete B. Grupioni, pp. 93–104. São Paulo: Secretaria Municipal de Cultura.

Moreira Neto, Carlos de Araújo. 1988. *Índios da Amazônia: De maioria a minoria, 1750-1850*. Petrópolis, Brazil: Vozes.

Morgan, Lewis Henry. [1877] 1963. *Ancient society*. New York: Meridian.

Morse, Richard. 1988. *O espelho de Próspero*. São Paulo: Companhia das Letras.

Morse, Richard, ed. 1965. *The bandeirantes: The historical role of the Brazilian pathfinders*. New York: Knopf.

Mossri, Sônia. 1994. Jaguaribe defende o fim dos índios até ano 2000. *Folha de São Paulo*, August 30, sec. 1, p. 4.

Mougeot, Luc J. A. 1988. Planejamento hidroelétrico e reinstalação de populações na Amazônia: Primeiras lições de Tucuruí, Pará. In *Fronteiras*, edited by Catherine Aubertin, pp. 231-50. Brasília: Editora Universidade de Brasília/L'Institut Français de Recherche Scientifique pour le Développement en Coopération.

Mueller, Charles. 1980. Rondônia, Brazil. In *Land, people, and planning in contemporary Amazonia*, edited by Françoise Barbira-Scazzocchio, pp. 141-53. Cambridge, England: Centre of Latin American Studies, Cambridge University.

Muggiati, André. 1996a. Justiça Federal proíbe disco que ataca índios. *Folha de São Paulo*, February 24, sec. 1, p. 8.

Muggiati, André. 1996b. Mineradora e índios tentam acordo no AM. *Folha de São Paulo*, October 11, sec. 1, p. 9.

Munduruku, Daniel. 1996. *Histórias de índio*. São Paulo: Companhia das Letrinhas.

Murdock, George Peter. 1934. *Our primitive contemporaries*. New York: Macmillan.

Nandy, Ashis. 1983. *The intimate enemy: Loss and recovery of self under colonialism*. Delhi: Oxford University Press.

Nascimento, Celso Gestermaier de. In press. Raízes distantes: José de Anchieta, S.J., e o teatro de conversão. In *Religiões indígenas e cristianismo no Brasil: Perspectivas antropológicas*, edited by Robin Wright. Campinas, Brazil: Universidade Estadual de Campinas.

Neri, Emanuel. 1996. Abandono provoca o suicídio de índios. *Folha de São Paulo*, May 12, sec. 1, p. 14.

Neto, Miranda. 1979. *O dilema da Amazônia*. Petrópolis, Brazil: Vozes.

Neto, Olímpio Cruz. 1996. Jobim ensina como alterar terra indígena. *Folha de São Paulo*, January 30, sec. 1, p. 12.

Newsweek. 1981. The vanishing tribals, September 21, p. 30.

Nogueira, Rui and Lucas Figueiredo. 1996. Militares planejam ocupação econômica da Amazônia. *Folha de São Paulo*, October 27, sec. 5, p. 9.

Nugent, Stephen. 1990. *Big mouth: The Amazon speaks*. London: Fourth State.

Nugent, Stephen. 1993. *Amazonian caboclo society: An essay on invisibility and peasant economy*. Oxford, England: Berg.

Nugent, Stephen. 1997. The coordinates of identity in Amazonia: At play in the fields of culture. *Critique of Anthropology* 17 (1): 33-51.

Nunes, Eunice. 1994. Caso Paiakan abre discussão sobre punições para os índios. *Folha de São Paulo*, December 4, sec. 4, p. 2.

Nuningo Sesén, Andrés. 1991. Isto é o desenvolvimento? In *Subsídios para a Discussão sobre Autosustentação*, by Helcio Souza and Marta Azevedo. Unpublished manuscript, 11 pp.

O Dia. 1980. Contestada competência do Tribunal Russell: Governo confirma proibição da ida de Juruna à Holanda. November 4, p. 5.

O Estado de São Paulo. 1977. Índios repelem a Funai e poderão ficar sem tutela. August 3, p. 13.

O Estado de São Paulo. 1980. Viagem surpreende na Funai. November 22, p. 10.

O Estado de São Paulo. 1981. Elogio para os Salesianos. April 11, p. 13.

O Globo. 1980. Ministro reitera veto à viagem do cacique Juruna. November 4, p. 3.

O Globo. 1981a. Santa Sé rechaça acusação de genocídio na Amazônia. January 28, p. 11.

O Globo. 1981b. Presidente da Funai visita na terça Alto Rio Negro. April 4, p. 15.

O Liberal. 1986. Ocupação e colonização da Calha Norte. December 28, pp. 16–19.

Oliveira, Ana Gita de. 1983. Missionários e índios do Alto Rio Negro. *Jornal de Brasília,* September 24, p. 15.

Oliveira Filho, João Pacheco de. 1992. Remilitarização, modernização e ambientalismo. *Políticas Públicas* 7 (80): 28–32.

Oliveira Filho, João Pacheco de. 1996. Os caminhos para o Évare: A demarcação Ticuna. *Povos Indígenas no Brasil, 1991-1995:* 307–309. São Paulo: Instituto Socioambiental.

Oliveira Filho, João Pacheco de, and Antonio Carlos de Souza Lima. 1990. Massacre d'indiens dans le nord Amazonien. *Brésil: Indiens et développement en Amazonie,* edited by Bruce Albert, special issue of *Ethnies: Revue de Survival International* (France) nos. 11–12: 136–41.

Ordem dos Advogados do Brasil. 1981. *O índio e o direito.* Rio de Janeiro: Ordem dos Advogados do Brasil.

Pagden, Anthony. 1982. *The fall of natural man: The American Indian and the origins of comparative ethnology.* Cambridge, England: Cambridge University Press.

Paoli, Maria Célia P. M. 1983. O sentido histórico da noção de cidadania no Brasil: Onde ficam os índios? In *O índio e a cidadania,* Comissão Pró-Índio/SP, pp. 20–34. São Paulo: Brasiliense.

Pãrõkumu, Umusĩ and Tõrãmü Kẽhíri. 1995. *Antes o mundo não existia: A mitologia dos antigos Desana-Khíripõrã.* São Gabriel da Cachoeira, Amazonas: União das Nações Indígenas do Rio Tiquiê/Federação das Organizações Indígenas do Rio Negro.

Pechincha, Monica. n.d. O ritual da pacificação. Unpublished manuscript.

Pereira, Maria Denise Fajardo. In press. Catolicismo, protestantismo e conversão: O campo da ação missionária entre os Tiriyó. In *Religiões indígenas e cristianismo no Brasil: Perspectivas antropológicas,* edited by Robin Wright. Campinas, Brazil: Universidade Estadual de Campinas.

Perrot, Dominique. 1991. Les empêcheurs de développer en rond. *La fiction et la feinte: Développement et peuples autochtones,* edited by Dominique Perrot, special issue of *Ethnies: Revue de Survival International* (France) no. 13: 4–11.

Pinto, Lúcio Flávio. 1980. *Amazônia: No rastro do saque.* São Paulo: Hucitec.

Pinto, Lúcio Flávio. 1989. Decálogo da Amazônia. *Tempo e Presença* 244/245: 5–7.

Prado, Caio, Jr. 1942. *Formação do Brasil contemporâneo: Colônia.* São Paulo: Livraria Martins Editora.

Prado, Paulo. [1928] 1997. *Retrato do Brasil.* 8th ed. São Paulo: Companhia das Letras.

Pratt, Mary Louise. 1992. *Imperial eyes: Travel writing and transculturation.* London: Routledge.

Price, David. 1977. Acculturation, social assistance, and political context: The Nambiquara in Brazil. *Proceedings of the XLIII International Congress of Americanists* 2: 603–609. Paris, 1976.

Price, David. 1981. The Nambiquara. In *In the path of the Polonoroeste: Endangered peoples of western Brazil.* Occasional Paper 6, pp. 23–27. Cultural Survival, Cambridge, Mass.

Price, Richard. 1995. Executing ethnicity: The killings in Suriname. *Cultural Anthropology* 10 (4): 437–71.

Queiroz, Ruben Caixeta de. In press. A saga de Ewká: Epidemias e evangelização entre os Wai Wai. In *Religiões indígenas e cristianismo no Brasil: Perspectivas antropológicas,* edited by Robin Wright. Campinas, Brazil: Universidade Estadual de Campinas.

Rafael, Vicente L. 1988. *Contracting colonialism: Translation and Christian conversion in Tagalog society under early Spanish rule.* Ithaca, N.Y.: Cornell University Press.

Raminelli, Ronald. 1996. *Imagens da colonização: A representação do índio de Caminha a Vieira.* Rio de Janeiro: Jorge Zahar Editor.

Ramos, Alcida Rita. 1979. Yanoama Indians in northern Brazil threatened by highway. In *Yanoama in Brazil, 1979,* edited by Alcida R. Ramos and Kenneth I Taylor. International Work Group for Indigenous Affairs Document 37, pp. 1–41. Copenhagen.

Ramos, Alcida Rita. 1980a. A emancipação revisitada: Projeto Hélio Campos. *O Estado* (Santa Catarina), April 13, p. 12.

Ramos, Alcida Rita. 1980b. *Hierarquia e simbiose: Relações intertribais no Brasil.* São Paulo: Hucitec.

Ramos, Alcida Rita. 1980c. Development, integration, and the ethnic integrity of Brazilian Indians. In *Land, people, and planning in contemporary Amazonia,* edited by Françoise Barbira-Scazzocchio, pp. 222–29. Occasional Publication No. 3. Cambridge, England: Center of Latin American Studies, Cambridge University.

Ramos, Alcida Rita. 1984a. O Brasil no movimento indígena americano. *Anuário Antropológico, 1982:* 281–86.

Ramos, Alcida Rita. 1984b. Frontier expansion and Indian peoples in the Brazilian Amazon. In *Frontier expansion in Amazonia,* edited by Marianne Schmink and Charles H. Wood, pp. 83–104. Gainesville: University of Florida Press.

Ramos, Alcida Rita. 1990. Indigenismo de resultados. *Revista Tempo Brasileiro* 100: 133–49.

Ramos, Alcida Rita. 1991. Report on a trip to Yanomami territory in Roraima, November 24, 1990–January 14, 1991. *Urihi,* no. 13. Bulletin of the Comissão pela Criação do Parque Yanomami, São Paulo.

Ramos, Alcida Rita. 1994. Nações dentro da nação: Um desencontro de ideologias. In *Etnia e Nação na América Latina,* edited by George Cerqueira Zarur, vol. 1 pp. 79–88. Washington, D.C.: Organization of American States.

Ramos, Alcida Rita. 1995a. *Sanumá memories: A Yanomami ethnography in times of crisis*. Madison: University of Wisconsin Press.

Ramos, Alcida Rita. 1995b. O papel político das epidemias: O caso Yanomami. In *Ya no hay lugar para cazadores: Procesos de extinción y transfiguración étnica en América Latina*, edited by Miguel A. Bartolomé, pp. 55–89. Quito, Ecuador: Abya-Yala.

Ramos, Alcida Rita. 1995c. Nation-states hot and cold. *Identities* 1 (4): 415–19.

Ramos, Alcida Rita. 1996a. Por falar em Paraíso Terrestre. *Travessia: Revista do Migrante* 9 (24): 17–20.

Ramos, Alcida Rita. 1996b. A profecia de um boato: Matando por ouro na área Yanomami. *Anuário Antropológico, 1995:* 121–60.

Ramos, Alcida Rita, Marco Antonio Lazarin, and Gale Goodwin Gomez. 1987. Yanomami em tempo de ouro: Relatório de pesquisa. In *Culturas indígenas de la Amazonia*, edited by Luis Yáñez-Barnuevo, pp. 73–83. Madrid: Biblioteca Quinto Centenário.

Rappaport, Joanne. 1994. *Cumbe reborn: An Andean ethnography of history*. Chicago: University of Chicago Press.

Reichel-Dolmatoff, Gerardo. 1972. El misionero ante las culturas indígenas. *América Indígena* 32 (4): 1138–49.

Reichel-Dolmatoff, Gerardo. 1996. *The forest within: The worldview of the Tukano Amazonian Indians*. London: Themis.

Reis, Elisa P. 1988. O Estado nacional como ideologia: O caso brasileiro. *Estudos Históricos* 1 (2): 187–203.

Reissner, Raul Alcides. 1983. *El indio en los diccionarios: Exégesis léxica de un estereotipo*. Mexico: Instituto Nacional Indigenista.

Renteln, Alison Dundes. 1988. Relativism and the search for human rights. *American Anthropologist* 90 (1): 56–72.

Retamar, Roberto Fernández. 1989. *Caliban and other essays*. Minneapolis: University of Minnesota Press.

Ribeiro, Darcy. 1962. *A política indigenista brasileira*. Rio de Janeiro: Ministério da Agricultura.

Ribeiro, Darcy. 1970. *Os índios e a civilização*. Rio de Janeiro: Civilização Brasileira.

Ribeiro, Darcy. 1993. A invenção do Brasil. In *A fundação do Brasil,* edited by Darcy Ribeiro and Carlos Moreira Neto, pp. 15–61. Petrópolis, Brazil: Vozes.

Ribeiro, Darcy. 1994. Os irmãos Villas Bôas. In *A marcha para o Oeste,* Orlando Villas Bôas and Cláudio Villas Bôas, pp. 11–12. São Paulo: Editora Globo.

Ribeiro, Darcy. 1995. *O povo brasileiro: A formação e o sentido do Brasil*. São Paulo: Companhia das Letras.

Ricardo, Beto. 1996a. A sociodiversidade nativa contemporânea no Brasil. *Povos Indígenas no Brasil, 1991–1995:* i–xii. São Paulo: Instituto Socioambiental.

Ricardo, Beto, ed. 1996b. A FUNAI é uma morta-viva que continuará pairando sobre a política indigenista até que haja alternativas consistentes (interview with Márcio Santilli). *Povos Indígenas no Brasil, 1991–1995:* 40–48. São Paulo: Instituto Socioambiental.

Ricardo, Beto, and Carlos Marés. 1996a. FHC reacende estopim anti-indígena.

Povos Indígenas no Brasil, 1991-1995: 64-65. São Paulo: Instituto Socio-ambiental.

Ricardo, Beto and Carlos Marés. 1996b. Decreto do medo. *Folha de São Paulo,* February 5, sec. 1, p. 3.

Ricardo, Carlos Alberto. 1991. Jogo duro na Cabeça do Cachorro. *Povos Indígenas no Brasil, 1987-1990: Aconteceu Especial,* no. 18: 101-103. São Paulo: Centro Ecumênico de Documentação e Informação.

Ricardo, Carlos Alberto. 1995. "Os índios" e a sociodiversidade nativa contem-porânea no Brasil. In *A temática indígena na escola,* edited by Aracy Lopes da Silva and Luís D. B. Grupioni, pp. 29-55. Brasília: Ministério da Educação e do Desporto/Mari-Grupo de Educação Indigena/United Nations Educational, Sci-entific, and Cultural Organization.

Ricardo, Carlos Alberto. 1996a. Quem fala em nome dos índios? (II). *Povos Indí-genas no Brasil, 1991-1995:* 90-94. São Paulo: Instituto Socioambiental.

Ricardo, Carlos Alberto. 1996b. A sociodiversidade nativa contemporânea no Brasil. *Povos Indígenas no Brasil, 1991-1995:* i-xii. São Paulo: Instituto Socio-ambiental.

Ricardo, Fany. 1991. As usinas hidrelétricas e os índios. *Povos Indígenas no Brasil, 1987-1990: Aconteceu Especial,* no. 18: 77-83. São Paulo: Centro Ecumênico de Documentação e Informação.

Rich, Bruce. 1986. Environmental management and multilateral development banks. *Multilateral banks and indigenous peoples: Development or destruction?* special issue of *Cultural Survival Quarterly* 10 (1): 4-13.

Ricoeur, Paul. 1978. *O conflito das interpretações.* Rio de Janeiro: Imago.

Rios, Aurélio Veiga. 1993. Os direitos constitucionais dos índios nas faixas de fronteira. In *Os direitos indígenas e a Constituição,* edited by Juliana Santilli, pp. 51-64. Porto Alegre, Brazil: Núcleo de Direitos Indígenas e Sergio Antonio Fabris Editor.

Rocha Pitta, Sebastião. 1950. *História da América portuguesa,* 1730. Bahia, Brazil: Livraria Progresso Editora.

Rosaldo, Renato. 1989. *Culture and truth.* Boston: Beacon.

Rossi, Clóvis. 1995. Decreto sobre áreas indígenas repercute mal. *Folha de São Paulo,* September 21, sec. 1, p. 8.

Rowe, William and Vivian Schelling, eds. 1991. *Popular culture in Latin America.* London: Verso.

Rufino, Marcos Pereira. 1996. A missão calada: Pastoral indigenista e a nova evan-gelização. In *Entre o mito e a história: O V centenário do descobrimento da América,* edited by Paula Montero, pp.137-202. Petrópolis, Brazil: Vozes.

Ryan, Michael T. 1981. Assimilating new worlds in the sixteenth and seventeenth centuries. *Comparative Studies in Society and History* 23 (4): 519-38.

Sá, Nelson de. 1997. O choro dos xavantes. *Folha de São Paulo,* April 12, sec. 1, p. 5.

Sahlins, Marshall. 1988. Cosmologies of capitalism: The trans-Pacific sector of the "world system." *Proceedings of the British Academy for 1988:* 1-51.

Sahlins, Marshall. 1992. The economics of develop-man in the Pacific. *Res* 21: 12-25.

Sahlins, Marshall. 1993. Goodbye to tristes tropes: Ethnography in the context of modern world history. *Journal of Modern History* 65 (1): 1–25.

Said, Edward W. 1979. *Orientalism.* New York: Vintage.

Salles, Ricardo. 1996. *Nostalgia imperial: A formação da identidade nacional no Brasil do segundo reinado.* Rio de Janeiro: Topbooks.

Salvador, Vicente do. [1888] 1954. *História do Brasil, 1500–1627.* São Paulo: Edições Melhoramentos.

Sanders, Douglas. 1978. The unique constitutional position of the Indian. International Work Group for Indigenous Affairs *Newsletter,* no. 19: 39–44.

Santilli, Juliana. 1996. A proteção aos direitos de propriedade intelectual das comunidades indígenas. *Povos Indígenas no Brasil, 1991–1995:* 17–21. São Paulo: Instituto Socioambiental.

Santilli, Márcio. 1989. Tratado de Cooperação Amazônica: Um instrumento diplomático a serviço da retórica nacionalista. *Tempo e Presença* 244–45: 40–41.

Santilli, Márcio. 1990. Projet Calha Norte: Politique indigéniste et frontières nord-amazoniennes. In *Brésil: Indiens et développement en Amazonie,* edited by Bruce Albert, special issue of *Ethnies: Revue de Survival International* (France), nos. 11–12: 111–15.

Santilli, Márcio. 1991. Os direitos indígenas na Constituição brasileira. *Povos Indígenas no Brasil, 1987–1990: Aconteceu Especial,* no. 18: 11–14. São Paulo: Centro Ecumênico de Documentação e Informação.

Santilli, Márcio. 1996. O Estatuto das Sociedades Indígenas. *Povos Indígenas no Brasil, 1991–1995:* 2–5. São Paulo: Instituto Socioambiental.

Santilli, Márcio. 1997. Facada na Raposa. *Parabólicas,* Bulletin of the Instituto Socioambiental, 26 (4): 10–11.

Santos, Fábio Alves dos. 1980. A palavra do regional. *Boletim do CIMI* 9 (63): 3–4.

Schaden, Egon. 1960. O problema indígena. *Revista de História* 11: 455–60.

Scharf, Regina. 1996. Índios conquistam prefeituras estratégicas. *Parabólicas,* Bulletin of the Instituto Socioambiental. 23 (3): 4–5.

Schmink, Marianne and Charles H. Wood. 1992. *Contested frontiers in Amazonia.* New York: Columbia University Press.

Schwartz, Stuart B. 1995. *Segredos internos: Engenhos e escravos na sociedade colonial.* São Paulo: Companhia das Letras/Conselho Nacional de Desenvolvimento Científico e Tecnológico.

Schwartzman, Simon. 1982. *Bases do autoritarismo brasileiro.* Brasília: Editora Universidade de Brasília.

Schwarz, Roberto. 1992. *Ao vencedor as batatas.* 4th ed. São Paulo: Livraria Duas Cidades.

Seed, Patricia. 1992. Taking possession and reading texts: Establishing the authority of overseas empires. *William and Mary Quarterly* 49: 183–209.

Seed, Patricia. 1995. *Ceremonies of possession in Europe's conquest of the New World, 1492–1640.* Cambridge, England: Cambridge University Press.

Seeger, Anthony. 1980. *Os índios e nós: Estudos sobre sociedades tribais brasileiras.* Rio de Janeiro: Editora Campus.

Seidl, Antonio Carlos. 1990. Britânica que ficou milionária com produto natural "explora" Amazônia. *Folha de São Paulo,* May 5, p. F-1.

Service, Elman. 1962. *Primitive social organization: An evolutionary perspective*. New York: Random House.

Seton-Watson, H. 1977. *Nations and states: An inquiry into the origin of nations and the politics of nationalism*. London: Methuen.

Shakespeare, William. [1611] 1987. *The tempest*. New York: Signet Classic.

Shapiro, Judith. 1987. From Tupã to the land without evil: The Christianization of Tupi-Guarani cosmology. *American Ethnologist* 14 (1): 126–39.

Smith, Anthony. 1981. *Ethnic revival*. Cambridge, England: Cambridge University Press.

Smith, Anthony. 1983. *Theories of nationalism*. New York: Holmes & Meier.

Sotero, Paulo. 1990. Feministas atacam ianomamis. *O Estado de São Paulo*, April 7, p. 10.

Souza, Octavio. 1994. *Fantasia de Brasil*. São Paulo: Escuta.

Souza, Sérgio de. 1994. A epopéia dos irmãos Villas Bôas. In *A marcha para o Oeste*, Orlando Villas Bôas and Claudio Villas Bôas, pp. 17–19. São Paulo: Editora Globo.

Souza Lima, Antonio Carlos de. 1990. *O santo soldado*. Comunicação 21. Rio de Janeiro: Programa de Pós-Graduação em Antropologia Social, Museu Nacional.

Souza Lima, Antonio Carlos de. 1991. On indigenism and nationality in Brazil. In *Nation-states and Indians in Latin America*, edited by Greg Urban and Joel Sherzer, pp. 236–58. Austin: University of Texas Press.

Souza Lima, Antonio Carlos de. 1995. *Um grande cerco de paz: Poder tutelar, indianidade e formação do estado no Brasil*. Petrópolis, Brazil: Vozes.

Stavenhagen, Rodolfo. [1965] 1972. *Sociologia y subdesarrollo*. Mexico: Editorial Nuestro Tiempo.

Stedman, Raymond William. 1982. *Shadows of the Indian*. Norman: University of Oklahoma Press.

Sting and Jean-Pierre Dutilleux. n.d. *A luta pela Amazônia: Histórias da floresta*. São Paulo: L & PM Editores.

Stoll, David. 1982. *Fishers of men or founders of empire? The Wycliffe Bible translators in Latin America*. Cambridge, Mass.: Cultural Survival.

Stravinsky, Igor. [1942] 1996. *Poética musical em 6 lições*. Rio de Janeiro: Jorge Zahar Editor.

Strong, Pauline Turner. 1996. Animated Indians: Critique and contradiction in commodified children's culture. *Cultural Anthropology* 11 (3): 405–24.

Strong, Pauline Turner, and Barrik Van Winkle. 1993. Tribe and nation: American Indians and American nationalism. *Social Analysis* 33: 9–26.

Sutherland, Anne. 1975. *Gypsies: The hidden Americans*. London: Tavistock.

Sweet, David. 1974. A rich realm of nature destroyed: The middle Amazon Valley, 1640–1750. Ph.D. diss., History Department, University of Wisconsin, Madison.

Taussig, Michael. 1987. *Shamanism, colonialism, and the wild man: A study in terror and healing*. Chicago: University of Chicago Press.

Taussig, Michael. 1997. *The magic of the state*. London: Routledge.

Taylor, Charles. 1994. The politics of recognition. In *Multiculturalism: A critical reader*, edited by David Theo Goldberg, pp. 75–106. Oxford, England: Blackwell.

Taylor, Kenneth I. 1979. Development against the Yanoama: The case of mining and agriculture. In *Yanoama in Brazil, 1979,* edited by Alcida R. Ramos and Kenneth I Taylor. International Work Group for Indigenous Affairs Document 37, pp. 43-98. Copenhagen.

Teixeira de Carvalho, Wanderlino, and Manuela Carneiro da Cunha. 1987. A questão indígena e interesses minerários na Constituinte. In *A questão mineral da Amazônia,* pp. 57-91. Brasília: Ministério de Ciência e Tecnologia/Conselho Nacional de Desenvolvimento Científico e Tecnológico.

Terena, Marcos. 1981. O índio exige respeito. *Veja,* February 11, p. 90.

Thomas, Georg. 1982. *Política indigenista dos portugueses no Brasil, 1500-1640.* São Paulo: Edições Loyola.

Time. 1976. Beastly or manly? May 10, p. 37.

Time. 1978. Death by emancipation, November 11, p. 29.

Todorov, Tzvetan. 1989. *Nous et les autres: La réflexion française sur la diversité humaine.* Paris: Seuil.

Torgovnick, Marianna. 1990. *Gone primitive: Savage intellects, modern lives.* Chicago: University of Chicago Press.

Torres, Alberto. [1914] 1982. *O problema nacional brasileiro.* 4th ed. Brasília: Editora Universidade de Brasília.

Trexler, Richard C. 1995. *Sex and conquest: Gendered violence, political order, and the European conquest of the Americas.* Ithaca, N.Y.: Cornell University Press.

Trouillot, Michel-Rolph. 1991. Anthropology and the savage slot: The poetics and politics of otherness. In *Recapturing anthropology: Working in the present,* edited by Richard G. Fox, pp. 17-44. Santa Fe, N.M.: School of American Research Press.

Turner, Terence. 1991a. Representing, resisting, rethinking: Historical transformations of Kayapo culture and anthropological consciousness. In *Colonial situations: Essays on the contextualization of ethnographic knowledge,* edited by George W. Stocking Jr., pp. 285-313. Madison: University of Wisconsin Press.

Turner, Terence. 1991b. *Baridjumoko em Altamira. Povos Indígenas no Brasil, 1987-1990: Aconteceu Especial,* no. 18: 337-38. São Paulo: Centro Ecumênico de Documentação e Informação.

Turner, Terence. 1992. Os Mebengokre Kayapó: História e mudança social, de comunidades autônomas para a coexistência interétnica. In *História dos índios no Brasil,* edited by Manuela Carneiro da Cunha, pp. 311-338. São Paulo: Companhia das Letras/Fundação de Amparo à Pesquisa no Estado de São Paulo/ Secretaria Municipal de Cultura.

Turner, Terence. 1995. Neoliberal ecopolitics and indigenous peoples: The Kayapo, the "Rainforest Harvest," and The Body Shop. In *Local Heritage in the changing tropics: Innovative strategies for natural resource management and control,* edited by Gred Dicum, pp. 113-27. Bulletin Series of the Yale School of Forestry and Environmental Studies. New Haven, Conn.: Yale University.

Turner, Victor. 1969. *The ritual process: Structure and antistructure.* Chicago: Aldine.

Vainfas, Ronaldo. 1995. *A heresia dos índios: Catolicismo e rebeldia no Brasil colonial.* São Paulo: Companhia das Letras.

Vainfas, Ronaldo. 1997. Moralidades brasílicas: Deleites sexuais e linguagem eró-
tica na sociedade escravista. In *História da vida privada no Brasil*, vol. 1: *Cotidiano
e vida privada na América portuguesa*, edited by Fernado A. Novais and Laura de
Mello e Souza, pp. 222–73. São Paulo: Companhia das Letras.

Valente, Rubens. 1996. Garimpo invade reserva e levanta cidade. *Folha de São Paulo*,
December 25, sec. 8, p. 1.

Varnhagen, Francisco Adolpho de. 1848. O Caramuru perante a história. *Jornal do
Instituto Historico e Geographico Brasileiro* 10: 129–52.

Veja. 1972. Sinais da crise. May 31, pp. 20–21.

Veja. 1980. Crime perfeito: Tukano engana a Funai e viaja a Roterdã. November 26, pp. 28–29.

Ventura, Roberto. 1991. *Estilo tropical*. São Paulo: Companhia das Letras.

Vespucio, Américo. 1951. *El Nuevo Mundo: Cartas relativas a sus viajes y descubri-
mientos*. Buenos Aires: Editorial Nova.

Viana, Gilney, and Marta Suplicy. 1995. Nova ameaça aos povos indígenas. *Folha
de São Paulo*, June 20, sec. 1, p. 3.

Villas Bôas, Orlando, and Cláudio Villas Bôas. 1994. *A marcha para o Oeste*. São
Paulo: Editora Globo.

Viotti da Costa, Emília. [1966] 1989. *Da senzala à Colônia*. 3d ed. São Paulo: Editora Brasiliense.

Viveiros, Esther de. 1958. *Rondon conta sua vida*. Rio de Janeiro: Livraria São José.

Viveiros de Castro, Eduardo. 1992. O mármore e a murta: Sobre a inconstância da
alma selvagem. *Revista de Antropologia* 35: 21–74.

Viveiros de Castro, Eduardo, and Lúcia M. M. de Andrade. 1988. Hidrelétricas do
Xingu: O estado contra as sociedades indígenas. In *As hidrelétricas do Xingu e os
povos indígenas*, edited by Leinad Ayer O. Santos and Lúcia M. M. de Andrade,
pp. 7–23. São Paulo: Comissão Pró-Índio de São Paulo.

Walther, Juan Carlos. 1980. *La conquista del desierto*. Buenos Aires: Editorial Uni-
versitaria de Buenos Aires, Colección Lucha de Frontera con el Indio.

Weber, Max. 1978. *Economy and society*. 2 vols. Berkeley: University of California Press.

Weckmann, Luis. 1993. *La herencia medieval del Brasil*. Mexico: Fondo de Cultura
Económica.

White, Hayden. 1973. *Metahistory: The historical imagination in nineteenth-century
Europe*. Baltimore, Md.: Johns Hopkins University Press.

Whitehead, Neil L. 1990. Carib ethnic soldiering in Venezuela, the Guianas, and
the Antilles, 1492–1820. *Ethnohistory* 37 (4): 358–85.

Whitehead, Neil L. 1993. Native American cultures along the Atlantic littoral of
South America, 1499–1650. *Proceedings of the British Academy* 81: 197–231.

Wilkie, Tom. 1993. *Perilous knowledge: The Human Genome Project and its implications*. London: Faber and Faber.

Williams, Raymond. 1985. *Keywords: A vocabulary of culture and society*. New
York: Oxford University Press.

Wolf, Eric. 1982. *Europe and the people without history*. Berkeley: University of California Press.

World Bank. 1981. *Economic development and tribal peoples: Human ecologic con-

siderations. Washington, D.C.: World Bank, Office of Environmental Affairs/ Projects Advisory Staff.

Wright, Robin. 1990. Guerres de l'or dans le Rio Negro: Stratégies indiennes. In *Brésil: Indiens et développement en Amazonie,* edited by Bruce Albert, special issue of *Ethnies: Revue de Survival International* (France), nos. 11–12: 38–42.

Wright, Robin. 1996. *"Aos Que Vão Nascer": Um etnologia religiosa dos índios Baniwa*. Unpublished manuscript.

Wright, Robin. In press. O tempo de Sofia: História e cosmologia da conversão baniwa. In *Religiões indígenas e cristianismo no Brasil: Perspectivas antropológicas,* edited by Robin Wright. Campinas: Universidade Estadual de Campinas.

Yafusso, Paulo. 1995. Suicídios crescem em reservas indígenas. *Folha de São Paulo,* May 21, sec. 1, p. 14.

Yoors, Jan. 1967. *The Gypsies.* New York: Simon and Schuster.

Zavala, Silvio. 1964. *The defense of human rights in Latin America (sixteenth to eighteenth centuries)*. Paris: United Nations Educational, Scientific, and Cultural Organization.

Index

321